Schism and Continuity in an
African Society

D1496430

Classic Reprints in Anthropology

Editors
Bruce Kapferer and Clyde Mitchell

This series reprints classic texts in ethnography and methodology which have exerted a major influence on anthropological thought. The series will span a variety of traditions and will also include translations. Each volume will be introduced by a preface placing it in the context of current anthropological debate. The overall aim is to re-sensitize students and researchers to key issues which have shaped the discipline and continue to have relevance today.

ISSN: 1354-3601

Schism and Continuity in an African Society

A Study of Ndembu Village Life

V. W. Turner[†]

BERG

Oxford • Washington, D.C.

First published in 1957 by the University of Manchester on behalf of
The Institute for African Studies, University of Zambia.

Reprinted in 1964, 1968 and 1972 by the University of Manchester and
in 1996 by:

Berg
Editorial offices:
150 Cowley Road, Oxford, OX4 1JJ, UK
13950 Park Center Road, Herndon, VA 22071, USA

Berg is an imprint of Oxford International Publishers Ltd.

Library of Congress Cataloging-in-Publication Data

A catalogue record for this book is available from the Library of
Congress.

British Library Cataloguing-in-Publication Data

A catalogue record for this book is available from the British Library.

ISBN 1 85973 110 4 (Cloth)
0 85496 282 4 (Paper)

Printed in the United Kingdom by WBC Book Manufacturers,
Bridgend, Mid Glamorgan.

CONTENTS

Map 3 and the Appendices have been omitted from this reprint.

PREFACE TO THE 1996 EDITION

VICTOR Turner's *Schism and Continuity* is among the more outstanding monographs that came out of the work of Max Gluckman's 'Manchester School' of anthropology. This group developed from a research tradition established by Gluckman at the then Rhodes-Livingstone Institute for Social Research (now Institute for African Research and part of the University of Zambia). Gluckman succeeded the former Director (Godfrey Wilson) in the closing stages of World War II and set up a programme for the thorough ethnographic study of the region which included what are now Malawi, Zambia, and Zimbabwe. When Gluckman was appointed to the Chair of Social Anthropology at the University of Manchester in 1947, the Rhodes-Livingstone Institute continued as the research base for the school of anthropology that Gluckman was to develop. Those who gathered at the RLI and who largely built the fieldwork and theoretical perspectives that made Gluckman's Manchester School an important development within British social anthropology included Elizabeth Colson, Clyde Mitchell, Bill Epstein, John Barnes, Max Marwick, and Victor Turner. These scholars in their own distinctive ways pursued Gluckman's insistence that any theoretical and conceptual understanding of social forms and their defining ideas must be grounded in the study of social practice. This approach which Gluckman himself elaborated from the example of Evans-Pritchard became known broadly as 'situational analysis' and the 'extended-case method'. The line that Gluckman encouraged was also informed by a mixture of Durkheimianism (largely through the interpretations elaborated by Radcliffe-Brown) and the ideas of Marx and Engels. Overall, the theoretical and methodological hallmark of the Manchester traditional concentrated on practices which were viewed as revealing the inner 'logic' of what Gluckman referred to as custom or more generally, these days, as culture.

It must be stressed that the Manchester position was innovative. Many in British anthropology at the time regarded the Manchester anthropologists to be marginal to the mainstream and the

Manchester/RLI group valued themselves in this way. They were left-oriented and opposed to conservative tendencies in anthropology. In Central Africa they became sharp critics of Colonial Rule and were criticized in the press. Gluckman himself was officially refused entry into the region (and other areas of colonial rule such as Australia-controlled New Guinea). Others in the Manchester group were similarly prevented from continuing their research. Many of the Manchester/RLI group were directly active in radical politics in England and elsewhere (although, Gluckman was more subdued in such affiliation, a fact that exposed him to friendly jibes from his colleagues and students). The Manchester/RLI group in the fifties and early sixties carried their generally radical attitudes into their anthropological practice. It was a distinctive feature of the Manchester School. They pioneered perspectives that only became widely accepted much later in the seventies and eighties. The events of 1968 in Paris were an important intellectual watershed for anthropology as for other academic disciplines.

The Manchester emphasis on practice was sometimes compared with Firth's contrast between organization and structure. They were very different. Firth's observation largely boiled down to the fact (in my view fairly trivial) that the representations that anthropologists and the subjects of their observation make of their forms of life diverge from what they actually do. He stressed the importance of exploring the actual fluid organizations of activity. Leach probably carried this notion further (a notion already implicit in Malinowski) as did Barth. The developments within the Manchester School were more profound. They were not interested in the contradictions within 'cultural systems' (Leach) or in the dynamics of individual rational choice (Barth)—aspects that they did not ignore—but were directed more fundamentally to the contradictions within historical, political and economic forces of a global nature which were part of the wider circumstance within which particular human populations struggled to recreate or reproduce their social and cultural ways of life. (Jonathan Friedman's critique of Leach for overlooking the historical forces should be noted.) The Manchester orientation was more developed than many later and more fashionable post-1968 attempts at a Marxist perspective in other major centres of anthropology in

England (for example, that at LSE where first Firth and then Bloch announced a commitment to a Marxism that manifested a far cruder functionalist economism that in fact had no need of Marx of Engels).

The originality and possibility of the Manchester anthropology perspective reached a milestone in Turner's *Schism and Continuity*. The argument extends from Gluckman's lead, focussing on the dynamics of social conflict and its foundation within contradictions at the heart of systems of relatedness through kinship and marriage. This is the central problematic that guides the analysis (the contradiction between virilocality at marriage and a pattern of matrilineal descent and inheritance). The everyday conflict and the course of this conflict was rooted in this contradiction which was further complicated by the fact that the Ndembu of the villages studied by Turner were embroiled in larger historical changes effected through Colonial Rule. Turner shows how the contradictions at the heart of Ndembu life became, in effect, more and more irresolvable in the context of larger economic and political developments. He centres his account around the ambitions of a key and in many ways a tragic figure, Sandombu. Through the struggles of Sandombu the reader is lead into a remarkably vivid account of the everyday life of Ndembu villagers and, in Marxist vein, how they come to participate in the transformations of their own world even as they are caught in structural processes that are ultimately beyond their control.

Turner's methodological innovations in *Schism and Continuity* overcame contradictions in social anthropology between actor-oriented and structure-oriented perspectives, whereby a concentration on one aspect obviated the other. The overcoming of this contradiction was one concern of Gluckman's methodological development of 'situational analysis' which Turner elaborated and transformed. Broadly, situational analysis expanded beyond the sociological use of cases or instances from life to illustrate larger systems of structure or institutions of the social order that the analyst discerned—the case as illustrative. The aim was to demonstrate the intricacies of larger processes operating within the dynamics of particular events. Thus Gluckman explored how a bridge-opening ceremony in Zululand in Natal revealed the complexities of a then emergent system of apartheid. He applied the method to the process of judicial decision in Lozi courts in Barotseland in Zambia. However, it was Turner in *Schism and Continuity* who realized the full possibilities of the approach. Not only did he demonstrate the 'logic' in the event, Turner (by taking a number of events in series involving the same actors) was able to demonstrate how participants changed and transformed the very structural circumstances of their own action.

The general significance here of Turner's innovation should not be missed. Gluckman's perspective opened out to the importance of considering how people themselves constructed their contexts of action; that is, they had a role to play in the making of their socio-political and cultural realities. It was a move away from the objectivist position of the anthropological observer, a 'thick description' in Geertz' sense well before the latter had formalized the idea. However, Gluckman and his colleagues, regardless of their insistence on practice, could not, in fact, escape the case or the event as an illustration of social principles that they devised independently of participants. Furthermore, although they stressed an attention to the change OF systems of social action and not their timeless repetition, they could not break out of a form of analysis that was more about how systems remained the same rather than how they changed or transformed. I note, that this was also the marked difficulty of other perspectives developing in British social anthropology at the time—those of Leach and of Barth. Turner's analysis in *Schism and Continuity* broke out of the mould. He did so in a marked Hegelian manner.

Thus Turner analysed each crisis in the constantly changing flux of Ndembu village life as a dynamic of rupture reaching towards its overcoming in a new synthesis (resolution) or organization of social relations. The wider environment or political economic field of activities at once external and internal to Ndembu village life (the colonial political order, capitalist economies manifest in urbanization, labour migration, market farming) generated forces that were expressed in the conflicts that Turner describes and which the villagers could not resolve. However, their efforts to 'control' such forces involved villagers, nonetheless, in constituting dimensions of their changing universe and developing and elaborating original cultural conception and practice.

Coming back to the Hegelianism in Turner's approach, he does have a notion of an ultimate 'higher' unity. This is established in ritual and the growth in importance of rites, such as the Chihamba curing rite, that cross-cut the social boundaries of kin group and village. The Chihamba and its political importance is driven in the unresolvable divisions and ruptures emergent not just from the contradictions underlying the 'traditional' order (the contradiction of the matrilineal and virilocal principles) but in embracing globally connected political and economic changes. In an important way the Chihamba rite is generated and reinvented in such circumstances. It does not maintain the system, as a more functionalist analysis might have it (e.g. Gluckman's analysis of the rites of Swazi and Zulu kingship that were influential on Turner but from whose implications Turner broke). Rather it is integral within a dynamic of Ndembu social and political reconstitution.

The discussion of the Chihamba and other rites in *Schism and Continuity* is preliminary to what became Turner's key focus—the symbolic processes of rite. His later work, Chihamba the White Spirit, is a wonderful elaboration on themes indicated in *Schism and Continuity*. In this later study he gives full flight to his own creative spirit, engaging a variety of perspectives from other fields of enquiry (literary studies, Jungian and Freudian psycho-analysis) to an understanding of Ndembu symbolic processes and how they extend a comprehension of the dynamics of human being that goes far beyond a particular cultural/historical context. British anthropology up to and beyond the work of Turner is often characterized as static British structural functionalism. This common enough stereotype can only be so if his work is ignored and attention is focussed on what turned out to be the far more conservative and stultifying efforts of those centres of anthropology located in London and Oxbridge. I emphasize that it is by reading *Schism and Continuity* that a full grasping can be achieved of the radical direction that Turner was to lead the anthropology of ritual and symbolism.

Turner (and his Manchester colleagues) are what might be generally referred to as 'practice theorists'. Turner should be compared with more recent developments in anthropology, for example, those of

Sahlins and especially Bourdieu. The latter explicitly sets his approach to practice in contrast to that developed from Manchester. He chooses to distinguish his line from that of Van Velsen (*The Politics of Kinship*). Van Velsen's study was conceived of as a development from that of Turner. It took an individualistic strategic choice direction. This was a possibility of the Manchester orientation but probably a retrograde step (I state this self-critically because it is also a direction in my own early work written in the Manchester context). Bourdieu's line on practice is also potentially individualistic as evidenced in his free borrowing from the American pragmatist traditions of symbolic interactionism and ethnomethodology. Turner's analyses never hinges on a simple politics of self-interest or of strategy and, in my view, extends beyond many of the otherwise positive and fruitful aspects of Bourdieu's work.

Bourdieu attempts a synthesis of Husserl's (also Heidegger's) phenomenology with a Levi-Straussian structuralism. His approach is extraordinarily illuminating but his synthesis is not thoroughly successful and the way human beings can shift their doxa or radically alter the circumstances of their habitus or habituated activities is never clear. Bourdieu is committed to dynamics of the reproduction of the same and is not oriented to the production of difference and originality. In this, I consider, Turner in *Schism and Continuity* and in later work is probably more successful. He does not attempt to force together two forms of analysis (structuralism and phenomenology) that in Bourdieu's treatment at least appear to be incompatible. Turner's is an approach to practice—an approach that never relents on the density of the cultural processes ingrained and developing out of practice—that indicates how new modes of symbolic comprehension and structures of daily activity can be generated.

There is much else I could say about *Schism and Continuity* by way of introduction. For instance, here is an orientation that does not see cultural/social forms as coherently bounded systems. Turner developed on discussion at Manchester concerning the use of the concept of social field—borrowed from the social psychologist Kurt Lewin (see Turner's later *The Drums of Affliction*)—which concentrated on the dynamics of social structuration with an open field of forces. Turner in his development was himself a generative centre for perspectives developed by others within the Manchester tradition (e.g. Epstein, Bailey). Although intellectually unrelated, Turner's unbounded field notion was 'reinvented' within the contemporary suggestions of a postmodern anthropology. In Turner too we have a sense of the many voices of Ndembu villagers as they participate in the fashioning and refashioning of their own existential realities.

Schism and Continuity is a central work in the history of anthropology. It is critical for a thorough understanding of Turner's later writing. But it has far more than a historical significance. It is exemplary of the creative possibilities of anthropological ethnography, the centrality of rigorous ethnography in the anthropological contribution towards more general human understanding. The work should be read and reread as one example of how anthropologists might go about their research and develop analytical understanding. This is particularly so at this historical moment in a general discourse within anthropology concerning new analytical directions and the role of ethnography in demonstrating them.

BRUCE KAPFERER

PREFACE TO THE 1972 EDITION

SOCIAL anthropology in its modern form is only about forty years old, and during its short history it has changed and developed fast. For from the time when anthropologists began to carry out intensive field-studies, they have experimented with many methods of presenting their increasingly rich data about social life. Dr. Turner attempts a new mode of presentation in this book, but it is a mode which grows out of the history of anthropology since the War. He has here combined general analysis with the individual case-study in what I consider a most fruitful and illuminating way.

When social anthropologists began to cope with the problem of handling their very detailed data on the tribal societies of Africa, Oceania, Asia and the Americas, they seem first to have sought to establish that some kind of system existed in these societies. Malinowski found the system in the interdependence of culture, Radcliffe-Brown found it in social structure. The next generation of anthropologists in the British Commonwealth, among whom I myself fall, continued this search for system. As I see it, our analyses abstracted a set of regular interconnections between various social relationships, ecological relationships, modes of belief, etc. From the time when Evans-Pritchard analysed the Azande beliefs and practices relating to witchcraft, oracles and magic, to show that these constituted a rational philosophy of causation and philosophy of morals, which were related to a particular mode of social organization, we have exhibited that there is a systematic structure in one field of tribal life after another. The evidence for the existence of these structures was mainly qualitative, and consisted largely in illustrations from different situations of action in a number of families, villages, or political groups. These illustrative data were rarely related to one another. In result, when one reads even the best books of this period, it is not easy to put the system into working operation in actual life. In order to demonstrate the existence of system at all, we discarded much of the living reality about which we had collected information.

I consider that this was a necessary stage in the development of our discipline. Faced with the great variety of custom and forms of social relationships which occur in the tribal societies, we had first to produce a morphology of their structures, and general analyses of how their systems worked, to exhibit some stability within constant change of personnel and relations between personnel. But I think all of us have felt that more could be done with the detail of our data. It seems to me that our systematic knowledge has now developed sufficiently for us to achieve the next step. *African Political Systems* (1940), a collection of eight studies, marked an important step in the systematic study of one field, and it was followed by a series of comparable, but fuller, monographs. Yet it is significant that political studies since the War have, so to speak, put their systems back into a particular history, while still aiming at the demonstration of systematic interconnections : this is marked in, for example, Evans-Pritchard's *The Sanusi of Cyrenaica* and J. A. Barnes's *Politics in a Changing Society*, an historical analysis of the Fort Jameson Ngoni. Some anthropologists, notably Schapera, have even moved fully into a method of work more like orthodox history, but still seeking for a systematic structure.

The same change is likely to occur in the fields which social anthropology has made peculiarly its own : for the problems we meet in the field of tribal politics and law, we share with political science, history, and jurisprudence. The other fields are the study of domestic and village life, of familial and kinship systems, and of ritual—religion, magic, witchcraft, etc. And here Turner has made a significant contribution, following leads set, for Central Africa, by Mitchell, Colson and Barnes. Great classics on domestic and village life, like Fortes's books on the Tallensi and Firth's on the Tikopia, analyse for us the regularities they find in a variety of actual situations and relationships, and the interdependence between those regularities. Theirs are magnificent analyses. But they use the method of appropriate, illuminating illustration, and hence, in a way, of chance illustration. We cannot from their analyses work out how any one group of people lived, at a particular time and in a particular place, within this social structure and using these customs. Turner has used a different mode of illustration, which I consider deepens the understanding which he gives us of Ndembu tribal life. Indeed, it would be more accurate to say that he abandons illustration altogether, to develop what is, for African studies, a new mode of analysis. He first gives us a systematic outline of the principles on which Ndembu villages are constructed, and measures their relative importance with unusually adequate numerical data. Then he takes the history of one village through twenty years to show how these abstract principles have operated through that history, within the chance occurrences of illness, death and other misfortune, of good luck, of individual temperament and ambition, and finally of the major changes which have resulted from British overlordship. He thus shows us how certain principles of organization and certain dominant values operate through both schisms and reconciliations, and how the individuals and groups concerned try to exploit the varied principles and values to their own ends. Turner himself would not claim any particular points he makes as original, for most of them he has taken individually from the works of his predecessors. But this use of the detailed case-study, in the background of general systematic analysis, combines what he has taken over into a pioneer study. The late Buell Quain in his *Fijian Village* attempted this task, but his death perhaps prevented the final pulling together of his analysis, and it did not quite come off.

One thing I can do, in this foreword, is to answer a possible objection to this method : how is the reader to assess that Turner has selected a ' typical ' village ? This question is partly answered in the careful numerical analyses of many villages which precede the ' village-study '. Secondly, I am in the privileged position of having heard Turner present analyses of other village histories ; and hence I can vouch that for all its uniqueness, the village of ' Mukanza ' is ' typical ' of Ndembu villages. Turner hopes to publish separately studies of some of these other villages ; and collateral validation for this present analysis will also come out of the study of Ndembu ritual which he is now writing. For he plans to use the same method of analysis in studying ritual : and again I consider this will mark a significant advance in this field of research.

Turner has built his study of Mukanza village around what he calls ' the social drama '—one of a series of crises occurring in the history of the village, when either a quarrel between some of the inhabitants, or a misfortune ascribed by the people and by divination to ancestral spirits or sorcery, precipitates threats to

the unity of the village. The village as a whole, and its neighbours, as well as component groups within the village, try to
use different forms of redress to meet these threats. Turner
argues that when the conflict emerges from the opposed interests
and claims of protagonists acting under a single social principle,
judicial institutions can be invoked to meet the crisis, for a rational
attempt can be made to adjust claims which are similarly based.
But when claims are advanced under different social principles,
which are inconsistent with one another even to the point of
contradicting one another, there can be no rational settlement.
Here recourse is had to divination of sorcery or ancestral wrath,
causing misfortune ; and ultimately to a ritual reconciliation
which can reassert all the values held by decent Ndembu, under
the pretence that harmony is restored within those values. He
shows that after this situation has occurred, there is a temporary
respite ; but the deep conflicts between groups and individuals
in the village continue. Through the intervening, comparatively peaceful period, struggles continue till they precipitate a
new crisis. Each crisis marks the culmination of a period of
altering alignments of power and shifts of allegiance within the
village—though matrilineal attachment is always dominant in
the end. The crisis itself, through four stages which he carefully
delineates, is temporarily solved; but again this involves a
definite shift in the village's internal balance of power.

I have sketched something of Turner's method : he can speak
better for himself. But I make a few points to support him.
First, I hope no one will turn away from his analysis in dislike
of the phrase ' social drama '. Several of us have tried, with
Turner, to find another phrase which is less likely to meet objec-
tions : we have failed to, and he would be grateful for suggestions. Secondly, I warn readers that it is not easy to follow the
complicated story of this village, with its complicated internal
genealogy and its important links in other villages. Turner has
done what he can to help the reader, with a main genealogy and
periodically with subsidiary genealogies of those involved in each
drama. But the labour of learning who the characters are, and
how they are related to one another, is well worth while. The
reward is equal to the labour. I myself found that I soon got
the main characters clear, and the rest followed easily. Then I
became absorbed in the story itself, and particularly in the tragic

story of Sandombu—moved not only by his personal ambition, strong though that was, but also moved by the pride of his lineage, to struggle for the village headmanship when everything was against him.   With his generosity and capacity for affection, he fought with his quick temper and the curse of his sterility, to achieve a headmanship ; and Turner shows clearly out of his general analysis, that Sandombu was doomed to lose, and on the way to defeat to incur a reputation for sorcery.   He is a tragic figure, indeed.   But we learn too that his rivals could not wholeheartedly take advantage of his weaknesses ; for when they had overcome him, they in turn were moved by guilt, for, under the dominant value of Ndembu, was he not born from the same womb as they ?

Into this story, Turner has woven a striking general analysis, of schism of groups and relationships, and of continuity of society and principle and value above the schism—a continuity of a ' community of suffering ', for it is misfortune which assembles the cult-groups whose rituals dramatize that continuity. Thus incidentally as the story unfolds we learn what are Ndembu beliefs and customs.   We see these working in the process of social life, where they both control people, and are exploited by people.   Customs and beliefs are real, systematized through social relationships : they are not mere adjuncts.   In working all this out, Turner also—and this is an achievement—brings in the changes of values and principles of organization which are emerging out of British overlordship—the development of wage-earning and cash-cropping, the establishment of peace, the killing out of game which has struck at the dominant male value of hunting.   In all this I see a contribution to our knowledge of Africa, and to anthropological theory and method.   It is achieved in a book which will fascinate anyone.

MAX GLUCKMAN

UNIVERSITY OF MANCHESTER,
   June 1956

PREFACE TO THE 1968 EDITION

IT is now more than a decade since *Schism and Continuity* was first published. Seen from this perspective it emerges clearly as a transitional book between the prevalent structural-functionalism of British anthropology in the 1940s—the period in which I received my training—and the processual analysis of the 1960s. Whatever influence it may have had seems to have lain in the rapidly advancing sub-disciplines of diachronic micro-sociology and micro-politics. Yet it has sometimes been forgotten by those caught up in the first enthusiasm for 'processualism' that 'process' is intimately bound up with 'structure' and that an adequate analysis of social life necessitates a rigorous consideration of the relation between them. Historical hindsight reveals a diachronic profile, a 'temporal structure' in events, and this structure cannot be understood in isolation from the series of synchronic profiles which make up the structure of a social field at every significant point of arrest in the time flow. Processual studies can never be the negation of structuralism; rather do they put the discoveries of structuralism to new use in the perspectives of history.

In his introduction to the first edition of this book Professor Gluckman has called attention to the way in which case material is used to facilitate what he has later described as 'the intensive study of the processes of control in a limited area of social life viewed over a period of time' (Introduction to *The Craft of Social Anthropology*, 1967 by A. L. Epstein, London: Tavistock Publications, xvi). He contrasts this 'extended case method' with 'the method of apt illustration' (of abstract structural principles), and suggests that its systematic use would deepen our understanding of law and morality. But it was not solely with the collection of a different kind of data that I was concerned, even at the time of writing the book, but with a different kind of analysis. In formulating the notion of 'social drama' I had in mind the explicit comparison of the temporal structure of certain types of social processes with that of dramas on the stage, with their acts and scenes, each with its peculiar qualities, and all cumulating towards a climax. In other words, I was groping

towards the notion of studying the structure of successive events
in social processes of varying scope and depth.   But while the
synchronic structures investigated by many anthropologists could
be shown to rest upon custom and habit, and very often to remain
beneath the level of conscious awareness, the diachronic structure
or ' processional forms' that I was interested in exposing and
analysing developed out of clashes and alignments of human
volitions and purposes, inspired by private and public interests
and ideals.   Yet the social drama itself represented a complex
interaction between normative patterns laid down in the course
of deep regularities of conditioning and social experience, and the
immediate aspirations, ambitions and other conscious goals and
strivings of individuals and groups in the here and now.   At the
time, however, I was only able to raise some of the problems of
processual analysis, not to provide any of the answers.   Thus, I
was able to suggest that to the different phases of the social drama,
breach, crisis, redressive action, and immediate result, there
corresponded a particular style of social interaction, particular
patterns of norms and values, specific types of goals and goal-
orientated behaviour and specific forms of conjunctive and dis-
junctive behaviour.   But I was unable to probe these differences
minutely or especially cogently.   For one thing, there was little
at that time in the way of comparative data of this type.   Since
then there has been a considerable accumulation of extended case
material, for example, in the works of van Velsen (*The Politics of
Kinship*, 1964, Manchester University Press); Gulliver (*Social
Control in an African Society*, 1963, London: Routledge and Kegan
Paul); and Abner Cohen (*Arab Border Villages in Israel*, 1965,
Manchester University Press) to name but a few, while new
theoretical perspectives on the study of social processes (particu-
larly political processes) have been opened up by such scholars as
Gluckman (*Politics, Law and Ritual*, 1965, Chicago: Aldine); Bailey
(*Politics and Social Change*, 1963, Berkeley: University of California
Press); Adrian Mayer (The Significance of Quasi-groups in the Study
of Complex Societies, 1966, in *the Social Anthropology of Complex
Societies*, A.S.A. Monograph No. 4, London: Tavistock Publications) notably his concept of the ' action set', a concept further
elaborated by Gulliver (Dispute Settlement without Courts :
the Ndendeuli of Southern Tanzania, paper given in Wenner-
Gren Symposium No. 34, 1966, Ethnography of Law) ; Swartz,

Turner and Tuden (Introduction to *Political Anthropology*, 1966, Chicago : Aldine) ; Swartz (Introduction to *Local Level Politics*, 1968, Chicago : Aldine) ; Nicholas (Factions : a Comparative Analysis in *Political Systems and the Distribution of Power*, 1965, A.S.A. Monograph No. 2, London : Tavistock Publications) and the articles on case method by A. L. Epstein and van Velsen in *The Craft of Social Anthropology* (op. cit.). Other scholars are making contributions to a steadily broadening stream of studies in processual analysis, but clearly a great deal remains to be done if serious and rigorous comparisons are to be made in cross-cultural terms between diachronic structures.

To end on an ethnographic note : I have but recently learnt that headman Mukanza died at a ripe old age in 1967 and was succeeded by Kasonda. I predicted in this book that Kasonda would found a new farm and that Sakazao would remain in Mukanza Village with most of his lineage kin. This is one illustration of the difficulties besetting prediction in anthropology, for in 1954 when I left the field I did not anticipate that Sakazao would die within a few months and that Mukanza would live for a further thirteen years. But since my main doubt as to Kasonda's succeeding to the Mukanza headmanship was based upon his relative youth in 1954, and not upon his capability or the extent of his potential political support, my error was not perhaps so grave. In 1967 Kasonda was sufficiently mature to meet the tacit age requirement for a headman—and a headman he became !

PREFACE TO THE 1957 EDITION

'General Forms have their vitality in Particulars, & every Particular is a Man.'
WILLIAM BLAKE, *Jerusalem.*

IN this book I attempt to isolate the cardinal factors under-lying Ndembu residential structure. I focus the investigation upon the village, a significant local unit, and analyse it successively as an independent social system and as a unit within several wider sets of social relations included in the total field of Ndembu society. Interwoven with the analysis of structural form I present detailed studies of situations of crisis, which arise periodic-ally in village life. These crises make visible both contradictions between crucial principles governing village structure, and con-flicts between persons and groups in sets of social relations governed by a single principle. From repeated observation of such situations I have evolved the concept of the 'social drama', which I regard as my principal unit of description and analysis in the study of social process. On pages 91-3 I divide the social drama into four phases—its 'processional form'—and present reasons for doing so. Through the social drama one may sometimes look beneath the surface of social regularities into the hidden contradictions and conflicts in the social system. The kinds of redressive mechanism deployed to handle conflict, the pattern of factional struggle, and the sources of initiative to end crisis, which are all clearly manifest in the social drama, provide valuable clues to the character of the social system.

But the study of social dramas must be based on numerical analysis of village census data and the critical examination of genealogies. Before one can study breach one must be aware of regularity. I have therefore tried to discuss in quantitative terms such factors as the magnitude and mobility of villages, individual mobility, and the social composition of villages, before undertaking the analysis of social dramas.

Hence I have approached my major field of study in two ways. First, I have compared a number of villages with reference to such measurable criteria as size and genealogical composition. Secondly, I have analysed a sequence of social dramas involving the membership of a single village, and the members of other villages linked to it by ties of kinship and spatial propinquity. In the first instance I have examined regularities of *form* occurring throughout *many* villages ; in the second, I discuss regularities of *process* in the social maturation of a *single* village. The two approaches complement one another.

By numerical analysis of genealogical and census data I was able to infer the effective principles determining village structure. These on the whole were in conformity with the ideal pattern of residential relations presented by informants. Within villages the dominant principles influencing residence were maternal descent and virilocality.[1] Under Ndembu conditions conflict between them was ineradicable and accounted in considerable measure for the unstable and fissile character of village organization and for the high degree of individual mobility. It is possible that hunting, a purely masculine pursuit, and virilocal marriage, which binds together male kin in local descent groups, are parallel expressions of structural opposition between men and women in this matrilineal society. Hunting, the men's sphere in the basic economy, is socially valued above its objective contribution to the food supply, and is highly ritualized. Cassava cultivation, the women's sphere, is correspondingly undervalued, and is ritualized to a lesser extent. Yet women's work ensures the physical survival of the group, since hunting is fitfully pursued and success in it is uncertain. Hunting implies a rather greater stress on economic co-operation than cassava growing, although in all sectors production is mainly individualistic. Throughout the West-Central Bantu, hunting is linked with eminence or aristocratic ranking. Among Ndembu, professional hunters are highly honoured, and all men hunt to some extent. Hunting is equated with virility and reinforces in some ways the structural opposition between men and women. For marriage, as noted above, is virilocal ; women, on whom the social continuity of villages depends, reside at their husbands' villages after marriage. Nevertheless, maternal descent governs prior rights to residence, succession to office and inheritance of property,

---

[1] 'Virilocal' in this book refers to the post-marital residence of a woman in the village to which her husband takes her. 'Uxorilocal' refers to the post-marital residence of a man in his wife's village. 'Patrilocal' refers to residence in one's father's village. 'Avunculocal' refers to residence with one's mother's brother. 'Matrilocal' refers to residence with one's mother.

even of guns, the professional hunters' most cherished items of equipment. The nuclear residential group consists of male matri-lineally related kin. To remain together this set of kinsmen must import their wives from other village lineages and export their sisters. But with maternal descent as the basis of village continuity a contradiction arises between the role of men as fathers who wish to retain their wives and children with them, and their role as uterine brothers and uncles who wish to recover the allegiances of their sisters and sisters' children. Without that allegiance men cannot found enduring villages nor can they effectively press their claims for headmanship within their villages. Thus both marriages and villages are inherently unstable and in-laws struggle continually for control over women and their children.

Another consequence of virilocal marriage making for in-stability in residential structure is the great measure of auto-nomy it confers on the matricentric family. Frequent divorce weakens the link between father and children but strengthens the tie between mother and children. But virilocal marriage separ-ates a matricentric family from its maternal kin-group during the minority of the children who are reared in their paternal village. If they return to their maternal kin after the divorce or widowhood of the mother, the narrower loyalty of the members of the matricentric family to one another tends to come into conflict with their wider allegiance to the village as a whole. A matricentric family matures into a uterine sibling group which is the most frequent unit of secession to form new villages. Radical incompatibility, then, between maternal descent and virilocality gives a keen edge to conflicts between uterine kinsmen and husbands of women, which result in quarrels between vil-lages; to marital conflicts, producing a high divorce rate; and to conflicts of loyalties between narrow- and wide-span maternal descent groups, which inhibit the development of deep localized lineages.

Another effect of virilocal marriage is a high rate of patri-locality for children of male village kin. Children adhere closely to mothers, and while a marriage lasts the children stay at their father's village. Since villages are small (mean size—10·6 huts), they tend to be at once shallow lineages with a fringe of seminal children and cognatic kin, and bilateral extended families, i.e.

often the headman's uterine sibling group, brothers outnumbering sisters, and their children. There is a tendency to merge kin on the mother's and on the father's side as members of a genealogical generation. Within the village, membership of a genealogical generation cuts across affiliation by matricentric family and unites cross-cousins with parallel cousins. The senior of two adjacent genealogical generations exerts authority over and levies respect from the junior. On the other hand, alternate generations joke with one another and behave more or less as equals. Adjacent generations tend to build huts in separate arcs of the village circle, alternate generations in the same arc. Generation oppositions and alliances tend to reduce tensions in the relationships between matricentric families and lineage segments, and between children and sisters' children of headmen.

Marriages between classificatory grandparents and grandchildren who frequently belong to the same maternal descent group, and marriages between cross-cousins, also tend to bind the various components of the village together.

Nevertheless, despite these centripetal and accretive tendencies Ndembu villages remain inherently unstable. Ndembu have the ideal aim of building up large villages although this is unceasingly rebutted by reality. For the Tallensi described by Professor Fortes the deep localized lineage is the skeleton of the social structure. For Ndembu, on the other hand, a deep lineage is a seldom-realized goal, the end-product of the sagacious manipulation by headmen of a number of organizational principles which conflict with one another in various situations.

Ndembu villages have a wide range of spatial mobility and each maternal descent-group in the course of time is scattered throughout different vicinages (discrete clusters of adjoining villages) over the whole region. Thus vicinages are heterogeneous in composition, for adjacent villages are seldom linked by maternal descent. The mobility and instability of villages partly determines and partly is determined by the absence of political centralization. The Lunda ancestors of the Ndembu came from the great pyramidal state of Mwantiyanvwa's empire in the Congo, but in course of time succumbed to the decentralizing influences of their way of life, accelerated by the slave-trading and -raiding of the nineteenth century. But a vestige of the Lunda state power remains in the ritual role of the Ndembu chief, Kanongesha. The chieftainship symbolizes the unity of Ndembu and their ownership of a common territory.

The instability of the secular social structure can be palliated but not controlled by secular means. Ritual associated with corporate groups such as lineages and villages is meagre and can only act as a temporary brake against fission. But ritual performed by cult associations that cut across villages, vicinages and even adjacent chiefdoms of Lunda origin, acts to keep the common values of Ndembu society constantly before the roving individualists of which it is composed. These values include historical renown, hunting and virility, fertility and motherhood, and health and strength. The mobility of the society is reflected in the contingent and occasional character of the ritual. The misfortunes of life, including bad luck for men at hunting, women's reproductive disorders, and severe illness for both sexes, are attributed to the punitive action of ancestor spirits, who are exorcised and placated in rituals specific to each mode of affliction. The cult association is made up of doctors and adepts who were themselves once patients and candidates in that cult. The widest community of Ndembu is therefore a community of suffering. In the context of the ritual the common values of the whole society are stressed in symbol, mime and precept. The associations are transient groups called into existence by the unpredictable misfortunes of mobile individuals. Hence the cult groups are too fleeting and shifting in composition to develop internal stresses and divisions. It is, I suggest, because the organizational principles which govern the secular structure are contradictory and produce perennial conflicts between persons and groups, that rituals are constantly being performed by unitary though transitory associations, and that these rituals stress common values over and above the clash of sectional interests. Ndembu ritual does not reflect or express, as does Tallensi or Swazi ritual, the structure of a stable society, with ritual role corresponding, as it were, to secular role ; rather, it compensates for the integrational deficiencies of a politically unstable society. Poverty of secular status is confronted with rich development of ritual roles in many cult associations. The range of effective political or economic co-operation is small ; at some performances of ritual more than a thousand people may attend.

In Chapter One I briefly describe the historical and ecological background to this study. Chapter Two presents the relevant demographic information, while in Chapter Three I attempt to isolate structural principles governing the social composition of villages on the basis of genealogical and census information. The next four chapters are centred on the theme of maternal descent as the main principle underlying village continuity. In Chapter Four the concept of social drama is first introduced, and it is further refined in the course of this and the following chapter which deal mainly with struggles to succeed to headmanship between the matrilineal kinsmen in a single village. In these social dramas the pattern of factional intrigue is revealed and its consistency with, or degree of departure from, the basic social structure under varying circumstances is discussed. Chapters Six and Seven are concerned with village fission and with the pattern of secession. Chapters Eight and Nine deal with the second major determinant of Ndembu village structure, virilocal marriage, and how it operates within, and then between, villages. In Chapter Ten the integrative role of the cult associations is analysed. In Chapter Eleven the chieftainship, in its ritual importance and secular weakness, is briefly discussed.

That the pervasive theme of the book is conflict and the resolution of conflict arises from my predilection for the views, fast becoming a theory, of that school of British social anthropologists who are coming to regard a social system as ' a field of tension, full of ambivalence, of co-operation and contrasting struggle '.[1] For these anthropologists a social system is not a static model, a harmonious pattern, nor the conceptual product of a monistic outlook. A social system is a field of forces in which, to quote Fortes,[2] ' centrifugal tendencies and centripetal tendencies pull against one another ', and whose power to persist is generated by its own socially transmuted conflicts.

Underlying the whole study is the concept, most recently reformulated by Gluckman and Colson,[3] that groups have ' an

[1] Gluckman, M., *Rituals of Rebellion in South-East Africa* (1954), p. 21. Gluckman has recently developed and expanded this theory in his *Custom and Conflict in Africa* (1955).

[2] Fortes, M., *The Dynamics of Clanship among the Tallensi* (1945), p. 244.

[3] Gluckman, ' Political Institutions ', in *The Institutions of Primitive Society* (1954), pp. 66-80 ; Colson, E., ' Social Control and Vengeance in Plateau Tonga Society ', *Africa*, xxiii, 3 (July 1953).

inherent tendency to segment and then to become bound together by cross-cutting alliances . . . conflicts in one set of relationships are absorbed and redressed in the countervailing relations'. My analysis of village structure is influenced by this conception. But it must be pointed out that among the Ndembu, conflicts in secular, non-ritual, relations speedily sharpen to the point of irreconcilability in terms of the maintenance of local cohesion. The high rates both of divorce and of village fission attest to this. But conflicts which split sub-systems tend to be absorbed by the widest social system and even to assist its cohesion by a wide geographical spreading of ties of kinship and affinity. Centrifugal tendencies prevail on the whole over centripetal tendencies at the level of corporate kinship and local groupings, but centrifugality is confined within the bounds of the total socio-geographical system of the Ndembu nation. An overall ritual unity is contraposed to the fissile nature of secular life. Secular life shows unceasing attempts to build up coherent groups, but these attempts are as unendingly frustrated by centrifugal and fissile tendencies. The concept of Ndembu unity, transcending all the divisions of the secular system, is the product of innumerable, fitfully performed occasions of ritual, each couched in the idiom of unity through common misfortune.

ACKNOWLEDGEMENTS

THIS account of the Lunda-Ndembu is based on two periods of field research carried out between December 1950 and February 1952, and between May 1953 and June 1954, after my appointment as a Research Officer of the Rhodes-Livingstone Institute. I have no skill adequately to express my debt to the Ndembu people of Mwinilunga District for their contribution to this book. Many more than I can name instructed me patiently and painstakingly in their way of life. Villagers were never offended by my presence at many of their sacred or intimate occasions. From them I learnt not only some fascinating facts, but also that human frailty must be forgiven—in oneself as in others—if human social life is to be enriching. My especial thanks are due to Musona, my shrewd assistant, to Samutamba, to Sakazao, and to Headman Kajima. Others who gave me unstinting help were Windson Kashinakaji, Muchona and Chief Ikelenge. I am grateful to Mr. R. C. Dening, the District Commissioner, for access to his excellent maps and to the District Notebook.

Indeed, many persons have contributed, directly and indirectly, to the shaping of this book. Many separate skills and much collective knowledge and wisdom were put at my disposal as field-report became thesis and thesis was fashioned into book.

From Professor Forde I received my first training in social anthropology. It was in his lectures and seminars that my enthusiasm for the subject received form and direction.

During my field-work and while writing up, two sets of colleagues, several of whom belonged to both sets, gave me invaluable assistance. I refer to the Research Staff of the Rhodes-Livingstone Institute and to the Department of Social Anthropology at the University of Manchester. Professor Max Gluckman, a former Director of the Institute and present Head of the Department, has given me training, guidance and criticism of the highest order throughout this period. It is widely acknowledged, among those who have worked under his direction, that he has the gift of arousing in his students a zest for anthropological theory which enables them to keep on working with a will in spite of the many and often formidable difficulties and discomforts of field-work. I am deeply grateful to Professor Gluckman for his inspiring teaching, keen criticism and generous friendship.

Several members of the Department and the Institute have greatly helped me by reading the manuscript of this book with critical attention. Professor Elizabeth Colson, a former Director of the Institute, made many constructive comments during the crucial period between spells of field-work. Professor John Barnes read the manuscript at a late stage of preparation with incisive thoroughness. His advice on the layout of tables, diagrams and genealogies was of exceptional assistance. I would also like to thank Dr. A. L. Epstein for many valuable observations on my general argument.

I owe a special debt of gratitude to Professor Clyde Mitchell, who was Director of the Institute while I was in the field, for his unfailing help and encouragement. He gave me my first practical training in field-work methods during a happy fortnight of research in Lambaland. His studies of Yao village life opened up several fruitful lines of thought to me.

Mr. C. M. N. White, M.B.E., for a time Acting Director of the Rhodes-Livingstone Institute, gave me the benefit of his wide knowledge of the western tribes of Northern Rhodesia.

The influence of Professor Fortes is writ large in this book. Many of his ideas, first encountered during my student days, had already become part and parcel of my thinking when I entered the field.

My wife collaborated actively in all aspects of my field-work. Her contribution included most of the photography and much of the measuring of gardens and mapping of villages. In addition, she drew the maps for the book. Her comments on the argument have helped to shape its form.

In short, this book is in a very real sense the product of collective authorship.

V. W. T.

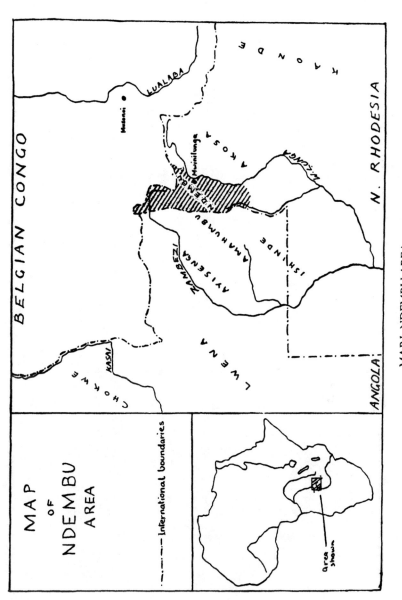

MAP 1 NDEMBU AREA

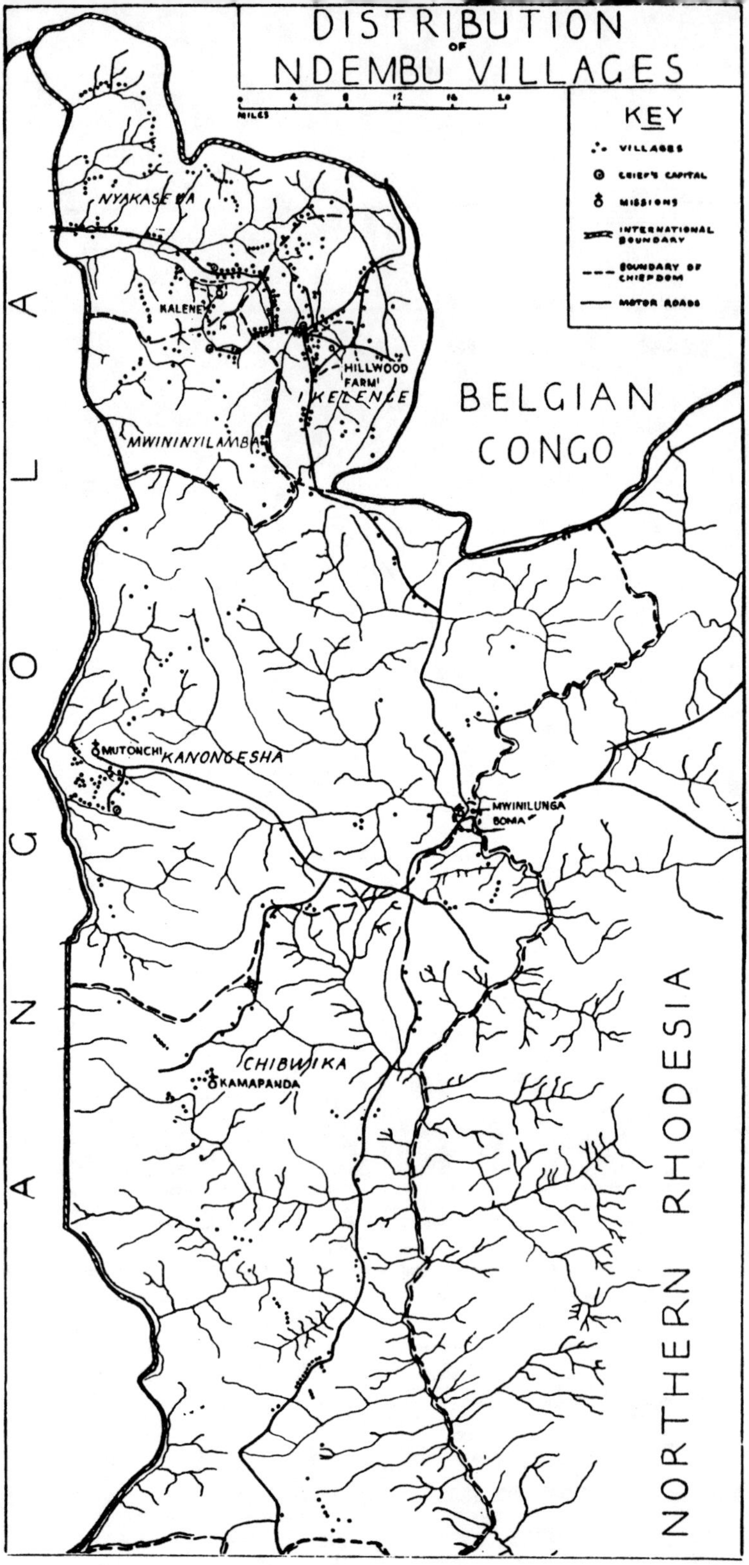

DISTRIBUTION OF NDEMBU VILLAGES
0 4 8 12 16 20
MILES
KEY
VILLAGES
CHIEF'S CAPITAL
MISSIONS
INTERNATIONAL BOUNDARY
BOUNDARY OF CHIEFDOM
MOTOR ROADS
NYAKASEWA
KALENE
HILLWOOD FARM
IKELENGE
MWININYILAMBA
BELGIAN CONGO
ANGOLA
MUTONCHI
KANONGESHA
MWINILUNGA BOMA
CHIBWIKA
KAMAPANDA
NORTHERN RHODESIA

MAP 2 DISTRIBUTION OF NDEMBU VILLAGE

CHAPTER I

HISTORICAL AND ECOLOGICAL BACKGROUND

THIS book is primarily what Professor Fortes would call a
'histological' study, an attempt to analyse in close detail
the form and functioning of a sub-system, the village, within a
wider system, the totality of Ndembu society. But something
must be said, however compressed, about the wider historical
and socio-geographical background of the village. Our village
microcosm is a component in a system of social relations existing
at a specific time and place. But it also has a specific history.
By European notions, this history is brief and blended with
mythology. Nevertheless, for Ndembu it is a history as a
record of successive, interdependent events, making an irreversible process, which in their view explains what they are and
where they are.

The Mwinilunga Lunda-Ndembu, hereinafter called Ndembu,[1]
numbering about seventeen thousand, today inhabit the western
portion of Mwinilunga District in the North-Western Province
of Northern Rhodesia, approximately between 11° and 12°
south latitude. Before European occupation the Ndembu chiefdom of Kanongesha comprised most of the territory between the
West Lunga, Zambezi and Lufwiji rivers. Now the tribal land
is crossed by the international boundaries that demarcate Northern
Rhodesia, Angola and the Belgian Congo. Kanongesha's chiefdom is virtually bisected by the Angola-Rhodesia boundary, and
on either side of the boundary there is a chief who calls himself

---

[1] A number of Southern Lunda groups call themselves *Ndembu*, including
the inhabitants of the chiefdoms of Kanongesha, Ishinde and Kazembe Mutanda
(or Izaizai). My informants say that Ndembu was originally the name of a
river at which these chiefs and their followers stayed together for several
years after their departure from Mwantiyanvwa's capital (see p. 2). I
employ the term *Ndembu* throughout this book to distinguish Kanongesha's
Lunda from the *Lunda-Kosa* (or Akosa) of Chief Musokantanda. This chief
lives in the Belgian Congo near Musonoi but has nominated Sailunga as his
representative in Northern Rhodesia. The Kosa occupy Mwinilunga District to the east on the West Lunga River. Government refer to Chief
Kanongesha's Lunda as 'Ndembu' and to the Kosa group as 'Lunda' in
official publications.

Kanongesha and is recognized as such by the colonial power. This book is based on research among the Rhodesian Ndembu and may not apply to Ndembu living in Angola or the Congo.

History and Traditions [1]

The Ndembu, like their Kosa neighbours to the east, claim to have come as invaders from the Northern Lunda [2] empire of Mwantiyanvwa between the Kasai and upper Bushimaie rivers, and to have conquered or received the submission of small scattered groups of indigenous Mbwela or Lukolwe. The invasion appears to have taken place before the beginning of the eighteenth century. According to Dias de Carvalho [3] the departure of Kanongesha and his followers from Luunda took place during the reign of the fifth Mwantiyanvwa, Ianvo Noeji, whose reign Verhulpen places between 1640 and 1660. [4] According to the traditions of both Ndembu and Kosa, Kanongesha's migration occurred at about the same time as the migrations of other Lunda leaders such as : (1) Kazembe Mutanda, who established a chiefdom just to the north of Kanongesha's ; (2) Musokantanda, who founded a chiefdom to the east of the Ndembu in what is now Musonoi District in the Katanga, and in eastern Mwinilunga ; and (3) Ishinde, whose chiefdom, like that of Kanongesha's, was later divided between Angola and Northern Rhodesia where it occupies the eastern part of Balovale District. For many years these chiefdoms, like that of Kazembe on the Luapula, described by Lacerda, Gamitto and others, were tributary to Mwantiyanvwa, and even today visits are made by

---

[1] A considerable literature exists on Lunda history, much of it represented in the bibliography attached to Miss McCulloch's *The Southern Lunda and Related Peoples*, Ethnographic Survey of Africa, ed. Daryll Forde (1951). In addition to works cited below in the text, Lewis Gann (' The End of the Slave Trade in British Central Africa : 1889-1912 ', *The Rhodes-Livingstone Journal*, xvi (1954), p. 36) makes some useful comments on the Angolan slave trade. See also my annotated translation of selected passages from Dias de Carvalho, ' A Lunda Love Story and its Consequences ', in *The Rhodes-Livingstone Journal*, xix (1955), for the Northern Lunda traditions.

[2] The land of Mwantiyanvwa is called *Luunda* or *Luwunda*, and his people *Aluunda*, by Ndembu.

[3] Dias de Carvalho, H. A., *Expedição Portuguesa ao Muatianvua* (1890), p. 541.

[4] Verhulpen, E., *Baluba et Balubaisés de Katanga* (1936).

Southern Lunda chiefs or their representatives to the potentate's capital on the Lulua river when a new Mwantiyanvwa succeeds.[1] When a Southern Lunda chief succeeds to office, confirmation is sought from Mwantiyanvwa. When the British Government sought to abolish the Ndembu chieftainship of Nyakaseya in 1947, the incumbent hastened to Mwantiyanvwa who wrote a letter to the Western Provincial Commissioner on his behalf. As a result he was reinstated.

According to White,[2] the Southern Lunda

largely retained their own language and to a greater degree their social system. One reason for this seems to have been that they migrated into a broken thinly-populated country where they had less chance of being absorbed by the people whom they found already there. The latter were of Lukolwe stock as evidenced by the names of rivers which they have left. . . . Indeed the Lukolwe, whose remnants today are a very primitive people, may have been one factor which was responsible for the failure of the Lunda to show the same degree of enterprise as their neighbours. . . . Lunda also suffered continuously from the incursions of their Lwena and Chokwe neighbours which may indicate that they were a later migration, at a disadvantage with their earlier established neighbours, which prevented their expansion and development. Hence the Chokwe and the Lwena were able to live in more open, flatter country, whilst the Lunda took refuge in broken hilly country between the Zambezi and Kabompo headwaters where they lived in small scattered communities.

There are today in the Mwinilunga Ndembu region some twenty-six villages, the residential cores of which claim to be of 'Mbwela' origin. The term 'Mbwela' appears to have been widely applied by in-coming groups of Lunda stock to the more primitive Bantu peoples, such as Lukolwe, whom they encountered to the south and west of their homeland. Ndembu today use the term *kabeta Kambwela* to denote 'the south'. Sometimes they group Mbwela and Kaonde together as having a cultural affinity. The Mwinilunga group of putative Mbwela origin are

---

[1] As in 1951, when Mbaka succeeded. Both Kanongeshas sent representatives, Musokantanda and Kazembe Mutanda went in person, and several Native Authority Sub-Chiefs such as Ikelenge, Nyakaseya and Mwininyilamba visited the new Mwantiyanvwa, each with his entourage who were given food by the potentate.

[2] White, C. M. N., 'The Balovale Peoples and their Historical Background', *The Rhodes-Livingstone Journal*, viii (1949), pp. 35-6.

generally known as 'Kawiku', after the name of a plain to the
north-east of Mwinilunga Boma, where they are first said to
have been encountered by Kanongesha's invaders. According to
Ndembu and Kawiku traditions they resisted the invaders for
many years before they submitted. In Angola, the Ndembu apply
the name ' Humbu ' to a population of Mbwela origin in the
south, and the senior Humbu headman Kafwana plays an important role in the Angolan Kanongesha's installation ritual.
Today Kawiku and Humbu are culturally and linguistically
almost indistinguishable from Ndembu, but on occasion still
maintain that they are ' the owners of the country '.
Ndembu did not establish themselves as a higher caste or class
above the Kawiku. Both groups intermarry freely and live at
the same economic level. Ndembu, however, consider Kawiku
to be turbulent, clownish and discourteous people and jibe at their
selfish and quarrelsome behaviour. Kawiku take delight in
fostering these beliefs by joking about their own uncouthness.
It is doubtful whether Ndembu have retained the social system
practised in their homeland to the extent indicated by White.
Several well-informed accounts of Mwantiyanvwa's state of
Luunda exist which give the picture of a highly centralized
political system.[1]   In the royal capital a host of nobles and officials
were permanently stationed, supported by the tribute that flowed
in, at the height of Lunda power, from chiefdoms as widely
separated from one another as Kapenda-ka-Mulemba to the west
and Kazembe on the Luapula to the east, a distance of more than
seven hundred miles. Not only tribute but trade contributed
to the surplus which maintained the Lunda nobility. Mwantiyanvwa had trade agreements with a number of Ovimbundu
chiefs who despatched caravans into the interior bearing trade
goods in exchange for slaves, ivory and, later, rubber and bees-
wax.[2] Capello and Ivens [3] wrote in 1882, when the empire was
already on the wane, ' at a short distance from the *mu-sumba*
[*Musumba*, " state capital "] are established vast markets, true

---

[1] Dias de Carvalho ; Buchner, M., ' Das Reich des Mwata Yamvo und
seine Nachbarländer ', *Deutsche Geographische Blätter*, I (1883) ; Pogge, P.,
Im Reiche des Mwata Yamvo (1880).
[2] Childs, G. M., *Umbundu Kinship and Character* (1949), p. 205.
[3] Capello, H., and Ivens, R., *From Benguella to the Territory fo Yacca*, translated by A. Elwes, (1882), vol. I, p. 389.

bazaars containing straight lanes or streets where flour of various kinds, ginguba, palm-oil, fresh and dried meat, massambala, salt, tobacco, maluvo (palm wine), mabellas, and other articles are displayed, and are bartered for merchandise, such as blue and red baize, cottons, printed calico, large white and small red beads, powder, arms and bracelets '. Verhulpen mentions how the razzias of the Lunda and Luba states swept the Central African area for slaves to sell to the Bangala and Ovimbundu middle-men of the Portuguese in exchange for guns and trade goods.

To maintain this system of tribute, trade and pillage, Mwanti-yanvwa had at his disposal a powerful army quartered in the capital and divided into advance, flank and rear guards, each army corps having a reserve of liaison personnel and scouts. Capello and Ivens [1] mention ' wars of extermination ' waged by Mwantiyanvwa against ' recalcitrant tributaries ' and dynastic rivals.

The Ndembu, on the other hand, seem never to have had anything like the same degree of political centralization as their Lunda ancestors.[2] It is said that Kanongesha, ' a son of Mwanti-yanvwa ', was accompanied, or followed shortly afterwards, by twelve senior headmen drawn from various Lunda noble families, when he first entered the present Mwinilunga area.[3] Each of these was accompanied by relatives, male and female, and a retinue of warriors. It took at least a generation of intermittent raiding to subdue the indigenous peoples, and the invaders were scattered far and wide over the country in pursuit of them. Eventually, so the tradition goes, the Southern Lunda chiefs, together with some neighbouring Lwena chiefs such as

[1] Capello and Ivens, vol. 1, pp. 390-2.

[2] For instance, Livingstone writes in his journal for 1854 that in the Lunda area of Kazembe (immediately north of Kanongesha's Ndembu), ' the frequent instances which occur of people changing from one part of the country to another show that *the great chiefs possess only a limited power* ' (my italics)—*Missionary Travels and Researches in Southern Africa* (1857), p. 305.

[3] Campbell, D. (*Wandering in Central Africa* (1929), p. 52 et seq.) is, I think, substantially correct when he attributes the ' colonial expansion ' of the Lunda—of which the Ndembu migration was a part—to ' wars of jealousy and internecine strifes that scattered leaders, who, with ambitious followings went farther and farther afield . . . nibbling into the weak frontiers of other tribes '.

c

Chinyama and Nyakatolu, whose forbears had come from Mwantiyanvwa in an earlier wave of migration, met together and divided up the conquered Mbwela and Lukolwe land between them, using the larger rivers as boundaries. Kanongesha received as his share the land between the Zambezi, West Lunga and Lufwiji, with Ishinde as his southern neighbour, Musokantanda to the east, Kazembe Mutanda to the north, and the Lwena chieftainess, Nyakatolu, to the west. Kanongesha recognized the claims of his twelve headmen to certain tracts of land which they had conquered, and later allocated further areas to certain of his sons and close matrilineal kin. He retained the largest share, including most of the Mwinilunga Ndembu region south of what is now the north-western pedicle of Mwinilunga District, and the Angolan region around the Lovwa river, to be under his direct control. The headmen and relatives to whom he had given areas were supposed to send him tribute of various kinds ; unrelated headmen had to send him tributary wives from their own matrilineages. He himself had to send a portion of the tribute thus obtained to Mwantiyanvwa, a custom which was discontinued several years before the Chokwe invasion of that potentate's territories in 1885.

After the division of the land, Ndembu tradition reports a long period of peace, during which there were no wars against neighbouring tribes. In this period, however, it would appear that the minor and minimal political units, the senior headmen's areas and the villages within them, became increasingly autonomous and independent of Kanongesha's control. Traditions exist of feuds during this period between senior headmen and even between individual villages and vicinages. Several factors are responsible for this regression towards local autonomy. Among these may be reckoned isolation from Luunda with its relatively high level of culture and social organization ; the small number of Ndembu invaders and Mbwela invaded alike, scattered over a wide region of forested terrain ; and the low level and rudimentary character of economic production associated with small shifting settlements. Villages were not permanently anchored to specific tracts of land but moved across the face of the Ndembu region with relative freedom. High spatial mobility contributed powerfully to the considerable political autonomy of the village.

The decentralization and mobility of Kanongesha's Ndembu were accelerated by the slave-trading and slave-raiding which reached their height in this region in the second half of the nineteenth century. Ovimbundu slave-traders made trade pacts with Kanongesha and important senior headmen such as Ikelenge, in north-west Mwinilunga,[1] and these powerful men raided their own tribesmen and sold them into slavery in return for guns and cloth. Later, Chokwe and Lwena, heavily armed with Portuguese muskets, attacked the Ndembu, who at first presented no united front to the slave-raiders and were defeated village by village, the unfortunate inhabitants being marched off to join the long lines of slave caravans that converged on Nyakatolu's Lwena capital from the interior. The Ndembu were rallied, not by a chief, but by a commoner, Chipeng'e, who went round the country urging them to sink their private feuds and jointly hurl out the invaders. He inflicted several defeats on a large war-party of Chokwe and Lwena who were under the leadership of the Lwena chief Kangombe (mentioned by Dan Crawford).[2] After this, the raiders withdrew into Angola.

But the Ndembu were not left long in peace, for in 1906, following the announcement of the King of Italy's arbitration of 1905, which settled a long-standing dispute between Great Britain and Portugal over the exact position of the western boundary of N. Rhodesia, officers of the British South Africa Company, accompanied by native police, commenced the administration of the new Mwinilunga District. As a result of the harshness of an early administrator, there was a mass migration of Ndembu out of the Company's territory into the Belgian Congo and Angola. The officer in question was discharged, but hardly had the people returned than there was a new exodus —in 1913, when taxation was first introduced. The senior headman Ikelenge, later to become a Sub-Chief under the Native Authority, was the only important Ndembu to remain, arguing that the taxes would produce benefits for the people in the form of roads, services and peaceful government. Chipeng'e, now an

---

[1] Gann, L. (p. 33), points out that the Angolan slave dealers, unlike the Arabs, never established political rule of their own, but preferred to work through native chiefs.

[2] Crawford, D., *Thinking Black* (1912), p. 116; Tilsley, G. E., *Dan Crawford, Missionary and Pioneer in Central Africa* (1929), pp. 104-5.

old man, encouraged the flight, realizing that the Europeans were too strong to eject by force. Gradually the population trickled back and were regrouped into villages by the Native Commissioner, the leaders of the malcontents being compelled to build near the Boma (a widely applied term for the head-quarters of the British District Administration) where an eye could be kept on them.

In 1906 Kalene Mission was founded by Dr. Walter Fisher of the Christian Mission in Many Lands at Kalene Hill in the northern pedicle, and a hospital and school for Africans were built soon afterwards. This event was to have important effects on the distribution of Ndembu villages and ultimately on their internal structure. For a time Ndembu regarded Kalene Hill as an alternative administrative centre and headmen took tribute to Dr. Fisher as a mark of vassalage. After each exodus from the Boma area, many headmen returned to Mwinilunga to build near the Mission, and others came from Angola where illicit slave-trading continued into the twentieth century. A trading store was early established at Kalene ; and in 1921, Dr. Fisher's son, ffolliot Fisher, started Hillwood Farm, near Ikelenge's vil-lage, twelve miles from Kalene, and a store was eventually added to this.

Some years later Sakeji School, a boarding school for the children of European missionaries of various Protestant denom-inations, was founded close to Hillwood Farm. In 1952 nearly sixty children were in attendance at the school. Altogether, in 1952, there were about a hundred Europeans, including teachers of European and African school children, doctors, state registered nurses, missionaries, and farm managers at Hillwood, in the pedicle area. Each of the three European centres employed a large African staff, including hospital attendants, farm hands, road labourers, school teachers, clerks and domestic servants. In addition to these, others were employed as store capitaos (foremen) and maintenance men by European commercial firms, whose headquarters were on the Northern Rhodesian Copper-belt. Each African in regular wage employment, whether he lived within the precincts of the European settlements or in an adjacent Ndembu village, tended to become surrounded by kinsmen who sought his patronage.

Three senior headmen in the pedicle became Native Authority

Sub-Chiefs under Government, and each of them is surrounded by an entourage of paid petty officials : clerks, *kapasus* (Native Authority Messengers), assessors, and the like. At each Sub-Chief's capital village there is a Lower School under the supervision of the Christian Mission in Many Lands at Kalene Hill. At one, that of Chief Ikelenge, there is a dispensary, a Post-Office, and a Native Authority Market.

The tendency to cluster round a European settlement in villages which began in Dr. Fisher's time has continued, and today each European centre, and indeed each Native Authority headquarters, has become the focus of a large African population. Not only those already employed, but those who seek wage employment, come to settle in villages and other local units in the pedicle, either by attaching themselves to already existing villages where they have kin, or by coming in kinship groups and founding new residential units. The fact that the soil in the pedicle is considered by Ndembu to be especially suitable for cassava cultivation is a further strong inducement to settle there.

Payment of domestic servants and labourers and the creation of opportunities for buying trade goods and selling native produce in the northern pedicle led to further increases in its population. Game was virtually exterminated in the pedicle by Africans with muzzle-loaders and Europeans with rifles. ˙ Local trade in dried meat and fish developed with Angolan and Congo Africans who exchanged these commodities for cash and store goods. This area was the first in Mwinilunga to grow crops for cash as well as for subsistence. Today this priority in development is reflected in the existence of a number of African traders, especially in Ikelenge's area near Hillwood Farm, who buy cassava meal from the villagers for re-sale to the Boma and to Belgian traders in the Congo. The pedicle area exhibits the highest degree of disruption of the traditional social system seen in the Ndembu region.

Many immigrants, including some Lwena and Ovimbundu, have entered the area since 1920, often to seek asylum from the Portuguese who had put down several rebellions of the interior tribes. The social composition of the pedicle has thus become extremely heterogeneous and its position astride labour routes from the adjacent colonial territories to the Rhodesian line-of-rail have made it subject to continual stimuli from alien cultures. In the last few years profound changes have occurred in the residential structure in this area : the most noteworthy has been the breakdown of traditional villages into small units headed by younger men who participate in the encroaching cash economy. These units known as *mafwami* (from the English ' farms ') increased enormously in number between my first and second periods of field-work. But since change is not proceeding evenly either in tempo or direction in all areas alike, I found it possible to observe many villages which retained the indigenous structure, even in the pedicle, and whose inhabitants still tended to conform to traditional norms of behaviour.

The traditional village was a circle of pole-and-mud huts typically containing a core of matrilineally related kin under the leadership of a member of the senior genealogical generation chosen by the villagers. The *ifwami* or ' farm ' consists of one or more Kimberley-brick houses bordered by a few mud huts and it is occupied by the farm head, his elementary family and a small fringe of kin and unrelated persons. In the pedicle near European settlements and Native Authority Sub-Chiefs' capital villages a ribbon-development of farms has begun along the Government motor roads. In this book I lay major stress on the problems posed by the structure of traditional villages and leave over for a further study the social organization of the farm. But this sudden multiplication of farms in a few years was only the outward manifestation of changes in values and of conflicts between old and new principles of social organization, which had been going on with gathering intensity within the framework of the traditional village for some time. I have tried to indicate some of the effects of social and cultural change on the rate and type of village fission at different periods in this century in Chapters Four to Seven. But until about 1950 the major effect of economic and political changes was to increase the rate and not to alter significantly the type of fission. The basic unit of fission was a maternal descent group. Today there are signs that the elementary family is becoming the typical unit of fission and that the links binding together uterine siblings and matrilineal parallel cousins are wearing thin. I mention these tendencies but do not discuss them in detail. In the group of villages I selected for particular study (most of them in the area of the deposed Native Authority Sub-Chief Mukang'ala), the effects of change on the social structure were visible, but they were far less pronounced than in the pedicle.

When Indirect Rule was introduced in 1930, the Northern Rhodesian claimant to the Kanongesha chieftainship was given the status of Senior Chief, and six senior headmen were made Sub-Chiefs.[1] These were : Chibwika, Ikelenge (or Ikelengi), Nyakaseya, Mwininyilamba, Mukang'ala, and Ntambu Lukon-kesha. Chibwika—like Kanongesha reduplicated in Angola—is the title given to the nominated successor of Kanongesha. His area lies to the south of Kanongesha's with which it is contiguous. Ikelenge is descended from an official called *Kalula* who accompanied the first Kanongesha. At the installation ritual of a Kanongesha his duty is to remove the lion and leopard skins from the chiefly chair. Today his area lies in the south-east of the pedicle.[2] To his west is the area of Mwininyilamba whose ancestor was the *Ifwota* or ' scout ', the leader of a war-party which went in advance of Kanongesha's forces during the invasion. Nyakaseya (' she who pours out ') is a title made for the first Kanongesha's senior wife (*mwadyi*) whose duty was to pour out beer when the chief offered it to his guests. Today Nyakaseya is a male Sub-Chief in the north of the pedicle. Mukang'ala's title was created by the second Kanongesha, Kabanda, for his son who subdued the Kawiku. His village was situated fairly near the Kawiku Plain in order that he might prevent rebellion. The senior Kawiku headman Nsang'anyi paid him tribute and

[1] Actually, Government had given *de facto* recognition to these headmen as ' Sub-Chiefs ' long before 1930. C. M. N. White (personal communication) prefers to call them ' Sub-Chiefs ' rather than ' senior headmen ' in the pre-European organization. White writes that ' they have always had royal insignia, their titles go back to the early days of the Lunda chiefs' coming, and the Lunda themselves in any interpretation of what the vernacular means, regard them as Sub-Chiefs '. I use different terms for their traditional and modern positions because I believe, as I have argued in Chapter Eleven, pp. 323-7, that their status rested on different criteria before British rule. In the past they enjoyed moral and ritual pre-eminence, but did not necessarily possess effective political authority. Today, since they are supported by the Administration, they have greater powers of coercion and are organized into a hierarchy of authority, but some of them, whose status rests on insecure or inadequate traditional foundations, do not command the respect senior headmen formerly possessed.

[2] See Map 2.

acted as his *Chivwikankanu*, a ritual office which gave him an important role at the installation ritual of a Mukang'ala. Kafwana, the senior headman of the Humbu in Angola, was Kanongesha's *Chivwikankanu*. Kafwana's office, which means literally ' he who puts on the *lukanu*', involved the investing of a new Kanongesha with the *lukanu* bracelet of human sinews and portions of genitalia, the supreme symbol of Lunda chieftainship, and thereafter the periodical renewal of its ritual powers by washing it with special medicines.   The other Sub-Chief recognized by Government in 1930 was Ntambu Lukonkesha. Ntambu was not tributary to Kanongesha in the past but paid tribute directly to Mwantiyanvwa.   Although his territory was much smaller than Kanongesha's his status was just as high.   The father of the present Angolan Kanongesha was Chief Ntambu and the father of Ntambu was a former Kanongesha.   Traditionally, Ntambu had the right to sit on a chair in the presence of Kanongesha, but Kanongesha's senior headmen, some of whom are now Sub-Chiefs, had to sit on the ground.

In 1936 Ntambu, and in 1947 Mukang'ala, had recognition withdrawn from them.   McCulloch, on the basis of information from White, writes : [1] ' Formerly these Sub-Chiefdoms seem to have been quite firmly established, but today political boundaries have been greatly altered and in the interests of centralization recognition has been withdrawn from " redundant " Chiefs and several areas have been amalgamated.' The areas of both ' redundant ' chiefs have been incorporated in Kanongesha's own area.

Few of the modern Sub-Chiefs were in fact ' firmly established '. Of the twelve headmen who came originally with Kanongesha, or followed him shortly afterwards, some are now ordinary headmen.   These include Chibwakata, the present incumbent of the office of *Kambanji* (' war-leader ' and ' executioner '), whose village is a few miles from Mwinilunga Boma, Kabung'u and Nyachilesya in Angola, and Mwanta waLuunda, Nyachikanda, Kabuya and Chota in Mwinilunga District.   By an odd quirk of fortune, Kakoma, the ' war-leader ' of Musokantanda (one of the senior migrant chiefs from Luunda), has been appointed a Sub-Chief ;   and Musokantanda's ' emblem-purifier ' (*Chiv-*

---

[1] McCulloch, p. 26.

wikankanu) Sailunga, has been appointed Senior Chief of the Akosa. Sub-Chief Mwininyilamba's original area was on the east of the Lunga River near the Kasanjiku Stream, in what is now ' Sailunga's Area '. Towards the end of the nineteenth century the incumbent of the time fled after a quarrel from this area and settled in what is now the pedicle. The senior headman there was a perpetual ' son ' [1] of Kanongesha, called Kafweku, who collected tribute from village headmen for Kanongesha. When Authorities were appointed in 1930, Mwininyilamba, although a refugee from another area, was appointed Sub-Chief of Kafweku's area. Ndembu say this was done because the Mwininyilamba of the time was a forceful character with a large village, whereas the Kafweku was a timid man who avoided meeting Europeans.

It is doubtful in fact whether the headmen recognized as Sub-Chiefs by Government were ever regarded as ' chiefs ' [2] by Ndembu with the exception of Ntambu Lukonkesha. They were simply village headmen who possessed important historical titles. Certain of them claim to have received their insignia from Mwantiyanvwa. If they were strong men with large villages Kanongesha might have entrusted them with certain tasks. Finally, if he were not related to them by ' perpetual kinship ',

---

[1] The son of a Lunda chief who has been granted his own area and at the same time excluded from the succession to his father's title is called *Mwana awuta* or *Mwanawuta*. Mukang'ala is also a *Mwanawuta* of Kanongesha. I. G. Cunnison (*A Social Study of a Bantu People*, unpublished thesis, Oxford University, p. 116), defines *perpetual relationship* as a relationship between the titles of headmen and chiefs which always remains constant irrespective of the actual genealogical relationship of the individuals holding titles, and which expresses the political relationships between the different chiefs and headmen. Cunnison has recently published a paper on ' Perpetual Kinship : a political institution of the Luapula peoples ' in *The Rhodes-Livingstone Journal*, xx, pp. 28–48.

[2] All were entitled to the respect due to their historical status as founders of the Ndembu people and all had certain insignia such as wooden slit-gongs, xylophones, bangles, short swords, etc. Some utilized the initial advantage given them by this status to dominate small areas. Harding (*In Remotest Barotseland* (1904), p. 146) describes Ikelenge (' Eakaling ') as a ' very important chief under Kanongesha '. His capital village was then at Kalene Hill, which was an important centre in the slave-trade with the Ovimbundu. It is likely that the Ikelenge headmen built up wealth and influence by trading in slaves. Harding published his book in 1895. He visited Ikelenge in the 1880's when Ovimbundu slave-traders still dealt with Ndembu headmen.

he might marry into their families. But although the boundaries of their areas have been rigidly demarcated by the Administration it appears as if many of them ranged widely over the Ndembu region in the past. Mukang'ala, for example, during part of the nineteenth century made his capital village well to the east of the Lunga. I mention below the spatial mobility of other important villages, including Chibwakata, and in the last chapter discuss in some detail the role of the senior headmen in the indigenous social system.

The Kanongesha in Angola is regarded by most Ndembu in Mwinilunga District as their authentic chief, since he possesses the *lukanu* given by Mwantiyanvwa to Kanongesha Kabanda (see p. 320). The first Kanongesha to enter Mwinilunga District, Mulumbi, took this *lukanu* with him when he left Angola in the early 1920's. Meanwhile a new Kanongesha was elected by the senior headman of the Angolan Ndembu who blamed Mulumbi for leaving the Isenga River Island area where the graves of former Kanongeshas were located. In 1927 the Angolan Kanongesha, Sakayoli Chifuwu, conspired with Kafwana, the Angolan Humbu senior headman, who then obtained the *lukanu* from Mulumbi on the pretext that it had been defiled and had lost its virtue. Kafwana told Mulumbi that he would wash it with medicine at the cross-roads to the west of the capital village at midnight to cleanse it. He took the *lukanu* and went straight to Angola where he gave it to Sakayoli. Mulumbi tried to obtain a new *lukanu* from Mwantiyanvwa, but according to most Ndembu was not given an audience by him. He returned indeed with a new *lukanu*, but this is said to have been made by a Luunda court official,[1] not by Mwantiyanvwa.

The formal structure of the Ndembu political system under the Native Authorities Ordinance and the Native Courts Ordinance presents a rigid hierarchical appearance quite foreign to the indigenous structure. In the past there was only a single Ndembu 'chief' (*mwanta wampata*) confirmed in his office and tributary to Mwantiyanvwa, and his effective authority was confined to his own immediate area. The first senior headmen (*ayilolu*)[2] were initially allocated tracts of bush in which they had rights

---

[1] Chipawu.
[2] For a discussion of the meaning of this term see p. 323.

to hunt and cultivate and to exact tribute from incomers who wished to hunt and cultivate there. In return for these rights they had to give Kanongesha tribute when he asked for it and tributary wives from their own matrilineages. But with the continual movement of villages from site to site, and with the frequency of village fission, it became extremely difficult for senior headmen to exert political authority over the inhabitants of their areas. The basic economy of the Ndembu, cassava-growing and hunting, did not compel any individual or group to remain in one specific area. In the period of slave-trading and -raiding, ties between groups and localities must have been further loosened both by internecine raiding and by the instant necessity to be ready to flee before an external enemy. In such an unstable and highly mobile society Kanongesha could not enforce his rule on senior headmen and the latter could not exact obedience from the villagers in their areas. Villages resorted directly to force in the form of self-help in defence of the rights of individuals and groups. If a chief or a senior headman managed to establish some degree of centralization in his area this was due more to personal qualities than to his social position. Unlike such chiefs as Kazembe of the Luapula Valley or Chitimukulu of the Bemba, the Kanongeshas had no military forces permanently stationed at their capitals. They had to rely on possessing rather larger followings of kin and slaves than other headmen, even to enjoy local political pre-eminence. In Chapter Eleven I argue that the position of the Kanongesha was ritually rather than politically important and that he was respected rather than obeyed.

The position of the Chief and of those senior headmen who have been appointed as Sub-Chiefs has been considerably strengthened by Government. McCulloch, following White, writes that [1]

today all civil cases and lesser criminal cases can be tried by the court of the Native Authority (the Chief's court) as constituted by the Native Courts Ordinance. The Chief is officially supposed to preside at trials, but in practice cases are often heard only by assessors. From this court, appeal lies in the first instance to a special Appeal Court of the Native Authority, then to the District Commissioner, and

---

[1] McCulloch, pp. 26-7, see also p. 71, based on MSS. and personal communications.

finally to the High Court of Northern Rhodesia. More serious crimes are taken directly to the District Commissioner, who may remit to the Native Authority any cases which he considers to lie under his jurisdiction. Imprisonment can be given for certain criminal offences by courts of the Native Authorities, but this happens comparatively rarely, and the usual penal sanction is a fine. Both fines and court fees are paid to the Native Treasury. In fact many minor cases tend to be settled out of court, but the Lunda Chiefs discourage this. . . . Cases concerning land rarely come into the Native Authority courts, but are usually settled by village heads.

In the past there do not appear to have been such centralized judicial institutions. Kanongesha and his important headmen— and their importance it must be remembered varied with personal and other adventitious factors—might on application test a diviner's attribution of witchcraft or sorcery to a person by recourse to their own poison oracles. Occasionally they might officiate in the ritual of *Musolu* to bring on belated rains and confer fertility on crops, animals and men. But in general most disputes were settled at the level of the vicinage (*chitung'ili*). Men skilled in the advocacy of cases, known as *mahaku*, or in judgment, known as *akwakusompesha*, were jointly invited by a plaintiff or his representative and a defendant or his representative to discuss the case and give their verdict. Such men were often, but need not necessarily have been, headmen. If there were a senior headman (an important *chilolu*) in the vicinage most cases in that vicinage would be settled in his village. Cases were seldom brought to Kanongesha's court on appeal. Kanongesha in fact was politically hardly more than a senior headman writ large and his effective authority was confined to the few vicinages of his immediate area.

The Native Authority and Sub-Chiefs are allowed to legislate under the guidance of the Administration. But there is much passive resistance against the implementation of Native Authority Rules and Orders by villagers who resent the political powers vested in the Native Authority.

Apart from those areas in the pedicle nearest to European settlements and Sub-Chiefs' capital villages, many features of the indigenous social system have tended to persist in much of western Mwinilunga, especially at the village and vicinage levels. This is probably due to a series of factors, including the thinness of

European settlement in the District, the distance from urban centres, the inadequacy of roads until recently, and the high cost of transport.   Little stimulus has been given to agriculture and consequently the traditional system of subsistence has not been greatly modified.   Since this mode of subsistence was congruent with the pre-European social organization the effects of modern changes on the Mwinilunga Ndembu have, until the post-war period, been much less radical and far-reaching than in other parts of Northern Rhodesia, such as the Northern Province.   In the last few years, however, changes brought about by the growing participation of Ndembu in the Rhodesian cash economy and an increased rate of labour migration, have in some areas, notably the pedicle, drastically reshaped some institutions and destroyed others.   In this book I shall consider in greatest detail the more conservative area of ex-Sub-Chief Mukang'ala where the effects of change have been hitherto less prominent.

Social change of the type we have been considering is to some extent reflected in Table I where population densities in the pedicle chiefdoms are compared with those in other Ndembu chiefdoms. Population figures were kindly made available to me by the

TABLE I

TOTAL POPULATION IN NDEMBU AREA

Native authority	Area (sq. m.)	Population	Density (per sq. m.)
Pedicle chiefdoms :			
Ikelenge	230	6,927	30·12
Nyakaseya	288	3,614	12·55
Mwininyilamba	162	978	6·04
Total pedicle chiefdoms . . .	680	11,519	16·91
Other Ndembu chiefdoms :			
Kanongesha	1,098	3,476	3·17
Chibwika	1,216	3,351	2·76
Total other chiefdoms . . .	2,314	6,827	2·92
Total Ndembu	2,994	18,346	6·13

District Commissioner, Mr. R. C. Dening, and are based on tax-registers. The areas of chiefdoms were plotted on a map of Mwinilunga District made by Mr. Dening. Table I shows the much higher density of population in the pedicle, especially in Chief Ikelenge's area,[1] some reasons for which have been previously considered. Mukang'ala's area, where most of the field research for this study was conducted, is included in Kanongesha's area by Government and must have roughly the same population density as the latter. It is an area of low density, and in Mwinilunga District by and large low density is associated with cultural persistence and higher density with culture change. In Mukang'ala's area, and particularly among the Kawiku, the traditional economy is still dominant, including a certain amount of hunting and collecting. In the next section of this chapter my account of the Ndembu economic system is founded on observations I made in that area.

Ecology

McCulloch [2] has summarized the available literature on the physical environment and the main features of the economy of the Mwinilunga Ndembu. I give below an outline of her account of the physical environment.

The Ndembu region is part of the Plateau region of the north-western area of Northern Rhodesia,[3] a very ancient land surface formed upon the basement complex of Archaean rocks (intensely folded and metamorphosed gneisses or schists, quartzites, limestones and shales, with intrusive granites). Altitude at Mwinilunga station is 4,500 to 5,000 feet. Most of the District is flat woodland with outcrops of hills at Kalene.

The rains usually begin in October but sometimes in September. The heaviest rain falls during November and December, the main planting months, and the wet season ends in April. During the period between 1926 and 1937 annual rainfall at Mwinilunga ranged from 47·88 in. to 74·83 in. with a mean of 54·75 in.

The mean maximum temperature is 84°, and the maximum monthly temperature remains very constant except in September

---

[1] See also Map 2, showing high concentration of villages in the pedicle.

[2] McCulloch, pp. 2–4, 14–17.

[3] Trapnell, C. G. and Clothier, J., *Ecological Survey of North-West Rhodesia* (1937). ·

and October, when it rises to 89·6°. The monthly minima show a greater range of fluctuation, from 44·6° in June and July, to 60·8° in January and February. The year thus falls into three regimes of temperature : November to April, an equable period, during which the maxima and minima show a small range ; May to August, characterized by low minima ; and September and October, when high maxima are registered. In the cold season night frosts sometimes occur.

The soils of Mwinilunga [1] are mostly of the Kalahari contact type, ranging from pale-coloured sandy loams and clay-sand soils to better-class light-reddish and brown soils of similar texture, and representing denuded or modified remains of a greater extension of the sands. With the exception of redder samples in Mwinilunga District they are of low productivity.

Most of the District is covered with *Brachystegia* woodlands. Thick *Cryptosepalum* forest occurs in the south of the Ndembu region between the Kabompo, Lunga and Manyinga rivers. Due to its situation close to the Zambezi-Congo Divide, Mwinilunga District is well watered and in fact is a source-area of many rivers, most of them perennial. The Lunga is the only fairly large river in the region of the Mwinilunga Ndembu. Grassy plains sometimes surround rivers for some distance from their sources. Dry patches of grassland are not infrequent.

Game was formerly abundant, especially on river plains, and in grassy tracts where woodland is stunted : but the game has been almost exterminated in the pedicle of land in the north-west of the District that projects between Angola and the Belgian Congo. In the rest of the District woodland, duiker and bush-buck, and grassland dik-dik, are still quite plentiful. But hunting, formerly the dominant masculine activity, has been considerably restricted by Government and Native Authority rules and orders. Men must obtain a licence to purchase a gun and the number of licences issued every year is small. Permits must be obtained to buy gunpowder or cartridges, and these are granted only for limited quantities. Certain types of traps such as pitfalls and snares are forbidden. There is a system of Controlled Areas by which the District is divided into First and Second-Class Controlled Areas

---

[1] Trapnell and Clothier. May be consulted for details and for an excellent map showing the distribution of soil and vegetation types.

and Uncontrolled Areas. In a First-Class Controlled Area, where game is plentiful, even residents need a permit to hunt. These are given only to known hunters in the area, and the District Commissioner has arranged with the Game Department for the Government Chief to have a major hand in control. In Second-Class Controlled Areas, those who do not reside there must have permits to hunt.

The Ndembu region is classified as Native Trust Land with the exception of some Crown Land near the junction of the Lwakela and West Lunga rivers, set aside as Forest Reserve in 1952, and the territory occupied by Mission Stations and by Hillwood and Matonchi Farms.

Agriculture

Ndembu are shifting hoe cultivators and hunters.[1] Their staple crop is cassava, of both the sweet (*manihot palmata*) and the bitter (*manihot utilissima*) varieties. Finger-millet is grown, mostly for the making of beer. Maize is cultivated in streamside gardens (*matempa*) in black alluvial soil and also around villages. In addition a wide variety of subsidiary crops are cultivated, including beans, groundnuts, sweet potatoes, yams, cucurbits, tomatoes, onions, potatoes, cabbages and a number of small relish plants. But with the exception of beans and sweet potatoes these are grown only in small quantities.

The main gardens (*maha*) are those containing cassava and, in the first year of cultivation, some finger-millet. In the area with which I am most familiar, that of the deposed Sub-Chief Mukang'ala immediately to the north of the District Head-quarters, the usual practice is to clear high *Marquesia* or *Brachystegia* woodland growing on red or orange loams and to heap up the felled branches in irregular piles, occupying anything from an eleventh to an eighth of the cleared area. These are then burnt and the resulting ash-patches (*mashita*) are broadcast with finger-millet. Some maize, pumpkins and other cucurbits are planted on the ash-patches, but many *mashita* may not be planted at all if seed is not available. The finger-millet is generally sown in December and harvested in May and June, when the rains are

---

[1] McCulloch, p. 14, writes that 'the Southern Lunda were in the past primarily hunters and subsistence cultivators'.

over. At the onset of the next rains, in October, the garden is hoed up into mounds and planted with cassava cuttings. At the end of the following rains, i.e. about eighteen months after planting, some cassava is taken from the garden and thenceforth continuously for about two-and-a-half years until the crop has been used up. The land is abandoned after one or sometimes two plantings of cassava on it, and the bush is then allowed to regenerate completely, resulting in a fallow period of about thirty years.   We studied the pattern of land-holding of a vicinage in September 1953, in the neighbourhood of Mwinilunga airfield between four and seven miles from the Boma [1] along the Boma-Kalene motor road. The gardens were plotted by compass and tape by my wife and an African assistant trained in surveying methods by the Agricultural Department. It was found that for a total population of 461 the area under finger-millet and cassava cultivation totalled 441·1 acres, or ·96 of an acre per person. Streamside gardens under maize cultivation totalled 52·5 acres, or ·11 of an acre per person. Taking both bush and streamside gardens into account the total land-holding of the vicinage amounted to 493·6 acres, or 1·07 acres per person.

I showed these figures to Mr. Allan, former Deputy Director of Agriculture in Northern Rhodesia. He considered it reasonable to assume that cassava gardens are cultivated continuously for either four or five years and then left for thirty years to regenerate, and that the cultivable percentage of land suitable for the fertility requirements of cassava under the vegetation-soil conditions prevailing in Mwinilunga lay approximately between 20-40 per cent of the land surface. On this basis he calculated that the critical population or land-carrying capacity for the Ndembu system of land usage probably lay between 17-38 persons per square mile. These figures represent the approximate population limit which cannot be exceeded without setting in motion the process of land degradation. They will be examined later in relation to village magnitude and distribution.

The Social Organization of Gardening

In general it may be said that tree-felling and clearing and burning the undergrowth are the work of men, while planting,

---

[1] Headquarters of the District Administration.

D

weeding and harvesting, save for cassava which is planted by both sexes, are women's work.

Gardens are owned and worked individually and may be made wherever suitable land is available. Usually the individual members of a family make adjacent gardens. A polygynist husband's cassava garden is in the centre of a clearing and those of his wives at either side. A common pattern is for a man, his wife or wives and a favourite sister to work contiguous gardens. Brothers and male matrilineal parallel cousins tend to cultivate in separate blocks of gardens. As may be seen in Map 3, the holdings of a single village may be scattered in discrete blocks over a wide area.

The cutting and clearing of bush, and later the initial hoeing up of the cleared ground into mounds, may involve a collective work-party (*chenda*) of kin and neighbours. When a man wishes to fell trees and clear bush for a finger-millet garden he lets it be known that he has brewed beer or killed game for those participating in a *chenda* to be held in a few days. Such a *chenda* is restricted to men and older boys. The beer is displayed at the beginning of the work which commences at dawn and continues until the sun becomes very hot. If much beer has been brewed much bush will be cleared ; if little, a much smaller area. The productive individualism of Ndembu finds expression in the grumbling and mutual recriminations over the amount of work to be done, which take place between the sponsor of the *chenda* and the volunteers who attend. Since most adult men sponsor working parties, it means in effect that the majority of men in a vicinage work collectively for each other in turn. Each man sponsors a single *chenda* only, so that when it is over he has to complete the clearing by himself.

Hoeing parties for first-year cassava gardens may be sponsored by men or women and contain members of both sexes. The men proceed in advance of the women hoeing up the rough ground, and the women follow, breaking up the soil more finely and making neat mounds. Men and women usually work as married couples, although a brother and sister or father and daughter may work together. When the working party is over the sponsor subsequently works alone or in partnership with his or her spouse.

Streamside gardens are owned and worked individually by

women only.   Gardens around the village peripheries or in old
village sites are owned and worked individually by members of
both sexes.   Village gardens, in contrast to bush and streamside
gardens, may be owned by young unmarried individuals of
either sex.

In the past marriage was uxorilocal for the first year, in the
course of which the husband had to build a hut for his mother-in-
law and clear and hoe up a garden for her with his wife's help.
Then he took his wife to his own village and cut, cleared and
hoed up the rough ground into a garden for her.   In subsequent
years a much larger share of cultivation fell to the wife's lot and
she was also expected to help her husband in his own gardens.
Nowadays, the work for the mother-in-law is often commuted
into a cash payment, ranging from 10s. to £1 or more, depending
on the wealth and status of the parties involved.

Agricultural production, then, is pronouncedly individualistic
in character.   Collective working-parties do take place but they
are brief and sporadic and performed for individuals.   There is
no concept of a joint estate, worked collectively by a village or
lineage-segment, the produce of which is owned in common.
Marital and family teams frequently work together but by no
means necessarily or invariably.   Men and women own their
own gardens and spouses have no rights in one another's gardens.
On divorce a woman may continue to work in, and feed her
children from, her own garden at her ex-husband's village if she
lives nearby.   If a man dies his widow's standing crop is sold on
her behalf by her nearest matrilineal kinsman when he comes
to take her back to his village after the period of mourning is over.
Today, when the surpluses of subsistence crops are sold for cash,
and when in some areas newly introduced crops such as rice are
grown solely for the cash they bring in, husband and wife retain
for their separate use the money obtained from the sale of all
their respective produce.   When my wife and I attempted to
collect 'family budgets' we found that spouses never pooled
their incomes and that few of them knew how much cash the
partners had obtained.

Consumption

Although agricultural production is dominantly individualistic,
consumption is mainly communal.   In villages the men eat in

the central thatched shelter (*chota* or *njang'u*) and the women take turns in cooking for the whole group.   In the village I knew best there was a clockwise rotation in which each adult woman in the circle of huts cooked successively for all the men.   Cassava mush, the invariable staple of every meal, was prepared by a woman and her daughters.   The dried cassava roots had been previously pounded into flour by one woman, or more rarely a team of women, ranging from two to four.   Such pounding teams consisted of a pair of co-wives, or a group of sisters, or a mother and her daughters.   Women, girls and uncircumcised boys ate their food, cooked on a separate fire from that on which the men's food had been prepared, in the kitchens, either in family groups or with friends.   Sometimes an elementary family, including the husband, would eat together in the wife's kitchen.   In the northern pedicle this arrangement is becoming more common today than the collective meal of the men's group.   This is yet another aspect of the general breakdown of the traditional social organization in this area where subsistence cultivation is steadily giving way to petty commodity cultivation.   It will give way more rapidly when access to urban markets becomes easier and when new local markets come into existence.

Generally speaking, the bulk of the cassava required for the men's food is taken from the men's gardens and the major quantity for the family meals from the women's.   Visiting kin and friends are fed from the gardens of their hosts, not those of the spouses of their hosts.   But wives are required to process the food and cook for their husbands' guests, and failure to do so is placed high among the causes of early divorce.

In the total agricultural system, from the clearing of gardens to the cooking of food, women play a much more important role than men.   Men work in short spectacular bouts of energy ; the regular patient labour of the women in hoeing up mounds, weeding, digging up roots, soaking, carrying, drying, pounding, and sifting, and finally in cooking the cassava mush provides the steady sustenance of the group.   Ndembu consider a balanced meal to consist of cassava mush and relish.   Even when meat or fish is unavailable as relish women can substitute beans, cucurbits and small relish plants from their streamside gardens.

Male activity, generally in the co-operative form of the *chenda*, sets in train, as it were, an agricultural process which is then maintained throughout the year by women, each working alone in her garden or fitfully assisted by her husband. In agriculture, as in other aspects of Ndembu life, femininity may be equated with continuity, masculinity with discontinuity.

Nevertheless, the overall productive role of men is not regarded by Ndembu as being merely ancillary or peripheral to that of the women. The men have a role in the productive system which is autonomous and from which women are debarred not merely by its inherent dangers and difficulties but in addition by a number of ritual taboos. This role is that of hunter.

Hunting : A Masculine Occupation

It may almost be said that the Ndembu social system is pivoted on the importance of hunting.[1]   This importance does not derive from the objective contribution to the food supply made by the chase. Hunting owes its high valuation, on the one hand, to an association consistently made among many Central and Western Bantu between hunting and high social status, and on the other, to an identification made among these peoples of hunting with masculinity.

There are numerous traditions ascribing the foundation of Central and West-Central African states to hunters. In other societies in this area hunters appear as an aristocratic class. The Lunda empire in the Congo was said to have been founded by a Luban hunter called Chibinda (meaning ' hunter ') Ilunga, whose son became the first Mwantiyanvwa. The Luba state itself was established by ' a tribe of hunters coming from the great lakes to the north '.[2] The Ovimbundu chiefdom of Viye (Bihé) was founded by a hunter of Lunda origin. According to Capello and Ivens [3] the ' real aristocracy among the Jinga of western Angola was composed of hunters and warriors '. Baumann points out that the *muri* class of nobles among the Mbala were hunters. Torday [4] writes that ' the chief character in the

---

[1] In this they appear to resemble the Northern Chokwe of whom McCulloch, p. 35, writes : ' Northern Chokwe society is oriented around the importance of hunting in its economy.'

[2] Dias de Carvalho, p. 54.

[3] Capello and Ivens, vol. II, p. 69.

[4] Torday, E., ' On the Ethnology of the South-West Congo Free State', *Journal of the Royal Anthropological Institute* (1907), p. 152.

peculiar politico-religious revolution which resulted in the institution of the *riamba* cult among the Bashi-lange was a hunter, and
the *pakassero* revolutionary society [sic.] of Ladislau Magyar
(p. 266) was a society of hunters '. Baumann [1] writes of the
Chokwe that there is a ' hunting class ' with special privileges
and a high social status, and Chokwe religious and magical rites
emphasize the importance of hunting.[2] The Bangala tribe of
Western Angola were founded by a Lunda hunter, Chinguli.

These examples could be greatly multiplied from the literature,
and are cited here merely to demonstrate the high value set on
hunting throughout the Central Bantu culture area, especially
among groups of Lunda and Luba origin or affinities. Many of
these tribes have traditions of protracted migration from one
region to another, during which they raided settled peoples for
their crops and killed game for their meat supplies. Even when,
like the Bangala and Shinje of western Angola founded by Lunda
leaders, they finally established themselves in a single area, their
villages still practised a semi-nomadic way of life, living in more
or less temporary villages and moving to new sites when game
was scarce. It has been pointed out by de Préville [3] that many of
these hunting tribes inhabiting the forest country to the south of
the Congo Bend grow cassava. He endorses Dr. Livingstone's
observation ' that cassava-growing involves very little work '
and that it is mainly carried on by the hunters' wives. This is
certainly true when one considers the extent of masculine participation in the agricultural work of a millet or sorghum economy,
carried on by *chitemene* ash-planting techniques. I do not mean
to suggest that grain cultivation is incompatible with an emphasis
on hunting but merely wish to indicate that the extremely important status of hunting in the Ndembu hierarchy of values is
congruent with a type of cultivation which does not make heavy
demands on men's time and energy.[4] Since cassava was intro-

---

[1] Baumann, H. von, *Lunda : bei Bauern und Jägern in Inner-Angola*, Ergebnisse der Angola-Expedition des Museums für Volkerkunde (1935), p. 11.

[2] Torday writes (*Camp and Tramp in African Wilds* (1913), p. 208) : ' the
most striking feature of the Kioko in later times is that they were essentially
a nation of hunters and ironworkers, but principally the former.'

[3] Préville, A. de, *Les Sociétés africaines* (1894), p. 195 et seq.

[4] Cassava certainly anchors a group to the ground for at least four years
after planting, but during this period men are less heavily involved in agriculture than in a grain economy.

duced into Central Africa only in the sixteenth century and most authorities are in agreement that the first migrations from the Lacustrine Region took place at an earlier date, it must be assumed that the original hunting invaders did not possess cassava. But its rapid and ready acceptance by tribes with a hunting tradition attests to its compatibility with hunting in the total system of subsistence.

The importance of hunting, then, among the Ndembu, a migrant group from Luunda, has its roots in tradition. But its value is also accentuated by its role in the conflict between the sexes.[1] In the idiom of Ndembu ritual, hunting and masculinity or virility are symbolically equivalent, and the symbols and gear of huntsmanship are reckoned to be mystically dangerous to female fertility and reproductive processes. Thus, when a woman is in labour, her husband must remove his hunting equipment and medicines from her hut and kitchen, otherwise his luck and skill at the chase will fail and she may die in labour or have a miscarriage. Conversely, a woman must not approach too closely a hunter's village shrine or she will have a protracted and painful menstruation. The same supernatural penalties will also be imposed on her if she approaches too near to the circumcision medicine of a senior circumciser (*mbimbi*), which, like many hunting-medicines, is placed in the cleft of a forked stick (*chishinga* or *muchanka*). This medicine (*nfunda*) is the supreme symbol of masculinity as opposed to femininity, and the close parallel between the effects of its supernatural sanctions against women and those of hunting medicine and apparatus supports the association with huntsmanship. ' For the man, huntsmanship ; for the woman, procreation ' (*neyala wubinda, namumbanda lusemu*), is the Ndembu saying. This is illustrated by a folk-tale in which a man, when his village is raided, snatches up his gun and hunting gear, while his wife's first thought is for her baby. She runs into the bush with her child, while he flees with what he most values, his hunting things. Later she goes to her relatives. When her husband follows afterwards she refuses to return with him. He

---

[1] Conflict between the sexes is ritually expressed among a number of related tribes in western Northern Rhodesia and eastern Angola, including Lunda, Lwena, Chokwe, Mbunda and Luchazi. Cf. M. Gluckman's ' The Role of the Sexes in Wiko Circumcision Ceremonies ', in *Social Structure : Essays Presented to A. R. Radcliffe-Brown*, ed. Fortes (1949).

demands his child. Her relatives say, ' No, the child is hers, for she has saved its life. The gun and axe are yours, for your only wish was to save them.' Ndembu, both men and women, put forward this story as an argument in favour of matrilineal descent.

Cassava, maize, sweet potatoes and other crops cultivated and tended by women frequently appear in rituals as emblems of female fertility. The conflict between male and female is ritually expressed in terms of each sex's dominant contribution to the mode of subsistence. Hunting and cultivation are complementary activities but they are also opposed and competitive. In the past, when hunters went into the bush they left their womenfolk undefended. If a hunter was killed his wife and children were for a time left unprotected. At certain times of the year, a man's economic roles as hunter and gardener might come into competition. The first rains which softened the earth and made it pliable for the hoe also stimulated the flush of fresh leaves and grass which attracted the antelope and made them easy prey to the gun and bow. Hunting brought men together and divided them from women. As we shall see, this probably had important effects on the social composition of residential groups, and the form of post-marital residence.

The Social Organization of Hunting

Hunting, like agriculture, may be carried on either collectively or individually. Ndembu classify hunting techniques into two major categories and to some extent these determine the social organization of the hunt. Hunters are divided into hunters with guns [1] (*ayiyang'a* ; sing. *chiyang'a*) and hunters with bows and traps (*ayibinda* ; sing. *chibinda*). The *chiyang'a* tends to make a profession of hunting, devoting as little time as he can to gardening activities and as much as he can to roaming about in the bush

---

[1] Gann, p. 36, states that ' in 1897 the Western Lunda had still been reported to be without guns, but by the time the officials of the British South Africa Company began to enter their country [1904], they were well supplied '.

The Ndembu themselves say that they first obtained guns from Ovimbundu traders and already possessed a limited number of muzzle-loaders before the Chokwe raid (*c.* 1885). One old man of about eighty years of age told me that when he was a boy (*c.* 1880), the cult for hunters with firearms, called *Wuyang'a* (see Chapter Ten) had only recently been introduced from tribes to the west (Lwena and Luchazi). It is likely that Ndembu have had guns since about 1870.

PLATE I

THE VALUE SET ON HUNTSMANSHIP

Four hunter-adepts play wooden stridulators before a shrine for hunter-spirits during a performance of the *Wuyang'a* ritual. The winnowing basket on the antelope horns contains herbal medicines to make the hunters invisible to their prey and to attract animals within range of their ancient and unreliable firearms.

in search of game. Frequently, he obtains vegetable produce in exchange for meat. *Ayiyang'a* participate in a cult in which there are four degrees of initiation. Membership in this cult enables them to range freely over Ndembu and indeed over Lunda territory, for wherever they go they are sure to find a cult-fellow who will give them temporary hospitality in return for a share in their kills. The *chiyang'a*, the ' big hunter ', who is also a ' gun-hunter ', tends to seek out the bigger game, such as buffalo, eland, gnu, and roan and sable antelope, although most of his kills consist of woodland buck such as duiker and yellow-backed duiker and small plains animals such as dik-dik. He is not infrequently a solitary, going whither he will, and returning to his own village when he chooses. However, *ayiyang'a* occasionally form temporary partnerships with other hunters, especially if dangerous animals such as buffalo are being pursued. Sometimes, too, they take with them young men who have shown an early flair for hunting and who have been apprenticed to them by their fathers or mothers' brothers. Most *ayiyang'a* endeavour to train their sons in hunting and woodcraft, and the father-son link among hunters is ritualized in a number of ways. A hunter father is also entitled to bestow one of a limited number of names normally reserved for hunters on his son, even although the latter may not be a hunter. In his life-time a hunter may train a number of apprentices : sons, matrilineal kin, and even the junior relatives of his friends and neighbours.

A *chiyang'a* may lead a small band consisting of men and boys of his own village or of contiguous villages into the bush on quite long expeditions lasting a week or more. On such an expedition the party build grass or leaf huts near an area known to be frequented with game and continue to hunt until they have killed several animals. The meat is cut up into joints which are smoked on a rough frame of branches to preserve them. The size of the band varies from about three to ten. The boys, often in their early teens, are taken into the bush for training and to carry the meat back. If the expedition is a long one the boys carry supplies of vegetable food such as cassava roots and green maize-cobs for the party.

In the past there were annual organized game drives in the so-called *ikuna* areas, where the trees are short and stunted and the grass long and rank. These drives no longer occur among the

Mwinilunga Ndembu, but Singleton-Fisher [1] has described a game drive among the related Lunda of south-western Katanga. The *ikuna* areas provide shelter for game when the surrounding bush has already been burnt, and the remaining *ikuna* is burnt in an organized way. The operation is directed by the ' village headman '. The *ikuna* is fired, and about thirty men and boys armed with guns and bows and arrows encircle it and kill the animals as they run from the flames. According to Singleton-Fisher, the village headman, with the headman from a neighbouring village, presides over the distribution of the game obtained. Each hunter who has killed an animal is given a special ritual portion, including head, neck, heart, lungs and intestines. This portion, called the ' head ' (*mutu*) or *yinjila* (literally ' forbidden ' or ' sacred ' things), may be eaten only by the hunter and is thought to maintain his mystical powers of huntsmanship. He is also given a leg. The remainder is shared out among all those who have taken part in the burning. Such drives are apparently organized by any headman who takes the initiative, and not necessarily by a chief or senior headman.

Hunters with bows and spears possessed much the same type and range of organization as hunters with guns. But whereas almost every man hunted with bow and trap, hunting with guns was confined to a select few, and of those few only hunters with great skill and ritual prestige belonged to the higher grades within the *Wuyang'a* cult. Nearly all men made traps and snares, of a wide variety of kinds, and each trap and the animals caught by it belonged to the individual who made the trap. I have recorded several disputes in the village courts between trap-owners and men detected in the act of stealing game from their traps.

It may be said that although in many respects hunting conforms to the pattern of productive individualism [2] found in agriculture, nevertheless, it involves on the whole a greater degree and intensity of co-operation than does crop-growing. Men hunt in bands, men and women perform much of their gardening

---

[1] Singleton-Fisher, W., ' Burning the Bush for Game ', *African Studies*, vii, 1 (1948), pp. 36–8.

[2] Cf. Torday, op. cit., p. 152 : ' the profession of hunting naturally induces an adventurous and self-reliant character, and encourages a roving disposition.'

alone. It should be noted that the majority of productive activities involving collective work are carried on by men—clearing the bush, hunting, and also hut-building, which will be referred to below.

Ndembu might hunt anywhere within Lunda territory and were not confined within a restricted area.[1] It was customary for a hunter to give the chest or a thigh of any large animal he had killed to the senior headman of the area in which he happened to be hunting. He could then carry the rest of his kill back to his village for distribution. Certain plains and thicket forests of *Cryptosepalum* trees (*mavunda*) had a wide reputation for containing much game, and hunters would come to them from far and wide. The hunters' cult and the great lateral range of remembered kinship ties were utilized by hunters to obtain hospitality and shelter in areas other than their own.

Meat Distribution and Consumption

The pattern of distribution of meat varies with the size and composition of the residential unit. If this unit is small, containing a small bilateral extended family (*ntang'a*), in addition to the portions reserved for the hunter and those given to the senior headman or chief, a back leg will be given to the hunter's brother or mother's brother or is divided between several brothers ; a back leg or a front leg will be given to his mother ; a front leg will be divided among his sisters ; the saddle will go to his wives ; the breast will go to his father ; and any small pieces that remain will be distributed among boys too old to live in their parents' huts. In the larger villages containing two or more minimal matrilineages (see page 80n.), a leg may be allocated to the senior man of each lineage, and it will be further subdivided by the latter among the married men of his lineage.

Consumption of game, like consumption of cassava mush, tends to be collective. It is considered to be good manners for each man or woman who has received meat to have a portion of it cooked for the men's eating-group in the village shelter, each

---

[1] McCulloch, p. 16, writes that ' most hunters confine their activities to within twenty miles of their village, and to their tribal areas '. But I have known hunters who have gone forty to sixty miles from their village to hunt. This may have been due to the disappearance of game from much of north-western Mwinilunga, compelling hunters to rove further afield.

retaining a share for his or her own elementary family. A good deal of grumbling goes on both over the precise division of the meat and over the amounts cooked for the men's group. Again, hunters are frequently accused of having made a kill and eaten the meat themselves in the bush, feigning on their return that they were unlucky in the chase. Throughout the economic system a tension is set up between the individual producer or killer of food and the group who by custom have claims in it. A 'greedy person', one who persistently retains what he produces for himself, ultimately may be expelled from the village. Conversely, a professional hunter who resents the claims of remote classificatory kin on the product of his hunting may lead away from a village a small group consisting of his wives, and children, and his sister's children, to found a new village.

Successful gun-hunters are regarded as sorcerers,[1] who acquire their power in hunting from killing people by means of their familiars. That is why great hunters seldom become successful headmen, in the opinion of Ndembu. Their nomadic inclination, their tendency to favour primary rather than classificatory kin in their own villages, and their association with sorcery, disqualify them from performing a role which requires tact, generosity to classificatory kin and strangers, and constant participation in the group life, for its successful functioning. A bow hunter may often make a good headman, a gun-hunter but seldom does so.

Summary of the Main Features of the Mode of Subsistence

Ndembu practise a form of subsistence cultivation in which cassava-growing is associated with hunting. In addition to

---

[1] The rancour and jealousy aroused in the situation of meat distribution are not only expressed in a number of folk-tales (*tuheka* or *ayishimu*) but also appear to influence strongly many beliefs about witchcraft and sorcery. A witch or sorcerer kills his victim 'for meat', whatever his other motives for killing are thought to be. Witches gather in covens to participate in necrophagous feasts on the bodies of their victims. In Social Drama I (p. 95), and IV (p. 148), quarrels over meat distribution provide grounds for subsequent accusations of sorcery and witchcraft.

Professor Monica Wilson discusses a similar connection between witchcraft and the lust for meat among the Nyakyusa of Tanganyika ('Witch Beliefs and Social Structure', *The American Journal of Sociology*, lvi, 4, Jan. 1951). She writes that 'witches lust for meat and milk—the prized foods of the group —and it is this which drives them to commit witchcraft. They delight in eating human flesh and gnaw men inside, causing death to their victims'.

cassava, finger-millet is grown by small circle ash-planting (*chitemene*) methods mainly for beer-making, and maize is cultivated in streamside gardens for food and beer. Other crops are grown in bush, village and streamside gardens mostly to provide relishes. In agricultural production and in the preparation of food women have the dominant role. Hunting is a male monopoly. Although in both agriculture and hunting production tends to be individualistic in character, where co-operation is wider than that between members of a family it tends to be between men, while women work on their own. But members of an elementary family often work together, though co-wives seldom assist one another in gardening. In the sphere of consumption, on the other hand, the emphasis is on sharing the product of gardening or hunting among kinsfolk living in joint residence. Here again the larger collective units of consumption tend to be male village kin, while the women eat separately with their unmarried daughters and uncircumcised sons.

CHAPTER II

THE VILLAGE: TOPOGRAPHY AND DEMOGRAPHY

Introduction

THE Ndembu are settled in discrete circles of huts which are not scattered evenly over the whole region but tend to be loosely grouped into spatially distinct vicinages. These circles of huts are traditionally known as *nyikala* (sing. *mukala*). This term may be translated as 'village'. Today, Ndembu distinguish villages entered on the Government Tax Register (and still called *nyikala*), from other residential units which have not yet been so entered. The latter are known as 'farms' (*mafwami*), an English term said to have been borrowed from African tribes living near the Copperbelt who possess similar units. Few farms are older than eight years. The term 'farm' conceals two clearly distinguishable types of residential grouping. The first of these represents the first stage in the life-cycle of the traditional Ndembu village; formerly such incipient villages were known as *nyana ya nyikala*, 'the children of villages',[1] the original village being regarded as the parent of the new one. The second is a new kind of settlement, possessing certain special features of hut arrangement and social composition unknown to the pre-European Ndembu social organization. These features will be discussed in subsequent sections.

I propose to use the term 'registered villages' for the villages appearing in the tax register, 'unregistered villages' for newly established villages organized on the basis of traditional principles of social structure, and 'farms' for the new type of settlement. It must be noted, however, that at the present time there exist a number of transitional types between these kinds of residential unit, and that it is often difficult to distinguish 'unregistered villages' from 'farms' unless one has personal knowledge of the economic interests and social ambitions of the headmen.

---

[1] Sometimes the new village was known as *mukala watwansi*, 'village of the juniors'.

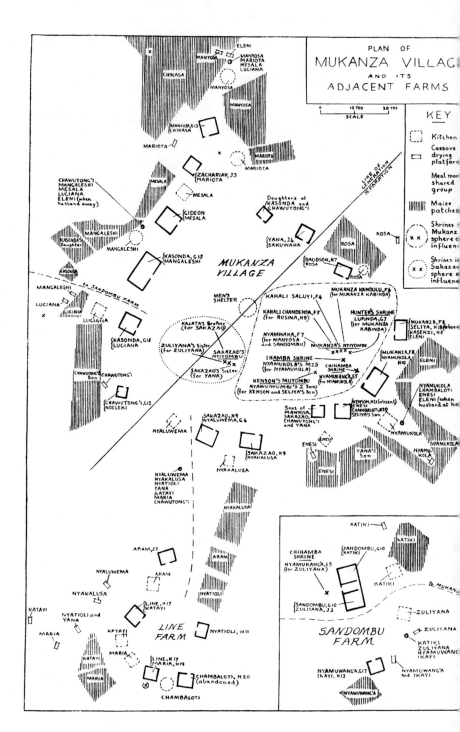

MAP 4

Village Topography

The registered village consists of a roughly circular or oval arrangement of huts around a cleared space in the centre of which is a round unwalled shelter (*chota* or *njang'u*), used as a men's palaver hut and mess-room. Map 4 shows a typical registered village, Mukanza.[1] Conspicuous features include the concentration of ancestor shrines before the huts of the headman and the senior representative of another village lineage, the maize patches around the village periphery manured by kitchen rubbish, the meal mortar sites shared by specific groups of women, the cassava-drying platforms, and the absence of grain granaries.

The ancient hut type was the round or square grass hut, and it was replaced in the present century by the pole-and-mud hut, which was introduced, say informants, from Angola by Lwena immigrants. The grass huts survive as seclusion huts for girls undergoing the puberty ritual and as hunters' temporary bush camps. I am told that villages in the remote past were merely hunting camps of grass huts, easily made and easily abandoned. However, during the slave-raiding epoch they were usually palisaded with strong stakes and sometimes were encircled with high earthworks.

The diameters of village hut circles are fairly small and range between about thirty and seventy yards.

The most common type of hut when I was first in the field was the rectangular or square pole-and-mud hut. Hut measurements lie between 9 ft. by 9 ft. to about 15 ft. by 25 ft. for this type. When I left, the pole-and-mud hut was everywhere giving way before the house of sun-dried Kimberley brick. Some of these exceeded 60 ft. in length, although the average was about 30 ft. Pole-and-mud huts usually contain only a single room, although some may have two. Most Kimberley-brick houses have at least two rooms, and a few, the houses of chiefs, have as many as six. At one time there was a certain correlation between size and type of hut, and social status ; but the recent

---

[1] As it was in 1953. Frequent reference will be made to this village in the text. I have concealed its identity under a pseudonym and altered the names of its inhabitants. I have adopted this procedure elsewhere in the book wherever necessary.

Government policy of inducing all men to build brick houses is obliterating this distinction.

The forest is cleared all round Ndembu villages in a wide ring to prevent damage from trees blown over by the dry season winds or felled by the lightning strokes of the rainy season. Since the first cassava-gardens are made close to a new village if soil conditions permit, most villages are clearly set off from the environing deciduous forest of the District.

When a village moves to a new site—in the past this took place every four or five years at the end of the rains—circular grass huts are built for the first few months or sometimes even for the first year of residence. Then the pole-and-mud huts of the headman and senior men of his genealogical generation are built for them by the younger men, in an approximately semi-circular formation, leaving fairly wide intervals between huts. When these are completed the men of the junior proximate generation build pole-and-mud huts in a semi-circle opposite their seniors, assisted by their sons and sisters' sons. Mature men of the junior alternate generation to the headman may then build huts between those of their grandparents.

Unregistered villages are often built today, when village mobility is less, with wide intervals between the huts to leave room for future members. In the past this was less common since the diameter of the hut-circle could soon be altered at the next village move.

Farms present a quite different spatial arrangement from villages. They are no longer a circular grouping of huts but typically consist of one or more Kimberley-brick buildings flanked on either side by a few small pole-and-mud huts and kitchens.[1] Occasionally, a hedge of flowering shrubs may be planted in front of a farm to screen it from the motor road. Most true farms are situated beside the motor roads, for the typical farm-head is a man who has earned money, often on the line-of-rail, and who intends to earn more locally. He may be a petty trader, a tailor with his own sewing-machine, a ' tea-room ' proprietor, a ' beer-hall ' owner, or a peasant producer raising cash crops. For all these purposes easy access to motor roads is necessary and propinquity to administrative and trading centres

---

[1] See inset, Map 4, Sandombu Farm.

advantageous. For these reasons most farms are found in the northern pedicle, or near the Boma, or close to chiefs' capitals, or in the vicinity of Mission Stations—i.e. wherever there are large concentrations of population and good communications with urban areas.

Village Magnitude

Ndembu villages have a smaller average magnitude than those of most other Central African peoples about which data are available. I mapped, and collected genealogies in, fifty registered villages, eighteen unregistered villages, and nine farms. In addition, I obtained census information in sixteen of the registered villages, eleven of the unregistered villages, and two of the farms, in which I collected genealogies. These genealogical and census studies were examples, rather than a random sample. They include a high proportion of settlements near to my first and second tour camps in Ikelenge area and Kanongesha area and along or within easy reach of the motor roads. The proportion of registered to unregistered villages and farms is definitely incorrect, since in Ikelenge Area alone, in 1953, there were 152 unregistered villages and farms as against 101 registered villages. Nevertheless, I believe that the information regarding the relative average magnitude of registered and unregistered villages and farms is not far from being correct. Estimates by eye of the number of huts in many settlements [1] where I did not collect genealogies suggest that these settlements had closely similar means and ranges to those in my sample.

There was a total of 657 huts in the 50 registered villages where I collected genealogies, the smallest having four huts and the largest fifty-four. The mean number of huts per village was 13·1 and the median was 12.

For unregistered villages there was a total of 135 huts in 18 villages, the smallest having one hut and the largest 16. The mean number of huts per village was 7·5 and the median was 8.

For farms there was a total of 23 huts in 9 farms, the smallest having one hut and the largest 5. The mean number of huts per farm was 2·6, and the median was 3.

---

[1] I employ the term 'settlement' as a generic name for registered and unregistered villages and farms.

E

The distribution of huts over the three types of settlement is shown in Table II.

For all types of settlement it was found that in 77 settlements there was a total of 815 huts, or an average of 10·6 huts per

TABLE II

NUMBER OF HUTS IN SETTLEMENTS

	Number of huts in settlements : 1 2 3 4 5 6 7 8 9 10 11 12 13 14 15 16 17 18 19 20+	Total	Mean	Median
Number of registered villages .	0 0 0 4 2 1 6 1 5 2 3 3 2 3 1 3 5 0 3 6	50	13·1	12
Number of unregistered villages .	1 1 0 1 1 2 2 4 1 1 2 1 0 0 0 1 0 0 0 0	18	7·5	8
Number of farms	3 1 3 1 1 0 0 0 0 0 0 0 0 0 0 0 0 0 0 0	9	2·6	3
Total . .	4 2 3 6 4 3 8 5 6 3 5 4 2 3 1 4 5 0 3 6	77	10·6	9

settlement.   The median was 9 huts per settlement.   But it must be remembered that my sample was not stratified in accordance with the proportions existing between these three categories of residential unit in the total Ndembu area.   In the pedicle, for example, farms and unregistered villages outnumber registered villages.   On the other hand, in the rest of the Ndembu area, registered villages probably outnumber the other two categories.

From the census sample it was found that there was a total number of 467 inhabitants living in 198 huts in the sixteen registered villages, or an average of 2·35 persons per hut.   In the eleven unregistered villages 158 persons occupied 72 huts, or an average of 2·2 persons per hut, while there were 15 persons living in the six huts of the two farms, or an average of 2·5 persons per hut.   In the total sample 640 people occupied 276 huts, or an average of 2·32 inhabitants per hut.

Thus the average registered village of about 13 huts contains about 30 persons, the average unregistered village of 7–8 huts about 16–17 persons, and the average farm of 2–3 huts about 5–8 persons.

In all villages with more than twenty huts, it was found that the main village circle contained in no case more than twenty huts. When this number was reached, either a new hut circle was started a score or so yards away, or new huts were built outside and along the periphery of the main ring.

I summarize below some information on the size of Ndembu villages as compared with the size of villages in a number of Central African peoples.

People	No. of huts per village	No. of taxpayers per village	Mean population per village
Luchazi [1]	Up to 200–300 (divided into sections of 20 huts each)		
Ngoni of Fort Jameson [2] . . .	6–120		
Bemba : [3]			
Commoners	30–50		
Chiefs	300–400		
Nyakyusa [4]	30–40		
Plateau Tonga [5]	30	20	
Unga of Lake Bangweulu [6] . .			69
Lwena [1]		20–30	
Lamba, Mushiri reserve [7] . . .			42·1
Lamba : [8]	17 (mean)	7–27	
Old Area			50·1
New Area			40·0
Intermediate Area			38·1
Kaonde [9]	11·1 (mean)		
Lunda Ndembu	10·6 (mean)		22·1

[1] McCulloch, M., pp. 66–7.

[2] Barnes, J. A., 'The Fort Jameson Ngoni', *Seven Tribes of British Central Africa*, ed. Colson and Gluckman (1951), p. 206.

[3] Richards, A. I., 'The Bemba of North-Eastern Rhodesia', *Seven Tribes*, p. 171.

[4] Wilson, Godfrey, 'The Nyakyusa of South-Western Tanganyika', *Seven Tribes*, p. 270.

[5] Colson, E., 'The Plateau Tonga of Northern Rhodesia', *Seven Tribes*, p. 111.

[6] Brelsford, W. V., *Fishermen of the Bangweulu Swamps*, Rhodes-Livingstone Paper No. 12 (1946), p. 31.

[7] Allan, W., *Studies of African Land Usage in Northern Rhodesia*, Rhodes-Livingstone Paper No. 15 (1949), p. 27.

[8] Mitchell, J. C. and Barnes, J. A., *The Lamba Village*, Communications from the School of African Studies, New Series No. 24 (1950), pp. 21, 29.

[9] Watson, W., 'The Kaonde Village', *The Rhodes-Livingstone Journal*, xv (July, 1954), pp. 6–7.

These figures are presented merely to give a rough impression of comparative magnitudes, and not to make precise distinctions. The material available is in some cases not strictly comparable. For instance, the data cited from Richards and Wilson were collected before the Second World War, and it is highly probable that there has been a marked reduction in the average size of villages in both areas since 1946. Only in the cases of the Unga, Lamba, Kaonde and Ndembu were the total number of villages and their range of size stated. But in spite of the obvious deficiencies in the data it would seem that Ndembu villages have a markedly smaller average size than those of the other peoples shown, with the exception of the Kaonde, eastern neighbours of the Mwinilunga Lunda. Today Ndembu villages probably have a smaller average size than the figure given (10·6 huts) since there has been a big increase in the number of farms since 1950.

In *The Lamba Village* (p. 2) the term 'Old Area' refers to Reserve No. 1, Ndola District, which was considered to be overpopulated in relation to the requirements of the agricultural system. 'Intermediate Area' refers to an area of Crown Land reopened to Lamba settlement where the people were bound to observe certain agricultural rules, and where their villages were laid out for them. In the 'New Area' the boundaries of the area within which a village could make gardens were mapped by agricultural officers according to the estimate of its needs of arable land.

For the Mwinilunga Lunda, White [1] gives a historical reason for the small size of villages. The Lunda were never strong enough to repel Chokwe and Lwena invaders, even if concentrated, and therefore preferred to seek safety in dispersion. White suggests that the continued preference of the Lunda for living in small villages is due to their 'general conservatism': 'kinship ties remain stronger, and the village headman is more respected, than among the Lwena or Luchazi.' However, my older informants have repeatedly declared to me that when they were young (some fifty years or so ago, when the slave-raids had hardly ceased), some villages were much larger than those of today. Some of them have even told me, from memory,

---

[1] Cited by McCulloch, p. 24.

how many huts there were in the village in which they grew up,
and some villages today which have only a dozen huts once
contained about thirty. Early travellers among the Southern
Lunda,[1] admittedly for the most part among the Lunda of Chief
Ishinde to the south of Kanongesha's chiefdom, mention 'large,
stockaded villages' in the Kabompo area. Harding, for instance,
writes of 'a Lunda *induna* who resided in a fortress of no mean
dimensions, enclosed with a high earthen wall'. On the other
hand, older Ndembu have told me of a tradition that 'long,
long ago', *before the slave trade*, their ancestors used to live in
small encampments of grass huts, of similar shape to those
described and illustrated by sketches for the Lunda of Mwantiyanvwa by Dias de Carvalho.[2] These settlements were apparently little more than hunting camps ; after destroying the game
in a given area the village would move on. If there is any
historical truth in this tradition then, the present small size of
villages represents partly a return to an ancient type, and partly,
in the case of 'farms', a response to changing socio-economic
conditions in Central Africa. This response has been assisted,
no doubt, by the fact that Government in spite of its 'ten taxpayers rule' did not make determined attempts to impose on the
Mwinilunga Lunda the rule that a village should contain a
minimum of ten taxpayers. Since 1950, in fact, the policy of
the District Commissioner has been to allow the unchecked
growth of small farms, so that in accordance with central government policy the 'parish' rather than the village should in time
become the basic unit of Native Administration. It would
seem, however, that some District Officers made sporadic
attempts to combine several small villages into single residential
units (see, for example, p. 182).

Further evidence against the view that dispersion in the face
of slave-raiders was the only cause of the small size of villages is
found in the fact that the major slave-raiders of the epoch in
West Central Africa, the Chokwe and Bangala, themselves lived
in small villages. Capello and Ivens,[3] when passing through

---

[1] Livingstone, op. cit., p. 283 ; Harding, p. 137 ; Cameron, V. L., *Across
Africa* (1885), p. 405 (of Lunda 'between sources of Lulua and Zambezi ').
[2] Dias de Carvalho, p. 220.
[3] Capello and Ivens, vol. I, pp. 236–8.

Chokwe territory in 1877, mention many small 'hamlets', 'miserable little hamlets' (vol. I, p. 216), and they insert illustrations of villages ('*senzalas*') of eighteen huts and less. In Bangala territory (vol. I, p. 362) they mention 'a *libata* or village [which] is a favourable specimen of its kind. The stockade by which it is surrounded encloses an ample space containing a couple of dozen habitations.'

Baumann's descriptions of Chokwe villages, summarized by McCulloch,[1] show that they had a remarkable similarity to Ndembu villages. In the northern savanna country, where hunting is the main activity, 'straw houses are more frequent, palisades are rare, and settlements are more or less temporary'. Within the villages houses are arranged round a cleared space, in the centre of which is the *tsota* or meeting-house. The two village plans which McCulloch reproduced from Baumann show that in one village, from the northern, mainly hunting, Chokwe, there are 14 huts ; and in the other, from the southern, mainly agricultural, Chokwe, there are 31 huts.

Capello and Ivens (vol. I, pp. 217-23) describe two hunting camps of Chokwe they found in the bush, 'of grass-thatched huts in an irregular circle', containing 'a score or so of men', which resemble those described by older Ndembu.

It is indeed quite probable that an ecological factor, i.e. a common emphasis on hunting, played a prominent role in restricting village size among both Chokwe and Ndembu. Later the effects of various sociological factors will be discussed for Ndembu in this connection, but these too will be shown to be directly and indirectly related to the high value attributed to hunting. On the basis of their agricultural system alone there is no reason why Ndembu should not live in larger villages.[2] Indeed, today, in the north-western pedicle where hunting is obsolescent, high population densities actually do subsist on agriculture. But even in this area individual villages tend to be small and are in fact becoming smaller with the rapid growth of 'farms'. What one finds here is ribbon development along the road of small settlements, a few hundred yards away from one another, each with its own headman and each containing a small

---

[1] McCulloch, pp. 40-3, gives Baumann's hut diagrams.
[2] See p. 21 for Allan's estimate of carrying capacity of land under Ndembu system of cultivation.

corporate grouping of kin.   Here the factor of cultural persistence or inertia seems to be important.   But even in areas where game is still plentiful, and where European contact and influence is less marked, villages tend to average about a dozen huts.   It is possible that village size is here regulated rather by the game resources of the surrounding bush and neighbouring plains than by the fertility requirements of cassava, the staple crop.   In the case of the few larger villages for which I have records I shall show that special factors are involved which maintain the integrity of the settlement under a single headman.

It should, of course, be mentioned here that the current growth of small villages is a phenomenon found throughout Northern Rhodesia.   It is partly due to Government policy which now encourages the parish system at the expense of the traditional village ;   to the *pax britannica* which has abolished slave-raiding, blood-feuds and inter-tribal war ;   and to the rapid extermination of lions.   Everywhere the need to rely on one's kin and neighbours is being reduced by these factors.   Quite as importantly perhaps, labour migration to the urban industrial areas is positively emancipating the individual from his obligations to his kinship group.   Again, if a man wishes to accumulate capital to set up as a petty trader or tailor, or to acquire a higher standard of living for himself and his elementary family, he must break away from his circle of village kin towards whom he has traditional obligations.   Everywhere, we see the spectacle of corporate groups of kin disintegrating and the emergence of smaller residential units based on the elementary family.[1]

In most cases where fission has occurred I shall show that the parent village seldom contained at the time when it split more than twenty huts.   In all extant villages containing around twenty huts powerful social tensions exist and the lines of imminent fission are clearly marked.

My own hypothesis, necessarily tentative, about the historical development of Ndembu villages is that before the period of the slave-raids most villages were about the same size as those found today in areas remote from European settlements, and that during those raids, some villages tended to unite into larger

---

[1] For a more detailed examination of changes brought about by the modern cash economy see my article (with E. L. B. Turner) on ' Money Economy among the Mwinilunga Ndembu ', *The Rhodes-Livingstone Journal*, xviii (1955).

concentrations while others dispersed into still smaller units.[1] Several large composite villages have been mentioned to me by older men. One such village was under the leadership of the 'national' hero Chipeng'e, who organized his people against the Chokwe, and it contained several groups of Ndembu and Kawiku who formerly lived in independent villages. Senior headmen such as Mukang'ala Ibala controlled similar composite villages. Other headmen, such as Nyachiu, formed composite villages from which they raided the traditional small villages of their fellow-tribesmen to sell the inhabitants as slaves to Ovimbundu traders. Later, under the *pax britannica*, these composite villages broke up again into their component groups of closely related matrilineal kin who founded separate villages.

I have discussed this question of village size at some length since, given the fact that Ndembu villages are inhabited by kinsmen, limitations on their magnitude impose limits on the number of kin who can dwell together. If maternal descent is an important principle governing residential affiliation, and if in small villages lineages are stunted, it is probable that the social mechanisms for promoting cohesion and reducing conflict in the residential unit will differ from those in societies practising maternal descent where the large village is typical. I will return to this question later, merely pointing out at this stage of the enquiry that there is probably a functional relationship of some importance between the size and the structure of the residential unit.

Village Mobility : The Changing Composition of Vicinages

In the past (and in some areas today) Ndembu villages changed their sites very frequently. One village, Nyaluhana, the core of which is composed of matrilineal kin of the Senior Chief Kanongesha, is said to have moved its site 17 times since it was founded about 75 years ago. Its average duration of occupation of a residential site is, therefore, about 4·4 years.[2] Most of these

---

[1] See p. 220 for a further discussion on this point. Whether village members dug themselves in and built stockades or dispersed and hid in the bush depended on the fortunes of war.

[2] This agrees with Trapnell's and Clothier's estimate that Lunda villages generally move 'after some four to six years' (Trapnell and Clothier, p. 38).

moves have taken place in a narrow orbit within a few miles from the present village, but its fifth move took it to the vicinity of the traditional capital of Kanongesha in Angola, and in 1908, after returning to its present area, it went to Angola again for about ten years to escape from the British South Africa Company's administration. Since its return it has remained more or less in its present vicinage. Another village, Mukanza, of Kawiku origin, is said to have moved twenty-six times since its foundation about a hundred years ago. This village again has tended to remain within about seven miles of its present site, although, when taxation was introduced in 1913, its members fled from the vicinity of the Boma to Ikelenge's area in the pedicle about 40 miles away, returning in 1919. But other villages have ranged more widely across the face of the country. The village of Chibwakata, for example, founded by the war-leader or *Kambanji* of the first Kanongesha, at various times has occupied sites in the extreme south-west of Mwinilunga and in the Kosa chiefdom of Chief Sailunga, sixty miles to the south-east of its present location which is five miles from Mwinilunga Boma. Other villages have migrated into Mwinilunga, before the Europeans came, from Lunda chiefdoms in the Congo and Angola. In general the Kawiku villages, containing descendants of the auto-chthonous population, have tended to remain more firmly fixed in a particular locality than villages descended from the Lunda invaders. In the past two or three decades many villages have migrated to the pedicle area where European settlement has held out hopes of employment for the men and markets for vegetable produce for the women. Today, a tendency towards permanent settlement in one site, noted above, is becoming clearly discernible. After villages have moved near a mission station, the Boma, a Native Authority centre or a European farm, they tend to become stabilized. At the present moment a process of fragmentation of traditional villages into small farms, containing elementary families with a small fringe of matrilineal kin of the headmen, is going briskly ahead. Since at most farms Kimberley-brick houses are being built it seems likely that these new settlements will remain in their present sites for a long time.

I have made many enquiries about why villages moved in the past and in no case was it stated that they moved because accessible land suitable for cassava cultivation had become exhausted. The most frequent explanation for change of site given me was that in the past older people were buried under the floors of their huts which were then burnt down, followed by the movement of a village to a new site.[1] Fear of the spirits of the dead led to change of site. For many years, however, it is said, Ndembu have followed the European practice of burying everyone in graveyards. These are situated in the bush a few hundred yards from the village. As a result frequent change of location has become unnecessary. Another reason for movement was alleged to be feuds between villages in the same or in adjacent vicinages. Feuds were sometimes prolonged and the weaker villages fled to new areas. Again, I have been told that when a village has remained on the same site for a number of years, larger game and small mammals get destroyed in its immediate neighbourhood, and the village moves nearer to new hunting resources. Thus the conscious motives for change of site are given as ritual, political and economic, in that order. The economic motives are couched in terms of the exigencies of hunting although there is little doubt that the proximity of suitable soil (Ndembu are soil-selectors, choosing land for cassava cultivation by the dominant species of trees on it) helps to determine their choice of one site rather than another. But it is unlikely that villages were compelled to move every four or five years by the exhaustion of local soil. Given a cultivable percentage of about 20 per cent, a village of thirty inhabitants, using the five-year garden system described above, would require about 1,000 acres to maintain it in perpetuity. Theoretically, therefore, if the population remained stationary and the forest regularly regenerated, there is no reason why a village should move its site at all. Factors other than those inherent in the agricultural system were probably at work. An attempt will be made later to isolate and analyse the most important of these factors. Meanwhile it can be stated that Ndembu villages were small, changed their sites often, and frequently moved considerable distances from one site to the next. When the new site was within a mile or so of the old one, the old cassava gardens con-

---

[1] It is said that after the death of a headman, or after the consecutive deaths of two mature villagers, a village always moved.

tinued to be utilized from the new site until they were used up. In the past, when a village moved to a completely new area, its inhabitants are said to have made large finger-millet gardens in the first year, for food as well as beer. Finger-millet is a quick-maturing crop (sown in December, harvested in June), while cassava roots take eighteen months to mature sufficiently to be used as food. Again, when a village moved into a new area its members used to borrow portions of the standing crop in cassava gardens from villages established there, cultivating extra land for the donors the following year. Or they might exchange meat, honey or craft products for cassava until their first crops had matured.

Villages are rarely built in complete isolation from neighbours. Map 2 shows how villages tend to be grouped in discrete clusters, of varying numbers and formation. Each such cluster is called a *chitung'ili* (from *ku-tung'a*, ' to build '). This term may be translated as a ' vicinage ' or ' neighbourhood cluster '. The vicinage has certain jural, economic and ritual functions which will be discussed in subsequent chapters. Here I wish to examine it in relation to village mobility. Vicinages are not spatially defined areas with permanent boundaries. The vicinage is not an objectively based enduring unit. In this respect it differs from a traditional senior headman's area or a modern sub-chiefdom. A vicinage is a cluster of villages, of changeable territorial span, and fluid and unstable in social composition. It has no recognized internal organization which endures beyond the changes in the identity of the villages making it up. But it is not just a neighbourhood round *any* village. As I will show in Chapter Eleven, the vicinage becomes visible as a discrete social entity in several situations, and a particular headman within it usually exercises moral and ritual leadership. Villages in a vicinage, however, do not move as a unit, but each village in its own time and to its own site either within the same, or another, vicinage. The frequency with which villages change their sites means that the composition of vicinages is constantly changing, new villages coming in from other areas and old villages moving out. It means that each vicinage is sociologically heterogeneous, few of its villages having mutual ties of lineal kinship or even originating in the same chiefdom. For example, in the small vicinage in which Nyaluhana is the most important headman [1] there are eleven villages and farms within an area of about twelve square miles. Nyaluhana was founded by the sister of a Kanongesha who reigned about 1880. One unregistered village, Wukengi, has recently split from Nyaluhana and has built about a quarter of a mile away. A mile away is Wadyang'amafu, which came in the nineteenth century from the Lunda-Kosa chiefdom of Nyamwana, in the Belgian Congo. Two miles away is the Kawiku village of Kafumbu, which broke away from Mukanza Village in another vicinage. A mile and a half on the other side is Sampasa which came from Chief Chibwika's area fifty years ago. Four miles away in another direction is Machamba, which recently broke away from Mwenilunga Village, founded by a son of the first Kanongesha more than two centuries ago. Near Kafumbu are Sawiyembi and Mukoma Villages which came from senior headman Chikeza's area in Angola thirty-five years ago and separated from one another recently, the Sawiyembi lineage having originally been slaves of the Mukoma lineage. Near them again is Nyampasa, recently founded by a woman-headman matrilineally related to the Kawiku senior headman Nsang'anyi, whose village is in another vicinage. A few small farms have detached themselves from some of these villages and built at some distance from their parent villages. Numerous ties of affinity and kinship now interlink the earlier established of these villages but few belong to the same maternal descent groups. Villages which formerly inhabited this vicinage have now settled elsewhere. One village in the vicinage is already making plans to move far to the south of the District. In the remoter, less stabilized areas I have visited, I have seen marked changes in the composition of vicinages between 1950 and 1954.

Fission of Villages

Ndembu thus live characteristically in loose and temporary collocations of small neighbouring villages. Both size and mobility are influenced by the fission of villages which divides larger villages into small units. If fission has been accompanied by violent quarrels the seceding group often builds far from the

---

[1] See also Chapter Nine for a detailed analysis of the social composition of another vicinage.

parent village. The sociology of the situation of fission will be discussed at length below : here it is proposed to examine its demographic effects only, the way in which settlements with a common origin have been dispersed after fission across the Ndembu region.

Chibwakata Village has already been mentioned in connection with village mobility. This village in the course of its history of perhaps two hundred years has ranged widely across Ndembu, and even into Kosa, territory. During this time it has given rise to no less than twenty further villages by fission, only one of which is not still in existence today. Some of them have given rise in their turn to further villages. In 1953, 3 of these offshoots were in Kanongesha Area, close to their parent village, 3 were in Chibwika Area to the south, 2 were in Nyakaseya and 1 in Ikelenge Area in the pedicle, a total of 9 villages in the Ndembu region.[1] In the Kosa Region, where Sailunga is the Senior Chief under the Native Authority, 5 are in Sailunga Area proper and one village has broken up there, 2 are in the former Chief Mpulumba's Area, and one is in Kakoma Area. One village is in Nyamwana Area and another in Kazembe Mutanda's Area in the Belgian Congo, a total of 11 in Lunda chiefdoms outside the Ndembu Region. Other long-established Ndembu villages have similar histories of fission.

There is plenty of evidence to show that the rate of fission has increased in the last three decades. All the Kawiku villages, containing descendants of the aboriginal population, claim to have split off from Nsang'anyi Village either by direct fission or by fission from one of its offshoots. I have collected information in all the extant Kawiku villages about the period at which they broke off from Nsang'anyi or one of its derivatives. This information has been checked against genealogical data and correlations have been made with historical events in the District the dates of which are known. Whereas during the whole of the nineteenth century there were only five remembered instances of the formation of new Kawiku villages, there were no less than five instances in the 1920's, three in the 1930's, and eleven since 1940, making nineteen in the first half of the twentieth century. Only four of these have been ' farms ', all founded since 1947.

---

[1] See Map 2 for these chiefdoms, p. xxiv.

Thus in the whole of the nineteenth century five villages hived off from one village while in half of the twentieth century nineteen villages have hived off from five villages.   If this rate continued it would mean that at the end of the century nearly eight villages would come from each village, an increase of 37·5 per cent.   It is, of course, possible that other Kawiku villages came into existence, only to break up again, during the nineteenth century, but careful enquiry did not reveal that this had been the case.   In the nineteenth century my informants say that several previously independent groups of Kawiku came together in quite large stockaded villages (which also contained some Ndembu) for self-defence.   The Kawiku, in contrast to the immigrant Ndembu, have tended to remain in the vicinity of the Kawiku Plain where they were first encountered by the latter.   Of the 25 villages 14, or 56 per cent, still reside within a few miles of the Plain, although their local mobility has been high.   As the result of a violent quarrel in one village, Mukanza, many villages seceded and later formed three villages far from the Kawiku Plain.   Several younger men have established farms in Ikelenge Area in the pedicle where they carry on trade.   But by and large the Kawiku have tended to remain in approximately the same area over long periods of time.   Each Kawiku village has moved its site many times but always within a much narrower orbit than the majority of true Ndembu villages.   Kawiku and Ndembu villages are interspersed in several vicinages.

Fission may occur without the seceding group's departure from the vicinage of its parent village.   This type of fission is becoming more common today when one sometimes finds a village surrounded by a number of farms built by enterprising younger men who desire a measure of economic and political independence from the old conservative headmen.   There has been no open breach in these cases and the older men are beginning fatalistically, if querulously, to accept the new order of things which is rapidly coming about with the spread of cash economy.

Undoubtedly, the accelerated rate of fission in recent years is related to a considerable increase in population in the District. This increase is the product of several factors.   Immigration from Angola, and, to a lesser extent, from the Belgian Congo into northern and western Mwinilunga is perhaps the most important of these.   The ending of the slave-trade and prohibition by the Government of internal blood-feuds are other causes of the increase. It is also possible that the introduction by missions and Government of hospitals and dispensaries has led to a reduction in the death-rate. On the other hand, the virtual extermination of game in some areas, a source of meat not yet replaced by cattle which could be kept in the fly-free north-west of the District, must have led to a decrease in the consumption per capita of animal protein. This lack of meat may have en-feebled resistance to disease and so prevented a marked reduction in the death-rate.

But the immigration from neighbouring territories of small discrete groups of kin who settle in every part of the Ndembu region has undoubtedly provided a stimulus to more rapid fission among villages already established there. Cash economy tends to destroy ties of corporate kinship *within* villages. Many small immigrant groups, each living separately, provide for established villages *external* models for a new type of residential group. But it must be stressed that these modern trends do no more than accentuate tendencies inherent in the indigenous social system. The local kin group appears never to have been extensive, the spatial mobility of villages was always considerable,[1] fission was relatively frequent and individual mobility was high. Modern changes have not so far struck at the basis of the indigenous system nor radically disrupted it. Because of the mobile fissile nature of its traditional residential units, the system has been able to absorb changes that promoted mobility and increased the rate of fission.

Individual Mobility

In addition to the high rates of mobility and fission of villages themselves, individuals also tend to circulate rapidly through villages in the course of their lifetimes. The sociological factors behind this mobility of individuals will be examined in detail in later chapters, but they must be mentioned at this point.

Men and women have different patterns of mobility. Most men are born in their fathers' matrilineal villages and some of

---

[1] See, for example, Livingstone's remark that 'people change from one part of the country to another' with frequency, quoted in a footnote in Chapter One, p. 5.

them go to their own mothers' brothers' villages in their teens. But if, as frequently happens, their parents are divorced, they go with their mothers in early childhood to their mothers' brothers' or mothers' mothers' brothers' villages. Some men remain with their fathers until the death of the latter. If a village splits, men often have a choice of matrilineal villages in which to live. The majority of adult men, however, reside avunculocally, unless they found new villages of their own. Women move more often than men. They are born in their fathers' villages ; they may return to their uterine uncles' villages for a while ; and they go to their husbands' villages after marriage. Since marriage is brittle among Ndembu,[1] they may spend their reproductive period alternating between their fathers' and mothers' brothers' villages, and successive marital villages. Many women, if widowed or divorced after they have passed the menopause, return to the villages of their nearest matrilineal kin to remain there for the rest of their lives. Thus the composition of a single village varies greatly from year to year as men, women and children enter and leave it. This natural fluctuation is supplemented by other movements dependent on the personality of the headman. If he is notorious as a sorcerer, or is unskilful as a judge, or mean and selfish, many people will leave him. If he has the reputation of being a wise and generous man he will build up a large village.

In Tables III and IV, I attempt to express certain aspects of individual mobility.[2] Table III shows minimum mobility. It is constructed from my village census figures and offers an indication of what proportion of adult men and women live in their natal villages.

These figures suggest that only one-seventh of adult men and women live in the villages where they are born, with no significant difference between the mobility of men and women. However, since Ndembu are often born in one village and reared in another we can obtain a further index of mobility by setting out a table which indicates the proportion of adult men and

---

[1] See Table VII for divorce ratios.

[2] The layout of these tables is based on Table I in E. Colson's ' Residence and Village Stability among the Plateau Tonga ', *The Rhodes-Livingstone Journal*, xii (1951), p. 42.

women who have been reared in their natal villages. By 'village of rearing' I denote for women the village in which they have spent the longest period of residence from birth to the puberty ritual (*Nkang'a*) which marks the entrance into womanhood at about the age of fifteen or sixteen. For men I have arbitrarily selected a similar age-range, birth to sixteen years of age, since

TABLE III

INDIVIDUAL MOBILITY : NATAL AND PRESENT VILLAGES, BY AGE

Age	Males			Females		
	Living in natal village	Living in other village	Total	Living in natal village	Living in other village	Total
20–29 years	11 (22·9%)	37 (77·1%)	48 (100·0) %	9 (17·0%)	44 (83·0%)	53 (100·0%)
30–39 years	8 (21·6%)	29 (78·4%)	37 (100·0%)	5 (9·1%)	50 (90·9%)	55 (100·0%)
40–49 years	3 (10·7%)	25 (89·3%)	28 (100·0%)	6 (18·7%)	26 (81·3%)	32 (100·0%)
50–59 years	3 (10·0%)	26 (90·0%)	29 (100·0%)	3 (12·0%)	22 (88·0%)	25 (100·0%)
60–69 years	0 (0·0%)	25 (100·0%)	25 (100·0%)	2 (9·1%)	20 (90·9%)	22 (100·0%)
70– years	2 (16·7%)	10 (83·3%)	12 (100·0%)	2 (20·0%)	8 (80·0%)	10 (100·0%)
Total . .	27 (15·1%)	152 (84·9%)	179 (100·0%)	27 (13·7%)	170 (86·3%)	197 (100·0%)

the boys' circumcision ritual (*Mukanda*) is often performed for boys of ten and under and is not comparable for our purpose to the girl's puberty ritual which is usually followed immediately by marriage. Table IV, therefore, shows the comparative proportions of those who have been reared in their natal villages and those who have been reared in other villages. Table IV shows that less than two-fifths of adult men and rather under a half of adult women were brought up in their natal villages. The slightly greater mobility of boys than girls is probably due to the fact that boys, after circumcision, may leave their fathers' villages for their maternal uncles' villages, or vice versa, more or less at will. Girls, on the other hand, tend to remain with their

F

mothers, or to move when they move. At circumcision a boy is symbolically severed from his mother ; henceforth he is a full member of a male moral community, free on the whole to choose his site of residence. But a girl does not lose her dependent status until she has borne several children. She passes from mother's to husband's village when she leaves mother for husband. Thus

TABLE IV

INDIVIDUAL MOBILITY : NATAL VILLAGE AND VILLAGE OF REARING,
BY AGE

Age	Males			Females		
	Reared in natal village	Reared in other village	Total	Reared in natal village	Reared in other village	Total
20–29 years	11 (22·9%)	37 (77·1%)	48 (100·0%)	21 (39·6%)	32 (60·4%)	53 (100·0%)
30–39 years	15 (40·5%)	22 (59·5%)	37 (100·0%)	23 (41·8%)	32 (58·2%)	55 (100·0%)
40–49 years	10 (35·7%)	18 (64·3%)	28 (100·0%)	17 (53·1%)	15 (46·9%)	32 (100·0%)
50–59 years	14 (48·3%)	15 (51·7%)	29 (100·0%)	10 (40·0%)	15 (60·0%)	25 (100·0%)
60–69 years	13 (52·0%)	12 (48·0%)	25 (100·0%)	13 (59·1%)	9 (40·9%)	22 (100·0%)
70– years	6 (50·0%)	6 (50·0%)	12 (100·0%)	8 (80·0%)	2 (20·0%)	10 (100·0%)
Total . .	69 (38·6%)	110 (61·4%)	179 (100·0%)	92 (46·9%)	105 (53·1%)	197 (100·0%)

women have greater individual mobility than men, but boys have greater mobility than girls.

The natal village is in several respects an unsatisfactory point of departure for a study of mobility. A person may be born either in his or her father's or mother's village. If the father's and mother's villages are fairly close neighbours the expectant mother is taken to her own village, usually the village of her close matrilineal kin, a few days before the confinement, and brought back to her husband's village after the birth of the child. Or a woman may go to her own village for the *ku-tena ivumu* ('mentioning the womb') ceremony, performed at a woman's first pregnancy, and come back to her husband's village to bear her child. These customs underline the basically matrilineal character of the social structure. But they have the effect of confusing informants as to what was really their natal village —the village where the mother actually gave birth, or the village where she was residing with her husband. A better measure

TABLE V

INDIVIDUAL MOBILITY : VILLAGE OF REARING AND PRESENT VILLAGE,
BY AGE

Age	Males			Females		
	Living in village of rearing	Living in other village	Total	Living in village of rearing	Living in other village	Total
20–29 years	15 (31·2%)	33 (68·8%)	48 (100·0%)	3 (5·7%)	50 (94·3%)	53 (100·0%)
30–39 years	9 (24·3%)	28 (75·7%)	37 (100·0%)	10 (18·9%)	45 (81·1%)	55 (100·0%)
40–49 years	5 (17·9%)	23 (82·1%)	28 (100·0%)	2 (6·2%)	30 (93·8%)	32 (100·0%)
50–59 years	2 (6·9%)	27 (93·1%)	29 (100·0%)	5 (20·0%)	20 (80·0%)	25 (100·0%)
60–69 years	6 (24·0%)	19 (76·0%)	25 (100·0%)	1 (4·5%)	21 (95·5%)	22 (100·0%)
70– years	0 (0·0%)	12 (100·0%)	12 (100·0%)	0 (0·0%)	10 (100·0%)	10 (100·0%)
Total . .	37 (20·7%)	142 (79·3%)	179 (100·0%)	21 (10·7%)	176 (89·3%)	197 (100·0%)

of mobility may perhaps be obtained by showing in a table what percentage of adult men and women continue to reside in their villages of rearing, whether or not these were their natal villages. Table V shows this.

Table V shows that adult men have a stronger tendency to remain in their villages of rearing than adult women. This is probably due to the fact that marriage is virilocal. Women are often brought up patrilocally,[1] marry virilocally, and after divorce reside

---

[1] 'Patrilocal' refers to residence in one's father's village. 'Matrilocal' refers to residence in one's mother's village. It should be stressed that my use of these terms refers to residence with a parent, and not with a spouse.

avunculocally until remarriage. It should be noted that a much higher proportion of men under than over forty years of age reside as adults in their villages of rearing : 25 per cent under forty and 14 per cent over forty. This is probably due to two main causes. The first is that the more able and wealthy men who have not become headmen often establish villages or farms of their own, and the second is the transfer of men from their fathers' to their uterine uncles' villages when their fathers have died.

In my sample I found that quite a high proportion of the population had been born, reared, and dwelt at the time of the enquiry, in different villages. 46 out of 179 adult men, or 25·7 per cent, and 57 out of 197 women, or 28·9 per cent, had been born in one village, bred in another, and lived at the time of the census in yet another.

To sum up : Tables III, IV, and V show that about one-seventh of the census population lived in their natal villages and six-sevenths in other villages ; that about three-fifths of adult men were reared in villages other than their natal villages, as were just more than half the adult women in the sample ; four-fifths of adult men currently resided in villages other than those in which they had been brought up, and nine-tenths of adult women did likewise. A quarter of the adult male population and nearly three-tenths of the adult women had been born, reared, and dwelt at the time of the census, in three different villages. These figures give little indication of the extent of spatial mobility of Ndembu but merely show transfers of residential affiliation from one headman's group to another. The few individuals who have remained in the same village all their lives may have travelled considerable distances across the region as members of that village. Those who have changed their village affiliation may have moved only a few hundred yards. Some idea of the extent of individual spatial mobility may be afforded by Table VI, which groups the census population into chiefdoms [1] of birth, rearing, and affiliation at the time of the enquiry.

---

[1] The term ' chiefdom ' here refers to a Sub-Chiefdom under the Native Authority. Mukang'ala, however, ceased to be a recognized Sub-Chief in 1947. His area has been incorporated in that of Chief Kanongesha.

Table VI shows that immigration into each chiefdom in which the census was taken, from other areas, has been considerable.

TABLE VI

INDIVIDUAL MOBILITY THROUGH CHIEFDOMS

Present chiefdoms of individuals in census	Males									
	P/R/N	%	P/R	%	P/N	%	O	%	Total	%
Mukang'ala .	29	43·3	9	13·4	2	3·0	27	40·3	67	100·0
Ikelenge . .	7	15·6	11	24·4	1	2·2	26	57·8	45	100·0
Nyakaseya .	6	18·3	11	33·3	1	3·0	15	45·4	33	100·0
Mwininyilamba	13	39·3	6	18·3	0	0·0	14	42·4	33	100·0
Total . .	55	30·9	37	20·8	4	2·2	82	46·1	178	100·0
	Females									
Mukang'ala .	40	57·1	6	8·6	1	1·4	23	32·8	70	100·0
Ikelenge . .	9	17·0	6	11·3	1	1·9	37	69·8	53	100·0
Nyakaseya .	12	27·3	8	18·2	1	2·3	23	52·1	44	100·0
Mwininyilamba	5	17·9	3	10·7	0	0·0	20	71·4	28	100·0
Total . .	66	33·8	23	11·8	3	1·5	103	52·5	195	100·0
	Males and Females									
Mukang'ala .	69	50·4	15	10·9	3	2·2	50	36·5	137	100·0
Ikelenge . .	16	16·3	17	17·3	2	2·0	63	64·2	98	100·0
Nyakaseya .	18	23·4	19	24·7	2	2·6	38	49·3	77	100·0
Mwininyilamba	18	29·5	9	14·8	0	0·0	34	55·7	61	100·0
Total . .	121	32·4	60	16·2	7	1·8	185	49·5	373	100·0

P/R/N = Chiefdom of birth, rearing and present residence the same.
P/R = Chiefdom of rearing and present residence the same.
P/N = Chiefdom of birth and present residence the same.
O = Persons born and reared outside present chiefdom.

The number of immigrants in the sample is nearly 50 per cent of the total population. I would like to repeat that the boundaries of chiefdoms have not been significantly altered during the period under consideration, although minor changes have been made by Government. In the past the areas of chiefs and senior headmen were demarcated by topographical features such as rivers and hills. Thus, in considering personal mobility through chiefdoms, I am no longer analysing allegiance to a spatially mobile unit (village), but am examining allegiance to a spatially fixed one (chiefdom). Indeed a person may meander through many chiefdoms while remaining the whole while in the same village. The percentage of persons born and/or reared in Mukang'ala area is markedly higher than that found in the other three chiefdoms, all of which are in the north-western pedicle where there is most European settlement. Mukang'ala is a deposed Sub-Chief of Kanongesha, his area is a ' conservative ' and traditional one, and many of his people are Kawiku, descended from the autochthonous inhabitants of the region. Most of the immigration into the pedicle has come from Angola and the Belgian Congo and has taken place since the beginning of the present century.

Summary

Ndembu society may be characterized as mobile rather than stable with regard to residence. Villages move through space and split through time. Individuals continually circulate through villages. There are two main types of village mobility : some villages tend to move in a relatively narrow orbit, for instance, Kawiku villages circulate around the margin of the Kawiku Plain ; others, especially those of Lunda origin, sometimes move considerable distances between successive sites. Individuals frequently change their village affiliations and few indeed of the adult members of my census sample were living in their natal villages and villages of rearing at the time of my enquiry. Since villages are seldom large, and there is nowhere to get away from one's neighbours within the village if one quarrels with them, people are constantly on the move. When villages reach a certain ' critical ' size they tend to split and the resultant immature villages often move some distance from the parent villages. I believe the critical sizes to have been, until very recently, in the neighbourhood of about 20 huts and 50 people ; since 1950 they are probably less. Just as the membership of villages is constantly changing so the membership of vicinages is also changing, although less rapidly. The rate of residential mobility considerably increased in the period between the world wars as the result of immigration into the Rhodesian Ndembu region from Angola and the Belgian Congo, and recently attempts by Government to stabilize the population have slowed down the rate of village mobility. But my evidence suggests that high village and individual mobility have always been features of the Ndembu social system. The accounts of ethnographers and travellers show that other groups of Lunda origin and affiliations possessed a similar unstable type of social system.[1] All these groups have traditions of migration ; and although they have settled in more or less defined territories in the last two or three centuries, within these territories villages and individuals have continued to range widely, while villages are ceaselessly coming into being. My genealogical data suggest that many small settlements have failed to become established and have died out.

This high mobility in the social system may be associated with a productive economy in which men hunt for meat and women grow crops, and in which the men's role is valued more highly than the women's. Women also tend to accept the men's valuation of hunting. The dominant characteristics of the social system at any given point in time may result from a male-dominated hunting economy in a bush-habitat, the characteristics being a high mobility, a limited degree of co-operation, and, where there is co-operation, this is mainly between men. Other characteristics, consistent with hunting, include personal independence, resentment of political control, and residential discontinuity of groups and individuals. On the other hand, there are regularities in behaviour which are consistent and constant through these changes. Regularity, cohesion and persistence, in the Ndembu system through time, are related to the roles of women both in production of crops and in reproduction. Undervalued though it is with regard to its actual contribution to the food supplies, the productive labour of women provides the regular staple for the physical survival of Ndembu society. Women bear and nourish the children, and where the mother goes, with or without the father, the children go also. The

---

[1] See, for example, Carvalho's (op. cit.) comments on the Chokwe, Bangala and Songo.

present belongs to the men, and the social order at any given moment bears the stamp of male activity ; the past and future of the society are dominated by the mothers. The group of male kinsmen forms the core of the village today : tomorrow its continuity will be found to have depended on their scattered matrilineal kinswomen. The men are present and together because of dead women ; the women are absent because they are married to other men, but their sons and daughters' sons will replenish the village. The conflicts and cohesion in the kinship and residential systems, associated with this dichotomy of productive and reproductive roles between men and women, will be the subject of subsequent analysis.

CHAPTER III

THE SOCIAL COMPOSITION OF THE VILLAGE

W E have already noted how, with the weakening of chiefly
authority, the village emerged as the significant local unit
among the Ndembu. But we have also seen that Ndembu
villages, like the Tonga villages described by Colson,[1] ' are not
necessarily enduring units with stable populations tied to particular localities . . . villages may shift from spot to spot, while
through them stream a succession of inhabitants '. Nevertheless,
at ·any given moment it will be found that the inhabitants of a
particular village are not merely a random grouping of unrelated
individuals but that the majority of village members are linked
to the headman by varying ties of kinship and affinity. An
Ndembu village, like the Lamba villages described by Mitchell
and Barnes [2] and the Kaonde village described by Watson, may
be defined in fact as ' a local residential group whose members
claim a genealogical relationship with one man, usually the
headman '.[3] In this the Ndembu, of course, resemble many
other Central African peoples.

In theory an individual, provided that he or she is not a slave,
a married woman, an uncircumcised boy, or an uninitiated girl,
may reside wherever he or she may please, but in practice his or
her choice of residence is usually circumscribed by a limited
number of modes of residential affiliation, based on kinship,
affinity and slavery. The most important of these is matrilineal
relationship to the village headman. However, this type of
affiliation is drastically modified by the virilocal residence of
married women. If matrilineal attachment to headmen and
virilocal marriage were the sole determinants of village affiliation,
villages would consist entirely of male matrilineal kinsmen, their
wives and dependent children. Adult men would reside avunculocally, adult wedded women virilocally, and their young

---

[1] Colson, op. cit., p. 41.
[2] Mitchell and Barnes, passim.
[3] Watson, p. 7.

children patrilocally. But structural rigidity of this order is
never found in the mobile Ndembu society. In practice, there
is a relatively high percentage of patrilocally resident, adult men.
A number of adult wedded women may also be found living
patrilocally. In the past, and in the more traditional areas even
today, marriage was uxorilocal for the first year and daughters
remained during this period in their fathers' villages with their
husbands. Again, young divorced women may return to their
fathers' villages if their mothers are living there. Indeed, divorce
powerfully affects the residential affiliation of adult women of

TABLE VII

DIVORCE RATIOS (TOTAL MARRIAGE EXPERIENCE OF LIVING INFORMANTS)

Ratio	No. in census sample	Value
A. No. of marriages ended in divorce expressed as a percentage of all marriages	347/658	52·7
B. No. of marriages ended in divorce expressed as a percentage of all completed marriages	347/429	80·1
C. No. of marriages ended in divorce expressed as a percentage of all marriages except those ended by death	347/576	61·4

all ages. Marriage is extremely brittle (see Table VII [1]), and
older divorced women usually go to live at the village of their
nearest male matrilineal kin until remarriage. After the death
of their husbands, widows also tend to live with their near male
matrilineal kinsmen until remarriage. When they have passed
the menopause widows and divorcees usually reside permanently
with their male matrilineal kin. There is a strong tendency for
mothers and children to gravitate together as the mothers grow
older. The mother-child bond is perhaps the most powerful
kinship link in Ndembu society. As minors both sons and
daughters tend to follow their mothers wherever the latter may
be living. Most children go with the mother on divorce. Boys
in their teens may sometimes leave their mothers and remain

---

[1] See pp. 263, 265 for discussion on small percentage of widows.

with their mothers' brothers, but girls usually stay with their mothers until the end of the puberty ritual which is customarily followed by marriage. Mothers rejoin their sons, daughters rejoin their mothers after widowhood or divorce. In their minority children live with their mother; in her old age the mother lives with her children again. In the intervening years mother, son and daughter may spend most of their time in different villages, although they may visit one another frequently.

Patrilocal residence and frequent divorce, then, have further modified the picture originally presented of a village occupied by a core of male matrilineal kin, their wives and children. What we now find is a group of siblings, brothers outnumbering sisters, and some of their children of both sexes. In addition we may find spouses of the above persons, with wives outnumbering husbands, and some grandchildren.

In long-established villages a number of classificatory as well as primary kin will be found. The senior generation will contain two or more groups of matrilineally related siblings and the junior adjacent generation will contain classificatory as well as full cross-cousins.

It will be remembered that the mean and median sizes of Ndembu settlements in my genealogical sample are small, 10·6 huts and 9 huts respectively. Now, given the tendency of full siblings and their mother to gravitate together, and given a tendency for a certain proportion of adult children of headmen and of other important elders to reside patrilocally during the lifetime of their fathers and while their parents' marriages remain unbroken, this means that in many long-established villages and in most recently established villages primary kin of the headmen outnumber their classificatory kin. Thus in a recently established village containing, say, 8 huts, the headman may be accompanied by his brother and widowed sister. If he has two wives each of them will have a separate hut, so that the sibling group in the senior generation will jointly possess 4 huts. The headman may have a married son living with him, and his sister a married son and divorced daughter, making three huts for the junior adjacent generation, and seven in all. The other hut might be occupied by a male or female parallel cousin of the headman, by the son or daughter of another sister residing elsewhere with her husband, or by a sister's daughter's child. Or it might be occupied by a member of a maternal descent group of slaves [1] owned by the headman's lineage, or even by a stranger.

Ndembu give different weighting to each of the factors affecting village affiliation. Matrilineal relationship with the founder of a village gives one the right to reside there permanently, other things being equal. A person may stay in his or her father's village until the latter's death, but must then leave. A free father's slave children are inherited by his heir and thus remain. This means that one's affiliation through one's mother is to a group, whereas one's tie with one's father is personal. A man is the end of a matrilineage, to paraphrase the Latin maxim, and his son does not belong to that lineage. A woman's real home is where her close male maternal kin (her mother's brothers, her brothers and her sons) happen to be living, usually together. These male members of her lineage transfer her economic and sexual services to a male member of another lineage, but never renounce their claim on her reproductive capacity. Eventually her sons and daughters' sons must go to them, and sooner or later she will probably follow them. But she spends most of her reproductive cycle in the village of her husband or in the villages of her successive husbands. In Table VIII an attempt is made on the basis of data supplied in the village census sample to discover whether minors, under the age of twenty, do in fact tend to reside with their mothers wherever the latter may be living.

Table VIII shows that about two-thirds of the population under twenty years of age, other than married girls living virilocally, were residing with both their parents, and about a quarter with their mothers only. A negligible percentage were living with their fathers only, and hardly more were living in their matrilineal villages with neither parent. More than nine-tenths were residing in the same villages as their mothers, and more than half of those who were not, were residing in villages whose nuclei were their own matrilineal kin.

Now let us try to find out at what period in the lives of sons this strong attachment to the mother is severed. Only a small

---

[1] Slavery was formally abolished by the British South Africa Company in the early years of the present century. But it lingered on as a clandestine institution in the villages for many years afterwards. See p. 187 ff.

sample could be obtained by comparing genealogical and census data, but the results are suggestive.

TABLE VIII

RESIDENCE OF UNWEDDED MINORS

With whom residing	Age groups								Total	
	0–4		5–9		10–14		15–19			
	No.	%	No.	%	No.	%	No.	%	No.	%
Males :										
Mother and father .	41	39·8	18	26·1	24	32·4	15	31·2	98	33·3
Mother only . .	10	9·7	5	7·2	10	13·5	9	18·7	34	11·5
Father only . . .	0	0·0	2	2·9	2	2·7	0	0·0	4	1·4
Neither : in village of matrikin . .	0	0·0	5	7·2	2	2·7	3	6·2	10	3·4
Total	51	49·5	30	43·4	38	51·3	27	56·1	146	49·6
Females :										
Mother and father .	39	37·9	28	40·6	20	27·0	8	16·7	95	32·4
Mother only . .	13	12·6	10	14·5	12	16·2	9	18·8	44	15·0
Father only . . .	0	0·0	0	0·0	1	1·4	2	4·2	3	1·0
Neither : in village of matrikin . .	0	0·0	1	1·5	3	4·1	2	4·2	6	2·0
Total	52	50·5	39	56·6	36	48·7	21	43·9	148	50·4
Both Sexes :										
Mother and father .	80	77·7	46	66·7	44	59·4	23	47·9	193	65·7
Mother only . .	23	22·3	15	21·7	22	29·7	18	37·5	78	26·5
Father only . . .	0	0·0	2	2·9	3	4·1	2	4·2	7	2·4
Neither : in village of matrikin . .	0	0·0	6	8·7	5	6·8	5	10·4	16	5·4
Total	103	100·0	69	100·0	74	100·0	48	100·0	294	100·0

According to Table IX, 21 out of 37 men in the 20–29 age group whose mothers were still alive were living in the same villages as their mothers. In the age group 30–39, 5 out of 11 men whose mothers were alive were living in the same villages as their mothers. In the whole sample rather more than half of the men whose mothers were alive were living with them in the same village.

According to my observations the mother-son link of common residence is only definitely snapped by the mother's death. A divorced or widowed mother of advanced years will usually spend her last years in her son's village. I have recorded a case in which an elderly woman actually divorced her husband in

TABLE IX

RESIDENCE OF ADULT MALES WHOSE MOTHERS ARE STILL ALIVE

| | | Age groups | | | | Total |
		20–29	30–39	40–49	50–59	
Men in same villages as own mothers	Married . .	18	3	4	2	27
	Unmarried . .	3	2	0	0	5
	Total . . .	21	5	4	2	32
Men in different villages from own mothers	Married . .	13	6	4	0	23
	Unmarried . .	3	0	0	0	3
	Total . . .	16	6	4	0	26
Total	Married . .	31	9	8	2	50
	Unmarried . .	6	2	0	0	8
	Total . . .	37	11	8	2	58

order to take up residence with her eldest son, who had just founded a village of his own. This mother-son tie of propinquity is all the more remarkable when the countervailing tendencies set up by virilocal marriage of women are considered. The mother-child, and especially the mother-son bond, emerges from these enquiries as the crucial link of kinship and determinant of village affiliation. Where adult children reside patrilocally this seems to be on account of the child's attachment to the mother rather than to the father. In Table VIII only 2·4 per cent of the 0–19 age group in the sample resided with their fathers only, while 26·5 per cent resided with their mothers only, following their divorce or widowhood. Of the four men who resided with their fathers only, I knew two very well, and in both cases special circumstances were involved. The mothers of both were dead and their fathers were headmen. These factors are, of course, infrequently combined. In one case the son feared witchcraft in the village of his near matrilineal kin. The matrilineal village of the other was in Angola and as a progressive young man who wanted to earn money he preferred to remain in Mwinilunga in the wealthier pedicle area.

The strength of the sibling bond and its importance as a determinant of residence also derive from this mother-child tie. In matters of inheritance and succession it is matrilineal descent that counts ; the children of one mother by several fathers regard each other as full (*chikupu*) siblings in every respect in the social context of their maternal village, although they may visit in their different paternal villages, and receive assistance from and assist their father's matrilineal groups independently of one another. As the analysis proceeds, it will be shown how a number of social mechanisms are brought into play to counteract this tendency for the minimal unit of mother and children to cohere too closely and intensely and prevent the growth of wider social units. Important among these—to anticipate—is an emphasis on the social and spatial separation of adjacent genealogical generations and on unity within each genealogical generation. This emphasis opposes mother to child in a relationship of authority on one side and respect on the other, and unites full siblings with parallel and cross-cousins against the senior generation as a whole. The persistence of the mother-child link as a determinant of residence attests to its strength in the face of generation separation and of other competitive modes of affiliation.

We are now in a better position to rate the various principles determining village affiliation according to their degree of emphasis in Ndembu culture. First, there is, as we have seen, an extremely powerful bond between a mother and her own children, acting against the dispersal of this matricentric family and towards its maintenance as a residential unit. But the principle of virilocal marriage disrupts the matricentric family by separating daughter from mother and sister from brother. Henceforth it is possible to regard the subsequent history of the original matricentric family as an effort to reconstitute itself as a local unit. Many sons remain with their mothers whether the latter live virilocally or avunculocally. If sons and mothers are temporarily separated, divorce or widowhood of the mother sooner or later brings the old woman back into the village of her son who by this time may be fully mature, and who may indeed have founded a new village of his own. Sisters return to brothers after their marriages have terminated and may often find their mothers there. The matricentric family, united in its early growth but divided as the children grow up and themselves reproduce, seldom comes together again in its full membership, but it always strives to do so against virilocal marriage and the many other centrifugal tendencies of Ndembu society.

Another important factor influencing residence is, as we have seen, the tendency of males to come together in kin groups to form the persistent core of villages. Their collaboration is couched in the dominant matrilineal idiom of Ndembu kinship so that the village is regarded at its inception as a group of uterine brothers. But a wider group than a pair or handful of brothers is required for effective collaboration in economic activities and in legal matters, and for offence and defence in feuds and raids. The concept of uterine brotherhood is extended to include in the residential unit, matrilineal parallel cousins. Virilocal marriage, which had broken up the matricentric family, now appears as the very means by which the 'adelphic group' of male uterine parallel cousins is enabled to remain together. Uxorilocal marriage would disperse this group,[1]

---

[1] Among the Nayar castes of Malabar in India, sisters remained in their brothers' house. The Nayar kinship grouping was a matrilineal lineage living on its own property. All Nayar women were married before puberty to men of their own caste and divorced after four days, so that children they bore subsequently to lovers of their own caste or higher castes would have the correct caste on the whole for 'father'. Thus uterine siblings and matrilineal parallel cousins remained together throughout life, for though each brother might have several 'mistresses' in other houses, he resided with his sisters. In a sense, the frequent divorce among Ndembu women parallels the Nayar situation, since there is hardly a village in which, at a given moment, one or more sisters are not found spending the intervals between successive marriages with their uterine brothers and matrilineal parallel cousins.

primary uterine kinship as the basis of local association would prevent its classificatory extension.

The unity of the matricentric family, virilocal marriage, and classificatory adelphic co-residence, are principles of local groupings which give rise to continual conflicts within the village. We have seen how the ecological system of the Ndembu, with its complementary and opposing poles of hunting and cassava-cultivation, may itself be a direct source of residential instability. This instability is considerably aggravated by conflicts which arise out of the social structure. In subsequent chapters I shall examine in turn each of the principles determining residence and show how each interlinks persons and groups divided from one another by other principles of social affiliation. In the course of the analysis it will be shown, for example, how conflict between the principles of the unity of the matricentric family and virilocal marriage tends to break up the marital group, especially in the early years of marriage, and on the other hand, how stable marriage tends to retard the growth of villages by keeping men apart from their uterine sisters with their children. It is to a considerable extent by divorce and widowhood that a village is enabled to persist through time. With a woman come her children, and if she is divorced or widowed after she has passed her menopause she and her sons come back permanently to the village of their matrilineal kin and replace the wives and children of their male kin who have gone out of it. Thus divorce and widowhood act simultaneously as principles of village recruitment and attrition.

What are the visible effects of these principles of local organization on the social composition of villages that I have actually observed ? Is it possible to infer regularities in residential composition from field data ? Is it then possible to construct models of different types of village structure on the basis of such observed regularities ? An attempt to answer these questions is provided in Tables X and XI. The universe on which these tables are based consists of hut-owners in villages where I have collected full genealogies. Of the 77 villages in which I collected genealogies (see p. 37), I have used material from 68 villages for the purpose of making these tables. The nine discarded villages are those in which the genealogical data are too scanty and fragmentary to be suitable for use.   Since in the great majority of villages most members are kin of the headmen I have classified hut-owners according to the kind and degree of kinship or affinal links they have to headmen.   Where a person has more than one tie of consanguinity or affinity to the headman of his village I classify him by the relationship which Ndembu hold to be the dominant one in the context of village membership.   In establishing which member of a marital pair or of a group of immature boys or girls inhabiting a single hut is the ' hut-owner ' I employ the criteria used by Ndembu themselves.   If a woman is living in a village where she has a primary or classificatory matrilineal relationship with the headman, and her husband has not, she is considered to be the hut-owner.   If both are matrilineally related, as in the case of a marriage between matrilineal kin of alternate genealogical generations, the husband and not the wife is taken to be the hut-owner.   If a woman is living in her father's village and her husband is not related or is a distant cognatic relative of the headman she is the hut-owner.   In a cross-cousin marriage, the spouse matrilineally linked with the headman, regardless of sex, is the hut-owner.   In a boys' or girls' hut the oldest, linked by whatever tie of kinship to the headman, is classified as the hut-owner.   If no link of consanguinity or affinity can be traced between a hut-owner and his or her headman, he or she is classified as a ' stranger '.   Strangers fall into two categories.   They may be first-generation slaves (sing. *ndungu*, pl. *andungu*) or maternal descendants of slaves, who even today may still be regarded as belonging to free members ; or they may be immigrants from other areas in Rhodesia, Angola or the Belgian Congo who have attached themselves or have been attached by a Government Sub-Chief to a particular headman.   I have not been able to determine in every case who was or was not a slave and have consequently been compelled to classify all hut-owners for whom it was impossible to trace genealogical connection with the headmen of their village as ' strangers '.   I have called a female stranger a ' hut-owner ' if she is so described by the headman of the village in which she is living.

By employing the descriptive system of kinship nomenclature used by anthropologists I was able to distinguish no less than 72 different categories of kin, in relation to headmen, living in these 68 villages.   These are subsumed in the Ndembu

TABLE X

RELATIONSHIP OF HUT-OWNERS TO HEADMEN IN 68 SETTLEMENTS
(male and female)

Category		Primary M.	F.	Total	Classificatory M.	F.	Total	Total M.	F.	Total
Ego (headmen themselves)		67	1	68	—	—	—	67	1	68
Matrilineal kin	mm	—	0	0	—	1	1	—	1	1
	m	—	4	4	—	12	12	—	16	16
	mG	1	0	1	6	0	6	7	0	7
	older G	2	7	9	16	7	23	18	14	32
	younger G	35	23	58	28	9	37	63	32	95
	zC	56	28	84	26	22	48	82	50	132
	zdC	11	9	20	5	6	11	16	15	31
	zddC	0	0	0	2	1	3	2	1	3
	Total . . .	105	71	176	83	58	141	188	129	317
Own descendants of male headmen	C	49	21	70	—	—	—	49	21	70
	dC	1	2	3	—	—	—	1	2	3
	SC	3	0	3	—	—	—	3	0	3
	Total . . .	53	23	76	—	—	—	53	23	76
Children of male matrikin	mBC	3	0	3	3	2	5	6	2	8
	older BC	3	3	6	0	0	0	3	3	6
	younger BC	9	0	9	0	0	0	9	0	9
	BC (unspecified sibling rank)	0	0	0	6	1	7	6	1	7
	zSC	2	0	2	3	3	6	5	3	8
	Total . . .	17	3	20	12	6	18	29	9	38
Patrilateral siblings	older FC	1	0	1	2	1	3	3	1	4
	younger FC	6	2	8	4	0	4	10	2	12
	Total . . .	7	2	9	6	1	7	13	3	16
Children of patrilateral siblings	FdC	2	1	3	0	0	0	2	1	3
	older FSC	3	1	4	0	0	0	3	1	4
	younger FSC	1	0	1	0	0	0	1	0	1
	FddC	0	0	0	1	0	1	1	0	1
	Total . . .	6	2	8	1	0	1	7	2	9
Total		255	102	357	102	65	167	357	167	524

Legend

m	Mother	z	Sister	d	Daughter	B	Brother
G	Sibling	C	Child	S	Son	F	Father

classificatory system under 14 kinship categories, or 18 if certain terms are qualified by adjectives denoting sex. In Table X I discriminate between matrilineal and patrilateral primary kin according to descriptive criteria, and subsume all other kin under Ndembu classificatory categories.

A number of inferences may be drawn from the material presented in Table XI. The first is that headmen and their kin outnumber strangers in villages by more than four to one. The second is that headmen and their matrilineal kin account for nearly

TABLE XI

THE SOCIAL COMPOSITION OF 68 SETTLEMENTS

Category of hut-owners	Males		Females		Total	
	No.	%	No.	%	No.	%
Headmen and primary matrilineal kin	172	25·7	72	10·8	244	36·5
Classificatory matrilineal kin . .	83	12·4	58	8·7	141	21·1
Own descendants of male headmen	53	7·9	23	3·4	76	11·4
Children of male matrilineal kin .	29	4·4	9	1·2	38	5·7
Patrilateral siblings and their children	20	2·9	5	0·8	25	3·7
Unspecified kin and affines . .	16	2·4	3	0·5	19	2·9
Total kin and affines	373	55·9	170	25·4	543	81·3
Strangers	97	14·5	28	4·2	125	18·7
Total hut-owners	470	70·3	198	29·6	668	100·0

three-fifths of all hut-owners in the sample. Children of headmen and of their male matrilineal kin account for just under one-sixth of all hut-owners and one-fifth of all related hut-owners. Another feature is the numerical preponderance of primary over classificatory matrilineal kin in a ratio of almost two to one. 130 out of 385 matrilineally related hut-owners, or 33·7 per cent, are women, an indication in a society practising virilocal marriage of the strong tendency of women to rejoin their male matrilineal kin. Since nearly all women are married just after their puberty ritual this means that women found in their matrilineal villages must have been divorced, widowed, or recently separated from their husbands, or with husbands who live

uxorilocally. The evidence of my village census suggests that
divorce is easily the most common reason why women reside
with their matrilineal kin. Women live in uxorilocal marriage
only for special reasons, except that a few men still live uxorilocally during the first year of marriage. The reasons behind
the matrilocal and avunculocal residence of adult women will
emerge in the course of the analysis.

Headmen and their primary and classificatory brothers in both
lines of descent account for 161 out of 542 related hut-owners,
or nearly three out of ten. With them are 49 women whom
they call ' sisters ', of whom 32 are their own sisters, making
up a sibling and classificatory sibling category which accounts
for two out of every five related hut-owners. In this category
we find that two out of every three are primary siblings. This
tends to confirm the previous statement that uterine siblings
rejoin one another in the same village as they grow older. The
table also demonstrates that whereas the ratio of male parallel
cousins to brothers is 53 : 47, the ratio of female parallel cousins
to sisters is as low as 35 : 65, a fact that indicates the importance
of the principle of classificatory adelphic co-residence.

The bilateral character of the junior adjacent genealogical
generation of hut-owners emerges from the analysis of the
data. Children of headmen and of those whom headmen call
' brothers ' total 94 persons, while those whom headmen call
' sisters' children ' total 134, a ratio of about 2 : 3. For males
the ratio of ' sons ' to ' sisters' sons ' is about 7 : 8, and for own
sons to own sisters' sons approaches one to one.

I found in the villages from which the figures were compiled,
that there was an approximate numerical balance between hut-
owners in the opposed generation categories. Thus if hut-owners
in the headmen's generation are added to those in the second
descendant and second ascendant generations from the headmen,
members of this linked generation category total 269 hut-owners.
If members of the first and third descendant generations and first
ascendant generations from the headmen are added together,
this opposed linked-generation segment possesses 273 hut-owners.
This numerical balance between the linked-generation segments
is to be expected, since in a given population, a hut-owner is
equally likely to belong to either generation-segment on a
random basis. Each linked-generation segment in Ndembu

society occupies its own section of the village, and, since villages are generally circular in shape, inhabits a semicircle of huts facing the semicircle of the opposed generation segment. In each village the number of members in each segment is seldom equal, but if a sufficiently large sample of villages is taken it appears that the linked-generation categories approximately balance one another numerically.

In order to bring out significant differences in social structure between long and recently established villages I compiled a further table illustrating such differences. For the purposes of this analysis I defined ' a long-established village ' as a village in which there had been three or more successive headmen, including the present incumbent, and ' a recently established village ' as one in which there had been less than three successive headmen. This distinction does not precisely correspond with the distinction previously made between registered and unregistered villages and farms. According to the earlier distinction both unregistered villages and farms are of comparatively recent establishment (cf. p. 34 and p. 36) since they consist of settlements not yet recorded on the Government Tax Register. Thus by this earlier reckoning I included as ' registered villages ' settlements that had been founded more than about five years before the enquiry and which had been granted official recognition as tax-paying units. Several of such villages indeed had been founded more than thirty years previously, but each village had been under the authority of a single headman throughout this period. A long-established village with three or more successive headmen is, in every case I collected, a village that was in existence before the European government began. There were 21 such villages in my sample and I compare the social composition of these villages with that of 47 ' recently established villages ' in Table XII.

Table XII shows that in long-established villages the ratio of primary to classificatory hut-owning matrilineal kin is about 1 : 1·1, whereas in recently established villages the ratio is about 3 : 1. In other words, recently established villages tend to consist dominantly of uterine siblings and their families, while in long-established villages uterine kin are just outnumbered by their classificatory matrilineal kin. In long-established villages also we find a significantly higher percentage of cognatic hut-owning kin than in recently established villages. This is because such villages are regarded as something more than a group of uterine siblings. Their membership is looked upon as a group with a persistent matrilineal core to which a fringe of other cognates

TABLE XII

THE SOCIAL COMPOSITION OF LONG-ESTABLISHED VILLAGES COMPARED WITH THAT OF RECENTLY ESTABLISHED VILLAGES

	Category of hut-owners	Males		Females		Total	
		No.	%	No.	%	No.	%
21 long-established villages	H.M. and primary matrikin.	52	18·2	23	8·0	75	26·3
	Classificatory matrikin . .	53	18·6	33	11·6	86	30·2
	Descendants of H.M. . .	20	7·0	9	3·2	29	10·2
	Cognatic, patrilateral and un-specified kin, and affines .	38	13·3	9	3·2	47	16·5
	Strangers	41	14·4	7	2·4	48	16·8
	Total	204	71·6	81	28·4	285	100·0
47 recently established villages	H.M. and primary matrikin.	120	31·3	49	12·8	169	44·1
	Classificatory matrikin . .	30	7·8	25	6·5	55	14·4
	Descendants of H.M. . .	33	8·6	14	3·7	47	12·3
	Cognatic, patrilateral and un-specified kin, and affines .	27	7·1	8	2·1	35	9·2
	Strangers	56	14·6	21	5·5	77	20·1
	Total	266	69·5	117	30·5	383	100·0
Total	H.M. and primary matrikin.	172	25·7	72	10·8	244	36·5
	Classificatory matrikin . .	83	12·4	58	8·7	141	21·1
	Descendants of H.M. . .	53	7·9	23	3·4	76	11·4
	Cognatic, patrilateral and un-specified kin, and affines .	65	9·7	17	2·5	82	12·3
	Strangers	97	14·5	28	4·2	125	18·7
	Total	470	70·3	198	29·6	668	100·0

attach themselves. In these villages the matricentric family has matured into the matrilineage. The principal factors influencing the persistence of settlements beyond their initial phase as uterine sibling residential groups is discussed on pp. 198–203. In a matrilineal society which practises virilocal marriage, if there is virtually unlimited access to resources so that settlements are under no constraint to occupy specific tracts of land in perpetuity, the transition from matricentricity to matriliny as the basis for local groupings must always be hazardous and uncertain. It is dependent on such factors as the ability of the headman to keep his following together, the maintenance of reasonably good relations between the men of the matrilineal core and their brothers-in-law, and the biological accidents of fertility and freedom from disease.

The core of the Ndembu settlement consists of a group of uterine or matrilineal kin, of whom the most senior is the headman. Virilocal marriage separates female and male matrilineal kin and at the same time enables men often to retain their children, especially their sons, in their own villages after the latter have matured. Nevertheless the dominant attachment of children is not to their fathers but to their mothers. Thus a man can only retain the residential affiliation of his children while his marriage to their mother endures. On divorce a woman usually goes to live with her nearest male matrilineal kin, and her children tend to follow her. The crucial bond of kinship is between a mother and her children, who form a matricentric family. This family may be attached for longer and shorter periods to a woman's husband or brother. As the children mature, daughters are separated from mothers, and brothers from sisters, by virilocal marriage. But there is a constant tendency, though it is seldom completely realized, for the matricentric family to reconstitute itself as a local unit. This is an important factor behind the mobility and instability of the individual's residence. It is also a cause of conflict between husbands and brothers-in-law and between sons-in-law and mothers-in-law. Virilocal marriage is related to the tendency for uterine brothers and male matrilineal parallel cousins to reside together. This is part of a general tendency among Ndembu to build up villages around a framework of close male kin : brothers, sons, sisters' sons, and sisters' daughters' sons. Evidence from matrilineal societies practising uxorilocal marriage such as the Bemba and Yao [1]

---

[1] Richards, A. I., 'Mother-right among the Central Bantu', *Essays Presented to C. G. Seligman*, ed. E. E. Evans-Pritchard, R. Firth, B. Malinowski,

suggests that where the link between male village residents and the headman is one of affinity, and these men are linked to one another not by kinship but merely by propinquity, they co-operate very little among themselves. This is probably because in most primitive societies social control at the local level is associated with position in the kinship structure. Senior kin exert authority over and command respect and obedience from their juniors, and between each category of kinsmen custom has prescribed an intricate and specific pattern of behavioural expectations which facilitates co-operation and inhibits dispute. Among Ndembu, male villagers co-operate in hunting and bush-clearing, and formerly assisted one another in offensive and defensive warfare. There was no strong central political authority and no national army, and a man's first loyalty was to his village. For all these purposes close and ready co-operation between men was necessary. It was therefore appropriate that men living together should be linked by consanguineal kinship, the major vehicle of social control. But the local attachment of male kin probably owed something of its intensity, as we have suggested in previous chapters, not only to such empirical factors, but also to masculine resentment of matrilineal descent formally expressed, as we shall see, in a number of ritual contexts, and the decisive economic importance of women. It is as though there were a general though unconscious male conspiracy to exclude their female kin from their local units. Nevertheless, men needed women for their personal and corporate survival. The individual man owed his care and nurture to a woman, his own mother. Similarly the group of male villagers needed their sisters to ensure the survival of their village as a social entity. To bring them back into the village entailed the male group's coming into conflict with other men. So that the very exclusion of female kin from villages in order that male kin might live together provided the principal source of conflict and unrest between Ndembu men as a whole. Again, since in the economy women's work provided the staple of subsistence, women were needed in the

---

and I. Schapera (1933), p. 267, and *Bemba Marriage and Modern Economic Conditions*, Rhodes-Livingstone Paper No. 4 (1940), pp. 33 ff. ; Mitchell, J. C., 'The Yao of Southern Nyasaland', *Seven Tribes of British Central Africa*, ed. Colson and Gluckman (1951), pp. 328 ff.

village. Men owned gardens, it is true, and worked in them sporadically, yet women had not only worked more regularly in their own as well as in their husbands' gardens but also dug up, carried, processed and cooked the daily, never-failing supply of cassava. If sisters were excluded, wives had to be included in the village personnel. In all their conscious statements about the relative importance of wives and sisters, Ndembu have continually stressed to me that wives outrank sisters, and that indeed the marital tie is the strongest and deepest they know. In ritual, too, husband and wife are regularly initiated together into curative and fertility cults. In a decisive aspect the girl's puberty ritual is a drama of marriage, emphasizing the importance of the conjugal tie. In spite of this verbalization and ritualization of the importance of the marital relationship, in fact Ndembu marriage is extremely brittle. This is due to the very real importance of the brother-sister tie which is the socially, although not biologically, procreative link in matrilineal society. Male kin can only live together through the exclusion of their sisters and sisters' daughters and the importation of wives linked to other corporate groups of male kin.[1] But having thrust their female kin out, the men must reclaim these women and their families if the village is to persist through time, and is not to die out for lack of replenishment. Unfortunately for the men, their own wives, closely bound to their children, are subject to the same 'gravitational' compulsion from their male matrilineal kin. Every adult Ndembu man, under the operation of the same set of social forces, is in the ambiguous position of striving to retain his own wife and children by his side and of simultaneously endeavouring to win back the sister whose absence is the price of his privilege of living with his brothers and sons in a matrilineal society. Put succinctly, to live with the male kin he loses a friend to marry an enemy. It is all part of the Ndembu male flight from the inexorable reality of matrilineal descent and female control of the economic basis of survival. Perhaps this is one factor in the Ndembu preoccupation

---

[1] In this discussion I have been considering some of the factors relating to the question of why Ndembu are virilocal. I have taken the fact that they are matrilineal for granted. I am also assuming here that there is a brother-sister incest rule.

with ritual, one aspect of which is escape, and another, compensation, although these constitute only a minute part of the whole story.

There is no guarantee, therefore, that a settlement will be perpetuated and will survive. If the sisters of the adelphic group have successful marriages, and providing that their husbands have long lives, it may be that their sons will live many years with fathers ; and that when these fathers die the sons will found sibling villages of their own rather than return to their uterine uncles. It may be that conflicts among the brothers themselves, arising from jealousies over succession and inheritance, will break up a village. Much depends in this society of individualists, only too ready to take offence, on the tact and diplomacy of individual headmen, whose best hope is not to browbeat or domineer but to persuade and reconcile. But once the essential link-up between first and third generations after the founding of a village has taken place, new sources of conflict within the settlement come into being. When a village contains only two generations of hut-owners it may still be regarded as a bilateral extended family. But when three generations of adult hut-owners form its membership, incipient cleavage along lineage lines becomes detectable. If a headman has two fertile sisters each has become the founder of a lineage. The principle of the unity of the matricentric family comes into conflict with the unity of the matrilineage, and each matricentric family or alliance of matricentric families with a common grandmother is a potential source of village cleavage and the potential starting-point of a new residential unit. Here the unity of siblings and the unity of classificatory adelphic male kin may be insufficient to hold the village together by cutting across lineage affiliation. It may be that the original sibling-group which founded the village has been reduced in numbers by death. In any case its authority is continually threatened within the village by the maturation of the junior adjacent generation, the leading men of which are eager to obtain the headmanship. To maintain its authority within the village on the one hand, and to prevent the disruption of the village as the result of struggles between lineages on the other, an alliance develops between the senior and the second descendant generations, an alliance sometimes cemented by marriage between persons who stand in the classificatory relationship of 'grandfather' (*nkaka*) and 'grandchild' (*mwijikulu*) to one another.[1]   Where such marriages occur they often link a ' grandfather ' of one lineage to a ' granddaughter ' of another. Thus the grandparent and his siblings secure the allegiance of the granddaughter's siblings against the thrustful middle generation. The middle generation, of course, exercises authority over the generation of grandchildren and also threatens the authority of the senior generation.   Grandparent-grandchild marriages also bind together potentially conflicting minimal [2] matrilineages and uterine sibling groups.   They are only made between classificatory kin and never between primary grandparents and grandchildren.   Thus they tend to occur mainly within long-established villages.   Nevertheless, in all villages containing at least three generations of hut-owners the alliance between alternate generations, whether intermarried or not, finds physical and spatial expression in the fact that both generations build their huts in the same village semicircle of huts facing and opposed to the semicircle of huts built by the intervening genealogical generation.   I use the term ' alliance ' and not ' unity ' or ' equivalence ' in describing the relations between alternate generations, since their mode of association approaches more closely that obtaining between cross-cousins (*asonyi*, sing. *musonyi*)[3] who intermarry, rather than that between siblings who do not.   Alternate generations, like cross-cousins, joke with one another and intermarry, although the joking is less ribald and more gently affectionate than the pleasantries of cross-cousin intercourse.   Joking, according to Radcliffe-Brown, implies a fairly even balance between hostility and friendliness, and in fact tension exists in grandparent-grandchild relations.   In the first place grandparents and grandchildren belong to different, and therefore potentially opposed, matricentric families, the basic

---

[1] It should be mentioned here that grandparent-grandchild marriages take place not only within villages but between villages of common origin (see p. 176).   Most, but not all, of such marriages are between a man and his ' granddaughter ' (see p. 246).

[2] In this book I regard a *minimal* matrilineage as a group consisting of the descendants through women of a common grandmother, a *minor* matrilineage as the matrilineal descendants of a common great-grandmother, and a *major* lineage as those of a common great-great-grandmother.

[3] See Chapter Eight for analysis of village kinship.

corporate kin units of Ndembu society and the starting-point of new residential units.   In the second place, grandparents, especially the senior male grandparent, belong to the generation which exerts gerontocratic political and jural authority in the matrilineal village or in other villages in which the grandchildren may reside.   Authority is ultimately in their hands.   At the same time, the position of these two generations is essentially similar *vis-à-vis* the middle generation as we have seen above. Again, the older needs the younger generation to replace as allies the siblings who have died, and the younger needs the older to mitigate the severity of the intervening generation of uterine uncles and senior affines.   Their mutual inter-dependence, strengthened by marriage and brother- and sister-in-law ties of familiarity and friendship, acts to bind together a residential group constantly liable to disruption from lineage and adjacent generation conflicts.

In the subsequent analysis I shall isolate each dominant principle governing village residence, and examine its operation, illustrated by case material, in promoting cohesion or generating conflict within the local unit.   This examination will concern itself not only with secular behaviour but also with ritual.   Afterwards, the working of each principle in the field of inter-village relations will be analysed.   Finally, there will be a discussion of modes of social integration, other than those derived from kinship, and these will be examined in terms of their congruence with and opposition to the kinship principles already considered.

CHAPTER IV

MATRILINEAL DESCENT :
THE BASIC PRINCIPLE OF VILLAGE ORGANIZATION

THERE is sense in regarding Ndembu villages as collocations of matricentric families interlinked by varying ties of
kinship and affinity. In addition, some measure of continuity
is provided by maternal descent which determines succession and
inheritance. In long-established villages with respected headmen something like hierarchically organized lineages of the type
made familiar in British anthropological literature by the researches of Evans-Pritchard and Fortes begin to emerge, although
such lineages are shallow by comparison with those found among
such matrilineal and uxorilocal people as the Hopi and Ashanti.
Table XIII shows lineage depth in 64 village genealogies. Farms
have been excluded from the sample and also several villages for
which my data are unsatisfactory. Table XV appears to indicate that there is a significant increase in the magnitude of a village
if six generations of matrilineal kin of its headman can be recorded
on a genealogy. Thereafter village magnitude seems to remain
fairly constant regardless of recorded lineage depth. The difference in genealogical recall between the older villagers of nine-
hut and thirteen-hut villages respectively tends to correspond
with the difference previously made between ' long and recently
established villages ' (see Table XII). It tends to correspond also
with differences in social structure. Recently established villages,
villages with less than three successive headmen, consist mainly
of uterine siblings, their adult children and a few mature grandchildren. Long-established villages, on the other hand, may contain many adult members of two or more segments of equal
status within a minor or major village matrilineage (see footnote
on p. 80). But few long-established villages, whatever the
generation depth of their nuclear lineage, attain to a great
population size. For fission, occurring most frequently between
uterine sibling groups and minimal lineages, and virilocal marriage, and various kinds of individual mobility, all prevent their
expansion.

Although there is no absolute correspondence between the limit of recall and the span of the residential segment, one tends

VILLAGE LINEAGES

TABLE XIII	TABLE XIV
LINEAGE DEPTH IN 64 GENEALOGIES	GENERATION OF HEADMAN

No. of generations in village genealogies	No. of villages
4	4
5	19
6	21
7	14
8	2
9	2
10	1
11	0
12	1
Total	64

Mean lineage depth . . 6·1
Median 6
Mode 6

Generation of headman	No. of village headmen
3rd	15
4th	26
5th	16
6th	4
7th	2
8th	0
9th	0
10th	1
Total . . .	64

Mean generation level . 4·3
Median 4
Mode 4

TABLE XV
VILLAGE SIZE AND LINEAGE DEPTH

No. of generations in village genealogy	Mean no. of huts in village
4	8·4
5	9·4
6	13·5
7	13·1
8 & over	14·0
Mean 6·1	11·9

to find a greater depth of recall by the headmen of long-established villages than by those of recently established villages. This is because it is of immediate interest to distantly connected kin in long-established villages, to trace precise genealogical relationship to one another as members of a single local community. Of course, one may find that headmen of recently established villages may be able to trace back their matrilineal ancestry to quite a considerable depth. This is especially the case if they belong to the maternal descent group of a chief or senior headman, and therefore are possible successors to an important office. But it is usual to find that headmen tend to trace back their descent from that ancestress whom the matrilineal core of the village have in common, and to forget her predecessors. Structural amnesia typically begins above the ancestress whose genealogical position is structurally significant for the living members of the village matrilineage. If remoter ancestresses are recalled, one finds oneself in the field of supra-village relations.

The lineage among the Ndembu is not, as among the Tallensi,[1] 'the skeleton of their social structure', so much as the end-product of a number of social tendencies which under specific circumstances place a curb on the mobility and instability of residential groupings. I discuss these tendencies in the subsequent analysis. Among them may be mentioned a time-honoured village title, continued proximity to an area where game is abundant, and the good reputation of its headman at the crucial transition period from sibling group to structured lineage. Among the Tallensi the lineage is *ab initio* a basic premiss of social organization. Among the Ndembu the local matrilineage is a goal, and an ideal to which ambitious headmen aspire. Once a village has become established and consolidated, great efforts are made not only by its headman, but also by those who hope to succeed him, to prevent the disruption of its widest span lineage. The form and direction of such efforts will be considered in a series of detailed studies in this and the following three chapters. In most cases these efforts are ultimately unavailing since the ecological and structural pressures making for fission are too strong, but the efforts are nearly always made. The basic unit in Ndembu society is not the lineage, but the matricentric family which in its life-cycle becomes, after the death of the mother, the uterine sibling group. This and not the elementary family is the basic unit, since frequent and easy divorce, often consequent

---

[1] Fortes, op. cit., p. 31.

on the conflict between a woman's husband and her brothers for custody of her and her children, renders the family unstable and impermanent. The uterine sibling group is a constant source of danger to the continuity of the village lineage ; the narrower unit is the foe of the wider. It will be shown below that the most frequent unit of secession from a village is the uterine sibling group and not a lineage of wider span. Each matricentric family is given an early autonomy from other maternally-linked matricentric families by the institution of virilocal marriage. Hence when the matricentric family finally returns to the village of its nearest matrilineal kin, it is seldom assimilated fully into the latter, and time and again its narrower loyalties prevail against the value set on village unity. We have seen how virilocal marriage disperses the members of the uterine sibling group for a time, and how they tend to divest themselves of other attachments in order to become reunited as a local autonomous group. The success of the narrower against the wider unit as a residential nucleus is attested by the small average magnitude of Ndembu settlements.

I cannot say with any certainty whether this structural weighting in favour of the narrower maternal descent group is directly associated with an ecological emphasis on hunting, with its concomitant mobility and productive individualism, or whether it is linked to hunting only through virilocal marriage which primarily consolidates *adelphic* relations. It may well be that a whole complex of ecological and historical factors is involved. But it is clear that the tension between the widest village lineage and its component uterine sibling groups, overlaid though it may be by sundry other sources of tension, nearly always asserts itself in situations of crisis and determines the dominant mode of fission.

Ndembu do not now possess structurally significant clans (*nyinyachi* or *nyichidi*) although they had them in the past, and a few older people remember their names. Most of the peoples who came from the Luunda homeland of Mwantiyanvwa possess a set of clans in common, several of them named after some legendary hero (such as *Saluseki* or *Sachingongu*). Among Lwena today individual members of these clans still have an obligation to offer hospitality to fellow clansmen, even those

H

of other tribes, who travel across Lwena territory. But for many years Ndembu have had no clan in the sense of a group consisting of a number of men and women, bearing a common name which passes matrilineally, dispersed widely over the country, forbidden to intermarry, and claiming vague kinship with one another, such as exist among other Central African peoples like the Bemba, Kaonde, Mazabuka Tonga, Lamba, Lunda of Luapula, and many other tribes. Ndembu may marry a primary (though rarely) or classificatory sister's daughter's daughter, a marriage which would have been forbidden by clan exogamy. Ndembu also have a fairly narrow range of incest prohibitions. Examples of marriages which occurred between reputedly forbidden categories of kin and which have been cleansed and made publicly acceptable by ritual, are given below in case histories. In one case a woman married her matrilineage brother descended from a common great-grandmother and the marriage, which served as an index of village fission, speedily achieved general recognition (see p. 208). The disappearance of clan organization is a further example of the persistent tendency towards the consolidation of narrower groups at the expense of wider groups in all sectors of the Ndembu social system, except in the field of ritual where, as we shall see in Chapter Ten, the reverse holds good.

Indeed, even villages whose nuclei claim common maternal descent cannot trace precise genealogical connection with one another, unless one has split off very recently from the other. As we have seen above, villages said to be inter-related by maternal descent may be scattered far and wide across the Ndembu region in different Government chiefdoms and in different vicinages.

Nevertheless, Ndembu possess a lineage group wider than the village lineage within which genealogical linking is possible. This group extends beyond the village matrilineage and includes all, or nearly all, of the living matrilineal kin of the village matrilineal core. The woman who has married out of a village, and her children, are not forgotten by her kin, even if she lives more than fifty miles away in her husband's village. The man who has quarrelled with his matrilineal kin and has gone to live with a paternal or other cognatic relative is similarly remembered. Sisters' children who as adults are living with their fathers are kept in mind. The continual flow of visits between matrilineal kin, however far apart in space, serves to maintain their connection. These dispersed matrilineal kin constitute a pool which may at some time be drawn upon to supplement and replenish the village of the nuclear maternal descent group. Again, if a man wishes to start a village or farm of his own he may attempt to attract to his new settlement such scattered kin. A man I knew who was thinking of starting a village told me of 17 men and boys and 10 women and girls of his lineage living in his village, and of 19 males and 19 females of his lineage living outside it. He had in the period during which I knew him paid a series of visits to many of these matrilineal kin in other villages to sound them about coming to join him in his contemplated new village. This example illustrates the point that Ndembu regard matrilineal kin as the primary and essential element in the social composition of a village. It is true to say that both a man and a divorced woman have a *choice* in the matter of residence in that they may decide to live either with their matrilineal kin or with their father, or, indeed, in other villages under special conditions ; but they have a life-long and automatic *right* to reside in the village of their close matrilineal kin, unless they have lost this right through some sin or crime they have committed such as sorcery, witchcraft or murder. A man has the right to remain in his father's village while the latter is alive, but after his death he must go to his matrilineal village, unless his mother was a slave, in which case he would belong to his father's uterine heir.

Succession to Office

Maternal descent determines succession and inheritance. In succession to headmanship uterine brother succeeds uterine brother, and if the village is a large one with a deep matrilineage it sometimes happens that matrilineal parallel cousins succeed one another. When the row of brothers and classificatory brothers has died out, or if there are no suitable candidates among them, the right to succeed passes down to the next senior genealogical generation of sisters' sons. Due to this tendency to confine succession within the membership of the senior genealogical generation, it not infrequently happens that sisters' sons become impatient for office from which they are barred by adelphic succession until ' hope deferred maketh the heart sick '. They hive off from the village with their own uterine sibling group and the children of that group and found new settlements. Table XVI, based on data I have collected about succession to village headmanship, supports this statement.

TABLE XVI

Relationships Between Headmen and their Successors [1]

| | Relationship of successor to previous incumbent | | | | | | | | |
	B	zS	zdS	S	mBS	mB	z	zd	*Total*
No. of instances	20	15	4	3	0	0	1	0	43

Legend

B   Brother
zS   Sister's son
zdS   Sister's daughter's son
S   Son
mBS   Mother's brother's son
mB   Mother's brother
z   Sister
zd   Sister's daughter

[1] Excluding the instance of succession in Chikang'a Village discussed on p. 211.

From Table XVII, p. 205, it would appear that sisters' sons and not brothers of headmen are the most frequent founders of *new* villages. This tendency would be less marked if there existed, as in many other matrilineal societies, a clear-cut norm enjoining nepotic succession to office. If we examine the pattern of succession to headmanship, Table XVI shows that brothers succeed more often than sisters' sons. When it is realized that the number of men in the senior genealogical generation is far less than in the junior proximal generation, which contains men of a lower average age, it is clear that the chance of succeeding to office is much greater in the former. Adelphic succession ensures that a number of aged office-holders will succeed one another, few of whom will live long. Even if a sister's son does succeed, he probably succeeds much later in life than he would have done if he had been his mother's brother's first heir. A value is attached in Ndembu society to the wisdom which comes from age, and

age-seniority is an important qualification for headmanship.
The older an heir is when he succeeds, the shorter the time he is
likely to hold office. Consequently, there tends to be a high
turnover of adelphic successors, who manage to obtain office
before they die. If heirs manage to succeed young, they remain
in office longer, which means that potential successors have to
wait for many years, and may eventually be passed over. For
these reasons, it is often a headman's sister's son who leads a
dissident group from a village. If he wishes to enjoy a long
period of leadership, he may well prefer to give up his chance
of succeeding to office in a long-established village, despite the
greater prestige of such an office, than to wait until he is old.
In this and subsequent chapters I present a number of case-
histories (social dramas) which throw light on the problems of
succession to headmanship. It is indeed distinctly unusual for
sisters' sons to succeed while a member of the mothers' brothers'
generation remains alive. Table XI shows that out of 385
matrilineal hut-owners only 7 were primary or classificatory
mothers' brothers of the headmen, and of these only one was a
headman's own mother's brother. This man, Biscuit (III, E7),
lived in Kamawu Village near Mwinilunga Boma ; he had spent
most of his life in Southern Rhodesia, and had returned as an old
man to live with his sister. She was a widow living in a village
which her sister's son had founded. When her brother returned
he had no wife to cook for him and no other kin except her to
look after him. He did not contest the headmanship of the
village with his sister's son, as he was feeble, forgotten by many
people, and an inveterate drinker. By and large, however, it
may be stated that in practice as well as in principle brothers
succeed brothers and cousins succeed cousins before nephews
obtain the right to succeed.

Conflict over Succession within the Matrilineage

This book is dominantly a study of social conflict and of the
social mechanisms brought into play to reduce, exclude or resolve
that conflict. Beneath all other conflicts in Ndembu society is
the concealed opposition between men and women over descent
and in the economic system. Influenced by this basic opposition,
but possessing their own autonomy, sets of struggles arise within
the social structure : conflicts between persons and between

groups who invoke different principles of residential affiliation to support and justify their own specific interests, political, jural and economic ; struggles between persons and groups couched in terms of a common norm which each party claims the other has broken ; and conflicts between persons, united by a single principle of descent and residence, for positions of authority determined by that principle. Struggles around succession to village headmanship are instances of the last type of conflict and it is with these that I wish to commence the analysis of what I propose to call ' social dramas '. Formal analysis of a social system enables us to locate and isolate critical points and areas in its structure where one might expect, on *a priori* grounds, to find conflicts between the occupants of social positions carried in the structure. In the examination of the Ndembu system I have in this chapter isolated the matrilineal descent group and shown how the office of village headman is vested in this group. I have looked at different categories of matrilineal kin and shown how struggles for succession may be expected to take place between adjacent generations and between specific kinship positions, notably between mother's brother and sister's son. It remains to test out these hypotheses in a number of cases, regarded as typical, and to see whether struggles do in fact take place. But the task does not end at this point. If conflicts occur we want to see in what way they are handled by the members of the society. In Ndembu society conduct has been regulated over what we can assume to have been a very long period of time by norms, values, beliefs and sentiments associated with kinship. Conflicts of interests arising out of the social structure are per-petuated by the observance of these norms. Hence the conflicts must also follow a regular course dictated partly by these norms, and take a shape grown familiar to the people through repetition. We can expect to find, in fact, a number of social mechanisms, of institutionalized ways of behaviour, which have arisen in response to an almost endless reduplication of such conflicts, and which have been designed by group experience to mitigate, diminish or repair them. Conflict and the resolution of conflict have effects which are observable in statistical and genealogical data. But the hints and indications afforded by such data must be followed up by a close study of social dramas. There we observe the interlinked and successive events which follow breach, and make visible the sources of conflicts. This in turn leads to action which may restore the earlier set of relations, or reconstitute them in a different pattern, or even recognize an irreparable breaking of relationships between particular persons or groups. These last, nevertheless, fit into the wider pattern of the Ndembu system.

The Concept of the Social Drama

On a number of occasions during my field-work I became aware of marked disturbance in the social life of the particular group I happened to be studying at the time. The whole group might be radically cloven into two conflicting factions ; the quarrelling parties might comprise some but not all of its members ; or disputes might be merely interpersonal in character. Disturbance in short had a variable range of social inclusiveness. After a while I began to detect a pattern in these eruptions of conflict : I noticed phases in their development which seemed to follow one another in a more or less regular sequence. These eruptions, which I call ' social dramas ', have ' processional form '. I have provisionally divided the social process which constitutes the social drama into four major phases :

(1) Breach of regular norm-governed social relations occurs between persons or groups within the same system of social relations. Such a breach is signalized by the public breach or non-fulfilment of some crucial norm regulating the intercourse of the parties.

(2) Following breach of regular social relations, a phase of mounting crisis supervenes, during which, unless the conflict can be sealed off quickly within a limited area of social interaction, there is a tendency for the breach to widen and extend until it becomes co-extensive with some dominant cleavage in the widest set of relevant social relations to which the conflicting parties belong. The phase of crisis exposes the pattern of current factional struggle within the relevant social group, be it village, neighbourhood or chiefdom ; and beneath it there becomes visible the less plastic, more durable, but nevertheless gradually changing basic social structure, made up of relations which are constant and consistent.

(3) In order to limit the spread of breach certain adjustive and

redressive mechanisms, informal or formal, are speedily brought into operation by leading members of the relevant social group. These mechanisms vary in character with such factors as the depth and social significance of the breach, the social inclusiveness of the crisis, the nature of the social group within which the breach took place and the degree of its autonomy with reference to wider systems of social relations.   They may range from personal advice and informal arbitration, to formal juridical and legal machinery, and, to resolve certain kinds of crisis, to the performance of public ritual.

(4) The final phase I have distinguished consists either in the reintegration of the disturbed social group or in the social recognition of irreparable breach between the contesting parties.

In short, the *processional form* of the social drama may be formulated as (1) breach ; (2) crisis ; (3) redressive action ; (4) re-integration or recognition of schism.

It must be recognized, of course, that in different kinds of group, in different societies, and under varying circumstances in the same kinds of group in the same society, the process may not run smoothly or inevitably from phase to phase.   Failure, for example, in the operation of redressive machinery, may result in regression to crisis.   In recently-formed groups institutionalized legal or ritual means of handling social disturbance may be lacking, and breach may be succeeded immediately by the irreversible fission or fragmentation of the group.

In Ndembu society, although villages arise and perish, the ideal form of the village persists.   Meanwhile, in order that any village life should be possible, it is necessary that members of a village should observe certain common values, and that the norms governing behaviour between village members, most of whom are interlinked by ties of kinship and affinity, should be upheld. Where customary norms and values are deeply entrenched it is usual to find institutionalized machinery of redress.   Each instance of breach in social relations is made the occasion of a restatement of their regulative norms.   The nature of redressive machinery and the way in which it functions in specific situations is discussed later.

I have found the social drama a useful descriptive and analytical tool when taken in conjunction with more orthodox techniques of analysis, such as the genealogy, the census and the hut diagram.

Analysis of numerical material obtained by the use of such techniques reveals regularities in social relations that we may call structural. Among Ndembu, for example, we find by these means that the core of villages tends to be the maternal descent group, that marriage is predominantly virilocal, that there is a high frequency of divorce, that alternate genealogical generations tend to build adjacently and adjacent genealogical generations in opposite sections of a village, and so on. We find that there is a tendency towards adelphic succession and that sisters' sons tend to be the most frequent founders of new villages. This leads us to suspect tension in the relationship of mother's brother and sister's son. The social drama shows vividly how these social tendencies operate in practice ; how, in a given situation, some may support and others oppose one another ; and how conflict between persons or groups in terms of a common norm or in terms of contradictory norms may be resolved in a particular set of circumstances. In the social drama latent conflicts of interest become manifest, and kinship ties, whose significance is not obvious in genealogies, emerge into key importance.

If we examine a sequence of social dramas arising within the same social unit, each one affords us a glimpse, as it were, of the contemporary stage of maturation or decay of the social structure of that unit. I hope to demonstrate this in presenting a set of five consecutive social dramas in a single long-established village. The social drama is a limited area of transparency on the otherwise opaque surface of regular, uneventful social life. Through it we are enabled to observe the crucial principles of the social structure in their operation, and their relative dominance at successive points in time.

Of the five social dramas based on material collected at Mukanza Village, the last three came under my direct observation. The first two rest on data collected from a large number of interviews and conversations with living persons who actively participated in them.

Social Drama I illustrates the conflict that may arise between mother's brother and sister's son, and between male parallel cousins, when only a few men remain in the senior, office-holding generation in a village, and there are several middle-aged men ripe for office in the junior generation. Other kinds of conflicts become overt within the framework of these crucial conflicts ; but the former will not be analysed here, since they involve other principles of village organization than matriliny.

This social drama is one of a series, each of which contains the same principal characters, and each of which reflects different aspects of the same structural conflicts. It may be objected that such factors as innate psycho-biological constitution and personality variations determined by differential training in the early years of childhood take precedence over sociological factors in shaping the events to be described. But it is clear that the different personalities involved occupy social positions that must inevitably come into conflict, and each occupant of a position must present his case in terms of generally accepted norms. A person can avoid disputes over succession only by renouncing the claim to office vested in his position. In a society governed by rules of kinship, he cannot abrogate his position, into which he is born and by virtue of which he is a member of the village community. Personality may influence the form and intensity of the dispute, it cannot abolish the situation in which conflict must arise. A person who endeavours to avoid pressing his claim to office when the position of headman falls vacant is subject to intense pressure from his uterine kin and from his children to put it forward. If he fails to do so, there occurs a displacement of the locus of conflict, not a resolution or bypassing of conflict. Instead of leading a group of kin against the representatives of other pressure groups, he becomes the target of criticism from members of his own group. At some point in the social process arising from succession he is compelled to turn and defend himself, whatever his temperament or character. The situation in an Ndembu village closely parallels that found in Greek drama where one witnesses the helplessness of the human individual before the Fates : but in this case the Fates are the necessities of the social process.

Since the struggles to be described below are determined by the matrilineal structure of a long-established and mature village, it is necessary to give an outline of this structure. Appendix I shows the genealogy of Mukanza Village. Mukanza is a Kawiku Village, but the conflicts within it are typical of those found in all Ndembu villages in similar situations of crisis.[1]

---

[1] I am preparing for publication a paper which deals with similar conflicts in Ndembu villages of *Lunda* origin.

SOCIAL DRAMA I

The Bewitching of Kahali Chandenda by his Nephew Sandombu
(compiled from informants)

One day, in 1947, Sandombu (I,G10) trapped a duiker and divided its meat between his village kin. His own mother's brother Kahali Chandenda (I,F5) was headman of the village and should have received by custom a back leg or the breast of the animal as his share. Sandombu, however, gave him part of a front leg only. Kahali refused to receive it, saying that Sandombu had shown that he despised his uncle. A few days afterwards Kahali went to a village in Chief Sailunga's area about eight miles from Mukanza Village and snared a bush-buck. He sent his daughter back to Mukanza with the meat. Sandombu took the meat and proceeded to divide it, retaining the breast, liver, a front leg and the head, for himself and his wives. Next day Kahali returned, and finding Sandombu away, asked Sandombu's wife Malona, a Lunda from Angola, for some food, for he had no wife of his own at that time. She was insolently slow in preparing the food, and in the end he went to his classificatory sister Nyamwaha (I,F7), who gave him beer as well as food. At night Sandombu's sister and Kahali's own niece, Mangalita (I,G11), came to him in private and told him, in anger and shame, how the meat had been divided.

Next morning Sandombu set off early to go to Hillwood Farm, twenty-five miles away, where he had seasonal employment as a capitao in charge of road maintenance. Meanwhile Kahali spoke bitterly in the village forum (*chota*) about Sandombu's action, and the latter's wife Malona wept tears at this public shaming of her husband.

After a week Sandombu returned to Mukanza Village and Malona reported Kahali's remarks to him. A fierce dispute arose between uncle and nephew, in the course of which each threatened the other with 'medicine' (*yitumbu*, a euphemism for sorcery, *wuloji*). Sandombu ended by saying, 'I am going to Sailunga Area. The people of this village are worthless. Some people must look out.' By this people took him to mean that he was going to seek out the services of a notorious sorcerer, thought to be Sakasumpa of Shika Village, to kill Kahali. It was believed by Mukanza people that Kahali kept his familiar, an *ilomba*, or water-snake which possesses the face of its owner, in a stream in Sailunga Area; and that Sandombu had gone to pay Sakasumpa a fee to shoot the *ilomba* with his *wuta wawufuku* or 'night-gun', a piece of human tibia carved in the form of a muzzle-loader and primed with graveyard earth and decomposing pieces of

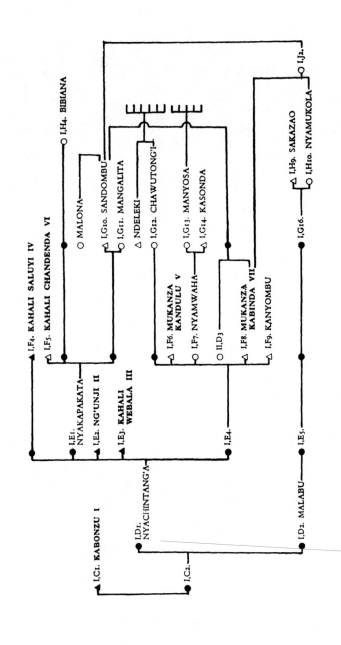

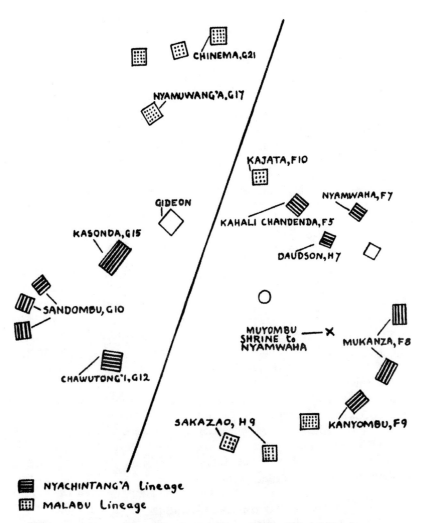

CHINEMA, G21

NYAMUWANG'A, G17

KAJATA, F10

NYAMWAHA, F7

GIDEON

KAHALI CHANDENDA, F5

KASONDA, G15

DAUDSON, H7

SANDOMBU, G10

MUYOMBU
SHRINE to — X
NYAMWAHA

MUKANZA, F8

CHAWUTONG'I, G12

SAKAZAO, H9

KANYOMBU, F9

▤ NYACHINTANG'A Lineage
▦ MALABU Lineage

MAP 5. HUT PLAN OF MUKANZA VILLAGE IN 1947–48
Illustrating Social Dramas I and II
(Line down centre shows the separation of adjacent
genealogical generations)

human bodies. When an *ilomba* has been killed its owner also dies.
After a few days Kahali fell ill, and died shortly afterwards. A
rumour came to Mukanza Village that Sandombu had boasted in
Shika that he would kill his uncle by sorcery. No divination was
made into the death since the people feared prosecution by the Government for making accusations of witchcraft. Besides some, including
Mukanza Kabinda (I,F8) and Kanyombu (I,F9), classificatory matrilineal brothers of Kahali, said that Sandombu had condemned himself
out of his own mouth both in Mukanza and in Shika Village.
Sandombu returned to his place of employment and Mukanza people
said that Sandombu must not succeed Kahali, for he had shown himself
to be a man with ' a black liver ' (*muchima bwi*), a selfish person and
a sorcerer. The question of succession was left over for a time.
Sandombu was not expelled from the village because there was no
positive proof of his guilt, such as might be obtained from the diviner's
basket. He had only spoken in heat as had Kahali himself, although
good men did not speak in this way.

Mukanza Kabinda was made headman with the approval of all,
and confirmed in his office by the Government Sub-Chief Mukang'ala.

Analysis

The account presented is a digest of information given me,
four years later, by most of the senior residents of Mukanza
Village including Sandombu himself. Sandombu, however,
denied that he threatened to bewitch Kahali, although he admitted
that he went to Shika Village after the quarrel. He said that he
did this in order that peace might be restored in the village.
Kahali, he said, was an old man, and old men always die some
time or other. This rationalistic attitude was not, however,
typical of Sandombu in other situations, as we shall see presently.
All the other members of the village concurred in the view that
Sandombu had bewitched Kahali and asserted that he had
publicly avowed that he would do so.

It is impossible to get any closer to the actual facts of the case
for the events are no longer susceptible to enquiry and the
account has acquired a mythical character. Why has it by the
consensus of all save one acquired this character ? The answer
lies, I think, in the genealogy of Mukanza Village itself, and in the
operation of the principles of residential affiliation discussed in
Chapter Three. The myth of the bewitching of Kahali
Chandenda had already in a short period of time become the

' mythological charter ', to use Malinowski's expressive phrase, the social justification for the exclusion of Sandombu from the succession. Why had he been so excluded ? Was it simply because he was regarded as a selfish and a quarrelsome fellow and a sorcerer to boot ? I do not think that this explanation altogether fits the facts. Sandombu was a most generous host to me as well as to others. He was a diligent agriculturalist, who grew much finger-millet and gave away beer brewed from it free of charge. Although he might easily have followed the growing practice of selling beer, he preferred to give it to all and sundry. But there is no doubt that within the limits of his little world he was a highly ambitious man, eager for headmanship and the prestige that even today attaches to that office in the more conservative areas. This is why he gave away beer and also food, for he wanted to put many people under an obligation to him, and in time to build up a following who would come and live under his leadership in his village. This ambition was a little too obtrusive for his relatives to stomach, since he would boast, even when I knew him, that one day he would become headman of Mukanza Village. This meant only one thing to Ndembu, that he was impatient for office and would stop at nothing, not even sorcery, to obtain his ends. But his hospitality, his obtrusive ambition, and even his wild boasting in his cups, suicidal though it was at the time to his hopes, all stemmed from his position in the social structure.

It may be noted from Appendix I that Mukanza is a long-established village in which Kahali Chandenda (I,F5) was the sixth successive headman, and in which there were two well-defined lineage segments whose common ancestress was in the third ascendant generation from the present headman. Succession had been adelphic between the second and third headman and in the next genealogical generation three matrilineal parallel cousins had followed one another in the headmanship. In other words, the social composition of the village must have successfully undergone the qualitative change from bilateral extended family (i.e. uterine siblings and their children) to matrilineage, and had developed a precise and extensive system of complementary and opposed genealogical generations. But with the onward flow of structural time and the passage of successive genealogical generations the danger of fission became progressively greater.

The lineages of which NYACHINTANG'A [1] (I,D1) and MALABU
(I,D2) were the respective ancestresses were structurally ready
to divide from one another. A few years previously (1928)
another matrilineage had split off after actual fighting in the
village between the senior men of Mukanza ; and it was touch
and go, so to speak, whether the lineage (*ivumu*) of MALABU,
the senior man of which was Sakazao (I,H9), would not follow
suit. Sakazao, although in the second descendant generation
from Kahali Chandenda (I,F5) and Mukanza Kabinda (I,F8),
and in the first descendant generation from Sandombu (I,G10),
was older than the latter, and not many years younger than
Mukanza Kabinda. Mukanza Kabinda was in fact the person
who held the two lineages together, since his wife, by whom he
had many children, was own sister of Sakazao, head of the
MALABU lineage. He was thus a matrilineal relative of his wife
by grandparent-grandchild marriage. His wife Nyamukola
(I,H10) was the link that united the two halves of the village
and stood in an intercalary relationship between them. Her
children are children of the two lineages : outside Mukanza
Village they had nowhere to live. At the same time, Mukanza
Kabinda (I,F8), his sister Nyamwaha (I,F7), and his brother
Kanyombu (I,F9) were the last surviving members of the senior
genealogical generation after the death of Kahali. No male of
the MALABU lineage, to whom the headmanship might pass,
remained alive in that generation. Old Kajata (I,F10) was senile,
and at that time seemed likely to die in Kafweku, his wife's
village. Most of the senior members of MALABU lineage were
in the second descendant genealogical generation to Mukanza
Kabinda and his siblings, and were moreover allied to him by
affinity and sibling-in-lawship. One man and three women
of MALABU lineage and of G generation (to which Sandombu and
Kasonda also belonged), were alive at that time. The man,
Chinema (I,G21), was working on the Copperbelt as a road
labourer, and it was then considered that he would never return
to Mukanza Village. He had been headman of Kahali Chandenda's village in Ikelenge Area for a number of years after
Kahali had returned to Mukanza. But since his village there had
been composite in character, containing many members of

---

[1] The names of lineages are in capitals.

another lineage and few of his own matrilineal kin, he had been involved in many disputes with the other lineage. He returned to Mukanza Village about 1945, perhaps with the hope of succeeding Kahali Chandenda. But he had quarrelled with Nyamuwang'a, the notorious witch of Social Drama IV, and it was said that his fear of her led to his flight to the Copperbelt. Nyamuwang'a herself was barely tolerated in Mukanza Village, and, as we shall see, was subsequently expelled from it. Her sister Shimili (I,G18) was at the time of Social Drama I living virilocally with her husband in Chimbila Village in Ikelenge Area. Of her other sisters, Kalusa (I,G19) was living virilocally at Shika Village, while Nyamalita (I,G20) alternated between her virilocal village Chimbila and Kalene Hospital where she worked for long periods as a ward-maid. None of the living members of G generation in MALABU lineage entered the reckoning at the time of Social Drama I as candidates for office or supporters of a candidate. But Sakazao and his uterine sisters and their children could be regarded as more or less permanent residents in the village, and Sakazao's sisters were married to Mukanza and his brother Kanyombu. Mukanza Kabinda by a number of reckonings occupied a pivotal position with regard to the village as a whole ; most of its structural relations converged on his position in the kinship system.

Before considering the position of Sandombu in this situation, another potential source of danger to the continued existence of the major matrilineage should be mentioned. It has been noted that fission may, and frequently does, occur as the result of the secession of a family of mature uterine siblings and their children. The possibility of such fission existed in Mukanza Village at the time of Kahali Chandenda's death. Two women, Chawutong'i (I,G12) and Manyosa (I,G13), both sister's daughters of Mukanza, had large families, one with six and the other with five children. Both these women were living avunculocally with weak compliant husbands. The husband of one, named Ndeleki, in fact provides an illustration of the fate of a man who has not pressed his claims to the headmanship of a village. He was a quiet and self-contained person, a devoted husband and father, but without that stubborn individualism, barely concealed by the veneer of politeness and sociability, which is typical of Ndembu of both sexes. When the headman of his matrilineal village had died,

ı

he had not put himself forward as the successor. As a result people tended to despise him or at best to chivy him in a good-humoured way in his own village. He phrased his social rejection there in terms of witchcraft accusations against his kin and went to live at his wife's village. His wife Chawutong'i (I,G12), on the other hand, was an aggressive and ambitious woman, highly conscious of her importance as a mother of many children. Her mother's sister's son, her own parallel cousin, Kasonda (I,G15) by name, was an important man in the little village community, shrewd to observe the social norms of Ndembu life but also ambitious and seeking by devious means either to succeed to the headmanship, or better, to start a village of his own. The other mother of many children was his own sister Manyosa (I,G13), also a dominating personality. All three, Kasonda, Manyosa and Chawutong'i, were full sisters' children of Mukanza Kabinda (I,F8), who in former times would have had the right, as their mother's brother, to sell them into slavery. He still exerted considerable authority over them. But one factor in particular at that time militated against Kasonda's claim to succeed—his relative youth. Although he had lived for more than ten years in urban areas, five of them in Bulawayo, and although he had acquired a little education in Mission schools, traditional Ndembu notions rated him too young, at the age of thirty-five, to become a headman. In frank conversations I have had with Kasonda about the question of succession, he has told me that he saw his best hope in exerting his influence over his powerful sisters to support the claim to succession of his own uterine uncle, Mukanza Kabinda. The latter was by that time an old man of about 66 and could not be expected to live very long. If he died in a short time Kasonda would support Sakazao (I,H9), also in his sixties, for the headmanship. If Mukanza Kabinda's life lasted a further ten years Kasonda would press his own claims after his uncle's death. Kasonda, although he was careful to maintain the outward show of friendliness towards Sandombu, was privately jealous of him, hated him as a bar to his own advancement, and feared him on account of his widespread notoriety as a sorcerer and friend of sorcerers. If Sandombu were to succeed at the age of about fifty, it might be many years before Kasonda would get the chance to follow him into office, and therefore Kasonda was determined to keep

Sandombu out of the running at all costs, by the secret and devious ways of whispered slander. He, more than anyone else, was responsible for the story that Sandombu had bewitched Kahali Chandenda, and he never allowed the episode of the quarrel to become forgotten. For various reasons it suited him well that Mukanza Kabinda, and not Sandombu, should succeed. Mukanza Kabinda had a retiring and unaggressive character and at that period at any rate did not possess Kasonda's skill in the advocacy and judgment of cases. Judicial skill (*wuhaku*) is rated high among the accomplishments of Ndembu men, and Kasonda hoped that through his own gifts of eloquence and deliberation he would become the *de facto* headman of Mukanza Village. Kasonda could also speak with facility and assurance to such Europeans as District Officers and missionaries who came sporadically ' to trouble the people ' (*nakukabisha antu*), as Ndembu put it. His knowledge of English, and his familiarity with documents, would prove useful in this respect, and provide a sharp contrast with Mukanza's illiteracy and ineptitude with *mapaperi* (' papers ', a general term for tax receipts, gun and dog licences, bicycle tax, permits to buy gunpowder, etc.). Kasonda saw himself, in short, as the Grey Eminence of Mukanza Village, recognized by Ndembu as the effective village head, but delightfully free from official responsibility for the delicts of its members.

The links which bound Mukanza Kabinda, his brother-in-law Sakazao (I,H9), and his own sister's son Kasonda closely to-gether, were extended to include the close lineal kin and de-pendants of these important men. Three linked pressure-groups were thus formed, all of which supported Mukanza Kabinda's claim to succeed Kahali Chandenda (I,F5). Sandombu (I,G10), although anxious to succeed, was the odd man out. Why then was he unable to obtain support from the other members of the village? The principal reason for his exclusion from considera-tion lay in his structural position. Kahali Chandenda was his own mother's brother and if Sandombu had succeeded, members of one lineage segment of different generations would have succeeded to headmanship, while a senior of the other lineage segment was available. A principle of great importance in Ndembu political structure would thus have been broken, namely that no single lineage segment should obtain a monopoly over a long-established office, for such positions are few, highly valued, and jealously contested. For instance, the chieftainship of Kanongesha is vested in a dispersed maternal descent group which is scattered over the Ndembu region to form the nuclei of different villages. There is a rule of succession which states that no two successive incumbents should come from the same village. This mode of succession ensures that the honours should go round and not become the monopoly of a single village matrilineage belonging to the chiefly maternal descent group. In a similar way in long-established commoner villages, classificatory adelphic succession, often cutting across affiliation by lineage segment, is a means of interlinking discrete uterine sibling groups. If the leading men in each consider that they stand a reasonable chance of succeeding to office they may well hesitate before seceding from the village. The basic membership of long-established Ndembu villages consists of a rather loose association of free and independent elders who are not really constrained by economic exigency or political directive from above to remain together. Nevertheless, if the village is relatively ancient, powerful ties of historical pride may buttress those of kinship to retain the elders' joint allegiance. Perhaps their unity tends to be further stiffened by the possibility of succeeding to the headmanship. The prestige attached to living in a long-established village puts them under a certain amount of moral pressure not to secede from it and ' kill the village ', as Ndembu put it. Since the headman, among the watchfully egalitarian Ndembu, is hardly more than a *primus inter pares*, he cannot coerce village members to remain in the village. The unity and cohesion of villages depends on the fraternal association of generation mates, not on the dominance of a single lineage segment.

Another reason for the premeditated exclusion of Sandombu lay in the history of Mukanza Village. In most Central African tribes the name of a village is a hereditary title through which flows a succession of individual incumbents, who take the name of the founder of the village. In the case of senior headmanships this is also the case among Ndembu. Here the names of the founders become inherited titles. But commoner villages are constantly coming into being as the result of fission, and also villages frequently become extinct owing to the secession of the majority of their inhabitants. There is often, among

Ndembu, a period in the development of a village during which the village is generally known by the personal name of each successive headman. But when a village has become unquestionably established as a persistent social unit, the personal name of an outstanding headman tends to petrify into a title which is inherited by his successors.

Thus in the village now known as Mukanza, the founder was Kabonzu (I,C1), his first successor was Ng'unji (I,E2), while the next three headmen (I,E3 ; I,F4 ; I, F5) bore the title of Kahali. The establishment of this title marked as it were the social consolidation and maturity of the village, and it is likely that the village would have continued to bear this title had not the British Government intruded upon the continuity of Ndembu life. When taxation was introduced by the Boma in 1913, the village of Kahali Saluyi (I,F4), as it was then known, fled to what is now Ikelenge Area to seek the protection of the first C.M.M.L. missionary, Dr. Walter Fisher. There a great hunter from the village, Mukanza Kandulu (I,F6), killed a roan antelope and quarrelled over its division with Senior Headman Ikelenge, a descendant of one of the twelve headmen who had accompanied the first Kanongesha from Mwantiyanvwa. Ikelenge demanded a back leg of Mukanza's kill, as his right, since he was a senior headman whose ancestor had been appointed by Kanongesha, chief of the Ndembu. Mukanza refused to give him the meat and thus refused to recognize Ikelenge's authority in the area. But Ikelenge had more followers in his own area than Mukanza could muster ; and Mukanza, having heard that the British South Africa Company's administration was less harsh than had at first been feared, suggested to Kahali Chandenda (I,F5), uterine uncle of Sandombu, who had just succeeded Kahali Saluyi (I,F4), that the village group should return to their old site five miles from the Boma. Kahali refused to go and the village divided, some returning with Mukanza and some remaining with Kahali. In 1919 Mukanza Kandulu died, and some years later Kahali Chandenda, who had himself quarrelled with Ikelenge's people, came back to the village and resumed his position as headman. But in his absence, the village had generally become known as Mukanza, and although Kahali refused to take the title of Mukanza, the village continued to be called by that name both by its inhabitants and by other Ndembu. It was argued, I understand by the siblings and sisters' children of Mukanza Kandulu, that the name of Mukanza was now established as the title of the village. In fact, Kabinda (I,F8), who eventually succeeded Kahali Chandenda as headman and was still headman when I was in the field, went so far as to succeed in 1928 to the name Mukanza. By that act he secured for himself, in Ndembu belief, the tutelage of the spirit of Mukanza Kandulu (I,F6), in anticipation of his later accession to office. In a similar way, Sandombu, while I was residing at Mukanza, formally succeeded to the name of Kahali. Thus, as early as the twenties of this century, a cleavage had already developed between the followers of Mukanza Kandulu and those who remained in Ikelenge Area with Kahali Chandenda (I,F5). Among the former were Sakazao (I,H9) and his sister Nyamukola (I,H10), whom Mukanza Kabinda married, thus linking the matrilineages of NYACHIN-TANG'A (I,D1) and MALABU (I,D2). From this union many children were born both of whose parents belonged to the major matrilineage of Mukanza Village, and who could be counted upon by their father to support him when he claimed the headmanship. Sandombu (I,G10), on the other hand, remained with his uterine uncle Kahali Chandenda, and stayed for many years in Ikelenge Area, where indeed he secured paid employment as a road capitao at Hillwood Farm. He visited Mukanza Village often, however, and when he saw that most of Kahali's original following were trickling back to Mukanza, decided to build his own huts there, and eventually to try to succeed there. But by the time he had settled there a network of ties already united the members of the two lineages who had followed Mukanza Kandulu (I,F6). Not only affinity, but also the alliance of alternate generations (cf. p. 80 above), held together the senior members of these two groups. In the course of time genealogical generation and biological age had ceased to coincide as between members of the two lineages. This gave rise to a situation in which several members of the grandchild generation of MALABU lineage were chronological contemporaries of several members of the grandparent generation in NYACHINTANG'A lineage, and were in fact older than most of the senior members of the intervening generation in the latter. Due to the friendship that existed between these alternate generations it was quite possible that Sandombu, and indeed Kasonda (I,G15), would

PLATE II

SUCCESSION TO A NAME

Headman Mukanza pours out white maize beer at the base of a newly-planted
muyombu sapling (see Social Drama II) to the spirit to whose name Yana (see
Chapter Ten) is succeeding. Yana is on the left. She will later wear the
white head-cloth draped over the *muyombu*. She will also wear a white bangle.
Manyosa, to the right, is anointed with powdered white clay (*mpemba*), and
holds some in her hand with which she will later anoint the whole ritual assembly.
White stands for health, good luck, strength, fertility, good will between persons,
atonement with the ancestors. The *muyombu* tree has white wood and exudes
white gum.

be passed over in the succession, and that Sakazao (I,H9), the 'grandchild' and brother-in-law of Mukanza Kabinda (I,F8), would follow the latter if he succeeded to Kahali Chandenda (I,F5). This situation gave to Sandombu's ambitions an edge of desperation that caused his desire for office to become a little too obtrusive for Ndembu tastes : he made statements publicly which proclaimed this desire and brought upon him the suspicion that he would not hesitate to use sorcery to realize it.

An important factor operating to defeat Sandombu's ambitions in the period immediately prior to Social Drama I, was the absence from Mukanza Village of close maternal kin descended from his mother's mother Nyakapakata (I,E1). His sister Mangalita (I,G11) appeared to be sterile and his mother's sister's daughter's daughter Bibiana (I,H4) was residing on the Copperbelt with her husband. He could thus invoke no local support from close maternal kin to counter the powerful local pressure-group mustered by Mukanza Kabinda and Sakazao (I,H9).

Other factors arising from biological and psychological accident conspired to harden suspicion against Sandombu into what for Ndembu was virtual certainty. Paramount among these was the fact that Sandombu had no children, save for one daughter—whom scandal hinted was not his child. Indeed, it is certain that when he had gone to an urban area to work in 1927 he contracted gonorrhoea which seems to have rendered him permanently sterile. Now for Ndembu a sterile man is often regarded as a sorcerer. It was said that his semen (*matekela*) was not 'white' (*atoka*), a colour symbolically associated in many ritual and ceremonial contexts with purity, health, strength, piety towards the ancestors, and good will towards one's fellows. Instead, his semen had become 'red' (*achinana*), a colour often linked with witchcraft, aggressiveness, and evil power obtained through a wilful breach of the social norms. Sandombu, owing to his infection, had yellow semen (called 'red' by Ndembu) ; and this was common knowledge among his fellow-villagers, perhaps because he had married successively two of Mukanza Kabinda's daughters, the first of whom died. He had often beaten both of them, and caused them to seek the protection of their parents, whom they had doubtless informed, in the circumlocutions (*ku-didyika*) employed between members of adjacent generations, of their husband's misfortune.

Sterility is also a misfortune for an ambitious man in other respects. When a man wishes to succeed to office or to found a village of his own, he looks for the backing of his own children in these ventures, as well as to his uterine kin. A man's major unit of political support is the circle of his closest kin, called by Ndembu *ntang'a*, or by the plural form *antang'a*. In addition to his own and his sisters' children, these kin include his brothers and their children. Such a group contains the nucleus of a new generation, the junior adjacent genealogical generation over which he and his siblings exercise authority and control. Sandombu was doubly unfortunate in that his only full-sister Mangalita (I,G11) was barren, so that he had neither children nor own sister's children to support him.

Finally, the fact that Sandombu was a diligent and tireless gardener set the seal on the view that he was a sorcerer, a *muloji* or *mukwa kulowa*. It was said that he had a familiar, a wooden figurine of the type called *katotoji*, which was activated by the blood of his previous victims, and which worked beside him, invisible to others, in his cassava gardens, heaping up countless mounds. Sandombu from the fruits of his labours was able to dispense to many people, most of them strangers, a lavish hospitality, and to earn golden opinions from them. Thus he aimed to lay the basis for the inclusion in his future village of strangers who might be attracted thither by his reputation for open-handedness. This again constituted a threat to the closely-knit and partly endogamous traditional community of Mukanza Village.

In summary, Sandombu was from many points of view an outsider, an atypical, marginal man in Mukanza Village. He belonged to the Kahali faction who had remained in Ikelenge Area when Mukanza Kandulu (I,F6) and his close kin and the sibling group of Sakazao (I,H9) had returned to the traditional area where Kabonzu founded the village. He was outside the mesh of interlocking relationships that united the majority of members of NYACHINTANG'A and MALABU lineages. He was a member of the intervening genealogical generation, which at the time was out of power in the village. He was sterile and industrious, both indications of sorcery. If he succeeded to office a single minor lineage would gain control of an office that should have been shared in turn by all the lineages of the village.

Finally, he was a channel through which strangers might flow into the tightly organized and highly conservative community of a typical Kawiku village. Who better than he could serve as a scapegoat for misfortunes befalling the village ? Who better than he could serve to unite the potentially fissile components of the remaining membership, in terms of opposition to his ambitions and to his immoderate way of life ? He tried to attach himself to the CHINENG'A sub-lineage of NYACHINTANG'A lineage and to MALABU lineage by marrying daughters of Mukanza, one by Nyatungeji (II,D3), and one by Nyamukola. By this last marriage he made himself the two lineages' ' son-in-law ' (Ndembu *muku*, properly speaking an affine belonging to an adjacent generation to EGO). But this very relationship is one involving avoidance of female in-laws, and unwilling submission to male in-laws, of the senior adjacent generation. It is not a relationship of friendship and familiarity. Yet still this odd man out was audacious enough to aspire to be the man at the helm.

Why was it, then, that the marriage of Mukanza to Nyamukola proved to be a structurally effective alliance between lineage segments, whereas that between Sandombu and Zuliyana was fraught with conflict ? Part of the answer lies undoubtedly in the fact that the former marriage was fruitful and the latter barren. It was a source of chagrin to Sandombu that Zuliyana had no children and he was wont to blame her infertility and not his sterility for this misfortune. In fact, he paid several ritual specialists to treat her with medicines to render her fertile. In Chapter Ten I discuss one such ritual in which Zuliyana underwent treatment. But other factors were, in my opinion, no less important in rendering the alliance structurally ineffective. The marriage between Mukanza and Nyamukola did not markedly increase the social distance between the spouses and members of the intervening genealogical generation, since the parents of Mukanza and of Nyamukola were dead, and neither had close in-laws in the senior adjacent genealogical generation. But Sandombu, and for that matter Kasonda, ranked as classificatory affines of an adjacent generation to both spouses, and this relationship by marriage, added to the tense relationship between adjacent generations, did nothing to bring Sandombu closer to Mukanza and his wife. On the other hand, Mukanza's marriage to Nyamukola strengthened the antecedent tie of alliance between alternate genealogical generations that connected Mukanza and Sakazao, head of MALABU lineage. The children of their union were Sakazao's sister's children and classificatory 'children' of Nyamukola's sister Nyatioli (I,HII).

Biological and structural factors, interacting in the process of social life, limited the effectiveness of Sandombu's cross-cousin marriage and increased that of Mukanza's grandparent-grandchild marriage. The unfruitfulness of the former led to frequent quarrels between the spouses and Zuliyana was usually able to run to her parents for solace and protection against her husband. The fruitfulness of the latter gave Mukanza and the senior members of MALABU lineage a joint interest in the children born in it.

The relative duration of the respective marriages at the time of Social Drama I must also be taken into account. Mukanza's marriage had stood the exacting test of time. Nearly all the children of Mukanza and Nyamukola were full-grown adults, and some had children of their own. The marriage was everywhere held up as a shining example of matrimonial happiness (*wuluwi*). On the other hand, Sandombu had only recently married Zuliyana, a pretty and rather flighty girl, and the first years of marriage among Ndembu always possess an experimental character, frequently terminating in divorce. Even in 1953, Sandombu was still almost pathologically jealous of Zuliyana. Once he showed me a spear that he kept in a corner of his hut. He said that he would stab anyone with it whom he found making advances to Zuliyana. He did not trust her for a moment out of his sight. But he was determined to keep his marriage in being, for although it was unsatisfactory in many respects, it still gave him a footing in the village community.

I have set out the sociological and historical background to this first social drama at some length, and delineated the personalities of its main protagonists, because without this preliminary work it would be impossible to make a satisfactory analysis of the subsequent social dramas, each of which represents a further stage in the conflict over succession implicit in the matrilineal structure of Mukanza Village.

It is evident from the events described at the beginning of Social Drama I, that tension had existed in the relationship

between Kahali Chandenda and Sandombu for some time before
the episodes involving meat distribution had precipitated a
situation of open hostility. My informants told me that Sandombu had neglected for several years before this to supply his
widower uncle with cassava meal from his own gardens. Nyamwaha (I,F7), Manyosa (I,G13) and Kasonda (I,G15) had combined
to feed the old man. Kahali Chandenda, even by Ndembu
standards, was a very poor man. Part of his leg had been
amputated, and when he travelled he had to enlist the help of a
younger man to push him on a bicycle. On the credit side of the
balance, he had been a famous *chiyang'a*, a hunter with a gun, and
was in addition a great 'law-man' (*ihaku*), judging and advocating cases with forensic skill and knowledge of custom. But
he was old-fashioned and could not cope with the modern duties
of a headman. He was also feared as a sorcerer. Hunters are
thought to possess exceptionally powerful familiars ; their
strength and skill in killing animals is acquired initially from
killing their junior relatives by medicine. Thus Kahali's accomplishments belonged to a rapidly passing social order, and
physically he was a burden to the village and a reproach to
Sandombu. His reputation as a man with bad medicine was all
that restrained the hostility, felt by several persons against him,
from breaking out.

Sandombu, who had lived and worked in Ikelenge Area most
of his life, had also gained a certain notoriety as a sorcerer there.
I have been told by members of a village in Ikelenge Area in
which he lived for a long time, that when he left it finally, a large
hole was found under the floor of his abandoned hut, in which it
was supposed he kept his *ilomba*, a serpent familiar with a human
face. If there really was a hole, it was probably used for urination
at night. I have seen similar unhygienic devices in huts elsewhere in Mwinilunga, and Ndembu consider that people who
have these holes are disgusting. But, whatever the 'circum-
stantial evidence', it is certain that Sandombu had a bad reputation
as a practitioner of the black art among the local inhabitants of
Ikelenge Area. I myself have often discussed sorcery and
witchcraft with him, and although he always spoke indignantly
against it, he had undeniably a wide knowledge of its putative
techniques and *materia medica*. It is possible that Sandombu,
finding himself dubbed a sorcerer on account of his sterility,

deliberately fostered the belief, by innuendo when sober, and by the violence of his behaviour when in his cups, in order to inspire fear in people and so to get his own way in a number of situations. But it was even more in the interests of his rivals for the village succession, particularly Mukanza Kabinda and Kasonda, to harden suspicion of his sorcery into popular certainty and to establish it as a local dogma.

Ndembu headmen pray to their ancestors before boys' and girls' initiation rituals : ' Give us in this village only the meat of animals, not the meat of men.' This means, ' Exclude sorcerers and witches from our midst.' If the headman himself is a sorcerer, in Ndembu belief, the village is in terrible danger, for it is thought that headmanship adds additional power both for good and evil to what a man already has in the way of mystical acquirements. If Sandombu were branded with this evil reputation, his chance of succeeding to office would be eliminated, except under special circumstances which I will mention in the analysis of a subsequent drama.

By giving Kahali an inferior share of his own meat and by eating a major share of Kahali's meat, Sandombu made it clear that he no longer respected Kahali as an uncle and a headman, and would be glad to see the last of him. The fact that in the subsequent quarrel Mukanza people alleged that Kahali too used threats of sorcery against Sandombu indicates that they considered that uncle and nephew were equally evil. From this the people argued that their lineage should no longer enter into the succession.

It may be asked why, if Sandombu had the reputation of being a sorcerer, people thought it was necessary for him to go to the black-hearted old Sakasumpa to enlist his aid against Kahali. The answer lies in the belief that when a man wishes to kill an office-holder, such as a headman or a chief, he does not wish to take the full responsibility himself for the sorcery. It may be also that the diviner, to whom the kin of the dead headman may repair, will be deceived by this device. There are innumerable Ndembu tales, told round the *chota* fire or in the privacy of huts and kitchens, of claimants for office who have sought for sorcerers to slay by medicine the present incumbents. It is told how payment of guns, cloth and money, and formerly slaves, were made for these services. It is also told how a great diviner will detect this device and how he will lay the blame for the sorcery on the claimant and not on the sorcerer who actually 'shoots the medicine'. He was only doing a job for which he had been hired, the people say, a wicked job it is true. But the real guilt lay 'in the liver', as the seat of the will and source of power, of the relative who wanted to succeed. In such divinations the name of the hired specialist is never mentioned, perhaps because of the mode of questioning employed by diviners which makes the initial assumption that kin bewitch kin. Only if they receive negative answers, on consulting their oracles, to questions embracing the whole gamut of kinship, will they seek for a sorcerer or witch outside the victim's kin-group.

This point is relevant to the analysis for later we shall find Sandombu accused by the headman of a neighbouring village as the sorcerer called in by that headman's relative to bewitch him.

In this narrative of the bewitching of Kahali, coloured though it is by the inclusion of mythical material, we detect the presence of those elements considered typical of all social dramas. There had been a breach in the customary regularity of social relations between Kahali and Sandombu, and between the members of Mukanza village as a whole. This breach took on decisive and dramatic form as the breach of a crucial norm governing the relations of mother's brother and sister's son in Ndembu society. A sister's son should give his uterine uncle a specific joint of meat when he has made a kill. This is one of the major obligations inherent in the relationship. If it is not carried out, without the excuse of exceptional circumstances, this is tantamount to a refusal on the part of the nephew to accept the continued authority of his uncle. But it goes further than that. It is a challenge to one of the most deeply entrenched principles of Ndembu social organization, that by which the senior adjacent genealogical generation is given authority over the junior generation, and the latter must respect and obey the former. Where generation authority is linked with matriliny, as in the uncle-nephew relationship, the authority of the senior generation is exceptionally strong. It is not simply a breach in the relationship between two persons, but a matter involving the whole group; for it is a challenge to the authority of the senior generation as a whole and ultimately to the system itself.

The challenge is also one which not only jeopardizes the general authority structure, but which involves succession to office in the group. It is argued by Ndembu that no-one would make such a challenge against gerontocratic authority, and assert his claim to office, unless he possessed special powers, beyond the power inherent in his kinship position alone. To make such a breach in the social order, an order validated by Ndembu animistic religion, a man must have powers of an anti-social kind, which in this society are hostile to kinship. To counteract these powers, the forces of the constituted order must be mobilized. This is done by a conscious and public statement of official norms of correct behaviour and by a public condemnation of the actions of the delinquent.

But why, in this case, was no recourse made to a diviner, who would almost certainly have given the Mukanza people the answer they desired, that Sandombu was a sorcerer and should be expelled from the community ? The answer given by the community that Government would get to hear of it and take action against the accusers is important, but it is not the whole truth. An active and aggressive man like Sandombu might have reported to the Boma an accusation of sorcery made against him. I say he ' might have reported ' the matter because this betrayal would have led to his banishment from the village, which he did not want. But the people feared he might so report them, in which case the other senior men of the village, who made the charge, would undoubtedly have been sent to prison. And it is for this reason that Ndembu rebuke Government in private discussion for ' protecting witches and allowing them to multiply '.

But over and above this cogent argument there was the important consideration that, objectively speaking, Sandombu was an asset to the community. He was in regular employment and his position as capitao enabled him to obtain labourers' jobs at Hillwood Farm for other men in the village. He was said to have the ear of Mr. Fisher, the employer, and could find places for his own kin. Again, there were several boys in the village who had passed Standard II at the local mission out-school and required money for their boarding fees at the Middle School at Kalene Mission. These boys were partly financed by Sandombu. From Kalene they might go on to Mutanda School at Solwezi where, if they passed Standard VI, they would obtain a qualification for the lucrative job of clerk. Then they would be in a position to assist their elders with money. On the whole, it was better to retain Sandombu as a village member than to incur his determined hostility by expelling him. But he must at the same time be prevented from succeeding to the headmanship. The upshot of the case was that Mukanza Kabinda became headman, an appointment confirmed by the Government Chief Mukang'ala, although he did not have a formal installation ritual. This appointment was engineered by imputing Kahali's death to Sandombu's sorcery by word of mouth, but not by invoking the crucial test of divination. Sandombu could not argue against this course, since the majority of villagers gave Mukanza Kabinda their support when Chief Mukang'ala came to the village to ascertain their views about who should succeed. Nor could he demand a divination to clear himself, for it would almost certainly have gone against him. All he could do was to prepare the ground for an attempt to succeed to Mukanza Kabinda.

This drama thus began with the breach of kinship norms between Sandombu and Kahali. This breach led to a public quarrel between them, in which the whole village took an an interest. When Kahali died the quarrel gave rise to accusations of sorcery against Sandombu behind his back. The accusations eliminated his prospect of succeeding to headmanship. The drama culminated in the appointment of Mukanza Kabinda. This appointment led to the restoration of a social order in which Kahali's and Mukanza's generation continued to hold office and the possibility of fission on lineage and on sibling-family lines had been at least temporarily averted. Sandombu had not been expelled from the village but had been excluded from headmanship. The village had maintained its unity and even strengthened it by finding a scapegoat for its internal dissensions.

But at this stage Sandombu was still smarting from his defeat and further outbreaks of hostility on his part occurred against those who had ousted him. The most serious of these led to Social Drama II, which brings out clearly the lines of tension in the village structure of Mukanza.

SOCIAL DRAMA II

The Expulsion and Return of Sandombu
(compiled from informants)

Sandombu had married Mukanza Kabinda's daughter, Zuliyana (I,J2). It may be supposed that he hoped by this means to attach himself securely to the two village matrilineages of CHINENG'A (I,E4), and MALABU (I,D2), since she was connected to both through her mother and father. He also hoped that she would give him children, for although he had married eight times, no wife, except his first, had borne him a child, and this was thought not to be his. He had divorced Malona (see Social Drama I) before marrying Zuliyana, because she was not acceptable to Mukanza people, being reluctant to give them food and hospitality. One of the psychological drives behind Sandombu's persistent and openly expressed desire for headmanship probably consisted in the fact that the names of sterile persons are not given to children, or rather, to put it in Ndembu idiom, do not ' come back to children to give them a name '. Their spirits are called *ayikodjikodji* (sing. *chikodjikodji*) and in ritual concerned with female fertility are given special offerings of beer and food by way of placation at one side of the temporary shrine, to keep them away from the afflicted woman patient. Sterile people ' die for ever ', in that their names are not remembered and no *muyombu* shrines of quickset saplings are planted to honour them. Sandombu probably feared that his name, i.e. his social personality, would be forgotten, unless he became a headman, in which case he would be remembered as the occupant of a political position. After a year Zuliyana had borne no child although she came from a fertile family, and Sandombu, while he was living at Hillwood Farm, used to vent his spleen on her by frequently beating her.

Towards the end of 1948 an *Nkula* ritual was performed at Mukanza Village for Nyatioli (I,H11), sister-in-law of Mukanza (I,F8), own sister of Sakazao (I,H9), and classificatory mother of Zuliyana (I,J2). *Nkula* is most often performed for women with menstrual troubles, and it appears that Nyatioli was experiencing a difficult menopause, with much menstrual bleeding.

Sandombu, who was by this time working as a Road Capitao for the Public Works Department in a camp about a mile from Mukanza Village, was under the impression that an *Nkang'a* girl's puberty ritual was to be held that weekend, and not *Nkula*. He ordered Zuliyana to brew many calabashes of beer for the occasion, for at *Nkang'a* nearly all the people in a vicinage attend. At the concluding phase of *Nkula* many people also usually attend, but this was only a ' small *Nkula* '

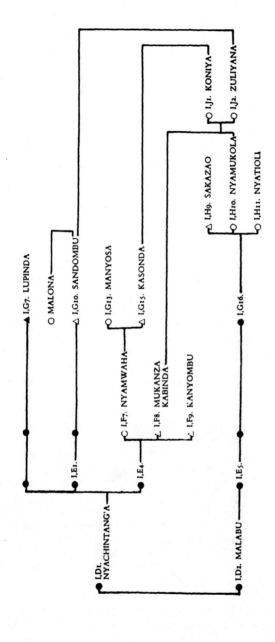

K

confined to Mukanza Village and a few external kin and neighbours. Zuliyana, who was living in Mukanza Village itself at the time, brewed only two calabashes for this small ritual. When Sandombu came off duty—most Ndembu rituals today are held at weekends to accommodate those at work—he found only two calabashes of beer. Without waiting to hear the explanation he began to beat Zuliyana, who called out to her kinsfolk for help. Kasonda (I,G15) entered Sandombu's village hut, and according to his own account, remonstrated in a brotherly way with Sandombu. The latter's only response was to take a bamboo cane and thrash Zuliyana with it. Then a young man called Benson, a member of the neighbouring village of Ng'ombi, just back from the Copperbelt, came n, snatched the cane from Sandombu and broke it across his knee. Sandombu lost his temper and his head completely, according to Benson and Kasonda, and accused Benson of being Zuliyana's lover. Others, by this time assembled in the doorway, heard him go on to say that he would make the members of Mukanza who were interfering with his married life pay for their intervention.

Next day, Sandombu was observed by Kanyombu (I,F9), Mukanza Kabinda's younger brother, and by their sister Nyamwaha (I,F7), as he was stooping over the footpath between Mukanza and Benson's village of Ng'ombi. Then he circled the huts of Mukanza and Nyamwaha. He was heard, it was alleged, to have invoked the spirit of his deceased parallel cousin Lupinda (I,G7), a hunter and powerful personality in his life-time, to punish his enemies. He is then alleged to have said to those sitting in the *chota*, 'I am now returning to Sakeji [i.e. to Ikelenge Area]. Tomorrow someone will die in this village. Mukanza people have no sense.'

Early next morning while the aged Nyamwaha, sister of Mukanza and mother of Kasonda, was pounding cassava, she felt a spasm of pain and fell down in a helpless condition. Kasonda, who had been working as a garden boy for the D.C., was informed of this and obtained permission to return to the village, five miles from the Boma. Nyamwaha was gravely ill. Her last words before she died were 'Sandombu has killed me.'

Kasonda wrote an angry letter to Sandombu, retailing his mother's last words and demanding that he return to Mukanza and give a full explanation of his suspicious behaviour. Sandombu came back and all the senior men of Mukanza assembled in the *chota* to hear what he had to say. It was put to him by Mukanza that he had cursed the village by invoking Lupinda's ghost. This form of curse is called *ku-shing'ana* by Ndembu and is classed with sorcery (*wuloji*). Sandombu denied that he had cursed the village in this way, but he admitted that he had been angry, and expostulated that he would never, under any circumstances, have killed his 'mother', whom he loved. He took out a 10s. note and said : 'Here is my money. Go yourselves to a diviner in Angola, and find out the truth.' (The Portuguese, according to Ndembu, do not regard witchcraft accusations as a criminal offence, so that divination is legal in their territory.) Kanyombu (I,F9), Mukanza's brother, took the money and demanded £3. 10s. in addition, saying that the compensation he should pay for causing Nyamwaha to die must be set at £4. It was no use, he went on, denying that he had threatened the village with sorcery. Many people had heard him, so that there was no need for a divination. But Sandombu insisted with tears in his eyes that under no circumstances would he kill his mother, or indeed, any of his kin. Kanyombu then said that after the mourning ritual (*Mudyileji*) Sandombu must leave the village, and stay away until he showed by his behaviour that he could live properly with his kin. The others agreed, and Sandombu left the village for about a year. In the end he humbly asked Mukanza for permission to return.

In the meanwhile, in view of Sandombu's evident sorrow at Nyamwaha's death, public opinion wavered as to the cause of death, and secret divination into it was made by means of a medicated pounding-pole (*ng'ombu yamwishi*), and blame was finally ascribed to the husband of Nyamwaha's daughter's daughter from Chibwakata Village in the same vicinage. It was alleged that Nyamwaha had tried to keep her granddaughter in Mukanza while her husband wanted to take her to his own village. In anger he had ' shot medicine ' at her and killed her.

Sandombu was absolved from blame and allowed to return. But in order to show finally that ' his liver was white ' towards the people of Mukanza, dead and alive, he paid Mukanza a goat and took part in a village ritual performed to placate the restless spirit of Nyamwaha who had caused many people to dream of her and caused a minor epidemic of illness. It was thought that she was disturbed by the ' troubles in the village '. Sandombu planted a *muyombu* [1] tree to his ' mother ' in front of Mukanza's hut, and Manyosa (I,G13) inherited Nyamwaha's name. Both Sandombu and Mukanza prayed to Nyamwaha, and mentioned that they were now reconciled. Through the planting of the tree, they said, she would be remembered by her relatives. Finally, three lines of powdered white clay were sprinkled on the ground from the base of the tree by Mukanza, and all the members of Mukanza Village who were present, matrilineal,

---

[1] Trapnell and Clothier, p. 80, give the botanical term for this tree, which they call *muyombo*, as *Lannea antiscorbutica*. *Check List*, issued by the Forestry Office, Northern Rhodesia, identifies *muwiombo* [sic] as *Kirkia acuminata*.

patrilineal and affinal, were anointed by Mukanza with white clay, symbolizing the basic values of Ndembu society—good health, fertility, respect for elders, observance of kinship dues, honesty, and the like.

The prodigal nephew had returned.

Analysis

In this drama the breach of relations which inaugurated the series of events was a quarrel between a married couple who not only stood to one another in the relation of husband and wife but were also cross-cousins. Furthermore, since Zuliyana (I, J2) was a child of both the village matrilineages whose members had effectively prevented him from succeeding, the cleavage between Sandombu and the rest of the village entered into his marriage relationship with Zuliyana. As usual, the breach of relations received visible expression in the violation of a crucial norm governing those relations. In this case the norm governed marital behaviour and can be stated as follows : ' No husband should beat his wife violently without good reason or without a fault on her part.' Zuliyana had brewed a smaller amount of beer than her husband had ordered, not because she was lazy or wilfully disobedient, but because her husband had misunderstood what ceremony was to be performed. Sandombu probably thought that she should have brewed a large amount of beer in any case, whether the ritual was a minor one or not, simply because he had ordered her to do so. The fact that she had not done so would almost certainly have been interpreted by him as agreement with her village relatives and disobedience to him, her husband. But to the other members of the village, his beating of his wife must have seemed a breach of the norm that a man must not beat his wife without good reason. They felt morally justified in intervening, although actual physical intervention was left to an outsider from another village. Their disapproval of his action was immediately interpreted by Sandombu, and probably not without reason, as a recrudescence of their hostile attitude to his claims for headmanship. He lost his temper, as I myself have known him to do on many occasions, and reviled everyone within range. It is impossible now to find out whether he merely reviled (*ku-tukana*) the villagers or cursed (*ku-shingana*) them. It is allowable, though frowned upon, to revile in Ndembu society. Outlets for suppressed feelings are sometimes venial in a small-scale society where personal relations are intense. But cursing, since it involves the raising of a malevolent ghost (*musalu*) to kill, is illicit, a form of sorcery. Sandombu's rivals say he *cursed* the village; he himself admits only to having reviled them.

Unluckily for Sandombu, the death of Nyamwaha, like the death of Kahali (I,F5) on a previous occasion, occurred just when it was most likely to confirm the worst suspicions of his fellow villagers. He was publicly denounced as a *muloji* (sorcerer), and in spite of his genuine and obvious grief which made a profound impression, he was temporarily banished from the village.

Unlike Drama I, the mechanisms used to seal up the breach between Sandombu and the rest of the village were of a more formal and institutionalized nature. In Drama I, it will be re-called that although the village informally discussed Sandombu's behaviour in the *chota*, he himself was not present and no action was taken against him. Just enough mobilization of public opinion was made to bar effectively his way to the headmanship and ensure that Mukanza Kabinda should succeed. But in Drama II Sandombu was formally excluded from the village for a probationary period by a general assembly of the village. Later, doubt arose in the minds of village members whether the grave accusation made against him was just, and by one mode of divina-tion he was adjudged innocent. Therefore he was received back into the fold by means of a ritual which reasserted the solidarity of the lineage of NYACHINTANG'A (I,D1), to which not only Sandombu but also headman Mukanza Kabinda, Kanyombu, Kasonda, and Manyosa among the living belonged, and ex-headman Kahali Chandenda and the victim Nyamwaha among the dead.

It will be noted that although action was taken against San-dombu, the matrilineal lineages of Mukanza Village were careful to appear to be morally justified in their actions and to avoid open violence against him. For example, it was Benson, an outsider, who broke Sandombu's cane. Kasonda, Sandombu's classifi-catory brother, confined himself to mere remonstration. Kan-yombu, Mukanza's brother, and not the headman Mukanza himself, pronounced the sentence of exile; and this was a temporary, and not a permanent, exile. Then a decision was obtained from divination which allocated blame for Nyamwaha's death to an outsider, and not to Sandombu. No attempt was made to bring a divorce suit on Zuliyana's behalf against Sandombu by her relatives of MALABU lineage. The door was left open for the reconciliation that finally occurred. At the same time it was made clear to all who might have supported Sandombu in the village that he was completely unsuitable for the position of headman.

By jural and ritual means the crucial norms of kinship and affinity had been reaffirmed, and Sandombu had been shown not to have conformed with them. Sandombu had been compelled to accept his junior status in the new order of things in which Mukanza Kabinda was village headman. Sandombu had been reintegrated into the village community, but the condition of his re-admission was that he had to return as a penitent and to renounce his claims to office. Conflict had been temporarily mitigated but not, of course, eliminated. Its inevitable revival lay coiled within the social structure. The *ilomba*, the poisonous snake with the human face which is used by Ndembu sorcerers as a familiar, vividly symbolizes the secret malignity and sudden emergence of masculine jealousy over succession to office.

The process of both these dramas has been shown to run from breach through crisis and redress to reintegration. Informal and formal jural mechanisms, and ritual, were brought into play to restore the equilibrium of the disturbed social groups. Is there any way in which we may distinguish between the implicit aims and functions of these different modes of redressing and adjusting conflict,—jural and ritual ? It would seem, at the present stage of anthropological enquiry, that jural machinery is employed when conflict between persons and groups is couched in terms of an appeal by both contesting parties to a common norm,[1] or, when norms conflict, to a common frame of values which organize a society's norms into a hierarchy. Thus, when Sandombu spoke angrily to his relatives, they all accepted a common norm governing social intercourse—namely, that no person should curse

---

[1] Cf. Professor Gluckman's discussion of how Lozi judges work with norms in cross-examination in *The Judicial Process among the Barotse of Northern Rhodesia* (1955), pp. 49–50.

another by raising a powerful ghost. In other words, human beings who were members of a single society had an interest in one another's welfare and should not wish one another dead. In Ndembu society the wish is thought often to be father to the deed ; in fact, when it is publicly expressed, it is stated by custom to have the mystical power to do the deed. Thus, Sandombu argued that he had not cursed but had only reviled, while his relatives held that he had not reviled but had cursed. Both sought to justify their actions in terms of the common norm that cursing is anti-social and immoral. The corresponding jural situation where two norms come into conflict but are hierarchically organized is exemplified in the history of Sandombu's marriage. Although Sandombu treated Zuliyana abominably in Ndembu eyes, beating her without cause, no divorce action was undertaken by her relatives. A norm of Ndembu society is that relatives should protect a married woman from an unjust husband. But the unjust treatment must continue for a long time and be exceptionally severe before they intervene to end the marriage. The norm that marriages should remain unbroken supervenes over the norm that relatives may at times offer sanctuary to an ill-treated wife. In this case Sandombu's beating of Zuliyana did not bring jural mechanisms into action although it might well have done so if Zuliyana had refused to go on living with her husband.

On the other hand, ritual mechanisms are invoked when it is felt that the fundamental norms of society themselves are threatened or challenged, not by a single individual but by the social group which operates by means of adherence to them. It is not that persons or groups phrase their disagreements in terms of a common norm to which all parties basically conform, but that hostility comes to be felt by all concerned against the constraints imposed by the norms themselves. Rebellion develops against the very way the social system is ordered, and a challenge is made to the established moral order, with its norms and their evaluative framework. I venture to suggest that every time a norm is broken by one individual, a temptation is experienced by every other individual in the group to do likewise. Breaches represent constant temptations to the members of the group to rebel against norms critically connected with the unity and persistence of the group. These tendencies to come into conflict with the norms must be purged of their socially disruptive quality if the group is to remain integrated. Ritual is the social mechanism by which a group is purged of the anarchic and disruptive impulses which threaten its crucial norms and values. These impulses are present in the majority of its members and come dangerously near to overt expression if there has been a long series of quarrels between its members.

But this temptation to rebel and even revolt, may also be fed by constant disputes between individuals and factions, which in fact manifest deeper conflicts between different social processes. In Ndembu society, we have discerned that certain principles of organization, which appear to give rise to consistent norms, in practice originate processes which work against one another. Over a period of time, conflict of process leads to breaking of particular relationships and fission of particular groups, but new relationships and groups on the old pattern are established. The contrary processes compensate one another within the structure of the changing, but repetitive, social field. But until the processes have worked out their mutual compensation, the conflict between them will continue to produce naggingly persistent quarrels, which are ineradicable until new relationships are formed. In a society which is not changing, the same processes will then produce similar quarrels in the new relationships.

On this view of society, norms and their supporting values can only *appear* to be consistent, since they must cover the presence of contradictions within the structure itself. The contrary processes are likely each to be stated in norms. Hence situations must arise where the norms which determine the course of action to be taken cannot be clearly and consciously affirmed for the acceptance of all parties, since each can claim some support from customary values. It is here that intrigue may become rife and disruptive. In Ndembu society, based as it is on close interpersonal ties, it is also at this stage that ill-feeling becomes charged with the malevolent, mystical power of witchcraft and sorcery. Ill-feeling is not merely immoral : it is charged with the danger of disease, death and other misfortunes to one's fellows.

Here judicial decision can condemn one or more of the disputants, but it cannot always relieve the quarrels so as to preserve the threatened relationship. Accusations of sorcery and witch-

craft may temporarily emphasize for the parties the mystical
danger of their ill-feelings, as happened to Sandombu when his
' mother ' died.   Ritual, like beliefs in witchcraft, is a customary
device which lifts the emotions of people and the values of society
to a mystical plane where they have power beyond their secular
effects.   It may be invoked to affirm the unity of a relationship
or group over and above the quarrels which are rooted in conflicts
between their organizing social principles.   It is significant that
as accusations of witchcraft and sorcery follow on what we call
natural misfortunes, which are ascribed to ill-feeling in the
group, so similar situations, rather than open dispute, lead to the
performance of rituals.[1]   Hence, it seems to me, after a major
crisis produced by these conflicts of process, rituals are employed
to affirm that reconciliation has been achieved.   These rituals
may even be employed after a judicial decision appears to have
settled rights and wrongs, when in fact the cause of dispute is
beyond settlement.   And finally, when all attempts to preserve
existing relationships have failed, final breaches, often provoked
by witchcraft charges, are confirmed by rituals which restate the
norms as consistent and enduring, even though new relationships
have been established.   Those who disputed bitterly for headmanship within a village, may become helpful relatives when they
reside in two different villages which each appear to conform to
the Ndembu ideal.

In the two dramas set in Mukanza Village, we have seen a
series of these conflicts and a series of attempts by members of the
village matrilineage to resolve them, first by informal, then by
formal, jural measures.   With the expulsion of Sandombu a new
level of conflict had been reached.   Doubts as to the justice of
their action in banishing him seem to have beset the leading
members of the village.   These found expression in the result
of the divination and in the belief that the spirit of Nyamwaha
was haunting the village.   They appeared to represent the
uneasy stirrings of a sense of collective guilt.   The people of the
village had exiled their kinsman, in whom flowed the blood of

---

[1] Cf. the views expressed by M. G. Marwick in ' The Social Context of
Cewa Witch Beliefs ', *Africa*, xxii, 2 and 3 (1952), and by J. C. Mitchell
in ' A Note on the African Conception of Causality ', *The Nyasaland Journal*,
v, 2 (July, 1952), pp. 51–8.

their common ancestress and who for long had been part of the collective life, a man who had in many ways treated them generously ; and perhaps they felt that they had sinned against the deep value set on kinship itself as an organizing principle of social life. I got the impression from the way they talked, that they felt guilty lest, in order to further their sectional and personal interests, they had excluded a brother and a benefactor from participation in their joint existence as a community of blood and place. When Sandombu expressed his sense of penitence and asked to return, there followed not merely an expression of his own contrition at the *muyombu* tree of his ' mother ', but prayers to her by her brother the headman, and by her very own daughter that all of them should be forgiven. The life of the community should begin anew with Sandombu in its midst once more. The *muyombu* tree, planted because there had been conflict between people and within people themselves, now stands, and will grow and branch out as a symbol that peace is restored and the values of kinship are once more renewed with fervour.

Judicial mechanisms tend to be invoked to redress conflict, where the conflict is overt, and these judicial mechanisms involve rational investigation into the motives and behaviour of the contending parties. Ritual mechanisms tend to be utilized where conflict is at a deeper level. Here conflict expresses itself through projection—that is, in the collective association of misfortunes with ill-feeling and the working of mystical beings and forces, with dreams, and with answers to divination. The conflict is between norm and impulse in each individual member of the group, but since in a tightly-knit group similar impulses assail common norms in situations which embrace the whole of its membership, this conflict attains social recognition through repetition down the years, and ultimately cultural techniques are devised to handle it. It appears to the members of the society as though mysterious forces are attacking the very foundations of the moral and social order, not from within, but by projection from without, in the form of witches, spirits and mystical powers which penetrate individual members or some representative individual in the group in the form of dreams, illness, infertility, madness, etc. Viewed in this way, the *muyombu* tree planted to the dead ' mother ' Nyamwaha may be regarded as a means by which the forces which are potentially disruptive of the village are drawn off; and the conflicting members of the group unite, purged of anger, in amity of common worship, around it. The very tensions and aggressions that arise in this social system thus become means to give its norms a new charge of energy so that not only are they reinstated but also they are the more fervently accepted. Thus, Sandombu may well have wept because he believed, with other Ndembu, that his norm-breaking behaviour and disloyal self-seeking impulses might have caused Nyamwaha's death. Pressure is exerted by such beliefs on the individual to conform to the norms of Ndembu society, because, if he persistently breaks them, people whom he loves will die. The overt expression of ill-feeling, especially during periods of crisis in the affairs of a group, is thought to render the objects of anger vulnerable to mystical danger. It is thought, for example, that the familiars of witchcraft and sorcery are emboldened by the anger of their owners to demand the ' meat' of those against whom their owners are incensed. If hasty anger ripens into a protracted grudge (*chitela*) the familiar cannot be gainsaid in its demand to kill. Violent persons are thus constrained not only by the public opinion that they are witches, but also by their own fears that inadvertently their anger might kill someone they love.

A further difference between the kinds of situation in which judicial and ritual machinery of adjustment are respectively employed may here be considered. Recourse is often made to law when the living quarrel. The nature of the conflict brought to light is usually specific ; attempts are made to find a remedy, and if possible to bring about a reconciliation between the opposing parties. The conflict is man-made and immediately intelligible.

But when a breach in social regularity is made by some natural misfortune such as the death of a member of the group, or a famine, or a plague, and if the natural order is thought to be sensitively responsive to the moral condition of society, then the calamity allows of a number of alternative interpretations. A wide range of conflicts between persons and factions in the disturbed group is brought to light. I take up this point in greater detail in the following chapter, in which I attempt to analyse the pattern of intrigue in Mukanza Village. But I would like here to emphasize what seems to me to be a significant difference. When rules are broken by living persons, judicial action can follow and this action can speedily seal off conflict within the orbit of a single relationship or within a small sector of the social system. But when a severe natural misfortune precipitates crisis, practically every latent source of conflict in the system is made manifest. These may be disclosed in accusations of witchcraft/sorcery, or in confessions of guilt by those who feel that they have broken some crucial norm governing the intercourse of the living with the living or with the dead.

Since no specific norm has been patently broken it is impossible to introduce judicial machinery of redress. Either ritual or the ascription of witchcraft/sorcery to one of its members is resorted to by the stricken group. In both events the fundamental norms and values of the community are emphasized in symbol, mime and precept. And by the purging of a witch the group reaffirms its solidarity. In such situations irremediable conflict has been felt to exist between the major principles by which the group is organized. There is nothing for it but to lay stress on values to which all men subscribe, regardless of their particular loyalties and interests.

It should be pointed out that while judicial machinery is often deliberately and consciously brought into play when men quarrel, ritual seems to emerge as the spontaneous response to the moral discomfort experienced by a group disturbed by some natural disaster. Law is thus directly related to man-made breach in social regularity, while ritual is obliquely related to natural breach in it.

Finally, when natural disaster strikes, there is no legal remedy for it. One cannot sue mystical beings and powers in any court and obtain compensation. Yet the disaster has to be made intelligible in terms of a moral order of the universe. This can be done, as I have mentioned, by a confession of one's own guilt in a ritual context, or by a projection of the guilt outwards onto an external enemy, a witch or a sorcerer.[1]

Summary

It has been shown how in a long-established village, matrilineal affiliation constitutes the crucial means of providing village inte-

---

[1] I am grateful to Professor John Barnes, of the University of Sydney, for making this final point.

gration. Both dramas reveal how powerful matrilineal ties can be, and how they resist disruptive forces put into action by conflicts of interest which arise within the institutional complex of matriliny itself. People live together because they are matrilineally related, but just because they are matrilineally related they come into conflict over office and over the inheritance of property.[1] Since the dogma of kinship asserts that matrilineal kin participate in one another's existence, and since the norms of kinship state that matrilineal kin must at all times help one another, open physical violence between them seldom takes place. Their struggles are phrased in the idiom of sorcery/witchcraft and animistic beliefs. Yet in spite of the fear aroused by witchcraft and sorcery, matrilineal kin may go to strenuous lengths to avoid finally ostracizing one of their number who is believed to be a sorcerer or witch. Conflict is endemic in the social structure but a set of mechanisms exists whereby conflict itself is pressed into the service of affirming group unity. In the next chapter I go on to show how the conflicts over succession to headmanship [2] inherent in the matrilineal structure of Mukanza Village broke

---

[1] When a person dies, his or her most senior matrilineal kinsman, usually an own mother's brother or uterine brother, becomes executor (*nyamufu*, literally ' mother of the dead one '). Traditionally, the standing crops in the dead person's gardens were consumed by the funeral gathering (*chipenji*) that came nightly to mourn for a month or more. The funeral camp consisted of kin and neighbours of the deceased. At the end of the *chipenji* (or *chibimbi*) the executor divides the dead person's movable property, including such items as guns, tools, utensils, cash, small stock, clothes, bows, spears, beds, stools, etc., among the matrilineal kin of the deceased. Uterine kin of the executor's own genealogical generation, i.e. uterine siblings, receive the largest share ; next, his or her sisters' children, then sisters' daughters' children. If any property still remains it is allocated to more distant matrilineal kin in order of seniority. It depends on the good will of the executor and the agreement of the matrilineal kin whether or not the wives and children of a dead man receive any of his property. The deceased's hut is burnt down and he is buried in his clothes and blanket, while many of his cups, plates, and other utensils are nailed on trees in the graveyard as a *memento mori*.

[2] Headmen in the past enjoyed a few privileges, such as gifts from their villagers of first fruits and the first calabash brewed of each kind of beer. At ritual gatherings and other public occasions when beer and food were distributed headmen were entitled to the first share. But the primary value of the headmanship of a long-established village, such as Mukanza, lay in its prestige—it is a great achievement to build up an enduring residential unit from Ndembu individualists.

out afresh in a new series of social dramas. Throughout my second tour of fieldwork it became clear to me that the village was rapidly approaching the major crisis of fission, which will probably take place when Mukanza Kabinda dies. I then go on in subsequent chapters to discuss a number of situations in which fission actually occurred in Mukanza and in other villages and analyse the tensions that led up to it in different villages. In spite of all efforts to maintain the unity of village members, fission frequently takes place. The circumstances in which it occurs and the different forms it assumed will be described and analysed, and the relationship between the sub-system of the village and the inclusive system formed by Ndembu society will be examined in a variety of aspects.

CHAPTER V

MATRILINEAL SUCCESSION AND THE DYNAMICS OF VILLAGE INTRIGUE

IN the last chapter I examined two social dramas which made visible and explicit the underlying social structure of Mukanza Village, and exhibited in action the lines of tension and struggle within the major matrilineage. I now wish to analyse a further set of dramas which arose out of the same fundamental structural situation after a passage of three years in Mukanza Village, as that village became the scene of new conflicts for power. But first I must outline the events that preceded the next overt rupture of relations between the leading persons in the village. After a social drama has passed a climax, and the group involved seems to have been reintegrated, there often follows, in Ndembu life, a period of apparent equilibrium during which, in the main, interpersonal behaviour is in consonance with generally accepted norms of conduct. But beneath the surface conflicts of interests go on and private intrigues provide means whereby individuals seek to realign the social structure in pursuit of their own advantage. Beneath the manifest pattern of daily interactions a re-shaping of the social group is taking place—transferences of persons from one faction to another, loss and replenishment of personnel in the followings of leading men—so that in effect a new and at first hidden set of power relations gradually comes into being. There comes a time when this realignment becomes visible in a fresh social drama. At the culmination of this drama, if unification is re-established, the group may exhibit a marked shift in the balance of power between various components.

In these intrigues the different principles of Ndembu social organization are manipulated by the major intriguers to further their own ends. These interim periods of seeming peace between struggles are really the continuation of struggles in a different and indirect guise. In them we find attempts being made by parties who have secured social gains in preceding social dramas to consolidate their position, and attempts by defeated parties to repair their damaged prestige, attach to themselves fresh

supporters, and win over to their side members of the opposing groups.

After the reconciliation between Sandombu and the other
members of the major lineage of Mukanza, several years elapsed
during which there prevailed on the whole an appearance of
outward harmony between Mukanza Kabinda (I,F8), Sandombu
(I,G10), Sakazao (I,H9) and Kasonda (I,G15), the leading men
of the village.   It is true that, on occasion, bickering took place
between Sandombu and the others over minor matters.   One
such dispute arose over the allocation of a goat paid to Sandombu
by the husband of his classificatory sister's daughter as a customary
gift to the local head of the nearest maternal descent group when
a wife bears her first child.   Mukanza Kabinda, as headman of
the village, said that the goat should be killed and divided immediately between all the village members for 'there was meat-
hunger in the village'.   But Sandombu pointed out that the
goat was in kid and that if they were patient they would have
several goats instead of only one to eat.   Mukanza became angry,
but Sandombu, claiming that he was the senior living 'mother's
brother' of the woman and thus had the right to do as he pleased
with the animal, sent it to a village some miles away to run with
the flock of his blood-brother.   Village opinion was divided on
this issue, some siding with Mukanza, others with Sandombu.

During this period of peace, Sandombu was careful on the
whole to avoid public dispute with Mukanza, and, in fact,
sought to ingratiate himself with the other village members.
From 1948 to 1951 he did not live in Mukanza Village but in a
camp of road labourers a mile away, where he was capitao or
'foreman'.   He managed to obtain the employment by the
Public Works Department of a number of Mukanza men and
youths, thereby putting them under an obligation to him.   In
his camp of mud huts he occupied a position analogous to that
of a village headman and at work he enjoyed greater authority
than Ndembu headmen normally possess.   This situation was
brought to an end in mid-1951 when an African Road Inspector
recommended to the District Commissioner that Sandombu
should be dismissed on account of the poor condition of the
stretch of road for which he was responsible.   Dismissed he
was, and it is interesting to note that in this situation all the
Mukanza people, including the headman, took Sandombu's part

in attributing his misfortune to the repayment of an old grudge by the Road Inspector, who had quarrelled with Sandombu when both were living in Chief Ikelenge's area.

Sandombu now decided to build near Mukanza Village. He did not build his new house in the village itself since there was little space in the hut-circle for such an edifice as he intended to erect. He selected a site about a hundred yards from the main village, next to the main Boma-Kalene road, where he would be in constant contact with the daily stream of people passing along it, could offer hospitality to the wealthier and more important, and be *au fait* with any District news he might turn to his advantage, such as advance information about paid employment. With his savings he employed an Ovimbundu bricklayer to make for him a large three-roomed house of Kimberley brick and a carpenter to make him a handsome door, window-frames and furniture. He then applied his indefatigable energy to the task of making large gardens of millet and cassava, and urged on his two hard-working wives to do likewise. His senior wife at this time, Katiki, was the daughter of a Lwena woman slave of Government Chief Nyakaseya, and had a well-grown family, one of whom, a son by a former husband, built a pole-and-mud hut beside Sandombu's. Sandombu's immediate aim was to build up by any means a following to settle with him, and when Mukanza died to make a renewed bid for the headmanship of the village. It is at this point that we must pose the question: why did Sandombu still desire to become a traditional village headman when through his participation in the modern cash-economy he might have expected to prosper as a petty trader and cash-crop farmer?

All over Mwinilunga, and especially in the northern pedicle where Sandombu had spent a large part of his working life, the traditional village was giving ground before the small 'farm' as the typical form of settlement. Farm heads were disencumbering themselves of many of the obligations of kinship, and retaining for their own use and for the use of their elementary families money they earned as wages and by the sale of cash-crops or surplus subsistence crops. But Sandombu still hankered after the headmanship of a traditional village. Why? The answer to this question lies, I think, in the fact that the kind of response made to socio-economic change in this region was largely a function of relative age. Old men like Mukanza remained obdurately conservative, and deplored the new ways, although they were indulgent towards the young people who practised them. Young men like Sakazao's uterine nephew, Pearson (I,J5), capitao of a European-owned store at the Boma, and Manyosa's oldest son Daudson (I,H7) who had worked in Chingola, had accepted the new order of things, and wore smart European clothes, owned bicycles and gramophones, played guitars, used Copperbelt slang, and attended traditional rituals only to join rings of young people, who danced the latest dances imported from the Rhodesian or Congo urban areas and sang the latest local or urban ' song-hits '. Between these two extremes, Sandombu, and to a lesser degree Kasonda, though they had grown up in the era of money-earning, still belonged to a generation which saw success in life as measured by the number of followers a man could acquire, and not by the insignia of conspicuous wealth that could be purchased by money. True, Sandombu, and also Kasonda, had large houses well equipped with furniture. They had mosquito-nets and oil lamps. But these signs of wealth were rather indices of success in the traditional order than signs of an altered way of life, involving the acceptance of entirely new modes of behaviour and of a new scale of values. Both these men continued to work in their gardens, to gossip and discuss cases in the village *chota*, to participate in ritual as cult-members and patients, to exercise their traditional rights and fulfil obligations as kin, and to interact with the older generation in terms of traditional norms. They were not ashamed, as many of the younger people were, of the ancient way of life ; they lamented that so much of it had already passed away, and more was passing beneath their very eyes. But they felt that the royal road to eminence within the village way of life now lay through the acquisition of cash. Possession of cash gave them large houses, bride-wealth for several wives who might give them children and enable them to offer hospitality, and the means of retaining their children and giving these a good education. They wanted money to better their position within the traditional system, not as a means of loosening their ties with it. For instance, for these men of middle years, a gun was better than a bicycle, and to obtain the wherewithal to buy one they would save up for many years, keeping the money in a bag or box buried secretly in the ground where even their wives could not find it.

I would like to emphasize at this point the main differences between two modes of incorporation in the modern cash economy. On the one hand, a man can acquire wealth by working in the White economy as a wage labourer, either locally or by migrating to the urban centres on the Rhodesian line-of-rail. On the other hand, a man can obtain money locally by selling surplus subsistence crops, by growing cash crops, such as rice or ground-nuts, for sale to European or African traders, and by setting up in business as a petty trader, tailor or 'tea-room' proprietor (i.e. by selling food and drink to travellers along a labour route). It seems often, even today, to be the aim of returned labour-migrants or of paid workers in local employment to obtain influence, and subsequently office, in traditional villages. Many of them see the village as their ultimate home, and regard their wage-labour as a means of acquiring the wealth that will give them prestige in the village sphere. But if they have substantial savings, it may happen that they wish to invest these in capital equipment, such as a sewing-machine, with the aid of which they make up store cloths into garments for payment, a bicycle, on which they can travel to buy goods cheap and sell them elsewhere at a profit, or a storehouse or tea-room made from sun-dried bricks, to serve as business premises. Once they have taken this step and have invested money to make more money, they find themselves increasingly embarrassed by the demands of their kin for presents in cash and kind. If they wish to become petty capitalists, they must separate themselves from the village sphere and the village way of life. That is why it is usual to find traders and tailors living with their families, in different vicinages, and even chiefdoms, from the villages of their close matrilineal kin. To a lesser extent the same set of conditions holds good for petty commodity cultivators, the incipient 'kulaks', who grow crops specifically for sale. If the making of money tends to supplant as a major aim in life the acquisition of a following, people try to accumulate money, to be turned into capital and the visible signs of a higher status in terms of European values. A large following then tends to become an embarrassment rather than an asset. In essence, the wage-earner, who acquires wealth at the expense of the Whites to strengthen his position in the traditional village, must be distinguished from the local money-maker who grows rich at the expense of his fellow-Ndembu.

But Sandombu, and for many years Kasonda too, sought to use their wages gained in working for Europeans (Kasonda since his return from the line-of-rail had worked as a domestic servant for a succession of District Officers) in acquiring friends and sup- porters among their kin and neighbours to prepare the way for succeeding to headmanship. Later on, towards the end of my second period of fieldwork, both men were coming to realize that the old order was doomed, and that to become eminent they must commit themselves whole-heartedly to the cash economy. But at the time of Social Drama III they were still caught up in the contradiction between participation in a modern way of getting a living and allegiance to an obsolescent set of values. The cash economy to which they were committed was breaking down the structure of the village : and yet it was their ambition to obtain authority over a disintegrating social unit of this kind.

Sandombu, then, used money to increase his influence within a system which was gradually breaking down as the result of the introduction of money. He was not satisfied to remain alone in his big house, or even to attract others to his settlement. He wanted eventually to become headman of Mukanza and to spend the evening of his life as a respected elder of the neighbourhood community, supported by emoluments from the salaried young men to whose education he had contributed when they were boys.

Meanwhile his prospective rivals for the office had been by no means inactive. A member of MALABU lineage, who had spent many years on the Copperbelt, Line (I,H17), returned in 1951 with his wives. Sandombu promptly found him a job as a road labourer, but Line soon quarrelled with him. Sakazao (I,H9) then persuaded Line to bring his uterine nephew Aram (I,J7) with him and found a ' farm ' just behind Sakazao's own huts. Nyamuwang'a (I,G17), the suspected witch of Social Drama IV, also had a hut built for her at Line's ' farm '.

Sakazao, it will be recalled, was the brother-in-law and classi- ficatory ' grandson ' of Mukanza Kabinda. He was rather older than Sandombu. Sakazao was much poorer both in cash and in

PLATE III

Mukanza Village in September 1951

The *chota* (men's forum) is in the centre of the village. Kasonda's Kimberley-brick house is under construction (see p. 138).

kind than Sandombu and Kasonda. His health was uncertain.
In his young manhood he had been considered something of a
'mischief-maker' (*chipapoki*). His favourite practice was to
travel to a part of the District where he was little known, offer
to sell a gun to a villager at a very cheap price, receive part-
payment for it in advance, and set off home, promising that he
would return soon with the gun. He never returned. He had
been cured of this practice by his village kin who grew tired of
paying damages to Sakazao's victims, most of whom tracked him
down in the end. His personality was a curious mixture of
naïveté and shrewdness, but it was universally regarded as
lovable. Sakazao was not respected as Mukanza Kabinda was
respected, but he was loved. When his youthful exploits were
recounted in the *chota*, people would grin and shake their heads,
clucking their tongues and repeating his name. When he made
his pretendedly grumpy sallies in response to teasing everyone
would be delighted. It was thought by most members of both
village lineages that Sakazao would make an excellent successor
to Mukanza, since he was unaggressive, hated no one, and,
though somewhat inactive, was hospitable to strangers. Most
important of all, no one had ever accused him of practising
sorcery. But if he became headman it was generally recognized
that the real management of affairs would devolve upon a younger
and more capable man. Sakazao would make an admirable
figurehead, but a poor representative of the interests, joint and
several, of his villagers. Yet in his own way, and during the
struggle for power described in this chapter, Sakazao was astute.

Sakazao played on the suspicions of his classificatory 'father',
Ntololu (II,D2) of Shika Village, that his relatives were bewitch-
ing him, in order to get Ntololu to come and live uxorilocally
in Line's farm. Ntololu, perhaps influenced by Sakazao, built
a hut there. Ntololu's wife Kalusa (I,G19) was the sister of
Nyamuwang'a (I,G17), and both these women, although about
the same age as Sakazao (I,H9), were his classificatory mothers of
MALABU lineage. Nyamuwang'a had a hut built for her beside
Kalusa's. Just previously, Kalusa's and Ntololu's daughter Ikubi
(I,H14) had undergone her puberty ritual at Mukanza Village.
Ntololu and some boys from Mukanza built a hut for Ikubi at
Line's farm, where she was to await her husband's return from
the Belgian Congo. Also at Line's farm were a woman of

MALABU lineage and her husband, a road labourer in Sandombu's gang.

Thus, at the end of the dry season in September 1951, it was already possible to observe in the spatial structure of Mukanza Village visible signs of gradually approaching conflict for authority.   Behind Sakazao's hut were five huts belonging to members of MALABU matrilineage, forming, as it were, a nucleus of social power.   A hundred yards from the village behind the circle occupied by his generation mates of NYACHINTANG'A lineage was Sandombu's great house, occupied by himself, two wives and a grandson of his senior wife, and her son's small hut.   In Mukanza Village itself Kasonda had built a large Kimberley-brick house and a smaller one for his recently married third wife.

SOCIAL DRAMA III

Kasonda is Accused of Bewitching his Uncle Kanyombu
(my own observations)

Before proceeding any further with this account I must mention my own impact and influence on the life of the village.   At the beginning of 1951 I employed Kasonda as a cook and general henchman. After a time I made a permanent camp in Chief Ikelenge's area, returning to Mukanza Village on intermittent visits to watch the progress of events.   In June of that year Kanyombu (I,F9), Mukanza's younger brother and a leading doctor in several cults, died after a protracted illness.   Kasonda told me that the cause of his death was probably Sandombu's sorcery.   He had received a letter from Sakazao asking him to return for the funeral ritual.   Since I was about to pay a protracted visit to some bush villages at that time I was unable to release Kasonda whose services I needed on tour.

In July Kasonda received a verbal message that his classificatory mother's brother, Kajata (I,F10), an extremely old man of MALABU lineage who had recently returned to his matrilineal kin after about fifty years' absence, had also died; and the message urged him to come to the funeral ritual.   It happened that I had planned to pass by Mukanza Village on my way to the capital village of a Kosa chief and I took Kasonda with me.   When we reached Mukanza we found the entire village in an uproar.   The day following Kajata's death Mukanza himself had been taken seriously ill.   Sakazao and Ikubi (I,H14), his young female relative in Line's farm, had been ill for about a week.   A social drama was, in fact, in progress.

This time the breach in regular relations between villagers had not

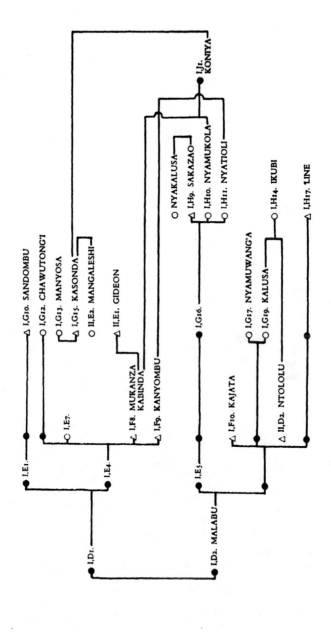

been caused by a dispute but by the natural calamity of what I took to be an epidemic of malaria. For among Ndembu unlucky events occurring in the natural order are thought to originate in breaches of the moral order. More explicitly, in the context of village life, these misfortunes originate either in the malignity of kin with evil powers against other kin or in the punitive action of ancestor spirits against their living kin who have forgotten them or transgressed kinship norms. The epidemic just mentioned was thought to have been caused by one or the other of these agencies.

I arrived at the phase of crisis while the people were still arguing about the origin of their troubles and about the best means to banish them. Kasonda was received with hostile looks, and it soon became clear that he was regarded as the sorcerer who had bewitched Kanyombu and Kajata, and who was now threatening Mukanza's life.

Presently, Nyamukola (I,H10), Mukanza's senior wife, and Nyakalusa, Sakazao's junior wife and slave, began openly to accuse Kasonda of having gone to Kalene Mission, where the missionaries have created a sanctuary for people banished from their homes in Angola as witches and sorcerers, in order to procure medicine to kill his three senior relatives of the first ascendant generation and his classificatory sister's son Sakazao (I,H9).[1] Manyosa (I,G13), Kasonda's uterine sister, and Chawutong'i (I,G12), his matrilineal parallel-cousin, strenuously defended him, as did his senior wife, Mangaleshi (II,E2), but they were in the minority. Kasonda had already begun, with the help of his cross-cousin Gideon (II,E1), Mukanza's son by a deceased wife, to build his Kimberley-brick house, and Nyamukola shouted that this was clear proof that he was planning to succeed Mukanza.

We went in to see Mukanza [2] who was lying on his bed, obviously in a condition of great fear and distress. Mukanza's two wives followed. An extraordinary scene took place beside what looked like becoming a death-bed. Kasonda became very angry and said : ' Alas, Africans are very, very stupid people. Kajata was an old man. God (*Nzambi*) has taken him. But if God has taken Kanyombu, it is obvious that Kanyombu's spirit (*mukishi*) is now troubling the village. Women are mighty fools and will tattle about anything. How could I have gone to Kalene Hill when I was working for Mr. Turner all

---

[1] Sakazao was grouped with the senior in the linking of alternate generations.

[2] Under normal circumstances Kasonda would not have entered Mukanza's and Nyamukola's hut; since Mukanza was his mother's brother and Nyamukola rated as his mother-in-law, to be avoided, since she was the mother of his divorced wife, Koniya (I,J1). But as my servant, the dominant role he chose to play, he ignored these customary rules.

the time? Why should I kill Kajata? For meat? I had plenty of beef, goat's flesh and duiker meat at Mr. Turner's place. *I do not eat human beings even if other people in this village do.'*

At this point I intervened and offered to take Mukanza without delay to Kalene Hospital. The old man accepted gratefully, not, I suspect, because he had much faith in European medicine, but because he longed with all his heart to get away from the situation in which sorcery was thought to be active. Once away from his relatives he would be safer.

Others demurred and we all went into the *chota* to discuss the matter fully. Sandombu was away at work at the time. Mukanza's two adult sons, Line (I,H17), Kasonda's two grown nephews, and the headman of a nearby village whose father had come from Mukanza Village, were present. The women sat outside the *chota* and took a lively share in the discussion.

But first I dosed the sick people with quinine and offered to take them all to hospital.

Manyosa (I,G13) said that her mother's brother, Kanyombu, had in his lifetime drunk *mwiyanawu* medicine, (that is, medicine which would enable him to come back as a ghost (*musalu*) and kill members of the lineage of the sorcerer who had bewitched him). She implied by this that since so many members of MALABU lineage were sick the sorcerer or witch had belonged to that lineage.

Nyamukola, wife of Mukanza, had now calmed down somewhat with the prospect of accompanying her husband to Kalene Hospital before her, and interjected that it might well be that Kanyombu was haunting the village, not because of revenge medicine, but because he had given Mukanza detailed instructions about how his funeral stretcher should be made and medicated, and Mukanza had omitted to carry them out. Perhaps he was angry at this neglect. If Mukanza were taken away from the village and given European medicine he might recover. Yes, he should go.

Sakazao's wife then interposed that Sakazao had been dreaming about Kanyombu all the time he had been ill. Yes, Kanyombu's ghost was to blame for the trouble, not Kasonda.

Kasonda spoke up at this point, saying that Mr. Turner had once given Mukanza some money to pay Fisher's lorry driver to transport Kanyombu to Kalene Hospital when he first became ill, but that Mukanza had divided the money among his wives and children and not sent Kanyombu at all. This was another reason why Kanyombu was angry. It was not Kanyombu's ghost (*musalu*), his evil power, that was active; Kanyombu, in spite of what Manyosa had said, had never drunk *mwiyanawu* for he had never observed the taboos of *mwiyanawu*, such as eating only one side of an animal or chicken.

But Kanyombu's spirit (*mukishi*), his moral power, was angry because his relatives had scorned his wishes and neglected to look after him properly. Kanyombu had died because he had not been taken to hospital. If, on the other hand, Mr. Turner took Mukanza to hospital he would recover.

As Kasonda made these points, most of the men clapped their assent, and cried ' *Eyo-o* ', ' that's it '. The upshot was that it was agreed that Mukanza should go to Kalene Hospital, but Sakazao and Ikubi (I,H14) refused with the excuse that my medicine would soon make them recover.

Mukanza and Sakazao both recovered, but the young woman Ikubi died.

Analysis

In this situation misfortune was interpreted by various people in terms of a breach of several different moral norms, and thus it brought to the surface a number of different latent conflicts within the village. This time the lines of conflict were not clear-cut. If there is a real dispute between living village members, created by a breach of rules, judicial action can follow. When serious illness occurs it is believed to be caused by one of a number of mystical beings or forces. The operation of all those beings and forces is associated with disturbances of the moral order. Therefore every known item of the patient's behaviour in the recent past is brought under review, in order to survey possible sources of disturbance, and to locate that which is responsible. This is done in all cases within my experience even before resort is made to divination. Various theories are advanced about the precise nature and name of the supernatural cause of affliction, on the basis of the patient's known conduct. Since it frequently happens that contradictory theories are put forward by parties whose interests in the patient are diametrically opposed, representatives of the major interest-groups go jointly to an accredited diviner, who is usually in a distant area where the villagers have no kin, in order to obtain a decision untinged by partisan bias and validated by mystical beliefs.

In situations of grave misfortune moral misdemeanour is involved in two ways. Either the misfortune is the result of the victim's own misconduct, or else it is due to the wickedness of others. In the first event, the cause of misfortune is believed to be the punitive action of ancestor spirits, the watchful and unseen guardians of kinship morality ; in the second event, the malevolence of witches, sorcerers or ghosts has been at work.

There are certain exceptions to this rule. It is thought that sometimes, in extreme cases, the killing by sorcery of a notorious sorcerer or witch is justifiable. But when a sorcerer is believed to have been killed by sorcery, a certain odium is still felt to be attached to the slayer, although in this case divination is seldom invoked and his identification is left to gossip and rumour. On the other hand, certain manifestations of ancestor spirits express unjustifiable malevolence towards their living kin. When a spirit is thought to have caused unjustified serious illness or grave misfortune, it is not execrated but placated, although elements of exorcism may be found in the ritual.

Whether misfortune or illness is ascribed to the unrighteousness of the victim, or to the unrighteousness of a corporeal or spiritual enemy, depends on a number of factors : the degree or kind of misfortune ; the sex, age or status of the victim in varying social situations ; and the current level of morale of his local group of kin. In most cases, both theories in various forms are put forward. Sometimes sufficient consensus is obtained about the particular cause to avoid recourse to a diviner, which is costly and today risky as well. For instance, when a certain pregnant woman became seriously ill, it was agreed by her kin and husband that the *Wubwang'u* or twin ritual should be performed for her, since both her mother and mother's mother had been mothers of twins, and it was considered likely that her grandmother's spirit was afflicting her reproductive processes. When the woman admitted that she had forgotten to make an offering of first fruits to her grandmother, her kin regarded it as established that the latter's spirit was offended and had afflicted her in this way. But it is more usual for two major theories to develop and the diviner in effect has to choose between them. This tendency for two theories to develop sometimes produces unexpected consequences. When I was in Mwinilunga, a song was current throughout Chief Mwininyilamba's area, the gist of which was that when a headman died in one village, the senior men of two village matrilineages each went to a different diviner and each obtained from his own diviner the name of his rival as the sorcerer who had bewitched the headman. The song related how they returned to the village at the same time and each promptly accused the other of the headman's death. A dispute arose and each led his kin group away to form a new village, so that the name of the old village ' died '. There is a droll irony in the flat account of the events which is irresistible. Ndembu, in fact, often express scepticism about divinations made for others, but seldom about those sought out by themselves.

The situation in Mukanza Village brought out into the open not only an important cleavage in the social structure, but also interpersonal grudges. When Nyamukola accused Kasonda of bewitching her husband she was not only attacking him out of jealousy because his improved financial position as my cook gave him additional qualifications for headmanship, but also because Kasonda had once been the husband of her favourite daughter Koniya and had treated her so badly that she had left him after a month of married life. And when Manyosa (I,G13) said that Kanyombu's ghost was attacking members of MALABU lineage because Kanyombu had possessed vengeance medicine, she was not merely defending her brother from Nyamukola but also revealing the hidden conflict that existed between NYACHIN-TANG'A (I,D1) and MALABU (I,D2) lineages ; for if Kanyombu's vengeance medicine were working, this could only mean that someone of that lineage had killed Kanyombu by mystical means. Later in fact the myth became established among members of NYACHINTANG'A lineage that Nyatioli (I,H11), sister of Nyamu-kola, and divorced wife of Kanyombu, had bewitched the old man. They had lived a married life of continual domestic bickering and Nyatioli had developed a grudge against her former husband. Women are believed to possess familiars of a kind different from, and more dangerous than, those owned by men. They are called *tuyebela, tushipa* or *andumba*, and have the variable forms of little men with reversed feet, hyenas, jackals, owls or small rodents. They are believed to be inherited matri-lineally and to make demands on their owners to kill junior relatives. They may be refused three times but after that, however hard the owner (*nkaka*) may plead, they kill their chosen victim. When the owner of *tuyebela* dies, they seek out one of her close kin, it may be a daughter or uterine sister, and attach themselves to her whether she desires them or not. Their victims are the husbands or junior matrilineal kin of their owners.

If a husband is killed his ghost becomes what is known as a *kahwehwi*, and leads the band of *tuyebela*. He is more powerful than they, and may only be gainsaid once. *Tuyebela* are exceptionally active if their owner has a grudge (*chitela*) against someone, when they are liable to take instant action against him without asking their owner. Nyatioli had been suspected for some time of having *tuyebela*, as indeed had her classificatory mother, the notorious witch Nyamuwang'a (I,G17), also of MALABU lineage, of whom more anon. No doubt, one of Nyamukola's (I,H10) reasons for pinning the accusation of witchcraft on Kasonda was her fear that she herself, coming from a lineage the women of which were suspected of witchcraft, might be accused if Mukanza were to die. His niece Manyosa's reference to Kanyombu's vengeance medicine was a fairly direct hint to that effect.

Kasonda's later handling of the situation, after his first outburst of anger, was extremely diplomatic. First of all he cleared himself by attributing the sickness in the village to Kanyombu's spirit. Next, he cleared Kanyombu from the imputation that he had used vengeance medicine, a practice bordering on sorcery. If this argument were pressed too hard he realized that it would be tantamount to a public recognition of the cleavage existing between the two village minor matrilineages. But if he could gain general acceptance of the view that Kanyombu's moral spirit and not his vengeful ghost was troubling the village, he would have produced a formula that would unite the village again. All members, including Sakazao, had erred in neglecting the interests and ignoring the last wishes of the old man. That was why he had afflicted so many people with illness, as a rebuke. Furthermore, since I had given them money to spend on Kanyombu, but Mukanza had spent it on his own family, Kasonda subtly implied that Mukanza was under an obligation to make restitution to me, and through me, to Kasonda himself, who had urged on them that Kanyombu be sent to hospital before he died. This Mukanza could do in two ways, first by absolving Kasonda from blame, and secondly by going to Kalene Hospital himself for treatment. If Mukanza did this he would show publicly that he accepted Kasonda's point of view and did not believe that he was bewitching him. In other words, Kasonda completely reversed the case against him by posing as the would-be benefactor of Kanyombu and by implying that Mukanza and the other elders of the village had wronged the old man. He omitted to mention the death of the other old man, Kajata (I,F10 ; see p. 138), for ghosts (*nyisalu*) are believed to have power to kill, though spirits (*akishi*) are rarely thought to do so. Later, he told me that it had been accepted, in village gossip, that Nyamuwang'a (I,G17) had killed Kajata and I have no doubt that Kasonda did not strive officiously to kill this imputation. Later, Nyamuwang'a was accused publicly by Sakazao and Ntololu (II,D2) of having killed Ikubi (I,H14), so that it became natural to believe that she had killed Kajata as well.

Kasonda's major political triumph was to have created a general opinion that everyone in the village had wronged Kanyombu and that the main burden of guilt was Mukanza's. He had kept the two lineages together, and strengthened the view that he and not Mukanza was the real peacemaker, the most important of an Ndembu headman's roles.

But why was Sandombu at no time accused of sorcery in this situation, except privately, to me, by Kasonda who was intensely jealous of him ? As always, where human beings are concerned, there is no simple and all-sufficient answer. One reason may have been that for several years now Sandombu had lived quietly in his Public Works Department camp and had secured work for village members, thus enabling them to pay their tax and clothe their families and themselves without having to leave their homes. The scars of the old conflict between Sandombu and the rest had healed. But a more cogent reason, I think, was the sudden increment of members of MALABU lineage to the village population, creating a numerical imbalance in favour of MALABU people over NYACHINTANG'A people, whose lineage had always held the leadership. This led to tension between the two groups, tension which was openly expressed in Manyosa's reference to Kanyombu's vengeance medicine, which formed a component of Nyamukola's accusation against Kasonda, and which later gave rise to the NYACHINTANG'A myth that Nyatioli (I,H11), a MALABU woman, had killed Kanyombu by witchcraft. The fact that Mukanza himself was so ready to lend an ear to Kasonda's arguments, which implied that NYACHINTANG'A people should perform a ritual to placate Kanyombu's spirit and thus consolidate the lineage, suggests that he himself was reluctant to believe that Kasonda, his uterine nephew, of NYACHINTANG'A lineage, was the sorcerer. Sakazao, too, Mukanza's grandson, brother-in-law and friend, was in agreement with Kasonda's view, for he also was partially responsible for not carrying out Kanyombu's last wishes, and the belief that Kanyombu's spirit was punishing the *whole* village probably seemed to him a means of reuniting a settlement of which he hoped at some time in the future to be headman. Kasonda's remark that ' women are mighty fools ' refers to the fact that Nyamukola, Nyakalusa and Manyosa attributed the common misfortune to personal animosities ; if their views had been accepted, the village would almost certainly have split into its component lineages.

Another important factor was my role in the situation as a stranger. Once Mukanza was in my vanette he was my responsibility and no longer that of the village members. Frankenberg [1] has pointed out, in an analysis of a village community in North Wales, how the responsibility for making decisions about matters on which the village members, interlinked by long propinquity, kinship, religion, etc., were divided among themselves, was often thrust upon strangers or village members who were structurally outside the particular situation of controversy. Similarly in this Ndembu village of Mukanza, if the headman had died at Kalene Hospital, according to Ndembu notions his death would have lain at my door, though as I was a European no action could be taken against me. Since I had taken the first step in asking Mukanza to come with me, Kasonda could not be held responsible for his fate. As it happened Mukanza made a speedy recovery and both Kasonda and I in consequence acquired enhanced prestige in the village.

In this situation the structural cleavage between NYACHIN-TANG'A and MALABU lineages came into the open in the form of accusation and counter-accusation phrased in the idiom of mystical beliefs. Although these two lineages were linked together by many ties of marriage and alternate generation alliance, at the same time the distance from their common ancestress was beginning to be reflected in social and spatial segregation. Most MALABU lineage members were now in Sakazao's section of the

---

[1] *Kinship and Community in a Welsh Border Village* (1954), unpublished thesis presented for the degree of Ph.D. at University of Manchester.

village. When meat was divided Mukanza gave a large share of the carcase to Sakazao who took it to his own hut and sub-divided it among his lineage kin. On marriage and divorce MALABU and NYACHINTANG'A people dealt with the bride-wealth matters of their respective kin separately. With the progress of structural time the village cell was developing two independent nuclei.

The next social drama is concerned with divisions within MALABU lineage itself and shows how such divisions were ex-ploited by Sandombu to build up his own following.

SOCIAL DRAMA IV

The Expulsion of the Witch Nyamuwang'a
(my own observations)

Shortly after the above events, the young bride Ikubi (I,H14) died, I believe of malaria, in Line's farm.

Ntololu (II,D2), her father, promptly accused Nyamuwang'a (I,G17), her classificatory mother, of having killed her by means of witchcraft-familiars *(tuyebela)*. The usual *post hoc ergo propter hoc* arguments were invoked. It was said that Nyamuwang'a had asked Ikubi for some meat that she had cooked shortly before her illness. Ikubi had said that it was for her parents and that she had not enough to give away. Nyamuwang'a had become very angry with her and had threatened her in a roundabout way.

Nyamuwang'a defended herself by saying that Ikubi's death was probably due to Kanyombu's vengeance medicine, not an argument likely to commend itself to Sakazao (I,H9) and his lineage kin, since it implied that Kanyombu's killer had come from their ranks.

Gideon (II,E1), son of Mukanza by a dead wife from Shika Village,[1] and uterine sister's son of Ntololu, father of Ikubi, then lost his temper and started to beat up Nyamuwang'a. Sakazao stopped him, but told Nyamuwang'a to leave the village, and stay with her sister in Chimbila Village in Chief Ikelenge's area ; not because she was a witch but because she was a trouble-maker. Line (I,H17) endorsed this, saying that he would have no witches in his farm. All formed a united front against the old woman. She collected her belongings and fled to Chimbila Village.

Later Sandombu said she had been accused without proof and offered her a hut site in his farm. Nyamuwang'a, who had met her

---

[1] See Appendix II for skeleton genealogy of Shika Village lineage.

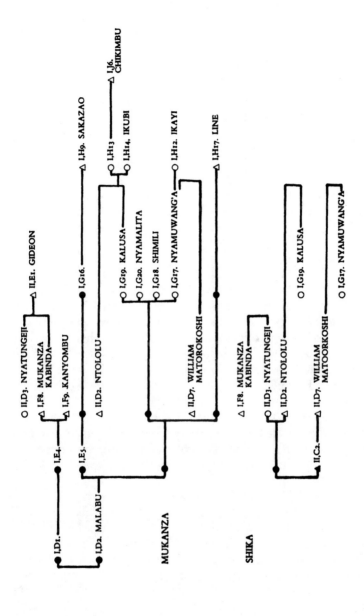

daughter Ikayi (I,H12) in Chimbila, came back with Ikayi in 1952 and Sandombu built them a small hut beside his house.

Nyamuwang'a's hut in Line's farm had been burnt and pulled down while she was in Chimbila. Ntololu returned, with his wife Kalusa (I,G19) and their remaining children, to his own village of Shika, saying that there was less witchcraft there than in Mukanza.

Analysis

This was not the first time by any means that Nyamuwang'a had been accused of witchcraft. In the summer of 1950 she had been accused by Mukanza Village of killing her uterine sister, Shimili (I,G18), at Chimbila Village, although Chimbila people blamed Shimili's other sister Nyamalita (I,G20) for her death. It was also said that Nyamuwang'a had killed her own children by means of *tuyebela*. Kasonda denied this, saying that Nyamu-wang'a first acquired her *tuyebela* from her mother-in-law, a slave of Shika Village. When I put it to Kasonda that the generally accepted belief was that *tuyebela* were matrilineally inherited, he admitted that that was usually the case, but said it had not hap-pened thus with Nyamuwang'a. This inconsistency is under-standable in terms of the social structure. Kasonda, for instance, had no hesitation in telling me privately at other times that women of MALABU lineage possessed inherited *tuyebela*, when conflict arose between the two lineages within Mukanza Village. But since Kasonda had acted as representative of Mukanza Village in the discussion of death-payment (*mpepi*) which fol-lowed Shimili's death at Chimbila Village, he had obviously tried to whitewash his own village matrilineal kin in a dispute with members of another village, by claiming that Nyamuwang'a *tuyebela*, if she had any, were acquired, not inherited. He had either come to believe this himself or else wished to clear the name of Mukanza Village in my eyes.

How, then, had Nyamuwang'a come to acquire her unenviable reputation ? In the first place, she was only half Ndembu, or rather half Kawiku, since her father had been a Lwena ; and she had spent many years in Angola at her father's village. Persons of mixed tribal origin, or who have been reared among other tribes, are frequently regarded as sorcerers or witches by Ndembu. Headman Chibwakata (cf. p. 160ff.) who was captured as a child by Chokwe and reared in a Chokwe village is a case in point.

They do not 'quite belong' to the local society, and as such make useful scapegoats for misfortune. In the second place she, like Sandombu, had been a prodigiously hard worker in her gardens, knew where to plant her crops so that she would obtain a higher yield than other people, and often went on working in the heat of the day when others had retired to gossip in the kitchens. And so the inevitable question was posed : from what sources did she draw her energy and why were her crops better than anyone else's? Obviously she had supernatural powers which gave her outstanding strength and luck. When she was a young woman she also had the reputation of being something of a nymphomaniac. Ndembu in conversation strongly condemn excessive sexual desire and associate it with propensities to sorcery and witchcraft. Like witchcraft, desire (*wuvumbi*) is 'hot', and in the boys' circumcision ritual, mystical protection in the form of medicines is used against both witchcraft and fornication. Again, like witchcraft, sexual desire causes social disturbance—marital infidelity, crimes of passion, and arguments over the repayment of bride-wealth. In the words of the most often sung Ndembu hunting song, ' the buffalo in the bush, the woman in the village, are the death of man'. The two beliefs coincide in the notion of the *kahwehwi*, the ghost of a witch's husband, killed by her sorcery. The *kahwehwi* is thought to be an incubus who continues to have intercourse with his widow, and to give her inordinate pleasure. On these three counts, then, her foreignness, her diligence, and her former nymphomania, Nyamuwang'a came to be reckoned a witch as she grew older. A series of deaths in her lineage were attributed to her witchcraft : those of Shimili (I,G18), Kajata (I,F10) and Ikubi (I,H14).

Old women are often considered to be witches. If they are widows or divorcees like Nyamuwang'a, with no sons or brothers, they have no one to obtain meat for them and have to rely on the uncertain generosity of remoter kin. They are constantly grumbling about lack of meat, and in a society with a lively belief in the necrophagous practices of witches, this is highly suspicious behaviour. It is believed that witches collect together in the bush with their familiars, and divide and eat the bodies of their victims. They substitute in the meanwhile a simulacrum of the deceased, fabricated from his faeces and body dirt, in his place in the village ; and this is mourned over and buried by his relatives.   It is, I think, significant in terms of this belief that the alleged cause of Nyamuwang'a's grudge against Ikubi was the latter's refusal to give her meat.[1]

Witches usually strike at their close maternal kin, on whom they depend and who therefore are those who neglect them by not fulfilling their obligations.   It is usually old women who are neglected because they tend to be an economic burden to the community.   Thus allowances are seldom made for old women detected as witches by any means of divination.   In the past, it is said, they were burnt to death.   Today, they are often driven from their villages.   According to my observations, old women who live with close kin such as sons or brothers, although they may be suspected of witchcraft, are never treated in this way.   It is the class of unfortunate old women who are without immediate male kin, but who are classificatory matrilineal kin of the village headman, that acquire the role of scapegoats for misfortune.   They consolidate the rest of the village or lineage membership against them.   However, in the case of Nyamu-wang'a, it would appear that Sakazao made a mistake in banish-ing her.   For unknown to him at the time, Nyamuwanga's daughter Ikayi (I,H12), with her own small daughter, had just returned from the Congo, having been away from Mwinilunga for five years.   She was staying at Chimbila Village.   Her husband had recently received a long sentence of imprisonment for manslaughter after a fight with Ikayi's current lover.   If Sakazao and Line had retained Nyamuwang'a they would have acquired two further women of their matrilineage who would have borne children for that group.

But it often happens that after a death has occurred, intense animosity is aroused, and if this is focused on a putative witch, a reasoned consideration of the resulting social situation is swept away by anger and hatred against her.   The prime movers in this matter appear to have been Ikubi's father Ntololu (II,D2) and her cross-cousin Gideon (II,E1), both from Shika Village lineage.   There is a long tradition of intermarriage between Mukanza and Shika villages.[2]   Kasonda's senior wife (II,E2)

---

[1] Cf. how quarrels in preceding episodes arose over the division of meat.
[2] See Appendix II.

came from Shika, Mukanza's first wife (II,D3) was a Shika woman, Kasonda's father (II,D1) came from Shika, and so on. For this reason, since marriage is liable to involve disputes between the kin of spouses, considerable tension as well as amity existed between the two villages. Nyamuwang'a's former husband, William Matorokoshi (II,D7), came from Shika, and she had stayed with him there for several years. William had recently divorced her because he said that he used to dream every night of 'animals' (*tunyama*), meaning that he feared that he was being bewitched by *tuyebela*. He said that these belonged to his wife, and sent her back to Mukanza Village. In addition, she had quarrelled continually with members of the Shika lineage, refusing to cook for the men in the *chota*, and squabbling with the women.

When Ikubi (I,H14) died all the accumulated dislike of Nyamuwang'a felt by Shika folk, and their suspicions of her witchcraft, broke loose and received expression in the beating given her by Gideon (II,E1). Sakazao, furious at the disruption of the following he was beginning to build up, ordered her out of Line Farm. She had already left her hut near the main village circle to build next to Ikubi's mother, Kalusa (I,G19), her uterine sister, because she had quarrelled with Gideon and Manyosa (I,G13), her neighbours. Gideon was now violently opposed to her return. In any case Sakazao had ordered her to go and live in Chimbila Village if the headman would allow her to do so.

When Sandombu heard that Nyamuwang'a's daughter had joined her mother in Chimbila he immediately saw this opportunity both to add to the strength of his own farm, and to ensure its continuity through time by inviting them to stay with him. At last he would be in a position to acquire the nucleus of a matrilineal group. Three generations of matrilineal kinswomen would be added to his following, even if one of them was a witch, another a prostitute, and the third a child in arms. In allowing Nyamuwang'a to reside at his farm Sandombu was openly defying the people of Mukanza Village, and behaving like the headman of a rival village. He was acting as though he intended to split Mukanza Village.

Nyamuwang'a eagerly accepted Sandombu's offer, for she was *persona non grata* at Chimbila on account of her reputation, and besides she had left her large gardens behind at Mukanza. She and Ikayi (I,H12) came and lived at Sandombu's farm where, at the time I left Mukanza Village, Ikayi was making money by selling her favours to passing lorry-drivers, African traders and other well-do-do Africans, although not to indigent villagers. She was reputed to give Nyamuwang'a and Sandombu a share of her earnings, and became a lively source of scandal among the respectable older women of Mukanza Village. About this time too Sandombu added to his following a young lad named Chikimbu (I,J6), daughter's son of Ikubi's mother Kalusa (I,C19). Chikimbu's mother had gone with her husband to the latter's place of employment in the Congo urban area. Chikimbu was too wild and wayward to be taken with her to her new husband's place, she said, and Nyamuwang'a offered to look after him. Soon he too acquired a reputation for sorcery in spite of his tender years : my wood and water carrier, a tall youth from a nearby village, gave notice because Chikimbu, half his size, had threatened to kill him as the result of a quarrel over a game of hopscotch. Chikimbu was the problem child of the local Mission out-school and his teachers could do nothing to discipline him.

I have given this thumbnail sketch of Chikimbu to show what kind of a following Sandombu had collected around him to further his unsatisfied ambitions. At this time his farm consisted of his senior wife's children by other men and a number of remote matrilineal kin of MALABU lineage who were social outcasts and misfits. But for this very reason they could be guaranteed to remain loyal to him and work hard for him according to their varied abilities. Chikimbu, for example, was always running errands and doing odd jobs for Sandombu, although he would do nothing for anyone else. Not unnaturally, the people of Mukanza Village referred to Sandombu's farm with a self-righteous shudder as ' that village of witchcraft ' (*mukala wawuloji*). But Sandombu continued to visit the *chota* every day, to take part in discussions on such important matters as bride-wealth, the holding of rituals, death-payments, cases of petty theft, slander, etc., and to state his opinions forcefully and authoritatively. It was clear that at some time or other he would make another bid for the headmanship.

By the middle of 1953 it became obvious that the headman

Mukanza Kabinda was becoming very old and infirm. He spent much of his time dozing in his kitchen, and although he still went into the bush to hunt, he seldom killed anything. The question of succession to headmanship was once more beginning to disturb the village. By this time I had made my permanent camp just on the outskirts of the village, not far from Mukanza's own huts. I was, therefore, in a position to observe the trend of events far more closely than before. Kasonda, still my cook, was now making plans to found a farm of his own. He said that when Mukanza died the village would break up, some going with him, others going to Sandombu, and others staying with Sakazao. Shortly after I arrived Mukanza publicly announced in the *chota* that he had appointed Sakazao as his *mulopu* or successor. This was done in the presence of Nsang'anyi, headman of the oldest Kawiku village, and of Nswanakudya, headman of an important neighbouring village belonging to the lineage of Chief Kanongesha. Sandombu was away at the time on a visit to Ikelenge Area. When he returned and heard the news, his first action was formally to succeed to the name of Kahali by asking Nsang'anyi's permission to use it, a name which, it will be remembered, was the ancient title of the Mukanza headmanship. Nsang'anyi, after demurring at first, agreed in the end to give permission. Mukanza publicly approved Sandombu's step, and said smilingly in the *chota*, when both Sandombu and I were present, 'Now there are *two* villages, Mukanza and Nswana-kahali.'[1] Sakazao will succeed in Mukanza Village, and perhaps [2] someone or other will succeed in Nswanakahali.' Sandombu said nothing but shortly rose and returned to his village. Trouble was patently brewing.

A week later Sandombu invited me to drink with him in his house. He was broodingly drunk when I arrived. Soon he asked abruptly, 'What is the name of this village in the Government tax-register?' I said that it was written down as 'Kahali-Mukanza'. 'Yes,' he said, 'in 1947 Bwana Heath [the District Commissioner] came to the village to collect tax and Kahali

[1] Literally, 'Heir-of-Kahali'.
[2] The use of this 'perhaps' (*kwiji*) was a powerfully compressed taunt which contained the notion that Sandombu's followers were all witches or sorcerers who might bewitch one another and was an oblique reference to Sandombu's sterility.

Chandenda, my uncle, told him to change the name in his book from Mukanza to Kahali, for the old name from long ago is Kahali ; but Mukanza Kabinda and Sakazao told him that the village had been founded by Mukanza Kandulu (I,F6) and was known by all as Mukanza. So Bwana Heath was very clever and wrote down Kahali-Mukanza. But he was wrong. You have written our history and you know that the true name of the village is Kahali. Please go to the Boma and tell the D.C. to change it to Kahali.' I replied that although it was true that the village used to be Kahali, the majority of people today thought that the village should be called Mukanza. At this point Kasonda came in, although he had not been specifically invited. He quickly picked up the thread of the discussion and said : ' A long time ago the Lenje people had a village in the place where Broken Hill now stands. Who remembers the name of that village now ? People only mention " Broken Hill ", " Broken Hill ", " Broken Hill "—even Africans. Now a long time ago there was a village called Kahali. That village divided and a new village was started by Mukanza Kandulu. Many people came and visited Mukanza Village. For many years people have only been speaking of Mukanza. It is like Broken Hill.' Sandombu angrily retorted that he had just visited Chief Ikelenge's area and that there people still thought of Mukanza Village as Kahali. Kasonda replied, ' Ikelenge Area is another place, not this place.' The conversation turned to other matters, and after a while I left.

But Sandombu went on drinking heavily, and in the evening another social drama began which revealed that the jealousy over succession had not been eradicated but had been festering beneath the show of outward harmony. Sandombu was well aware that Mukanza, Kasonda and Sakazao were attempting to seal him off from any possibility of succeeding, by asserting that his farm now constituted a separate village, and that Mukanza Village was not continuous with Kahali Village, which had, in their reckoning, become extinct. Perhaps he felt that he had made a mistake in taking the name of Nswanakahali, and that Mukanza and Kasonda were chuckling over their exploitation of that mistake. Whatever the cause the fact was that by nightfall he was in a prodigious temper, and threw over the restraints he had imposed upon himself for years.

SOCIAL DRAMA V

Sandombu Slanders and is Slandered
(my own observations)

While Sandombu was drinking great excitement was aroused in the village by the arrival of a masked *ikishi* dancer from a Boys' Circumcision Camp some miles away. At a certain point in the seclusion period of the boys, the dancers emerge from the camp and visit neighbouring villages, accompanied by ritual officials from the camp, to obtain gifts in cash or kind from the villagers or to extract various kinds of forfeits from them. The whole village was in a condition of social excitement, with drumming, dancing, singing, and drinking. This reached a high pitch when my kitchen accidentally caught fire.

Zuliyana (I,J2), Sandombu's junior wife and daughter of Mukanza and Nyamukola, went to join the other women who had assembled to sing and clap around the *ikishi* dancer. She came back in a temper because she did not possess a new dress as some of the other women did, and began to harangue Sandombu on this theme. She was assisted by Katiki, the senior wife, and both accused Sandombu of giving away large quantities of millet beer to ingratiate himself with people instead of selling some to buy them new cloths to be made up into dresses by Kasonda, who had by this time bought a sewing-machine. They said that apart from organizing the *chenda* collective tree-felling party, Sandombu had done little in the way of cultivating the millet, while they had weeded it, harvested it, thrashed and winnowed it, ground it and made it into beer. Certainly he was owner of the seed, but they were entitled to some reward for their labours. Zuliyana then said that Sandombu just wanted to make himself a big man ; that was why he had taken the name of Kahali. He wanted to become headman of the whole village. In view of the previous arguments of the day this was an unfortunate remark and Sandombu staggered towards Zuliyana to beat her. But he was extremely drunk and she easily evaded him and ran off to her mother and father for protection. Sandombu did not beat Katiki, who seemed to possess some sort of influence over him, and she persuaded him to sleep off his rage.

But when he awoke later that night, his wrath had not abated and he rushed to Mukanza's hut. Meanwhile Zuliyana had told her father that Sandombu had been boasting to many people that he was the elder (*mukulumpi*) of the village while Mukanza was his junior (*kansi*, literally, ' child '), and that the name ' Kahali ' was a ' heavier ' name than ' Mukanza '. Mukanza had also been drinking and a

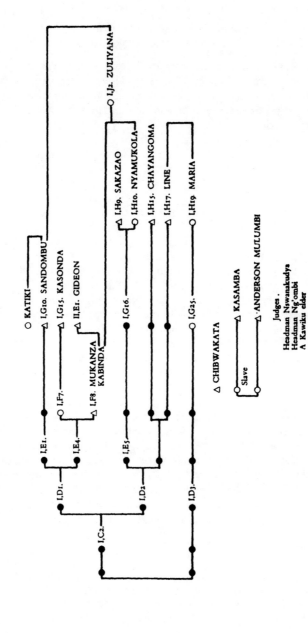

○ KATIKI

△ I,G10. SANDOMBU

△ I,G15. KASONDA

△ II,E1. GIDEON

△ I,F8. MUKANZA
KABINDA

○ I,F7.

I,E4.

I,E1.

I,D1.

I,C2.

○ I,J2. ZULIYANA

△ I,H9. SAKAZAO

○ I,H10. NYAMUKOLA

△ I,H15. CHAYANGOMA

△ I,H17. LINE

○ I,H19. MARIA

I,G16.

I,G25.

I,E5.

I,D2.

I,D3.

△ CHIBWAKATA

△ KASAMBA

△ ·ANDERSON MULUMBI

○ Slave ○

Judges .
Headman Nswanakudya
Headman Ng'ombi
∧ Kawiku elder

major dispute developed between them. Sandombu accused Zuliyana of trying to bewitch him with *tuyebela* which she had been given by her mother Nyamukola. Zuliyana began to deny this energetically from the kitchen where she was sitting with her mother, but both men told her to keep quiet. Mukanza said : ' Sandombu, you have slandered (*ku-tamukila*) my wife, and I will give you a big case. Also you have been heard by others to have threatened me. Why do you want to kill me ? Have I not given you my daughter ? You have a very bad liver to speak as you do to me. You must take your wife back again, treat her well, and buy her a new cloth. If you want to speak in this way you must stay away from the *chota* of Mukanza.' Sandombu refused to take back Zuliyana, and repeated that she and her mother wanted to bewitch him. He went back to his house and for a long time his voice could be heard roaring out abuse against the people of Mukanza, while those in the *chota* who were not immediately involved shook with suppressed laughter, especially the little boys. Zuliyana slept that night in the hut of Line's wife, Maria (I,H19), the latter's husband being away.

Next day Sandombu came to the *chota* and demanded the return of his wife. She came back with him but Sandombu was told to return the day after to explain his conduct at a meeting of village people. He did so and persisted in accusing his wife and mother-in-law of witchcraft. In such intra-village meetings in Mukanza the summing up (*ku-sompa*) was usually left to a blind member of MALABU lineage, Chayangoma (I,H15), who had lost his sight as the result of an industrial accident in a sawmill in Bulawayo. He had neither wife nor child, and used to stress that he felt free to say what he liked as he was a ' dead person ', a *mufu*. Since he was ' already dead ' no one had any motive for bewitching him, and he could speak impartially. In his summary of this case he said that grave charges had been made both by Sandombu and Mukanza, involving witchcraft. In the eyes of the Boma witchcraft accusations should be severely punished. Therefore he thought it wise if the affair were kept within the village and not discussed by the local ' law-men ', the *mahaku*, or vicinage elders with a high reputation for advocating and judging cases, since news might leak out to the Boma and their relatives would be arrested. Sakazao said that Sandombu was drunk at the time and could not be held responsible for his words. If he apologized and paid 10s. to Nyamukola and a new cloth to Zuliyana nothing more need be said.

But Sandombu refused to pay. He said that he had been wronged by his wife, who had first caused trouble in the house by starting an argument and had then borne tales to her parents against her husband to cause trouble in the village. He had accepted her back and yet they still wanted him to pay. As for the accusations of witchcraft, both parties had made them in anger.· He would pay nothing to Nyamukola, for he had been greatly provoked by both women.

It so happened that Sandombu himself at this very time was bringing an action for slander against the headman of a neighbouring village, Chibwakata (cf. p. 150). At a beer-drink at which I was present the day following the Zuliyana affair, headman Chibwakata had accused Sandombu of having accepted 10s. from Kasamba, Chibwakata's classificatory son by a slave mother, to kill the headman by sorcery. Sandombu at first thought that Chibwakata, who was his own classificatory grandfather, was joking with him, and laughed heartily. But Chibwakata, who was drunk, became very angry and said that Anderson Mulumbi, another classificatory son and Kasamba's mother's sister's son, had been witness of the transaction. Sandombu promptly charged Chibwakata and Anderson Mulumbi with slander (*mutamu*) and asked Chibwakata to settle with him on the names of *mahaku* who should discuss the case.

Thus Sandombu was in the odd position of being defendant in one slander case and plaintiff in another at the same time, both cases involving accusations of sorcery and witchcraft.

The Kasamba case was settled first. The *mahaku* were Nswanakudya, headman of a village of the Kanongesha lineage, headman Ng'ombi, and a Kawiku elder. Mukanza was invited, but he refused to discuss any case in which Sandombu was involved. Gideon (II,E1), son of Mukanza, acted as Sandombu's witness (*chinsahu*). Sandombu described how on the previous Sunday a quarrel had broken out at a beer drink between Kasamba and Anderson because the former had obtained the job of D.O.'s cook for which both had been competing, and Anderson had pushed Kasamba into the fire. Kasamba had attacked Anderson and chased him away. Now Anderson was trying to get his revenge by causing bad feeling between Chibwakata and Mukanza's people. If he said he had seen Kasamba and Sandombu conspiring to bewitch Chibwakata he had lied. Chibwakata, who had made the accusation, and Anderson should pay damages to Kasamba and himself. He demanded £5 from them. After much argument the court said that Chibwakata ought to pay Sandombu 30s., and Kasamba the same amount. Anderson had to pay each of the plaintiffs 10s. In this case Sandombu identified himself with Mukanza Village and with the exception of Mukanza and Nyamukola all the Mukanza people were pleased with the decision. They had old scores to pay off against both Anderson and Chibwakata. At a deeper level, too, the level of the Ndembu-Kawiku cleavage, they were pleased, for Chibwakata was the descendant of the Ndembu war-leader who had first attacked the autochthonous Kawiku. In addition, as we have said, he had been reared by Chokwe, the hated slave-raiders of the nineteenth century, and in certain circumstances was identified with the Chokwe.

Next day the Zuliyana case was settled, still at the intra-village level. Chayangoma (I,H15) was again asked to arbitrate. Sakazao was suggested, but turned down by all parties who claimed that he had no inherent faculty (*chisemwa*) for settling disputes. Besides, he was own brother of the co-plaintiff. Chayangoma said that Sandombu should pay Nyamukola 10s. for defaming her character, since the previous day he had obtained damages from Chibwakata for slander against himself. In both cases there had been witnesses and the fact of slander had been clearly established. Sandombu paid up, and people joked with him afterwards, saying that after all he had made a profit from his two cases. Peace was restored for a time in the village.

Analysis

It will be recalled that I divided the social drama into four main phases : breach, crisis, operation of redressive mechanisms, and either reintegration of the social group or social recognition of irreparable schism. Implicit in the notion of reintegration is the concept of social equilibrium. This concept involves the view that a social system is made up of interrelated units, of persons and groups, whose interests are somehow maintained in balance ; and further, that when disturbance occurs, readjustments are made which have the effect of restoring the balance. But it is necessary to remember that after disturbance has occurred and readjustments have been made, there may have taken place profound modifications in the internal relations of the group. The new equilibrium is seldom a replica of the old. The interests of certain persons and groups may have gained at the expense of those of others. Certain relations between persons and groups may have increased in intensity while others may have diminished. Others again may have been completely ruptured while new relationships have come into being. A social system is in dynamic movement through space and time, in some way analogous to an organic system in that it exhibits growth and decay, in fact the process of metabolism. In one aspect, the social drama is a process which reveals realignments of social relations at critical points of structural maturation or decay ; in another, it may be regarded as a trial of strength between conflicting interests in which persons or groups try to manipulate to their own advantage the actually existing network of social relations, both structural and contingent, within the system. Thus the social drama may represent either the natural, inherent development of a given social system through space-time at a distinct phase, at a critical point of maturation, or the deliberate attempts by some of its members to accelerate or retard that development. It may be either an index or a vehicle of change. In most cases both aspects are present. Thus in Social Drama III, the crisis which followed the death of Kanyombu (I,F9) indicated that there had been a change in the internal residential structure of Mukanza Village, in that MALABU lineage had increased in membership and strength. At the same time, through Nyamu-kola (I,H10) and Nyakalusa, slave-wife of the senior elder of MALABU lineage, an attempt was made by that lineage to impair the claims of Kasonda, then the most prominent member of NYACHINTANG'A lineage, to succeed, by fastening on him a charge of sorcery. Kasonda's new role as a man of relative wealth and influence residing outside the village with Europeans was also expressed in the charge ; in the course of the drama he used this new role to rebut the accusations, to mobilize NYACHINTANG'A lineage, and to further his own interest in the succession.

In this social drama it may also be noted that the socio-spatial system formed by Mukanza Village was by no means the same system as that revealed in Social Drama I at the time of the death of Kahali Chandenda. Former members had gone, new members had come into it. The conflict between Sandombu and the rest was in abeyance ; a new cleavage existed between the formerly allied lineages of MALABU and NYACHINTANG'A. Old members had formed new and broken off old attachments. The basic principles governing residential affiliation remained,—matriliny, the unity of male matrilineal kin, virilocal marriage, the relations between genealogical generations, the unity of uterine siblings, etc. But the relations between persons brought into daily contact by these principles had altered. And in the course of time the status of genealogically linked persons had changed asymmetrically. Mukanza was now a headman and Nyamu-kola a headman's wife. Sandombu was no longer a rival claimant for office but Mukanza's junior, under his authority. Kasonda was now old enough to be a powerful claimant in future, and as the result of external factors, had increased his internal influence in the system. Sakazao was older and had a large following within the village. As between groups MALABU lineage had gained and NYACHINTANG'A lineage had lost membership, but not office and influence, within the village. Social Drama III gave expression and ratification to the new situation.

Social Drama V brings to light further changes within the system, which had been unobtrusively taking place over a number of years. It was a repetition in many respects of Social Drama II, the bewitching of Nyamwaha. Like Drama V, that had speedily resolved itself into a trial of strength between Sandombu and headman Mukanza Kabinda. But this time, in Drama V, a clearly discernible improvement in the standing of Sandombu within the system becomes visible. This may in part be due to the less serious nature of the charge laid against him by Mukanza—slander instead of sorcery. But the case was undoubtedly brought in order to emphasize the fact that Sakazao and not Sandombu had been nominated by Mukanza as his *mulopu* and successor. It was brought to signalize Sandombu's exclusion from the succession and to show that Kahali Farm was subordinate to Mukanza Village, and not the reverse. It was perhaps unfortunate from Mukanza's point of view that Sandombu should have been involved at that precise moment in a case in which he stood as the representative of the Mukanza group against their inveterate enemy, Anderson Mulumbi, and against the successor of the ancient foe of the Kawiku, Headman Chibwakata. Anderson Mulumbi, a farm head, a man of wealth, trader and tailor, had long been engaged in disputes with Mukanza people, and indeed with other Kawiku villages. Recently, he had accused some boys from Mukanza Village of having wounded his hunting dog and killed one of his goats. He had taken this case to Chief Kanongesha's court and judgment had been given against him. Kasonda was his principal foe, and economic rivalry was involved in their relationship, since both were tailors. Kasonda was delighted to see him in trouble because Chief Kanongesha had said that if Anderson was mixed up in any more local disputes he would order him out of the area. In this situation, therefore, Sandombu had the tacit support of the majority of Mukanza people, and it would have been difficult to penalize him severely in one situation and applaud him in another on the following day.

But apart from these considerations, Sandombu had in other respects improved his position in the years that intervened between Social Dramas II and V. He was now a farm head with a following. He had obtained work for many Mukanza men. He had been liberal in offering beer to the villagers and to many others in the vicinage. There were even some who, like Manyosa's husband Chikasa,[1] and his mother's sister's daughter's daughter Bibiana (I,H4) in Ikelenge Area (just on the point of divorce and mother of four children), would support his future claims to village headmanship. Even if he did not succeed in Mukanza Village, he might yet be headman of a large farm and resuscitate the title of Kahali.

It is this heightened importance of Sandombu that was responsible for the way the case was played down and kept within the village, for the small amount of the fine imposed, and for the fact that Kasonda kept in the background instead of openly giving Mukanza his support. A conciliatory tone was adopted towards Sandombu throughout, no attempt was made to retain his wife, and after the case was over it was joked about. Although Sandombu paid damages to Nyamukola he did not lose face thereby. In the altered climate of opinion, as he had just scored a victory over Chibwakata and Anderson Mulumbi, it was in Sandombu's interest to make a gesture of goodwill towards the village. On balance he had considerably improved his position after these two cases, and Mukanza's refusal to have anything to do with a case involving Sandombu had not added to the old man's popularity when Sandombu had been disputing with a major enemy of Mukanza Village.

Nevertheless, by the end of Social Drama V, there is reason to predict that Mukanza Village will split up along certain lines after the headman's death. Kasonda told me shortly before I left that whereas he had once thought of supporting Sakazao's claim to headmanship and remaining with the latter, he, Kasonda, had become unpopular with the people of MALABU lineage and they would continually quarrel with him. He would start a farm near a former site of Mukanza Village, about a mile from

---

[1] Manyosa supported her brother Kasonda, but her husband, Chikasa, was very friendly with Sandombu. These two, Manyosa and Chikasa, had married late in life, after each had reared families with previous spouses ; and they quarrelled incessantly over almost every possible issue.

PLATE IV

A SYMPTOM OF SOCIAL CONFLICT

Headman Mukanza chats with his wife Nyamukola during an interval in an *Ihamba* ritual. An apprentice-doctor from Kafumbu Village (see Social Drama VI) is applying a cupping-horn to her back by suction. This ritual, to remove the tooth of a punitive dead hunter from the patient's body by 'catching' it in the cupping-horn, immediately preceded the *Chihamba* ritual described in Chapter Ten. Nyamukola, principal patient in both rituals, occupied a social position under severe strain at this time. Note the forked branch with a piece of ant-hill at the base set up as a shrine to the hunter's spirit. Nyamukola sits on a duiker skin. Traces of pounded herbal medicine adhere to her skin.

the motor road, with Manyosa's (I,G13) children, with Chawutong'i (I,G12) and some of her children, and with Gideon (II,E1), at once his matrilateral and patrilateral cross-cousin, and his children. He himself had two wives and five children, so that he would have a fairly large following. Manyosa's husband might go and live with Sandombu but there was a strong possibility that Manyosa would divorce him and come and stay with Kasonda. Again, the husband might accompany his wife to Kasonda's farm.

Sakazao would be left with most of his lineage kin. Some members of both lineages might build at Sandombu's farm. Sandombu, however, told me that if Sakazao succeeded, many would leave him and live at Sandombu's farm, for Sakazao had a poor head for ' speaking cases ', was idle and without wealth, and no-one really respected him. Sakazao said to me that if he succeeded, the village would not break up, because unlike both Sandombu and Kasonda, he had never been accused of sorcery and no-one feared him in this respect, and because some of Mukanza's children belonged to MALABU lineage and others to the lineage of his kinsman Line's wife (I,H19). He thought that Kasonda, Manyosa and Chawutong'i would remain with him, and if they stayed their children would stay also.

Of these appraisals that of Kasonda's is perhaps the most realistic. Sakazao, for instance, cherished the illusion that Kasonda would remain with him, whereas I was aware of Kasonda's plans to move, perhaps even before the death of Mukanza. The main link between NYACHINTANG'A and MALABU lineages is the marriage between Mukanza and Nyamukola. Since they have already become genealogically so distant, once that link is snapped there will be little to hold them together. When Mukanza dies, Kasonda will become the senior male of CHINENG'A (I,E4) lineage, the numerically predominant segment of NYACHINTANG'A lineage. If he founds a farm most of its members will follow him and not Sandombu. Basically then the division will probably follow the lines of lineage segmentation. Sandombu's lineage of NYAKAPAKATA (I,E1), with Bibiana as its foremost female, will live separately from the other sub-lineage of NYACHINTANG'A lineage, that of CHINENG'A. MALABU lineage will probably remain in the site of the present Mukanza Village, which will become Sakazao Village.

N

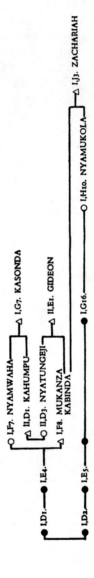

From beneath the manifold and transitory shifts and realignments of social relations from year to year in the village, we can
see the fundamental cleavages between maternal descent groups
emerge in the long run. Marriage and alternate generation alliance are means of delaying the final residential split between
lineages, but as the wedge of time drives deeper into their division,
so these lateral and supplementary linkages wear thin and break.

But at the same time this division into component lineages,
in another aspect, represents a division between genealogical
generations. Most of the leading members of NYACHINTANG'A
lineage belong to the senior adjacent generation (G) to the
leading members of MALABU lineage. Nyamuwang'a of MALABU
lineage belongs to the senior generation (G) but she lives with
Sandombu of her own generation, but of a different lineage-
segment. Chinema (I,G21), Sakazao's classificatory mother's
brother, also of MALABU lineage, who is working at Kitwe (a mining
township on the Rhodesian Copperbelt), has reported that
when he returns he will not live at Sakazao's village, for Sakazao
is his junior. Sandombu claims that Chinema will stay with
him. Mukanza's eldest son by Nyamukola, Zachariah (I,J3),
a member of MALABU lineage and sister's son of Sakazao, has
said that he will go with Kasonda, his cross-cousin, i.e. in his
own genealogical generation, reckoning through his father's side,
and in the alternate generation, through his mother's side.

Conflict between lineages and between adjacent genealogical
generations throws into high relief the role of alliance between
alternate genealogical generations as a means of integrating the
residential unit. In a sense the village of Mukanza was held
together by the grandparent-grandchild marriage of the headman
and Nyamukola. Tension between adjacent generations and
alliance between alternate generations were related to the unity
and continuity of the local group. Once the marriage between
the headman and his wife, the senior woman of the opposite
lineage, came to an end, lineage cleavage, which in this case
coincided with generation cleavage, would assert itself and irreparable breach between lineages would take place. In Chapter
Ten I will describe and analyse a major ritual which, to a sociologist, looked like a concerted attempt to overcome the widening
cleavages that were threatening to disrupt the unity of Mukanza
Village. In this ritual Nyamukola was the principal patient,

afflicted by the spirit of Nyamukang'a (I,E5), a daughter of Malabu ; Sandombu was the principal male organizer ; and Sakazao's senior wife was the principal female organizer. The ritual adepts were drawn from all the villages of the vicinage. But since this ritual appeared to have the additional social function of reconciling conflicts that had arisen between Mukanza Village and other villages with which it was connected by ties of kinship, affinity and spatial contiguity, the ritual cannot be discussed until a careful consideration of the sources of inter-village disputes has been made. In the next two chapters I present material indicating under what conditions fission of villages actually takes place, and what kinds of social grouping are involved.

CHAPTER VI

VILLAGE FISSION, SLAVERY AND SOCIAL CHANGE

BY 'village fission' I mean a situation in which a group or section within the total membership of a village detaches itself and builds a separate settlement. If a number of individuals leave a village and severally affiliate themselves to different headmen this is not fission. Similarly, if after the death of a headman or as the result of some disaster, a village breaks up completely and its members scatter in attachment to many different headmen, this is fragmentation, not fission. I define fission among the Ndembu as the division of a village community along lines of structural cleavage so that one section maintains continuity, usually symbolized by the retention of its name, with the original undivided village ; and the other section or sections, named after their leading elders, seek to establish themselves as independent villages. The lines of imminent fracture in Mukanza Village demarcated, as we have seen, three segments of a matrilineage, NYACHINTANG'A (I,D1) and MALABU (I,D2) lineages of equal span, and within NYACHINTANG'A lineage, NYAKAPAKATA (I,E1) and CHINENG'A lineages (I,E4), also of equal span. In the case of NYACHINTANG'A and MALABU lineages, genealogical distance from a common ancestress had led to their social differentiation as corporate units with certain independent social, economic and ritual functions. Breach of spatial relations of interdependence had been postponed by marital and alternate generation ties. Between NYAKAPAKATA and CHINENG'A lineages, the possibility of social severance had been accelerated by the ambitions of Sandombu, the leading elder of the former, and by social and economic changes brought about by the introduction of cash economy which facilitated the emergence of increasingly smaller settlements inhabited by ever narrower ranges of kin. But in both instances fission seemed about to take place dominantly along the lines of lineage cleavage. In many other villages for which I have records fission took place between segments of a local matrilineage. Nevertheless, fission does not always or even dominantly take place between segments of an equal order of segmentation. Very frequently the dissident group is a uterine sibling group, their children, and their mother, if she is still alive. The seceding section may not consist of matrilineal kin of the headman at all, but may be descendants of a female slave (*ndung'u*) of a village member. These, under the *pax britannica*, have experienced an improvement in status and wish to emancipate themselves in fact and in space from their former owners. Again, it may happen that a village is composite in membership, some of its inhabitants being matrilineally descended from a sister and some from a wife of the first headman. The matrilineal descendants of the wife may split off from those of the sister, and build separately. Or the sister's descendants may move. But in nearly all cases of fission the principle of maternal descent is crucial, and maternal kin almost always form the core of a new village.

Ndembu and Tallensi Social Organization

In order to bring out the essential character of Ndembu village fission it is instructive to compare briefly the main features of Ndembu and Tallensi social organization.[1]   Fortes writes :

Tale society is built up round the lineage system.   It is no exaggeration to say that every sociological problem presented by the Tallensi hinges on the lineage system.   It is the skeleton of their social structure, the bony framework which shapes their body politic ; it guides their economic life and moulds their ritual ideas and values.
[The Tale lineage is] a strictly unilineal, agnatic descent group, [and] eight to ten ascendant generations are usually reckoned between contemporary minimal lineages and the founding ancestor of the maximal lineage of which they are part (p. 31).
[All Tale lineages] are hierarchically organized between the limits of the minimum span, i.e. the minimal lineage, on the one hand, and the maximum span, i.e. the maximal lineage, on the other.   Thus every minimal lineage is a segment of a more inclusive lineage defined by reference to a common grandfather, and this, in turn, is a segment of a still wider lineage defined by reference to a common great-grandfather ; and so on, until the limit is reached—the maximal lineage, defined by reference to the remotest agnatic ancestor of the group. . . . Within a lineage of whatever span each grade of segmenta-

---

[1] Fortes, M., *The Dynamics of Clanship among the Tallensi* (1945), p. 30.

tion is functionally significant. Each segment has its focus of unity, and an index of its corporate identity, in the ancestor by reference to whom it is differentiated from other segments of the same order in the hierarchically organized set of lineages. Sacrifices to the shrine of this ancestor require the presence of representatives of every segment of the next lower order ; and this rule applies to all corporate action of a ceremonial or jural kind of any lineage. . . . A lineage of any span emerges in any of its activities as a system of aliquot parts, not as a mere collection of individuals of common ancestry (p. 31).

Tallensi do not live in discrete compact villages but in homesteads, containing on average some 12 to 14 people, scattered apparently indiscriminately, some close together, others farther apart, over the country, in irregular blocks which make up ' settlements '. There is a distinct though sometimes narrow territorial separation between the outermost homesteads of one settlement and those of another. According to Professor Fortes,

stability and continuity are essential characteristics of a settlement. They are implied in the native concept of a *teng'* (settlement) as both a definite locality and a fixed community. The ancient settlements have attained a very high degree of stability and continuity. . . . Precise local orientation is essential in the economic activities and social relationships of the Tallensi (p. 157).

' A settlement is a miniature of the whole society, and reveals all the basic principles of the social structure ' (p. 154). A settlement is a locality defined in relation to a corporate unit of social structure, a lineage, clan, or inter-connected group of clans.

Tale society, then, is built up round the hierarchically organized lineage system, and lineages of considerable depth are anchored to specific localities. Each segment of a single lineage of wide span

tends to form a coherent residential cluster, situated on land which has been owned by its members for several generations, and in close proximity to the graves of their ancestors. The lineage as a whole tends to form a local aggregate, though a somewhat looser one than any of its segments (p. 197).

According to Professor Fortes, ' neighbourhood ties are *ipso facto* lineage ties, and therefore economic, religious, jural and moral ties' (p. 211). Lineage proximity is correlated with local proximity.

This intense local fixation of the lineage is no doubt congruent with 'the rigorous precision with which its members fall into a set of hierarchically articulated segments, of homologous form but all exactly differentiated both genealogically and functionally' (p. 198).

Among Ndembu there is no close correlation between lineal and local ties. Local stability and continuity is typical of Tale, and spatial mobility is typical of Ndembu residential organization. Lineages are anchored to specific tracts of land among the Tallensi, and have deep genealogies ; and the fission of one homestead results in no more than the establishment of an adjacent homestead. Among Ndembu an articulated lineage has little depth (see Tables XIII, XIV and XV, p. 83), and its effective structure is confined within a single village. Fission is often accompanied by violent internecine conflict of the kind described in Chapters Four and Five, and results in the seceding group putting many miles between itself and the parent village. An Ndembu vicinage, which may perhaps be compared with a Tale 'settlement', is not a locality defined in relation to a corporate unit of social structure, 'a lineage, clan, or interconnected group of clans', but is extremely heterogeneous in character, so that in certain vicinages none of the component villages may be matrilineally interlinked. Certain villages, often dispersed throughout the entire Ndembu region, may claim relationship through putative maternal descent, but they do not trace descent to a named common ancestress and cannot place one another in a hierarchically organized maximal lineage with functionally significant grades of segmentation. Such a 'lineage' is not 'a system of aliquot parts', but 'a mere collection of [small groups of] individuals of common ancestry'.

The contrast between Tale and Ndembu lineage organization is strikingly displayed in the ancestor cult. Among the Tallensi ancestors have permanent shrines and graves, which are attached to specific localities, which are usually surrounded by the residential and farm land held by a maximal lineage, and which therefore serve as foci of the unity of the lineage as a whole and of its segments : hence, as Professor Fortes succinctly expresses it, ' the ancestor cult is the calculus of the lineage system.' But among the Ndembu, ancestor shrines consist of quickset *muyombu* saplings, planted to placate the spirits of deceased village members, who are still remembered as living persons by their kin. These spirits must be placated because they have returned to afflict individual relatives with misfortunes, as the result of neglect 'to mention their names' and pour them out beer when praying to other spirits, or because conflict has arisen between village members. Such shrines are abandoned when the village moves to a new site and it is very likely that new *muyombu* saplings will never be planted for the same spirits again. Remote ancestors are seldom worshipped except in a few important and infrequent rituals, such as the boys' circumcision ritual (*Mukanda*) or the great ritual of *Chihamba*; and in both these rituals the unity of all Ndembu, even of all Lunda, is emphasized rather than the unity of the particular village which sponsors the ritual. Graves are never used as shrines by Ndembu and are feared and avoided rather than tended and used as sites of sacrifice. For the Tallensi the ancestor cult is related to the land, to agriculture, and to permanent residence on the land of well-defined corporate lineages. For Ndembu, the ancestor cult is associated with the bush, its dangers and blessings, with the transience of settlement, with the hazards of life, and with the mobile human group itself rather than its specific habitation. It has been suggested in earlier chapters that the high mobility of Ndembu, and the small size of settlements and their frangible character, are congruent with the high value set on hunting, not only as a means of providing an appetizing and nourishing food, but also as an index of masculinity and as a historically validated means of acquiring prestige. The size and mobility of settlements seem to be more closely related to the local availability of game and sylvan resources than to the productivity of the soil.

Ndembu supernatural beliefs regarding the dead work towards the promotion of mobility rather than towards the creation of deep attachments to the sites where dead ancestors lie buried. In the past, when a person died, he or she was buried under the floor of the hut, and the village changed its site for fear of the ghost. Beliefs regarding the dead among Ndembu, then, accelerated the already high rate of mobility. On the other hand, the ancestor cult of the Tallensi tends to emphasize and validate the intense attachment of lineages to localities. Worship of the patrilineal ancestors and worship of the Earth are the deepest values of Tale religion. Although in some respects they are opposed, since the ancestor cult tends to emphasize the divisions between lineage and clan segments while the Earth cult tends to stress the common interests of the widest Tale community, the two cults are at the same time complementary, since the cultivations of individuals and of particular lineages are, as Professor Fortes puts it, ' but parcels of land cut from the limitless earth '. Tallensi are attached to the soil and, given the existence of patriliny as their dominant principle of social organization, local and lineal groupings tend to coincide, and to be interlinked within a common framework of overlapping clanship and lineage ties that embrace the entire socio-geographic region of Taleland. Ndembu move over the soil and across the bush in search of game, and given matriliny as their dominant mode of social organization, lineal kin tend to scatter across the region, local lineages tend to be small and unstable, and no deep interlocking local lineages and clans develop. Tale ritual expresses the unity of corporate groups from the unity of minor matrilineages to the unity of all the Tallensi, while in the great all-inclusive rituals the basic units in the composition of ritual assemblies are patrilineages. In Ndembu ritual, as we shall see, the basic ritual units are cult associations that cross-cut the relatively transient local and lineal affiliations. The dominant links between participants in Tale ritual are links of commonness and corporate identity ; in Ndembu ritual they are links of likeness and temporary association, lateral rather than lineal.

With this general background of comparison in mind, let us now consider the different modes of fission in the residential structure of these two societies. Among Tale fission does not represent a complete break between the groups involved. Rather, it represents a process of regular branching-off by means of which the formation of new local units advances and projects the social structure through time. The new group does not emancipate itself from the lineage ; it becomes a branch of that lineage. A cleavage occurs between two hitherto nascent segments of a minor lineage inhabiting one homestead ; and while this may give rise to the establishment of a new homestead, ties of jural and ritual co-operation between the two groups prevent radical breach and contain the cleavage within the framework of the maximal lineage.

But among Ndembu, the cleavage of a village, whether or not along lineage lines, results in the formation of a completely new unit. A hiatus is made in the genealogical structure of the original matrilineage in such a way that, after the passage of a single generation, no member of either village distinctly recalls the precise point of fission. After two or three generations all that is left is a vague sense of common maternal descent. Yet it often happens that while the name of the common ancestress and the relationship of the founding ancestor of the new village to members of the old village are forgotten, members of both groups continue to apply to one another kinship terms according to the nomenclature which expresses separation or equivalence in their genealogical generations. Thus the present Rhodesian Chief Kanongesha Ndembi calls headman Nyaluhana his 'older brother' (*yaya*), headman Nswanakudya his 'older brother', headman Shika his 'younger brother' (*mwanyika*), and headman Kajing'a his 'mother's brother' (*mandumi*), although the exact lineal relationship between these men can no longer be traced and all inhabit different villages widely separated in space. The facts of matrilineal kinship and the relevant genealogical generation category are recognized, but a more precise identification cannot be made. This system of nomenclature must be distinguished from perpetual kinship since the terms are applied between individuals and do not express the relationship between political positions in the social structure.

The generation principle governs the authority and marital structure of a settlement. It is important for members of a society which possesses a high rate of individual mobility, in which persons are frequently changing their village affiliation, to know in what relation they stand *vis-à-vis* the headman of a new village in terms of genealogical generation. Once this relationship has been established a new member of a village knows immediately whom to respect and from whom to levy respect, he knows which women he can marry and which he may not, he knows in what arc of the village circle he may build his new hut, and so forth. The stress laid by Ndembu on genealogical generation as a principle of local organization and as a means of facilitating inter-village mobility, may be regarded as an index of the brittleness of lineage structure. It may also be regarded as a means of organizing local units whose membership contains a high proportion of seminal children of the male matrilineal core, as well as a number of cognatic kin and slaves. In Chapter Eight I will discuss conflicts that arise in villages on the basis of their markedly bilateral composition, and the role of genealogical generation organization as a mechanism for containing such conflicts within bounds.

The point I wish to stress in this chapter is that, although at the level of lineage organization structural amnesia with regard to the precise genealogical links between villages separated by fission of a local lineage speedily occurs, memory is retained of common maternal descent and of the affiliation by genealogical generation between the detached groups. Separation has been effected between two sub-groups within one system of social relations, that of the village, but several sets of ties which formerly interlinked these groups as members of a single community continue to operate between them. Each group is now a unit within a wider system of social relations, and within that wider system each maintains with the other ties of a more durable nature than merely those of joint membership of a chiefdom, spatial propinquity, or affinity. After the feelings of animosity associated with the initial breach have died down, each has a special claim on the hospitality of the other, the members of both exchange long visits, and each may serve in turn as the base of the other's hunting expeditions. It is thought appropriate if cross-cousin and grandparent-grandchild (cf. pages 80, 246) marriage takes place between them.[1] It is an advantage to members of a highly mobile society to be able to obtain hospitality from distant matrilineal kin in remote areas through which they may wish to pass on their travels. Fission extends the geographical range of each village's ties of durable kinship, and each component village in a vicinage, through the frequent fission of villages, is interlinked by ties of common maternal descent with many villages in other vicinages. Among the Ndembu, therefore, the lineage principle operates to mesh together in a single system distant and discrete villages and vicinages

---

[1] See, for example, Appendix III for marriages between Nsang'anyi Village and its offshoots.

and to permit of a wide range of individual mobility. Among the Tallensi, the lineage principle operates to fix and consolidate lineal kin in specific compact blocks of land.

But it must not be thought that Ndembu consciously and purposefully utilize the fission and dispersal of villages to promote the closer cohesion of the wider social system, the tribe or tribal section. Independently of their wishes in the matter it may well be that centrifugal tendencies dependent on their ecological system constantly break up villages and change the composition of vicinages. It is more likely that the cohesion of the wider system is maintained *despite* these tendencies, and that Ndembu, in fact, make a virtue of necessity. Fission is usually regarded by the people themselves as something deplorable and they take every possible measure to avert it. In their conscious behaviour and judgments Ndembu act and speak as though the break-up of a village or its departure from a vicinage was a calamity, and the initiators of fission are always condemned, not only by members of the village from which they led away a section but by members of other villages in the vicinage. Again, if one asks the headman of a dissident settlement why he broke away from the original village, he will most likely answer that it was an unfortunate necessity. It was unfortunate that the village should have split, he will say, but the headman or one of his close relatives was a quarrelsome person or a sorcerer, or the headman failed to be impartial in his judgments, favouring his own primary kin in disputes with the seceding group, and so forth. Both groups, those who go and those who remain, will, in fact, stress the value of village stability and continuity, the original group emphasizing the wickedness or folly of the secessionists, and the latter the exceptional circumstances which compelled them to leave.

But after a lapse of time, and especially after the deaths of the leading disputants, the two villages tend to re-establish friendly relations in the way described above. The conflict has been absorbed by the wider social system, and what was originally a division between sections of its membership is gradually filled up by new sets of ties which reunite them at a different level of organization. Ultimately, a realistic attitude towards fission may be taken, and the members of the original group may admit that the headman of the seceding group was an elder with many close kin and had little chance of succeeding to office in an established village. How this process operates may best be illustrated by a social drama. The first of these is based on accounts given to me by members of all three of the groups involved. These groups are Mukanza Village and its offshoots Kafumbu and Yimbwendi Villages. I use material from Mukanza once more on account of its plentiful detail, because it provides an interesting comparison with the situations analysed in the two previous chapters, and because it illustrates two major types of village fission. I hope also that readers have begun to be acquainted with some of its inhabitants.

SOCIAL DRAMA VI

Yimbwendi and Kafumbu Secede from Mukanza
(compiled from informants)

In the period 1924–28 Mukanza Village passed through a crisis which almost resulted in its disintegration. At that time there were three major factions in the village. The cleavage between NYACHINTANG'A and MALABU lineages was then only incipient, and both these lineages were united as NYACHIPENDI (I,C2) lineage and as such were opposed to NYACHULA lineage (I,D3, see Appendix I), of the same genealogical depth and of equivalent span The common ancestress of all three lineages was Chipendipendi (I, A1), mother's mother of Kabonzu(I,C1), the founder of the village, but two intervening ancestresses between Chipendipendi and Nyachula had become forgotten. NYACHULA lineage had returned to Mukanza Village after many years' residence in Chibwika area. In the village also was a large group of hereditary slaves of Kahali Webala (I,E3), descended from a woman, Mpeza (I,F1), who had many daughters by two brothers of NYACHINTANG'A lineage. The eldest daughter was married to her cross-cousin Kafumbu (I,G1), also a slave belonging to NYACHINTANG'A lineage. Another daughter was married to Yimbwendi (I,F11), senior elder of NYACHULA lineage.

The village was a large one but full of constant bickering. One of the main reasons for this state of tension as given me by the present inhabitants of Mukanza, was that at this time there was no recognized headman. Kahali Chandenda (I,F5) had not yet settled permanently in Mukanza but spent his time alternating between his kin in Ikelenge Area and Mukanza Village. Mukanza Kabinda (I,F8) had inherited the name 'Mukanza' from his deceased elder brother Mukanza

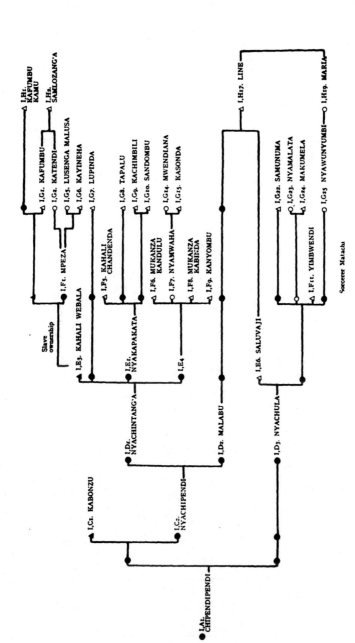

Sorcerer Matachi

Kandulu (I,F6) as an indication to all that he hoped to succeed to the headmanship. Yimbwendi (I,F11) and Kafumbu (I,G1) formed an alliance with their respective followings, and Yimbwendi strongly urged his own claims to office. When Kandulu died in 1919, Kafumbu had been suspected of killing him by shooting his *ilomba*, in the same way as Sandombu had later been suspected of shooting Kahali Chandenda's *ilomba* (see Social Drama I, p. 95). Kasonda told me that Kafumbu had called in a sorcerer from Angola, named Mapachi, to assist him in this deed, and that Mukanza Kabinda had consulted a ' great diviner ' with a divining-basket who had named Kafumbu as the sorcerer. I suspect that this tale is a myth retrospectively attributing evil qualities to Kafumbu in view of his subsequent defection from Mukanza Village. Although he was a slave (*ndung'u*), Kafumbu was a powerful man in Mukanza Village. He was a famous hunter, a skilled orator, and had a large following in the children of Mpeza (I,F1). He claimed that slavery (*wudung'u*) had been abolished by the European Administration and that Kahali Chandenda and Mukanza Kabinda no longer had any rights over the services and allegiance of their former slaves. He was constantly urging Yimbwendi (I,F11), whose two sisters had many adult children, to succeed to the headmanship. According to Mukanza Kabinda he knew that if Yimbwendi formally succeeded Mukanza Kandulu, the people of NYACHINTANG'A and MALABU lineages would leave the village and found a new settlement, and the group of slaves would be rid of their masters.

In NYACHINTANG'A lineage at this period there were a number of adult men who, on the whole, supported the claims of Kahali Chandenda (I,F5) and desired his permanent return to the village. These included the famous hunter Lupinda (I,G7), whose spirit Sandombu was later alleged to have invoked to bewitch Nyamwaha ; Tapalu (I,G8), later to become a wealthy African trader in Livingstone ; and Kachambili (I,G9), Sandombu's brother who fled to Broken Hill in 1928 to escape from the sorcery of Sandombu, according to some accounts, after a quarrel, and who has remained there ever since. Lupinda did not want to succeed, for he preferred the wild unanchored life of a hunter. In addition, he was feared as a sorcerer by the villagers.

In 1928 the simmering tensions in the village were brought to a head when Kahali Chandenda decided to take up permanent residence in Mukanza Village. This decision coincided with the decision of a special gathering of village elders to change the site of the village to the southern edge of the Kawiku Plain where the hunters of the village would be nearer to their major hunting ground. When Kahali announced his intention, Yimbwendi said that he could no longer remain in Mukanza Village as it was ' full of troubles ', ' people were not living well together', and so on. (In fact the change of site gave him a good opportunity to start a village of his own.) He was now, he said, a man with many children and sisters' children. He was an important elder (*mukulumpi*). He had been the headman of a settlement before coming to Mukanza. The time had come to divide off (*ku-baluka*). He pointed to the fact that Kanyombu, younger brother of Mukanza, had married his (Yimbwendi's) own sister's daughter Nyamalata (I,G23), who was Kanyombu's classificatory sister's daughter, without performing the ritual to cleanse an incestuous union (*kudisola*), as an indication that the lineages of NYACHINTANG'A and NYACHULA were no longer closely related.

He then asked Kafumbu to come with him as they had both married into the one lineage, that of MPEZA (I,F1). Kafumbu agreed and said that he was weary of the quarrelling in Mukanza Village. Kanyombu and Lupinda became very angry at this and said that, according to Lunda custom, Kafumbu and Mpeza's descendants belonged to them and had no right to dispose of their own future. Kafumbu said that a new law introduced by the British South Africa Company had ' killed ' the old custom and slavery had ceased to be. After some hot exchanges, fighting broke out in the village in the course of which Kachambili (I,G9) and Yimbwendi's uterine nephew Samunuma (I,G22) were badly beaten up. Yimbwendi and Kafumbu declared that the fight had clearly demonstrated that there could be no peace between the followers of Kahali and Mukanza, and the rest, and led their followers away to the far side of the Kakula river about seven miles from Mukanza Village, and nearer to the Boma. Possibly Kafumbu, who had chosen this site, thought he would be safer near the Boma if the Mukanza people tried to begin a feud.

Not all the followers of Yimbwendi and Kafumbu accompanied them. Nyawunyumbi (I,G25), uterine niece of Yimbwendi, remained at Mukanza Village, for the reason, as she told me, that Yimbwendi was a sorcerer, ' with a bad liver ', and she had three daughters and a son whom she wished to protect from sorcery. Mpeza's son, Kayineha (I,G6), also remained. He was married to Kasonda's sister Mwendiana (I,G14), daughter of Nyamwaha (I,F7), was personally friendly with Mukanza Kabinda, and in fact played a major part in bringing the fighting to an end. Nyamalata (I,G23) remained with her husband Kanyombu (I,F9). Line (I,H17), on the other hand, went with Kafumbu, although he belonged to MALABU, because he was the cross-cousin of Yimbwendi, and one of Kafumbu's sons was his personal friend. Later he married Nyawunyumbi's daughter (I,H19) and returned with her to Mukanza. Thus, although three major groups were clearly involved in the cleavage, several individuals

o

deserted from their own kinship factions and changed their allegiance. Such individuals, although acting apparently in accordance with their personal desires and interests, have an important role in reuniting the initially hostile factions at a later date. Each assumes an intercalary role in a wider social system, the units of which are villages and vicinages.

After the departure of Yimbwendi and Kafumbu the District Commissioner of that period wanted to combine Mukanza Village with Chibwakata and Nswanakudya Villages since the village had lost more than half its population. But an appeal was sent by Kahali (I,F5) to Ikelenge Area, to Sandombu and others living there to return and save the independence of the village. A number of them, including Sandombu, and their wives returned and the dreaded amalgamation was avoided.

In 1929, after one year, Kafumbu and Yimbwendi fell out over the headmanship of the new village ; there was a fight between their followers, and Yimbwendi left Kafumbu with his children and sisters' children to settle in Chief Chibwika's area, far to the south of the District on the edge of Mbwela country, where Kabonzu had once made a village about a century before, and where Yimbwendi had once had his own village, although in a different vicinage. When he died a few years ago his village split up once more after a quarrel between Samunuma (I,G22), son of his oldest sister, and Makumela (I,G24), son of a younger sister. Makumela, who had been nominated *mulopu* or heir by Yimbwendi, was a younger man than Samunuma, who hived off and made a farm of his own with his children and sisters' children. When Kafumbu died, his deceased sister's son (I,H1) claimed the headmanship but he was rejected by the overwhelming majority of villagers who chose Kafumbu's son, Samlozang'a (I,H2), as headman. Samlozang'a was the senior elder of MPEZA lineage to which most of the villagers belonged ; he had another claim in that he had 13 children, some of them adults. Samlozang'a was supported by Mukanza himself, by this time reconciled with the village through his friend Kayineha (I,G6). Kayineha, although mother's uterine brother of Samlozang'a (I,H2), did not succeed because he was working at the Copperbelt when Kafumbu died. Kafumbu's uterine nephew (I,H1) made a farm about half a mile from Kafumbu Village where he lives alone with his wives and children. His farm is called derisively by Mukanza and Kafumbu people ' Kafumbu Kamu ', meaning, ' the solitary Kafumbu ', while Samlozang'a's village is called ' Kafumbu Kevulu ', ' Kafumbu of many people '.

Commentary and Analysis

When a long-established village splits, it often happens that the seceding sections are highly unstable. They lack long-established bonds of discrete unity and they often break into small settlements of uterine siblings and their families, each under the leadership of the oldest brother. Once the strong bonds which hold together the members of a traditional village have been broken, the powerful individualism of the Ndembu ethos, nurtured by the self-reliant life of the hunter, asserts itself for a time and the dissident group breaks up into its basic units, the remnants of what were once matricentric families. But the original village slowly and painfully builds up its membership again. Ndembu take great pride in belonging to a village with a famous historical name, and although such villages are, like others, liable to fission, it is extremely rare for them to perish utterly. Villages founded by the twelve headmen who, according to tradition, originally accompanied Kanongesha, are still in existence, most of them large and thriving, as indeed are villages founded by the early chiefs for their close relatives. The ancient Kawiku villages too, such as Nsang'anyi, Mukanza, Kasai and Nyachiu, have persisted for many years in spite of frequent fission. The headmen of such villages enjoy greater respect than the headmen of newly-formed villages and farms, and if there is a gathering of local headmen at a ritual or at the hearing of a case they are always given beer or food before the newer headmen.

A few words must be said about the way in which this irreparable breach of intra-village relations has been recognized by the parties concerned and how new social relations have been established between the villages. The people of Mukanza Village say that both Yimbwendi and Kafumbu were sorcerers, and every death that subsequently occurred in their villages was laid at their door as proof of this statement. Kafumbu's slave status, and that of the MPEZA lineage is also mentioned, and blame is attributed to the Europeans who caused slavery to be abolished, thus allowing upstarts like Kafumbu to break away from their rightful owners (*ankaka*). They also allege that Yimbwendi was a quarrelsome man, not the kind to inspire respect or confidence in his judgment. Yimbwendi and

Kafumbu people, on the other hand, assert that Mukanza Village contained many sorcerers and witches, mentioning Kahali, Lupinda, Nyamuwang'a and Sandombu in this connection. Mukanza Kabinda was never considered a devotee of the black art, even by his enemies, but the dissident group say that at the time of the split he was a poor speaker in village lawsuits and was not sufficiently firm in his decisions to give a village good guidance. Kahali Chandenda was not acceptable to them as headman on account of his roaming propensities (*ku-kimboka*, ' to move about from one place to another '), his irritability, and his suspected sorcery.

But although there appears to have taken place a complete rupture of social relations between the leading actors in this social drama, Mukanza Kabinda, Kanyombu, Kafumbu and Yimbwendi, this did not occur between their several groups of followers, many of whom were interlinked by complex ties of kinship and affinity. Thus Sakazao's senior wife, Nyaluwema (I,G4), was the youngest daughter of Mpeza (I,F1) by Chisela Malwa (I,F2), brother of the fourth headman, and she was also sister of Kafumbu's wife Katendi (I,G2), so that Sakazao, according to Ndembu kinship nomenclature, called Kafumbu ' older brother ' (*yaya*). Chinema (I,G21), at that time headman of the village in Ikelenge Area abandoned by Kahali Chandenda, was the husband of Nyaluwema's and Katendi's other sister by the same father, Kawila (I,G3), and, it will be remembered, Yimbwendi was the husband of their other sister, Luseng'a Mulusa (I,G5), by a different father.

Eventually the children of all these men, who called one another ' older and younger brother', would form the residential core of the new unit founded by Kafumbu. This is probably the reason why Sakazao took no part in the fight which led to the secession of Kafumbu and Yimbwendi from Mukanza. Kayineha (I,G6) of the MPEZA lineage was, it will be recalled, married to Mukanza's sister's daughter, and was Mukanza's close friend, in spite of being his classificatory son-in-law (*muku*, a term employed not only by a woman's father, but also by her mother's brother, towards her husband). It is not frequently enough stressed by anthropologists that village kin, whatever their genealogical relationship, tend to develop new relationships of friendship or hostility based on their constant interaction and on temperamental affinity or animosity, which in the regular flow

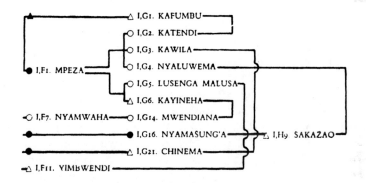

I,G1. KAFUMBU
I,G2. KATENDI
I,G3. KAWILA
I,F1. MPEZA
I,G4. NYALUWEMA
I,G5. LUSENGA MALUSA
I,G6. KAYINEHA
I,F7. NYAMWAHA
I,G14. MWENDIANA
I,G16. NYAMASUNG'A
I,H9 SAKAZAO
I,G21. CHINEMA
I,F11. YIMBWENDI

of the social process give rise to behaviour which cancels out in many situations the institutionalized behaviour prescribed by kinship rules.   Thus Mukanza and Kayineha should have participated in a relationship which formally enjoined the utmost respect on the latter in his dealings with the former, and gave the former peremptory authority over the latter.   But in practice the two men were friends, visiting Angola together, where they obtained a new variety of cassava which gave rich yields and which they introduced into Mwinilunga.   They slept side by side in temporary camps when custom decreed that they should never occupy the same dwelling.   In this case the fact that Mukanza and Kayineha were more or less contemporaries, and were brought up as adolescents in the same village, probably helped to mitigate the rigours of genealogical and affinal regulations.   Kayineha did not leave Mukanza with the others but remained until the death of his wife several years later.   He finally departed from Mukanza on the best of terms, and his friendship with that village probably had much to do with the re-animation of ties between the two settlements.   Line (I,H17), on the other hand, went with Kafumbu and Yimbwendi and eventually married the daughter of Nyawunyumbi (I,G25), Yimbwendi's sister, a woman called Maria (I,H19) with whom he eventually returned to Mukanza.   Nyawunyumbi [1] has remained in Mukanza Village, and after a few years married the headman of a nearby village, Mbimbi, son of a male member of MALABU lineage in Mukanza and her classificatory cross-cousin. The children of Nyawunyumbi played an important role in inter-linking the various sections within Mukanza Village, as well as in the re-establishment of relations with Yimbwendi's new village.   In addition to the daughter Maria (I,H19) who married Line of MALABU lineage, her oldest daughter, Seliya (I,H18), married Mukanza himself, of NYACHINTANG'A lineage ; and her son Kenson (I,H20) was brought up in Mukanza Village where he shared a bachelor hut with Pearson (I,J5), son of Nyatioli and sister's son of Sakazao of MALABU lineage, and with Daudson (I,H7), son of Manyosa of NYACHINTANG'A lineage.   Kenson is now affianced to his classificatory cross-cousin Mwendiana (II,F1), daughter of Kasonda of MALABU lineage.   In 1953 he

---

[1] Cf. p. 181.

paid several visits to Yimbwendi village to buy meat from the hunters there for resale in the vicinage of Mukanza. Mukanza and Kafumbu people regularly attended the others' rituals; but Yimbwendi people, although sometimes notified of such events as the funerals of important members of these two villages, never attended, and vice versa. I have heard Mukanza women wailing in the traditional fashion when news was brought to them of the death of an elder in Yimbwendi Village, but no representative was sent to the funeral ritual. On the other hand, when Pearson of Mukanza Village was killed in a motor accident in 1954, many people came from Kafumbu Village for the interment and mourning rituals. Again, I have known large parties of Mukanza people to go to Kafumbu, in the vicinage of which Headman Nyaluhana is the principal village headman (*mwenimbu*), when Kafumbu boys were initiated at the boys' circumcision ritual at Nyaluhana, and when a Kafumbu girl's puberty ritual was celebrated. I also attended the *Chihamba* ritual in 1954 at which a final reconciliation of the two villages tacitly took place, and at which I, an honorary member of Mukanza Village, was given the adept-name of *Samlozang'a Ndumba*, also possessed by the present headman of Kafumbu. The possession by two persons of the same name makes them *majinda*, ' namesakes ', a mutual relationship of mild joking and mutual assistance with goods and services.

In conclusion, therefore, it might be said that after the fission of Mukanza Village, new relations of cordiality, expressed in the maintenance and resumption of connubial and ritual ties, were formed between Mukanza and Kafumbu, each of which became points of contact between two discrete vicinages. But, on the other hand, while there has been a marked reduction of open animosity between Mukanza Village and Yimbwendi, the great spatial distance set between them fully reflects the continuing tension in their reciprocal relationship, and is perhaps a precaution against actual conflict.

Slavery and Social Change

For the purposes of this analysis, Social Drama VI may be said to have begun with the decision to change the site of the village, an event which may precipitate breaches of regular social relations which have been formed in a particular place. This decision coincided with the permanent return of Kahali Chandenda to the village as headman, an event which profoundly modified the internal relations of its members and precipitated a crisis. Yimbwendi and Kafumbu refused to accept Kahali as headman. For Yimbwendi had come to Mukanza Village with a large following about ten years before these events, and he had hoped perhaps to succeed himself; while Kafumbu wished to become independent of his traditional masters, the members of NYACHINTANG'A lineage. Redressive machinery was brought into action, in the form of a special meeting of the village's leading men. But the aims of the leaders of the different groups were divergent. Yimbwendi and Kafumbu wished to resolve the crisis by breaking away from Mukanza Village, i.e. by irreparable breach of intra-village relations. Kahali, Mukanza Kabinda, Kanyombu, and Lupinda, the senior men of NYACHINTANG'A lineage, wanted to retain the lineages of NYACHULA and MPEZA in the village. If Yimbwendi had confined himself to arguing a case for the secession of his own following there might have been no quarrel, at least no overt violence, especially since he and his kin had only been in Mukanza a short time. But when he openly urged Kafumbu to go with him, and when Kafumbu agreed to go, mentioning the discordant state of Mukanza Village, they touched off anger which culminated in fighting. For at this point one of the basic norms of the traditional social system was threatened, that which governed the relations between master and slave. It was threatened not so much by the demands and pretensions of individuals, but by major currents of social change set in train by British occupation and legislation. Kafumbu, like people everywhere and at all times, was merely utilizing new laws and norms to his personal advantage. Twenty years earlier he could not have made such a bid for independence. In the past runaway slaves were hunted by all free Ndembu, and if captured were returned to their owners who punished them severely. It was in the interest of all Ndembu to catch escaped slaves, for if they did not do so the system of slave-ownership would break down. But slavery had been speedily abolished under British Government and no-one dared to take action against slaves who had emancipated themselves by flight.

What were the main features of slavery among Ndembu

before British occupation ? Village slavery was distinguished from commercial slavery. Village slaves were paid as fines to terminate blood feuds, to settle debts, to compensate for homicide, to pay a chief or senior headman whose poison-oracle had cleared a person accused of sorcery, and to discharge fines for a number of other offences. The principal mechanisms through which payments of slaves were made were :—a chief's court ; a council of elders or *mahaku* ; direct negotiation between the parties involved in a dispute ; or the invocation by the wronged party of some famous warrior such as Chipeng'e who defeated the Chokwe and Lwena slave raiders, to press a claim against a transgressor. The persons paid as slaves were usually young children. Often they were already of slave status ; but if a man had to pay a relative, his choice usually fell on his own sister's child. Only as a last resort would a man pay a junior sibling and in custom he had no rights over the disposal of his own children in this manner. But in practice a man would resist the demands of a brother-in-law who wanted to pay his children, the latter's sister's children, as compensation for debt or homicide. For example, the mother's brother of one of my informants went to my informant's father about thirty years ago in Angola and tried to take his daughter to pay her as compensation for a large debt of long-standing. But my informant's father became very angry and told his brother-in-law to remove himself from the village forthwith, saying, ' If you take one of my children, one day, perhaps soon, we shall have a fight.' His brother-in-law replied, ' You have no cause to fight me. Are not these my sister's children ? I can do as I like with them.' The father retorted, ' No, they are my children. If you have got into debt because you love adultery and have had to pay many fines, perhaps you can pay your own children.' His brother-in-law then said : ' You are a bad brother-in-law (*ishaku*). You have no right to keep your children from me.' But he was afraid to take the girl, and went away.

In an egalitarian society like that of the Ndembu, slaves were not markedly exploited, and in fact were regarded more as relatives than chattels. If the slave was young and his or her master an elderly person, slave and owner initially stood to one another in the fictitious relationship of grandchild-grandfather. The term *nkaka* in Lunda means both ' grandparent ' and ' owner '.

This relationship provided a point of departure from which the slave could be assimilated into the kinship structure of the village. The owner's sister's son became his ' mother's brother ', the owner's son his ' father ', and so forth. Female slaves were often taken as concubines by their owners and a new pattern of kinship terms with corresponding rights and obligations developed from this relationship. The children of female slaves by free Ndembu remained in their slave status, the children of male slaves by free mothers—in the case of such marriages the slave husband had to pay bride-wealth—were regarded as free Ndembu and could go where they pleased. In other words, status was inherited matrilineally. Slaves were inherited in the same way as chattels, passing to the nearest matrilineal kinsman of the deceased. Slave widows, but not the widows of free Ndembu, could be inherited by the brothers of their dead husbands. Sister's sons also might inherit the slave widows of their uterine uncles. In the course of time, as in Mukanza Village, one finds in effect a large slave-lineage, like that of MPEZA, side by side with and owned by a free lineage. Often, indeed, the slave-lineage may be the larger, since most of its members may marry within the village while the virilocal marriage of female members of the free lineage may reduce its effective membership within the village. I have been told of powerful slave-lineages which, like cuckoos in the nest, ultimately ousted free lineages from the headmanship of villages. Perhaps Kafumbu had cherished hopes of doing likewise in Mukanza Village.

Slaves had to work in the gardens of their owners, even, in the case of male slaves, after they had married, an act that normally betokens among free Ndembu the assumption of adult status and economic independence. If they became hunters they had to give the whole of their kill, with the exception of the sacred portions reserved for the hunter, to their owners. If the owner of a female slave did not wish to take her as his concubine he received bride-wealth for her from any man who wished to marry her, and her children belonged to him and to his heirs.

A slave could, however, purchase his independence and that of his relatives. I have recorded several examples of this, which suggest that slaves were entitled to accumulate property of their own. I give one case here by way of illustration.

The father of Kasonda of Mukanza Village, a man named

Kahumpu (II,D1), was an elder of Shika Village, and his wife Nyamwaha (I,F7) of Mukanza Village was living with him viri-locally. One day, he caught his wife *in delicto flagrante* with a man called Kalubinji, classificatory brother of the headman of Kasai Village, one of the ancient Kawiku settlements. Kahumpu attacked Kalubinji and killed him with an axe. He then ran off and hid himself in the bush. News was brought to Headman Kasai of the murder and he gathered a force of armed men from his own and neighbouring Kawiku villages and came to the periphery of Shika Village. Headman Nsang'anyi, senior head-man of the Kawiku and son of a former headman of Shika Village, came also to arbitrate between the groups. Kasai shouted from the bush outside the village on two successive days and demanded and obtained from Headman Shika Ikubi (II,C2), a promise to pay two slaves, two guns, 10 yards of cloth and a conus mollusc shell (*imba*), as compensation for his brother's death. Kahumpu (II,D1) returned from the bush on the second day, and after pleading great provocation paid two slaves towards the total compensation, a young man of about fifteen called Sakutoha and his sister, together with a gun. Kasai received these. According to Kasonda, the reason why a large amount of compensation was made over to Kasai was that Shika and Kahumpu stood in great fear of the recently established European government (the murder took place in 1913) of the British South Africa Company which had made murder a capital offence. Kasai had taken advantage of the new situation to pitch his demands very high. It was tacitly agreed between the parties involved that no report would be made to the Boma if the Shika people agreed to Kasai's terms, which were, in fact, a form of blackmail. But after compensation had been paid, Kahumpu as a precautionary measure fled to Balovale District for many years.

The compensatory slaves, Sakutoha and his sister, were allo-cated by Kasai to his classificatory mother's brother, Kahona. They had come originally from Nsang'anyi Village and had been paid as slaves to Kahumpu's mother's brother, the late headman of Shika. But although they had thus been returned to a Kawiku village sprung from Nsang'anyi, they still retained their status as slaves. Every little Ndembu village, as long as it endures, may almost be likened to a sovereign and independent state. It was immaterial whether the slaves were Kawiku or not, or whether they came from Nsang'anyi Village or not. This did not give them freedom. Nsang'anyi and Kasai were independent villages, each had its own business to mind. In the late twenties Sakutoha purchased his freedom from Kahona with a muzzle-loading gun. A few years later he tried to obtain his sister, who had borne Kahona several children, by the offer of another gun. Kahona did not wish to lose his concubine and children, the major part of his following in Kasai Village ; he took the gun, feigning that he would release them to Sakutoha in a short while. Sakutoha, who had returned to Shika Village, was planning to break away and found a settlement of his own with as many of his siblings as he could muster. But Kahona then claimed that although Sakutoha had purchased the enfranchisement of his sister she still wished to remain with him, and he offered Sakutoha bride-wealth to legalize the marriage. He knew that Sakutoha could not prefer a charge against him in a chief's court, for the Boma might get to hear of it, and the British authorities might realize that slavery was still an active institution among Ndembu. This would mean much interference by Government in village affairs and possibly imprisonment for both disputants in the case. Sakutoha, whom I knew well, was a simple and straightforward man, traditional in the extreme, and he accepted the bride-wealth, although condemning in round terms Kahona's double-dealing. But his grudge against Kahona and his family did not die out, for when Set, Kahona's scapegrace son by Sakutoha's sister, who had been expelled from the Copperbelt for persistent thieving, was refused admittance to Kasai Village by the headman in 1953, Sakutoha would not allow him to build in his farm near Mukanza Village.

This case-history shows the tenacity with which Ndembu clung to the institution of slavery long after British rule had overthrown or greatly modified major aspects of the traditional political system. It also illustrates how Ndembu, both slave and free, played off the new laws against the old customs to further their own interests.

It also reveals that slaves, although they might be inherited or transferred like chattels and were compelled to remain in their owners' villages, nevertheless enjoyed certain rights. Sakutoha, for instance, had been able to obtain a muzzle-loading gun of his own with which he had bought his freedom. The status of slave could not have been very onerous, for Kahona's slave woman refused to leave him to join her brother, even though Sakutoha had obtained her liberty and guaranteed her an important position as the potential founder of a village matrilineage.

If many Ndembu continued to recognize slavery as an important institution in the thirties and looked askance on those who had resort to European-supported laws against it, feeling against those who refused to conform to its time-honoured norms must indeed have been strong in the twenties, when Kafumbu (I,G1) made it clear that he wanted to take advantage of the new ordinance. When Kafumbu and his followers joined the fight between Yimbwendi's and Kahali's parties, this act represented a violation of the norms governing relations between slaves and their owners. In the past slaves were expected to fight for their masters ; in this squabble the slaves fought against them. Formerly, the sanctions that would have been imposed against such recalcitrant slaves might have included the execution of their ringleader and the suspension of the rest by their necks from the forks of tall trees. If they had imposed these penalties, the people of Mukanza would have been supported by the other villages in their vicinage ; and Chief Kanongesha himself, if called upon, would have dispatched a punitive force from his own vicinage if Kafumbu and his group had offered resistance. But the alien European authority was known to possess overwhelming force in the form of armed police to back up its laws and render nugatory attempts to uphold the norms of the traditional political system. In short, the mechanisms which formerly maintained the norms governing the relations of slave-owners and slaves could no longer operate, although many Ndembu of both categories still adhered to those norms. Moreover new mechanisms had been introduced by the British which applied sanctions against Ndembu who were caught attempting to maintain the institution of slavery, mechanisms of a legal character designed to enforce conformity to norms which were opposed to those of the indigenous society. Since there was no way, therefore, of redressing a breach of traditional relations between slave-owners and slaves by traditional machinery, schism between members of the two categories within a single village resulted in the fission of that village.

Yimbwendi, on the other hand, was not condemned by the people of Mukanza for withdrawing his own lineage from the village so much as for conniving with Kafumbu at the secession of the slave lineage of MPEZA (I,F1) from their hereditary owners, the people of NYACHINTANG'A lineage. Yimbwendi's group, after all, had previously split off from Kahali Village and could no longer trace precise genealogical relationship with either NYACHINTANG'A or MALABU lineages, although they still remembered to what genealogical generation they belonged with reference to the founding ancestor Kabonzu (I,C1). The lineage of NYACHULA (I,D3) was sufficiently distinct from the combination of NYACHINTANG'A (I,D1) and MALABU (I,D2) lineages to constitute a virtually autonomous group. But it seems that Yimbwendi had at one time cherished ambitions to become headman of Mukanza and that he was encouraged in them by Kafumbu, even if this would have entailed the secession from the village of most of the members of the other two lineages. But he had not been successful in winning the support of any of the leading men of the established lineages without which he could not have become headman of Mukanza Village. He had to content himself with securing the temporary allegiance of Kafumbu. This was an uncertain asset, for Kafumbu was also an ambitious man, who wanted to use his relationship with Yimbwendi as a lever with which to secure his own emancipation and that of MPEZA's lineage, his personal following, from NYACHINTANG'A lineage. Later, when the two men founded their settlement, Kafumbu, whose following at that time outnumbered Yimbwendi's, claimed the headmanship of the new village and forced Yimbwendi, who naturally did not agree to this, to leave the area.

Why were ritual mechanisms not brought into operation to resolve the conflicts in Mukanza Village, as in the case of Social Drama II in which Sandombu was reintegrated into the Mukanza community? The answer probably lies in the nature of the social relationships involved in the respective dramas. Sandombu was a close kinsman of the principal actors in the earlier social drama and an almost life-long member of the residential group. Kafumbu and his faction were slaves, and breaches of owner-slave relations were traditionally settled by legal means supported by the sanction of organized force. Yimbwendi and his lineage kin were indeed matrilineal relatives of the Mukanza group, but only distant relatives, so distant in fact that two marriages had taken place between members of the respective groups which would have been considered incestuous had kinship nomenclature alone been the criterion. Before the split, Kanyombu (I,F9), of NYACHINTANG'A lineage, had married Nyamalata (I,G23), of NYACHULA lineage, whom he called ' sister's daughter ' ; and after the split Line (I,H17), of MALABU lineage, had married Maria (I,H19), of NYACHULA lineage, whom he called ' sister ' by one means of reckoning kinship. The sole common ancestress of these men and women was Chipendipendi (I,A1), mother's mother of Kabonzu (I,C1), the founder of the village that was subsequently known as Kahali, then as Mukanza. Chipendipendi was in the fifth genealogical generation before Kanyombu, the sixth before Nyamalata, and the seventh before Line and Maria, so that the relationship between these spouses was extremely distant. Yimbwendi and his group had lived separately from the rest of the village for about twenty years before they returned after Mukanza Kandulu's death, so that ties of spatial propinquity between the two sections had lapsed and had not been strongly revived in the short interval of nine years before the final split.

It would seem, therefore, and this view can be supported by evidence from other villages, that ritual mechanisms are only brought in to reintegrate a settlement group of relatively close lineal kin with a genealogical depth of about three generations at most between founding ancestor and the oldest living members of the lineage,—what I call a ' minor lineage '. Ritual mechanisms are only brought into operation, moreover, where ties of lineage kinship are supported by a long tradition of joint residence between the persons and sub-lineages concerned. Moreover, as a rule only a single type of ritual is utilized primarily for this purpose, the *ku-swanika ijina* ritual, in the course of which a *muyombu* tree is planted to a matrilineal ancestor or ancestress of a village member who inherits on that occasion his or her name (*ku-swanika*, to cause to inherit or succeed to, *ijina*, a name). Most other rituals, although they may have the subordinate function of reintegrating the ritual subject's village, dominantly emphasize the unity of all Ndembu, or even of all Lunda. But the lineage group which is reunited by the *ku-swanika ijina* ritual is the effective local lineage. Marriages between members of this lineage other than between classificatory grandparents and grandchildren are reckoned to be incestuous unions (*chimalwamalwa* or *chipikapika*), and a ritual (*ku-sola*, or *ku-disola*) is performed to cleanse the couple if they have a common great-grandmother. Within closer degrees of matrilineal kinship than this, in pre-European times the couple might have been permanently ostracized or put to death.

In Mukanza Village in 1954, when I left the field, the groups predominantly concerned in *ku-swanika ijina* rituals were tending to become, not the major lineage of NYACHIPENDI (I,C2), the mother of Malabu (I,D2) and Nyachintang'a (I,D1) ; but the separate minor lineages descended from these daughters (see Map 4). The children of Manyosa's, Chawutong'i's and Kasonda's generation, and the grandchildren of Nyamukola's, Nyatioli's and Sakazao's generation, when they grow up, will no longer constitute together an effective local lineage, and ritual mechanisms will no longer be able to reintegrate the whole village if there is a breach of regular social relations between the two sub-lineages. In any case, new social forces which are now rapidly developing will almost certainly accelerate fission of the larger villages into ever smaller residential units.

Social Drama VI well illustrates the type of fission which tended to occur in the first period of social change. Traditional ties became more brittle ; traditional social machinery for reintegrating a disturbed group became replaced in several situations by the legal machinery of the superordinate alien authority ; new norms regulating behaviour were introduced from above ; or new norms began to develop on the basis of nascent social relationships of a new type and came into conflict with old norms. But the first effect of these innovations tended to be the loosening of traditional ties rather than their replacement by new ones. The first of these ties to snap was the owner-slave link, and all over Mwinilunga District in the 1920's we find the growth of new settlements inhabited by former slaves. This territorial enfranchisement was everywhere accompanied by conflict between slaves and their former owners. But it was not long before the new situation was accepted by the majority of the people ; and although in private conversation a certain stigma is attached to membership of such a village by free Ndembu, the villages of slave origin are treated in most respects in the same way as villages of free men. Former slaves and free Ndembu intermarry freely and the children of former slave women are regarded as free.

Accretion

The role of NYACHULA lineage in the situation illustrates not only one type of fission, but also accretion as it operates among the Ndembu. When Yimbwendi returned to Mukanza Village after twenty years he was utilizing ties of matrilineal kinship which had not yet fallen into complete abeyance. His own uterine uncle Saluvaji (I,E6), the father of Line, moreover, had remained in Mukanza Village after the first secession of the NYACHULA lineage from Kahali Webala's village, and acted as a living link by means of which the lineage could be attached to the village once more. In most Ndembu villages one finds a few scattered classificatory matrilineal kinsmen of the headmen, members of sub-lineages that have split off, but who have re-mained perhaps on account of marital ties, as in Saluvaji's case, with the principal village lineages, perhaps because they have fallen out with their own primary matrilineal kin. These per-sons, for example, Nyawunyumbi (I,G25) and her children in Mukanza Village, in practice seem to assume the function of maintaining connection between the dissident and remaining sections of a divided village and to provide points of re-entry for members of the seceding group. In other words they have important roles in the system of inter-village and inter-vicinage relations, or from the point of view of members of a village in their system of external relations. Fission is seldom along abso-lutely clear-cut lines. Ties other than those of lineage affiliation may temporarily or even permanently prove stronger than the latter so that each core of primary matrilineal kin in a village may have a number of classificatory encrustations. Such per-sons must not be regarded simply as social isolates within a village ; they have functionally significant roles in the wider system. When Kayineha (I,G6), for instance, was living at Mukanza Village he held the door open, as it were, for a reconciliation with Kafumbu.

Lineage or Uterine Sibling Group ?

In effect, the groups which split off from Mukanza Village were groups of uterine siblings. Kafumbu managed to gain control over two of the daughters of Mpeza (I,Fi), and these, together with their children, formed the core of his new village. Kayineha should have been the leader of this group but his attempts to persuade his sisters to remain in Mukanza Village, where he had married, were resisted by them. Kafumbu had many children by Katendi (I,G2), and Katendi herself had con-siderable influence as the oldest sister and a strong personality in her own right over Kawila (I,G3) who also had many children. Here the powerful bonds between uterine siblings and between members of a matricentric family were exploited by the husband of the oldest sister in his own interests. The success achieved by Kafumbu (I,G1) against Kayineha (I,G6) in the struggle to control the all-important fruitful women is one case in which a husband defeated a brother. More often in such a struggle between brothers-in-law the brother wins ; but the outcome in Ndembu society is never a foregone conclusion. Undoubtedly the fact that Kafumbu was a cross-cousin of his wife and her siblings was of great assistance to him.

Yimbwendi's following consisted of his own group of uterine sisters, and their and his own children. But his youngest sister died ; and her daughter Nyawunyumbi (I,G25) suspecting Yimbwendi of having killed her mother by sorcery [1] to enhance his hunting powers, refused to leave Mukanza with him. His uterine uncle Saluvaji (I,E6), who also remained behind, was a feeble old man who had strong bonds of marriage and friendship with Mukanza Village and who, besides, would not accept the authority of his own sister's son. But Yimbwendi's other two sisters and their children remained loyal to him.

Later when Samunuma (I,G22) split off from Yimbwendi's village after Yimbwendi's death, he led away with him his own uterine sibling group, leaving Makumela (I,G24), his maternal parallel-cousin, with Makumela's own sibling group. The group of uterine siblings under the leadership of the oldest or most capable brother is the basic Ndembu residential unit and

---

[1] Cf. pp. 181, 186.

the most common nucleus of a new village. Happy is the ambitious man who has many sisters and unambitious younger brothers with children of their own. Sandombu is an example of a man who is not favoured with fertile siblings, and who has no children of his own. He must resort to discreditable means to scrape together what following he can, and is always regarded with suspicion. This nuclear sibling group has always been important as the pioneer element in founding a new village, according to my genealogical material and according to information collected from my older informants. But in the past, say the latter, fission was much less frequent, and in addition to his own uterine sibling group a man would hive off with other members of a three-generation or "minimal" lineage, the matrilineal descendants of a common grandmother. Today the ties of classificatory kinship are wearing ever thinner and each uterine sibling group is a potential unit of secession.

To achieve the qualitative transformation from a uterine sibling village to a three- or four-generation matrilineal village represented a substantial social achievement in this unstable and volatile society. It required the proliferation of a number of supplementary ties within the village interlinking members of potentially opposed lineage segments. That is why emphasis was placed in Ndembu culture on unity within the genealogical generation and on the alliance of alternate generations irrespective of the lineage affiliations of their members, and why succession and inheritance as far as possible ran laterally, even to cousins, rather than lineally. That is why so much intra-village classificatory cross-cousin marriage took place between the children of matrilineal parallel cousins of different sexes and lineages, and why grandparent-grandchild marriage is found between lineal kin belonging to different sub-lineages of a single matrilineage. That is why, also, members of a slave lineage in a given lineage were married by members of different village sub-lineages. For the slaves acted, as it were, as warp to the lineage weft. But the growth of such ties took time and meanwhile the independent and individualistic Ndembu personality proved a stumbling block to their development. Jealousy between classificatory mothers' brothers and sisters' sons and also between classificatory matrilineal brothers over headmanship, when the last headman of the senior generation died, and the extreme reluctance of the defeated claimant to submit to the authority of the successful one, were frequent causes of fission. The absence of a strong centralized political authority capable of compelling people to remain in a village after conflict had occurred also favoured village schisms. But once a village had become established great efforts were usually made, as in Mukanza Village, to prevent its disruption and to keep it alive.

Personal Factors

Much depended on the personality of the headman, the supreme agent of the transition from uterine sibling village to matrilineal village, if the group was to remain undiminished through the period of instability which supervened when the proximal generation to the village founders began to struggle among themselves for power. I found that successful headmen among Ndembu were firm but unobtrusive personalities, unaggressive, and ready to share what wealth they might acquire with their relatives. Scrupulous fairness is reckoned to be one of their most essential characteristics. But the best notion of what Ndembu consider the ideal personality type for headmen is afforded by the following text I collected about Headman Ng'ombi during a discussion with some members of the vicinage to which both Ng'ombi and Mukanza Villages belong :

Headman Ng'ombi, even before he succeeded to headmanship, used to laugh with everyone, elders and children alike. He liked both men and women. If his younger brother of his own lineage or of a senior or junior lineage, or his sister's son, or his father were hungry he would remember to offer them food. If they are very old (*adinawevu*, literally, ' those who have a beard ') he helps them (*wayikwashang'a*, literally ' he helps them all the time ' : *ku-kwasha* means ' to help in every way—with goods and services, to be solicitous to their every need ') ; if they are sick he helps them ; if they have come from another village he helps them with food, with beer, and gives them a place in which to sleep. And even if the Europeans send their messenger he will help him with one thing or another that he may require. If Chief Kanongesha is coming to call a meeting of headmen he will bring a calabash of beer or a sheep or cassava meal as tribute. Chief Kanongesha is very pleased and says ' You have brought me tribute as a village headman; that is a good thing to do.' He tells him ' The one who helps me in our village is a son in every respect.' Headman Ng'ombi has a good liver, he helps many people, he makes gardens for many people (i.e. to give them hospitality), he digs these gardens, he has strength, he has ability to argue cases, (*waheta wuhaku*), he does not steal nor tell lies, he does not slander people, he is not a sorcerer.

By way of contrast here is a text describing the personality of a headman who was feared and disliked :

He is a bad man, selfish (*waheta chifwa*), proud, quarrelsome, given to reviling people, lazy, a liar, without skill in legal argument, a thief, lustful, a slanderer and a sorcerer. He is *wafwaha walwa*, a person who scrounges beer from everyone without making a return. Such a person who takes without returning is like a mad dog. A man who has self-respect (*kavumbi*) [1] does not do so. He also respects other people, without regarding them as useless.

Ndembu do not admire overweening, domineering headmen ; men with such temperaments are condemned and although they not infrequently succeed to office seldom acquire a large following. Both Yimbwendi and Kafumbu appear to have been men of this type. Mukanza possessed many of the qualities attributed to Ng'ombi, although he was not such a good arguer of cases. Kasonda once told me that many headmen eat privately in their own kitchens, sending what is left of their food to the *chota* to be eaten by the *akwachota* (the group of male villagers, regardless of lineage or generation affiliations). But Mukanza, Ng'ombi, Kamawu and Mulila (other respected headmen in the vicinage) preferred to eat in the *chota* with ' their juniors and children '. They were ridiculed for their commensality by such headmen as Nswanakudya, Chibwakata and Nsang'anyi, but the people said that this behaviour proved that they were not sorcerers (*aloji*), since it is believed that sorcerers share their food with their creatures of sorcery, such as *malomba* and *tutotoji*. Only chiefs are expected to eat alone or with their children, apart from their people. On account of Chibwakata's pride (*winyi*), argumentativeness and reputed sorcery, four groups, led respectively by Ng'ombi's uterine uncle the founder of the village, Nyakapwipu, Sayifon and Makayi, divided off (*kubaluka*, literally ' to split a piece of wood ') from Chibwakata.

---

[1] C. M. N. White (personal communication) writes that ' *kavumbi* means "respect for others, not self-respect " '. My own informants, however, gave me the meaning ' self-respect ', ' care to be thought a good man '.

The good headman is the good fellow, the man who ' laughs with everyone ', who is hospitable, self-respecting, helpful and democratic. Perhaps the most significant section of the commentary on Headman Ng'ombi is that in which he is described as a man who would give food not only to ' a younger brother ' of his own lineage but also to members of other lineages in his village. His field of friendly co-activity is not circumscribed by narrow minimal lineage relations ; it extends outwards to include everyone of the village, regardless of their precise degree of relationship to him. The headman in his person should typify and exemplify the most general norms governing social interaction within the village. His generosity and range of interests should not be confined to his own village ; he should offer hospitality to visitors from other villages and should be able to argue cases in other villages with freedom from prejudice. Towards the agents and representatives of external authority, indigenous and alien, he should be courteous and respectful so that his village should be well thought of and he and his people should not incur the rancour of capricious officialdom.

Among Ndembu, however, it is not easy to find men who measure up to these exacting standards of generosity, impartiality, and unselfishness. For tradition and training uphold and produce among the majority of men a cast of personality in many ways opposed to the ideal type of headman. This is the ideal personality of the hunter. The professional hunter (*chiyang'a*) is a man of the bush who spends much of his life alone, pitting his wits against the fleetness or ferocity of animals, fierce himself, boastful, dreaded as a sorcerer, by character and mode of living unable to stomach the authority of another, patriarchal in his family life in a matrilineal society, a wanderer who may travel from Mwantiyanvwa's country to Ishinde's chiefdom in Balovale District in quest of game, and given to long and frequent drinking bouts round the calabashes of beer made from the honey which he fearlessly collects from the nests of wild bees in the woodland. A prayer made by hunters at the beginning of their *Wuyang'a* ritual defines the type of man that is meant by ' a professional hunter ' (*chiyang'a*). ' We want a man who can sleep with ten women in one day, a great thief of a hunter.' ' Thief ' actually refers to the ' theft ' of game from the bush, not to the stealing of property, but the bias of adulation for what in ordinary life

would be illegal acquisition is plainly evident.   Again, a headman should not be licentious ; in a hunter sexual potency—with
a fine disregard of its lawful direction—is reckoned a strong
qualification.   It is clear that such a personality type is diametrically opposed to that thought proper for a headman.   Few
Ndembu succeed in achieving a workable compromise between
these ideals.   Many professional hunters are headmen, but few
of them are successful headmen ; many successful headmen with
large followings are not professional hunters.   Both Kafumbu
and Yimbwendi were hunters, and acted as hunters, but not
headmen, were supposed to act.   One of the reasons why
Yimbwendi went south into Chibwika Area was because there
was much game there.   Although Mukanza was himself a
hunter he was not a great and dedicated hunter, and spent most
of his time in and around his village.

Because few men possess or develop the personality ideally
required for headmen new settlements often fail to become
established.   The spine of continuity which maintains a long-
established village is provided by its famous historical name or by
the mere fact that it has persisted from long ago and has thus
acquired the prestige of longevity.   Where these factors are
absent, when the founder of a village dies, fission often occurs
between uterine sibling groups sprung from different mothers.
Thus Yimbwendi Village split into the groups led by Makumela
and by Samunuma, and Kafumbu into those of Samlozang'a and
Kafumbu Kamu.   The name of the founder becomes extinct
in many cases, and new discontinuous settlements come into
existence.

CHAPTER VII

VARIETIES OF VILLAGE FISSION

IN order to demonstrate that the tendency for groups of uterine siblings to split off under the oldest or ablest brother is no unique or exceptional phenomenon, I present Tables XVII, XVIII and XIX compiled from data obtained from village genealogies collected in four Government chiefdoms and from discussion with the informants who supplied the genealogical material. Table XVII shows the relationship of the leader of the seceding group to the headman, whether classificatory or descriptive, and Table XVIII shows the span of the maternal descent group which formed the nucleus of his new settlement. I restate my use of terms : ' uterine sibling group ' refers to the children of a single mother ; ' minimal lineage ' to the matrilineal descendants of a single grandmother ; ' minor lineage ' to the matrilineal descendants of a single great-grandmother ; and ' major lineage ' to the matrilineal descendants of a single great-great-grandmother. I found no lineages of greater span than the ' minor lineage ' as nuclei of new settlements. Lastly, I give in Table XIX the relationship of the leader of the seceding group to the senior woman of his new settlement, in order to bring out the fact that there is often a struggle between brothers-in-law for the control over a woman and her children, and sometimes over her younger sisters as well, as in the case of the rivalry between Kafumbu (I,G1) and Kayineha (I,G6) described in the previous chapter.

Table XVII shows that 18 out of 33, or roughly half of the leaders of seceding groups were sisters' sons, primary or classificatory, of the headmen of the original villages. Of the 11 classificatory sisters' sons, 8 belonged to the same minor lineage as the headmen but to different minimal lineages within it, 2 belonged to the same major lineage as the headman but to different minor lineages within it, while one, Kafumbu, was more distantly related to the headman, Kahali Chandenda. It has already been pointed out that the secession of sisters' sons, both primary and classificatory, is often associated with the tendency towards adelphic succession in Ndembu villages (Chapter Three, p. 87). Only one uterine brother seceded from his older brother's village, and in this case he made a small farm with his two sisters and his and their

VILLAGE FISSION

TABLE XVII

RELATIONSHIPS BETWEEN LEADERS OF SECEDING GROUPS AND THEIR PREVIOUS HEADMEN

Relationship	Primary	Classific.	Total
zS	7	11	18
YB	1	4	5
S	2	1	3
Cross-cousin . .	2	1	3
mB	1	1	2
Not known . .			2
Total number of seceding groups . . . 33			

TABLE XVIII

LINEAGE SPAN OF NUCLEAR SECEDING GROUPS

Category of nuclear group	Number of groups
Uterine sibling group . . .	21
Minimal lineage	11
Minor lineage .	1
Total . . .	33

TABLE XIX

RELATIONSHIP OF LEADER OF SECEDING GROUP TO SENIOR WOMAN OF SECEDING GROUP

Relationship	Number
OB . .	8
YB . .	11
S . .	6
H . .	5
Class. B . .	3
Total . . .	33

Legend

OB	Older brother	Class. B	Classificatory brother
YB	Younger brother	zS	Sister's son
S	Son	mB	Mother's brother
H	Husband		

children about a hundred yards from his original village. Of the 4 classificatory brothers who hived off, one belonged to the same major, but to a different minor lineage as the headman ; one

to the same minor, but to a different minimal lineage ; and two
to different uterine families in the same minimal lineage. In
both cases where classificatory mothers' brothers split off they
belonged to the same major lineage but to different minor lineages
within it.

Abundant confirmation is offered by Table XVIII for the view
that the dominant nuclear unit of a new settlement is the uterine
sibling group.   In 21 out of 33 new settlements the nuclear group
consisted of uterine siblings ; in 11, of a minimal lineage ; and
in only one case of a minor lineage.   Secession of a minor lineage
occurred in one of the oldest villages in the Ndembu region,
Mwanta waLuunda in Nyakaseya area, the headman of which
used to have the office of supervising the caravan which took the
tribute that was irregularly despatched from Chief Kanongesha
to Mwantiyanvwa.   The classificatory sister's son of the headman
built a new settlement quite close to that of Mwanta waLuunda
Village and continued to pay tax through the latter.   The uterine
uncle of this leader of the seceding group had previously been
headman.[1]   In the majority of cases in which a *primary* sister's
son founded a new settlement this was built at a considerable
distance from the original village.   Why this should be so I do
not know, unless it is because conflicts between close kin of
proximal generations when they occur are liable to be more
violent than between distant kin, owing to the greater intensity
of their previous interaction.

This theme of the spatial dispersion of close lineal kin after
fission in a village pervades Ndembu society just as the theme of
lineal ramification in a single locality pervades Tallensi society.
If we examine the spatial arrangement of almost any vicinage
in the Ndembu region we shall find few adjacent villages indeed
that are linked by close lineal ties.   Close lineal kin do not seem
to make good neighbours if their leaders belong to adjacent
genealogical generations.   On the other hand, when uterine
brothers or parallel cousins of the same minimal lineage divide,
the new settlement may often be built adjoining the old.   Thus,
when Makayi, younger brother of Headman Chibwakata,
founded a farm in 1952, he built about a hundred yards from
his brother's village ; when Sakanya, parallel cousin of Headman

---

[1] Cf. the case of Sandombu in Chapter Four.

Machamba, made a new settlement he built about fifty yards from Machamba Village, and so on. When ties of genealogical generation affiliation are combined with lineal connections they seem to act against the breaking of links of spatial propinquity. When, on the other hand, conflict breaks out between close lineal kin of adjacent, and hence competitive, genealogical generations, ties of spatial propinquity are abruptly and irremediably severed ; and the seceding group moves out of the vicinage. Indeed, frequently it moves out of the senior headman's area to which the original village belongs, an area which may include several vicinages. In seven out of eight cases where fission took place between groups headed respectively by primary mothers' brothers and sisters' sons, I found that the seceding group had settled more than six miles from the original village. On the other hand, where classificatory mothers' brothers and sisters' sons had separated from one another, I found that in eleven cases the new group had settled within six miles of the original village, and in only one case more than six miles from it—although in five instances the new settlement was in a different vicinage from the old.

In the majority of cases (22–33), the leader of the seceding group was the oldest brother or classificatory brother in a group of uterine siblings or in a minimal lineage. In six cases he was the son of the senior woman in his following. This again illustrates the tenacity of the mother-son bond in Ndembu society. If the mother of a founder of such a settlement is alive he will take his mother with him. She will become the apical ancestress of the village lineage if the village becomes firmly established. In a sense, she is a living index of the matrilineal character of the Ndembu village, and she is her son's embodied hope that his sibling village will become a minor local matrilineage.

In order to bring out more fully the structural implications of fission in Ndembu society I give some examples of different types of village cleavage below.

(a) Fission in Shika Village [1]

Shika Village, about twelve miles from Mukanza Village today, is a village whose nuclear lineage belongs to the chiefly matrilineal

---

[1] Appendix II should be consulted for genealogical information.

group of Kanongesha.   In the latter half of the nineteenth century
its founder Kanjimana (II,B1), uterine nephew of Kanongesha
Kajing'a Mpata Yibamba (II,A1), left the area of Kanongesha
near the Lovwa River in Angola, on the occasion of his uncle's
death.   He moved because he feared the jealousy of the new
chief, the son of Kanongesha Kajing'a ; [1] and he settled near the
present site of Shika Village by the Lunga River with his brother
and three sisters, Wayanda (II,B2), Nyambunji (II,B3) and
Chilumbu (II,B4), his wives, and the children of the uterine
sibling group.   After his death he was succeeded by his uterine
nephew Ikubi Chingongu (II,C2).   The older brother of Ikubi,
Chanza (II,C1), resentful that his younger brother had been
preferred to him as headman, founded a new village with his
children, one of his sisters and her children, and his classificatory
sister Nyakawong'a (II,C3), daughter of Nyambunji (II,B3),
and her children.   Nyakawong'a's son Nswanakudya (II,D10)
became one of the first African Messengers of the British South
Africa Company's Administration.   Nswanakudya returned to
the new Boma near the Lunga, but after a short while left the
service of the Administration and rejoined his kin at Shika Village.
By 1914, five years after his return, he had become the leader of
a strong uterine sibling group and had hopes of succeeding Ikubi
(II,C2), now an old man.   He was older than Chipwepu (II,D4),
uterine nephew of Ikubi and his designated *mulopu* (deputy) ;
and had a larger following than Chipwepu.   But in this year
his sister Nyawatwa (II,D11) committed incest with her parallel
second cousin Samuheha (II,D6), uterine nephew of Ikubi.   The
old headman drove the pair violently from his village, which at
that time was quite near the present site of Mukanza Village.   The
incestuous couple lived for several years in the bush, shunning
the local villages.   Eventually Ikubi forgave them and the ritual
of *ku-disola* was performed to cleanse them, for they belonged
to the same minor lineage with a common great-grandmother.
But he said that they must live in another village lest his people
' should feel ashamed' by their presence.   Nswanakudya (II,D10)
may well have seen this expulsion of his sister as a blow to his
hopes of succeeding, for she had four children already by two

---

[1] Succession to the Kanongesha chieftainship was patrilineal until 1890.
Cf. p. 321.

previous husbands, a powerful pressure group to support his claim for headmanship. In the early 1920's he broke away from Shika Village and invited his sister and her husband to build with him. He started his new village [1] with his mother and his own uterine sibling group, including his older brother Matoka, two younger brothers, and two sisters, one of whom had been married to the late headman of the nearby village of Chibwakata. Nswanakudya's own father had been headman of Chibwakata Village, and many ties united and still unite the two villages, both descended from the first Lunda invaders. Later Nswanakudya was joined by his mother's matrilineal parallel cousin Nyakashilishi (II,C4), daughter of Chilumbu (II,B4), daughter of the apical ancestress of Shika Village lineage, NYACHIBAMBA (II,A2). Nyakashilishi had recently been divorced by her husband and had elected to go to Nswanakudya rather than to Shika, her village of origin. Perhaps this was because her mother was closer to Nswanakudya's grandmother in sibling order than to Headman Shika's grandmother from whom all the contemporary members of Shika were descended. One often finds on consulting Ndembu Village genealogies that the matrilineal descendants of adjacent siblings of similar age tend to live together, rather than with the descendants of a much younger or older sister.

In this case we find a marriage, reckoned incestuous, between members of a village lineage, as the prelude and catalyst of fission. Had there been any able senior men among the children of Nyambunji (II,B3) it is possible that one of them might have succeeded Ikubi, and the division of Shika Village might have been averted. But the senior lineage of WAYANDA retained the headmanship and rendered virtually certain the secession of Nswanakudya (II,D10) who belonged to a junior lineage. It is difficult to say whether the group which followed Nswanakudya was a minimal lineage or a uterine sibling group to which were attached Nyakashilishi (II,C4) and her daughter. Certainly with reference to the complementary and opposed lineage of WAYANDA, the split occurred between that lineage and those of NYAMBUNJI (II,B3) and CHILUMBU (II,B4), her sisters ; but in practice, the

---

[1] Nswanakudya told me that when he left Shika Village there were about thirty huts there.

seceding group consisted of Nswanakudya, his mother, and his siblings.

Finally, it should be noted that the breach of residential continuity which occurred when Nswanakudya and his uterine sibling group left Shika Village to go with Chanza (II,C1) probably helped to disqualify him for headmanship in the eyes of those who remained, the close lineal kin of headman Ikubi (II,C2) and his uterine nephew Chipwepu (II,D4). Members of groups which have once broken away from villages, like those of Nswanakudya in Shika and Yimbwendi in Mukanza, if they return are less likely to succeed to office than are persons who remain. Residential continuity, difficult to maintain, is prized in proportion to that difficulty.

(b) Fission in Nsang'anyi Village and its Offshoots [1]

Nsang'anyi is the senior Kawiku village in Mwinilunga District, and was already in existence when Lunda invaders came from Mwantiyanvwa. The headman claims also to have come from ' Luunda ', the homeland of all the peoples of Lunda stock, at a period long before the arrival of Kanongesha's Ndembu. Informants say that all the Kawiku villages and farms in the District, twenty-six altogether, hived off originally from Nsang'anyi. In spite of periodical loss of membership Nsang'anyi Village did not become extinct, but after each secession slowly but surely expanded once more. The following account attempts to trace briefly the history of fission in Nsang'anyi and its recent offshoots in the twenty-five years between 1929 and 1954.

The present headman (III,D4) succeeded to office in 1924. His predecessor had belonged to a different matrilineage within the village, and they knew of no common ancestress from whom both could trace matrilineal descent. The present headman called his predecessor ' older brother ', which implies that they were matrilineal kin. Neither lineage was reckoned by the people of Nsang'anyi village to have been of slave origin. Perhaps the lineage of the previous headman, that of NYANKUKA (III,B1), may be regarded as a group analogous to what Professor Fortes calls among the Tallensi ' an attached lineage ', linked to the authentic lineage, that of NYACHIMA (III,A1), by actual or putative cognatic

---

[1] See Appendix III.

ties, and in the course of time treated for all practical purposes as matrilineally connected. I have collected another village genealogy, that of Chikang'a, which shows that the founder's *son* succeeded him, and was succeeded in his turn by the founder's sister's son or sister's daughter's son. The uterine siblings of the founder's son remained in the village and his sisters' children regarded it as their primary local group. Thus in a single village were found two distinct matrilineages, one descended from the senior wife and the other from the mother or sister of the founding ancestor. In the second or third descending generation, members of the two groups began to call one another ' brother ' and ' sister ' instead of ' cross-cousin ', since they were genealogical generation mates primarily affiliated to the same village. Ties of co-residence and common genealogical generation affiliation took precedence over lineal ties which might have differentiated the two groups.[1] The same thing may have happened in Nsang'anyi Village, which is of considerable antiquity and enjoys great prestige. These factors may have induced both lineages to remain in the same village.

When the present Nsang'anyi succeeded, two men in particular were disappointed in their claims for office. One was his classificatory ' brother ', Matempa (III,D3), who was son of the new headman's mother's older uterine sister, and who was an able judge and advocate and one of Senior Headman Mukang'ala's councillors. The other was Nsang'anyi's classificatory sister's son, Mwanawuta Ikatu (III,E3), older than the headman, and leader of a large uterine sibling group which included five sisters. Mwanawuta Ikatu was the son of the older brother of Senior Headman Mukang'ala. In 1929 the District Commissioner made a road along the Congo Border connecting the Boma with Solwezi Boma. This road passed beside Nsang'anyi Village and, nearer the Boma, came within a mile of Senior Headman Mukang'ala's capital village. Mwanawuta Ikatu (III,E3)

---

[1] Yet, as we will see, Kamawu's brother, a member of NYACHIMA lineage, who called Makumela (III,F5), of NYANKUKA lineage, his ' older brother ', married Makumela's sister. This marriage was not regarded as incestuous. Thus in certain social situations, such as succession to headmanship, the two village lineages regarded one another as lineally related ; in others, such as marriage, distinctive matrilineal origin was stressed. See Chapter Eight for a full discussion of the dual character of Ndembu village structure.

informed Nsang'anyi (III,D4) that he wanted to ' split off ' and
make a village of his own near his ' father ' Mukang'ala and closer
to the Boma.¹ He said that he had many siblings with their
children, and that if he lived nearer the Boma and close to
Senior Headman Mukang'ala, who, in 1930, had been elevated
to the status of a Government Sub-Chief, there might be an
opportunity for his junior kin to find paid work. Nsang'anyi
tried to persuade him to remain, but he left the village and made
a new settlement near the Lwakela River bridge on the Government road, a mile from Mukang'ala's village and fifteen miles
from Mwinilunga Boma.

In 1940 Matempa (III,D3) also broke away from Nsang'anyi
and settled on the northern margin of the Kawiku Plain. With
him went his own uterine sibling group and all the members
of NYANKUKA lineage. The last two headmen of the village
had been members of that lineage. They could not expect to
supply a third successor, but they objected to the appointment of
Nsang'anyi on personal grounds.

In 1930, when the policy of Indirect Rule was first introduced,
Nsang'anyi had applied to the Boma for recognition as a ' Government Chief '. The District Commissioner had called in Chief
Kanongesha and Senior Headman Mukang'ala for consultation ;
and Nsang'anyi had admitted in their presence that formerly
he had paid tribute to Kanongesha through Mukang'ala, ' son '
by perpetual kinship, and representative, of the Senior Chief.
Kanongesha claimed that although an early Nsang'anyi had
resisted the efforts of the war-leader (*Kambanji*) of the first
Kanongesha, founder of Chibwakata Village, to subdue his
' Mbwela ' following, the second Kanongesha had sent his son
Mukang'ala Kabanda against Nsang'anyi. Mukang'ala had
defeated Nsang'anyi and compelled him to pay tribute, half
of which was taken by Mukang'ala for his own use and half of
which was sent to Kanongesha. In addition Nsang'anyi had to
give Mukang'ala a tributary wife (*ntombu*). In compensation
Nsang'anyi was allotted the ritual office of *Chivwikankanu* or
' emblem-purifier ' to Mukang'ala. The incumbent of this
office was entrusted with the medicines of Mukang'ala's senior

¹ Before Mwanawuta left Nsang'anyi there were more than thirty huts in
Nsang'anyi Village.

headmanship and performed an important role in his installation ritual. But the acceptance of this office excluded Nsang'anyi from political authority over any village except his own, in the indigenous political structure. Other Kawiku villages recognized Mukang'ala, not Nsang'anyi, as their senior headman. On hearing this evidence, the District Commissioner turned down Nsang'anyi's claim for Government recognition and appointed Mukang'ala as Sub-Chief of the area in which most of the Kawiku villages were situated. It is likely that the possibility of Nsang'anyi's appointment as a Sub-Chief had been instrumental in retarding Mwanawuta's secession from his village, since he might have hoped for an appointment in the Native Authority bureaucracy if he had remained. The rejection of Nsang'anyi's claim was probably an additional factor in his decision to build near Mukang'ala's village where some of his followers were later in fact appointed as councillors in the Native Authority Court. Matempa (III,D3) also, who became one of Mukang'ala's councillors before he broke away, probably left Nsang'anyi because he regarded his status as councillor as incompatible with his junior status within the village. For in the village he was subordinate to a headman whose claim for an important position in the new political order had been peremptorily dismissed by its authorities.

The nuclear group of Mwanawuta's village was a minimal lineage descended from his mother's mother, Nyachintang'a (III,C1). But in his village were three groups of uterine siblings, potential nuclei of new settlements. There was his own uterine sibling group, the children of his mother, Nyalubenji (III,D1). There was also the sibling group led by his parallel cousin Chipoya (III,E5), the children of his mother's younger sister, Nyamahandu (III,D2). Finally, there were the five children of his wife Nyampupa (III,E2), by a previous husband. Nyampupa and her brother Kakunda (III,E1) had fled originally from Angola as the result of a quarrel the nature of which I was unable to ascertain, and had been given sanctuary by Nsang'anyi. Kakunda went with his sister when Mwanawuta (III,E3) left Nsang'anyi, and neither he nor Nyampupa had any other home than Mwanawuta's village.

Mwanawuta, already quite an old man when he left Nsang'-anyi, had become more or less senile by 1947. In that year

o

John Kambanji (III,E6), his mother's sister's son, returned from the Copperbelt with some cash savings. He began to throw his weight about in the village and quarrelled with Kanema (III,F2) and Six (III,F3), two middle-aged uterine nephews of Mwanawuta, who had for the last ten years or so undertaken the practical running of village affairs. He also quarrelled with Sondash (III,F1), the oldest son of Nyampupa (III, E2) who by this time had become the leader of a thriving uterine sibling group. Kakunda (III,E1), the brother-in-law of Mwanawuta, was an old man now, almost as decrepit as Mwanawuta (III,E3) himself. In fact, in the village the management of affairs had fallen into the hands of the junior adjacent generation to the village founders. In 1947, Sondash (III,F1) told Mwanawuta and Kanema (III,F2) that he was now an elder (*mukulumpi*) with many siblings, children and sister's children, that he found it impossible to live in the same village as the obstreperous John Kambanji (III,E6), and that he proposed to found a new settlement about half a mile away. Little resistance was offered to his departure for he was not their matrilineal kinsman, nor was he Mwanawuta's own child. Shortly afterwards, John Kambanji, whose older brother Chipoya (III,E5) had died several years before, left Mwanawuta Village with his three wives, six children, and two sisters' children, and made what he called a 'farm' quite close to Mwanawuta. Mwanawuta's own younger brother Katoka (III,E4), an old man who had quarrelled with Kanema (III,F2), went with John Kambanji. Later, a Lwena Public Works Department road-labourer from a neighbouring camp married one of John's daughters and built a hut at his farm. But by 1954 John had lost nearly all his following except his wives and children. His sister's daughter married out ; his sister's son left him for fear of his irascibility ; his matrilineal parallel cousin Katoka died ; and the P.W.D. labourer also died. It was hinted in the villages of the vicinage that John (III,E6) or one of his wives practised sorcery or witchcraft. The fact that John was a blood-brother of Sandombu of Mukanza Village, the notorious sorcerer (see Chapters Four and Five), probably did not weigh in his favour either.

In 1954 Six (III,F3) also left Mwanawuta and founded a small farm, consisting of a single Kimberley-brick house occupied by his elementary family. This last type of fission is now greatly on the increase. In the pedicle area a rash of such farms has appeared in the last few years. Six has become a cash-crop grower.[1] He cultivates rice as well as taking in land for cassava over and above his subsistence needs. He sells to the Boma cassava meal which is mainly used to feed road-maintenance labourers in a large camp in the vicinity. Such petty commodity agriculturalists are tending to break away from their matrilineal kin in order to avoid the latter's claims on earnings. John, too, although his new settlement was originally an incipient village by traditional structural criteria, is now the head of a ' farm ' and relies on the cultivation of cash crops and sale of surplus subsistence crops for his income.

Since 1947, then, three groups have seceded from Mwanawuta Village. Little conflict accompanied these withdrawals, for it was generally recognized that the headman was extremely old and infirm and unable to perform his role effectively. Before the secession of Sondàsh (III,F1) Mwanawuta Village contained about seventy inhabitants occupying some thirty huts. It has been previously pointed out that today, when the population of a long-established village has reached about fifty inhabitants, it tends to exhibit signs of imminent fission. We have seen that the social unit which most frequently forms the nucleus of a new settlement tends to be a uterine sibling family, ranging from about ten to fifteen persons. A village like Mwanawuta, which contains three or more sibling families, some of which may be linked by a clever leader into a single minimal lineage, is more conspicuous for its divisions than for its unity. Only the joint operation of a number of factors making for cohesion (such as the capability of the headman, the historical fame of the village, or the existence of a number of supplementary ties of kinship, affinity, generation affiliation and friendship, which cut across lineal attachment) can hold together such a congeries of virtually independent groupings. Mwanawuta Village possessed few of these countervailing tendencies : the headman had little personal authority, the village was but recently established, it was situated about sixteen miles from the nearest European centre, and its component sections were interlinked by few of the ties mentioned. Sondash (III,F1) and his siblings were step-children of the

---

[1] Cf. p. 36.

headman and unrelated by consanguinity to the other village members ; one marriage only had taken place between members of his and the headman's matrilineal kin.   John Kambanji (III,E6) had spent many years on the Copperbelt and his experience and interests were different and opposed to those of the highly conservative old headman.   He was in the senior genealogical generation to Sondash and as the result of some early quarrel bitterly disliked him.   Six (III,F3), although he was the uterine nephew of the old man, had also been a labour migrant and saw his future in terms of personal advancement in the new cash economy.   In fact Kanema (III,F2) was the only senior kinsman of Mwanawuta (III,E3) who had remained with him at the time I left the field, and he had hopes of succeeding to the headmanship of the depleted village, according to informants who knew the situation.   The story of the foundation, rise and decline of Mwanawuta Village is typical of the fate of many Ndembu villages in the past twenty years as the cash economy has increasingly penetrated the traditional social system and corroded first the links of classificatory, and then of primary, matrilineal kinship.

The subsequent career of Matempa Village parallels in many respects that of Mwanawuta.   After Matempa's death his uterine nephew Nswanamatempa (III,E8) succeeded him and for a time the village maintained its unity and increased in membership. But in 1952, when Government delimited a new Forest Reserve, which included the Kawiku Plain and most of the bush adjoining it, Nswanamatempa's people, along with Nsang'anyi, Chibwakata, and other villages, were moved into the vicinage to which Mukanza, Nswanakudya and Ng'ombi belonged.   The leaders of two sections within the village took this opportunity of splitting off from Nswanamatempa Village with their followings.   The senior elder of NYANKUKA lineage was Makumela (III,F5), a man with eight living children, and he founded a farm, in reality an incipient traditional village in social structure, with two younger brothers, his mother's sister's son, their children, and a number of his sister's children.   His sister was the wife of the younger brother of Kamawu (III,F4), leader of the other seceding group, and she lived virilocally with her husband.   Kamawu was the sister's daughter's son of Matempa (III,D3).   His following basically consisted of the sister of his deceased mother and his mother's brother, his older and younger uterine brothers, his sister, and his and their children. Kamawu had become headman of this group, in spite of his low seniority, on account of his widely recognized qualities as a man of legal skill, as a hospitable and conciliatory person, as one possessed, in fact, of all the virtues regarded as desirable in a headman (see p. 200). His mother's brother Biscuit (III,E7) had returned as an old man after an absence of many years at Bulawayo, and had taken up residence with his sister at Kamawu's settlement. As a widower, he found it advantageous that the old widow was willing to cook for him. He was a sad-eyed humorist without ambition, his only requirement a steady supply of beer. Makumela built his farm facing Nswanamatempa on the other side of the motor road, and Kamawu established himself a hundred yards from Makumela on the same side of the road. All three headmen, Nswanamatempa (III,E8), Makumela (III,F5) and Kamawu (III,F4), had asked Mukanza Kabinda's permission to build in that locality, for Mukanza was generally reckoned to be *mwenimbu*, the headman longest established in that part of the vicinage. There were several abandoned village and garden sites and three separate graveyards of the Kahali-Mukanza village lineage near the three new settlements, and the ownership of these gave Mukanza his right to be reckoned *mwenimbu*. Over the whole vicinage Nswanakudya (II,D10) was recognized as possessing moral authority since he belonged to the chiefly lineage, but Nswanakudya had no say in the allocation of land that had once been occupied by Mukanza Village.

Nswanamatempa (III,E8) had the name of being one of the four most notorious sorcerers in the vicinage. He was thought to have caused the deaths of his two brothers, of a sister, and of Kamawu's mother's brother and mother's sister, by his 'medicine'. This, alleged Kasonda my henchman, was the 'real' reason why Makumela (III,F5) and Kamawu (III,F4) split off from his village. Kamawu and Makumela both told me, however, that all three groups remained friendly and recognized Nswanamatempa (III,E8) as their superior. In favour of their autonomy they argued that 'the big village was finished now',[1]

---

[1] Meaning that the type of large village containing a large group of matrilineal kin had been supplanted by the small farm inhabited by close kin.

that they were elders (*akulumpi*), and that each had a large following of his own close relatives. It is probable that both rationalizations for secession were actually advanced by them, the former privately, the latter in public ; but that really the prime cause of their secession was ambition to become leaders of local groups, ambition which had been given its opportunity to succeed by modern developments.

Thus in the course of twenty-five years (1929-54) Nsang'anyi Village has given rise to two villages by primary fission, Mwana-wuta and Matempa ; which in their turn have thrown off five further settlements, Sondash, John Kambanji, Six, Makumela and Kamawu.

The history of this little group illustrates a number of points previously made. The decline in political importance of Nsang'-anyi Village under the British Administration seems to have weakened the bonds that held this formerly large and hetero-geneous village together. But many of the headman's character traits were not such as to commend him to Ndembu. The leading elders of his village blamed him for not obtaining the good graces of the Boma, pointing out that another senior headman of Mbwela origin, Sailunga, had been persuasive enough to secure his own appointment by the District Commissioner as 'Para-mount Chief' of the Lunda-Kosa to the east of the Lunga River. They said that if Nsang'anyi had been firmer and more eloquent he might have become a Sub-Chief, and all his relatives would have benefited. He was garrulous but incompetent in discussing village cases. He was also much addicted to drinking. When I knew him he was regarded as a comic, but rather pitiable, old man. He used to have his xylophone and slit gong, emblems of a departed prestige, played at night in order to remind his departed kin that 'he was hungry and thirsty' and that it was their duty to help him. Although he was often neglected in secular contexts, Nsang'anyi was still, however, accorded con-ventional respect at rituals in Kawiku villages, where he was given beer and food before other Kawiku headmen. He continued to preside over the installation rituals of incumbents of the Mukang'ala senior headmanship, and to receive presents for it. But his glory had clearly gone, leaving only decrepitude.

The cumulative pressures of social and cultural change are

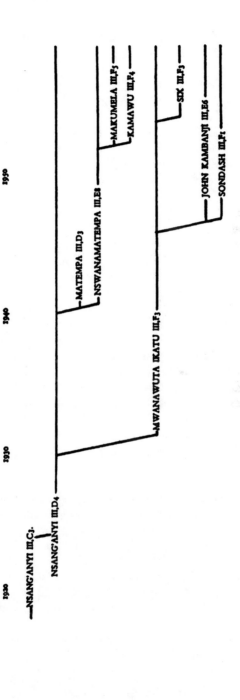

important factors behind these successive cleavages. We have already seen how in Mukanza Village much of Kasonda's and Sandombu's behaviour is explicable in terms of response to new incentives, and how the abolition of slavery by the British gave Kafumbu the opportunity to secede from Mukanza Village. Here again we find that on the one hand direct political factors such as the refusal of the Government to recognize Nsang'anyi as a Sub-Chief, and, on the other hand, the pervasive influence of the cash economy, have led to the gradual reduction of a large village into smaller and ever smaller components, most of which were hardly more than groups of uterine siblings, and in one case, a single elementary family. In Chapter Two it was suggested that in the latter part of the nineteenth century some Ndembu villages were quite large and others small,[1] both types representing different responses to the slave trade, and, later, to slave raids. The large villages were often composite, containing several unrelated matrilineages of relatively wide span who had settled together both for mutual protection against slave-raiders and in order to make successful raids on other villages. The small villages may have represented another way of escaping the raiders—by breaking up and scattering before them into the deep bush. In the present century, under British rule, with the abolition of the slave trade and of internal slavery, with the slow addition of a cash to a subsistence economy, and with a rapid post-war increase in the rate of labour migration, the large villages have tended to break up by successive stages of fission into the smallest possible matrilineal units, uterine sibling families. But change in the structure and stability of residence has by no means everywhere and invariably taken place at the same rate and in the same way. In a single area one may find traditional matrilineal villages side by side with modern family farms. Next to them one may find settlements which may be regarded as transitional types, consisting of depleted uterine sibling groups. Lip-service is still paid by the majority of Ndembu (despite the opinions, quoted above,[2] of Makumela and Kamawu), to the value of living in a large village of matrilineal kin. The members of some villages, for instance of Mukanza Village, until very recently have deeply respected this value. But with the breakdown of the

---

[1] Cf. pp. 43–4.   [2] See p. 217.

traditional authority of the old men of the senior genealogical generation in a village, and the emancipation of the younger men from this authority, the norms governing behaviour between generations have become enfeebled : younger men of wealth and ambition no longer feel constrained to obey the will of the headman and his generation mates, but assert their financial and political independence by seceding and founding farms. To some extent the values inherent in matriliny as a principle governing the composition of residential groups still persist : uterine siblings, that is, members of the same genealogical generation, between whom relations exist of approximate equality, still tend to build together. But today, especially in the northern pedicle, with its growing commitment to a cash economy, even the links between siblings are becoming more tenuous, and individuals are founding farms with their own elementary families.

Nevertheless, although modern developments have undoubtedly accelerated the rate of fission and perhaps reduced the span of the seceding matrilineal group, these developments have only recently, and in particular well-defined areas, produced the spectacular atomistic effects described above. In the past, as to-day, the Ndembu lineage seems to have been shallow by comparison with the lineage among such peoples as the Tallensi and the Ashanti ; and fission seems to have taken place within the minor or minimal lineage rather than dichotomously between structurally balanced and opposed major segments of a village lineage. Villages appear to have been small and spatially mobile in the past also, as Livingstone observed. If older informants are to be believed, Ndembu villages, before the epoch of slave-trading and slave-raiding, were hardly more than small hunting camps ; so that with regard to magnitude, if not to social structure, modern 'farms' resemble ancient villages. But the social core of the 'farm' is, as we have seen, an elementary family, while the core of an ancient village was probably a group of uterine siblings.

In the examples of village fission given above and from the tables constructed on the basis of genealogical data, the uterine sibling group appears as the basic unit of secession. But the seceding groups are not necessarily segments of a local matrilineage, since the group may be variously attached to its leader.

Kafumbu's (I,G1) followers were a group of uterine siblings and their children, related to him by ties of marriage and patrilateral cross-cousinship. The group led away by Sondash (III,F1) consisted of stepchildren of the village headman. Makumela's (III,F5) following were not matrilineal kin of Nswanamatempa (III,E8), although Makumela and Kamawu (III,F4) called one another respectively ' younger ' and ' older brother '. Appendix III, in fact, shows that Kamawu's uterine brother had married Makumela's sister. This marriage was not regarded as incestuous, since the people of Kamawu said, ' We have a different matrilineal ancestress (*nkakulula*) from Makumela.' Sometimes, it is true, segments of equal span broke away from one another. If, for instance, in Mukanza Village, MALABU lineage and NYACHINTANG'A lineage build in separate settlements, this will represent fission between two minor lineages. At a lower level of segmentation the secession of Matempa (III,D3) from Nsang'anyi Village and of John Kambanji (III,E6) from Mwanawuta, were divisions between two uterine sibling groups belonging to the same minimal lineage, divisions between the children of two sisters. The most common unit of secession is indeed the uterine sibling group led by a primary or classificatory sister's son of the village headman. Mwanawuta's secession from Nsang'anyi Village is an example of this kind of fission, as is Kamawu's from Nswana-matempa's Village.

Ndembu society, unlike Tale society, is not, in fact, ' built up round the lineage system '. A fully developed ramifying lineage system requires as a prime condition for its growth an ecological system in which limited access to resources is characteristic. Seen in structural terms, it also requires that the mode of post-marital residence should be consistent with the mode of descent. A system of patrilineages, if it is to be ' the skeleton of the social structure ', requires virilocal marriage ; a system of matri-lineages requires uxorilocal marriage. The patricentric family in the former is what Professor Fortes calls ' the growing tip ' of the lineage system, and like the lineage is attached to a locality. In matrilineal uxorilocal societies the local matricentric family is such a growing tip. If female members of a matrilineage remain in one settlement and import their spouses, each woman becomes the source and nucleus of a local lineage which may attain considerable depth in a society where settlement is anchored to limited resources. In the next chapter I propose to discuss the structural implications of virilocal marriage within and between settlements in Ndembu society in considerable detail. But some of the consequences of this antithesis between mode of descent and mode of post-marital residence have already become apparent in the last three chapters. In many of the simpler societies the tie between mother and children seems to be the closest bond of kinship. In societies with extended kinship systems, there is a tendency for members of the matricentric family to gravitate together in co-residence however far apart they may have been thrown by other social tendencies, such as virilocal marriage among many West-Central Bantu peoples. It is perhaps a tacit recognition of the strength of this bond that has given rise in many strongly patrilineal societies to institutions directed against divorce,[1] since the patrilineage of the father has a powerful interest in retaining his children to replenish its local membership, and there is a danger that where the mother goes her children will go also. In Ndembu society, virilocal marriage, coupled with and opposed to matrilineal descent, has the effect of weakening the local development of deep lineages ; and at the same time it makes every fertile woman who is living with her husband the potential starting-point of a totally new settlement of primary matrilineal kin. If for some reason a woman is unable to return to her own matrilineal kin, it is likely that when they mature her children will start a settlement of their own. Thus when slaves became emancipated, the children of slave women among Ndembu tended to form their own villages. The mother of Sondash could not return to Angola, and her many adult children, whose leader had been unable to succeed to head-manship in his stepfather's village, split off from Mwanawuta Village and made their own settlement. Again, due to virilocal marriage, a woman's children are frequently brought up in their father's village, among *his* matrilineal kin, and not in close everyday contact with their own matrilineal kin. Since they do not interact intensively with the latter, they do not develop strong sentiments of mutual interdependence with them. Each

---

[1] See Gluckman's argument on this point in ' Kinship and Marriage among the Lozi of Northern Rhodesia and the Zulu of Natal ', in *African Systems of Kinship and Marriage*, ed. A. R. Radcliffe-Brown and C. D. Forde (1950).

uterine sibling group tends to regard itself as autonomous. In their father's village uterine siblings are outside the matrilineal descent group which holds office. They do not interact in the affairs of daily life with their own matrilineal kin from whom they may be geographically separated by a considerable distance. Even when they return to the matrilineal kin of their mother, either in a compact block after the divorce or widowhood of the latter, or singly and severally in later adult life, the ties interlinking them among themselves are of a more durable and powerful character than those attaching them to more distant matrilineal kin—even to the children of a mother's uterine sister.[1]

A number of compensatory structural devices exist in the social system to prevent the secession of uterine sibling groups. Local exogamy, which is largely responsible for the initial cohesion and autonomy of such groups, later weakens their cohesion by dispersing their female members, as they grow up, among the villages of their respective husbands. The principle of classificatory adelphic co-residence, which associates male matrilineal kin of the same genealogical generation, establishes bonds of co-operation between men belonging to different uterine sibling groups and opposes them to members of adjacent genealogical generations. The children, and sisters' and brothers' children, of the head of a group of uterine siblings are classed as members of a generation opposed to that of their parents. The uterine sibling group begets the means of its own potential dissolution, since women may leave their brothers to accompany seceding sons. I have stressed the importance of the headman's reputation for justice and generosity as a means of holding together a settlement full of potentially disruptive tensions between its component uterine sibling groups and adjacent generations. The astute arrangement of marriages between his own and his sisters' children, and between members of his own and the junior alternate generation in a village, is another means by which a headman endeavours to maintain the continuity and integration of his following.

---

[1] Unless they have been reared in the same village as the children of a mother's sister. If members of a minimal matrilineage have been reared together they tend to form a potential unit of secession, e.g. the children of Manyosa and Chawutong'i in Mukanza Village.

Thus the unity of a village at any one time tends to depend on a precarious balance between different categories of conflicting alignments. Persons united as members of a single uterine sibling group are divided by virilocal marriage, and united with members of other uterine sibling groups by membership in a common genealogical generation. Male members of such a sibling group are opposed to their own children who belong to a different sibling group, belong potentially to a different village, and belong actually to a different genealogical generation which unites them with their primary and classificatory siblings and cross-cousins in the village. Female members of a uterine sibling group are opposed through marriage to their brothers. Normally, if their marriages are to remain in being they must live virilocally. Thus they set a limit to the ambitions of their brothers, who may wish to form a new village with their help, and in any case require the support of their children to further intra-village ambitions. They are opposed to their brothers' children if they live in the same village ; for their brothers tend to favour own children with food and attention rather than sisters' children, who will ultimately oust brothers' children from the village. Sisters are united with their brothers as members of the same genealogical generation, and with their other male and female classificatory matrilineal kin, against all members of the adjacent generations. In certain situations mothers are opposed to their own adult children, who, in seceding from the villages of their husbands or brothers, disrupt and weaken those villages. When, for example, Sondash made his own ' farm ', his mother remained with her husband, the old headman Mwanawuta ; and she scolded her son for ' spoiling the village '. She also scolded her brother, who went with Sondash because he was given the office of *mulopu* or second-in-authority to Sondash, although he was too old to perform the duties of a headman effectively himself.

Thus persons are interlinked in one set of relations with persons to whom they are opposed in others. Although these cross-cutting loyalties restrain and mitigate the powerful tendencies towards fission in the residential unit, the uterine sibling bond in its closeness and exclusiveness still tends to assert itself at the expense of all countervailing influences. The nuclear group in almost every instance of fission cited is clearly the group of uterine siblings and their children, although in many cases not all the living siblings of the leader of the seceding group have been with him at the point of fission. Sometimes one or more of the leader's sisters have been living with their husbands in other villages ; sometimes a brother has been elsewhere. Two of Matempa's (III,D3) sisters remained at Nsang'anyi and would not come with him. Kafumbu, who founded a village with his wife's siblings, could not get his wife's younger sister to leave Sakazao (I,H9) her husband, of Mukanza Village, nor his wife's brother Kayineha (I,G6), who preferred to live uxorilocally at Mukanza Village. Another of Kafumbu's wife's sisters accompanied her husband Yimbwendi (I,F11) to the village Yimbwendi founded after his quarrel with Kafumbu (I,G1). But in time most of the siblings of such a leader will come to his settlement. When his sisters are divorced or widowed they will join him with their children. The strong tie between uterine brothers also asserts itself. Gradually the uterine sibling group drifts together. Often the children of sisters who did not secede with their brother, join him when they grow up—boys when they marry and girls after divorce. Thus the children of Matempa's sisters who did not accompany him later built huts in his village.

The structural principles, then, which govern residential affiliation are manifold, complementary, and also conflicting. Matriliny is in the final analysis dominant ; but a peculiar cast is given to matriliny by virilocal marriage, which reduces the span of the effective matrilineal unit to the matricentric family. That the system is able to persist depends upon a number of compensatory principles : affiliation by genealogical generation ; opposition of adjacent, and alliance of opposed, genealogical generations ; and cross-cousin and grandparent-grandchild marriages. These are all means of interlinking matricentric families in a wider system of local ties and of reducing the strength of uterine siblingship. It is important to note, however, that the effectiveness of any one of these principles varies from settlement to settlement and depends on such local factors as the length of establishment of the settlement, the fertility of women and men, the strength of marital ties, the reputation and astuteness of the headman and of candidates for headmanship, the age and experience of these candidates, the local numerical strength of sibling groups and minimal lineages, and so on. Social change produces alterations in the relative weightings of these principles and gives rise to new types of interpersonal and inter-group relationships. For instance, ties between members of an elementary family are strengthened and ties between members of a local maternal descent group are weakened. Kinds of struggle arise within the village against which the traditional machinery for reintegrating a disturbed group may prove ineffective.

I am aware that when I wrote that 'virilocal marriage reduces the span of the effective matrilineal unit', I was guilty of over-simplification. In practice, the complex interaction of a number of ecological and political factors, and not virilocality alone, is responsible for the reduced span of the matrilineal unit. The same set of factors, which weakens the effectiveness of matriliny as a bond of local affiliation, assists, if it cannot be shown to determine, the emergence of virilocality as a competing principle of residential attachment.

In societies governed by matrilineal descent, wide-span local matrilineages tend to be found where access to land or other valuable natural resources is limited. Such extended matri-lineages tend to be associated with the possession of fixed estates. In the natural region inhabited by Ndembu, cultivable land is relatively abundant, while population density is low. Social groups are not constrained by natural exigency to remain permanently in particular areas, in pockets and tracts of fertile land. Indeed, since hunting is a highly valued activity, and game tend to move away from hunters, there are positive economic inducements to change the residential site periodically. These inducements are all the more effective for a population that does not invest in large, permanent houses, in long-growing and long-bearing trees, and in stumped land. Nor are Ndembu faced with the necessity of settling near limited water-resources, for their territory adjoins the Congo-Zambezi watershed and many streams and rivers take their rise in it.

Nevertheless, given abundance of land and lack of investment in immovable property, it would still be theoretically possible for a large matrilineal descent-group to move about together, and not to split up into smaller units. Why does this seldom happen ? Part of the answer lies undoubtedly in the individual-istic productive system. The limits of economic co-operation, as we have seen, are extremely narrow. Men hunt alone or in small bands. Communal working-parties to clear bush and hoe up mounds are infrequently mustered, and many Ndembu do not sponsor them. The elementary or polygynous family can, and today often does, satisfy most of its needs by its own labour. Not only is access to resources virtually unrestricted, but there is no concept of a joint estate worked collectively by a unilineal kin group. No one has a perennial interest in any one tract of land, owned jointly by his lineage.

Furthermore, Ndembu do not possess large herds of cattle, the joint ownership of which might under certain circumstances hold together a large nomadic group of unilineal kin. The most valuable item of movable property they possess is the muzzle-loading gun, and only a minority of men own efficient guns. Since such guns are scarce they are highly esteemed and are hotly competed for in situations involving inheritance. They tend to divide rather than unite matrilineal kin.

The true problem, indeed, for Ndembu society is not why local matrilineages are small, but rather why they exist at all. Why do Ndembu live in villages, the cores of which are male matrilineal kin, and not in family homesteads? In the past, at any rate, as we have seen, one of the reasons was provided by the necessity to unite in strong defensive groups against slave-raiders. One response to slave-raiding was to build palisades, throw up earth-ramparts, and dig ditches around large villages. Such villages were, in effect, fortresses, in a state of perpetual vigilance against siege. They seem to have been attached to the same tracts of land for long periods. Their male members must often have co-operated to repel raiders, and to defend their women, children and gardens.

On the other hand, an alternative response to slave-raiding was to scatter in small groups into the bush, each group holding itself in readiness for instant flight. Yet each such group, according to tradition, had a nucleus of uterine or matrilineal kin. Why were such groups wider than the family?

Ndembu have pointed out to me the practical advantages of living in villages. They say that when one family-head is short of food, especially of meat or fish, supplies of which are sporadic and uncertain, he can obtain it from a village kinsman or neighbour. Later, when he 'finds meat' he can make a return. In other words, living in villages under a subsistence economy raises the general level of consumption and safeguards against individual shortages.

Ndembu have also told me that before the Europeans came Ndembu used to raid each other to obtain captives whom they could sell to Ovimbundu traders as slaves in return for guns, powder and cloth. A large village was a more effective raiding and defensive unit than a small one in those troubled times. Then as now the local tie between uterine brothers was a very close one. A brother would help one in raids, and if a man was taken captive, it was his brother's duty to recover him, by force or payment, if he possibly could. The Icelandic maxim, which Dasent made the motto of his translation of Njal's saga, would be equally appropriate to Ndembu circumstances : ' bare is back without brother behind it.' Again, if a man were killed, it was his brother's duty to avenge him or to exact blood-compensation. As we have noted on many occasions, if uterine brothers are to remain together, they must marry virilocally.

We must regard matrilineal descent itself as given in this society. Matrilineal succession and inheritance are regarded as axiomatic by Ndembu. Matriliny is symbolized in many kinds of ritual, and is supported by the dogma of descent ; and its importance is emphasized in several folk-tales. If male kin resided together for defence, offence, and mutual economic aid, the majority of them would have had to be uterine and matrilineal kin. It is only the small span of the effective local matrilineal unit that we have to consider. It is probable that the external provision of law and order by the British authorities has contributed to the present small size of local matrilineages. Large units for defence and offence in raids are no longer necessary. Even before the introduction of cash, that solvent of corporate kinship groupings, the individualistic tendencies in production must have resulted in the breakdown of large local groups. These, as we have noted, had no permanent joint estates or communal movable property to keep them together. If a man wished to secede from a village with his family and kin who would follow him, he could always obtain residential and agricultural land elsewhere.

These factors, then—abundance of land, individualism in production, lack of investment in valuable fixed resources, and

R

external provision of law and order—do not provide favourable conditions for the formation of wide-span localized matrilineages. When, in addition, Ndembu observe the custom of virilocal marriage, a positive tendency making for the reduction of the span of the matrilineal unit may be said to be at work.

It is only by describing and analysing a number of cases of village fission in terms of the social drama, or, where there are insufficient data, in terms of the case history, that the precise effects of these principles and of social change in any given situation can be accurately assessed. For example, when one examines the composition of the seceding and remaining sections involved in village fission, one seldom finds that any one principle of social organization has clearly prevailed over the rest. In Nswanamatempa's Village one might have expected that Biscuit (III,E7), uterine uncle of Kamawu (III,F4), and not Kamawu, his nephew, would have become the headman of the new settlement, since uterine uncles have authority over their nephews. But when the particular circumstances of the case are considered, Biscuit is found to be a gentle, irresponsible drunkard, whereas Kamawu is a respected *ihaku* (law-man) with many siblings and children. These factors outweigh the values set on age and kinship position as criteria influencing selection for political office.

Ambition and ability become significant in any given instance, and have repercussions on the social structure of the local unit. In the social drama we can observe how particular individuals manipulate the organizing principles of social affiliation to serve their own purposes. Sandombu, although childless and without fertile siblings, exploited cleavages in other sections of Mukanza Village and invoked the principles of generation affiliation and the mother-child tie, to build up a following. By his hospitality to distant kin and strangers, he made apparent to all that he would give protection and assistance to persons who, for whatever good reason in Ndembu opinion, had been excluded from their own villages. Social prestige and authority in societies based on kinship principles are largely a function of the relative fertility of individuals and families. Sandombu was unlucky in this respect, and if he had been a less forceful character, he might well have resigned himself to be a man without a following, a social nobody. But he was resolved to be a headman, and consequently had to utilize other means of obtaining a following than those which lay to the hand of any fertile man with a fertile sibling group. In doing so he made many enemies since he was compelled to surround himself with strangers, social undesirables, or to attempt to win over by hospitality those whom more fortunate men would have regarded as their 'natural' supporters—close blood-kin.

Numerical analysis tends to ignore as irrelevant the unique features of each instance of fission and to stress regularities, the statistically normative pattern. Yet it provides the background against which each social drama assumes a significance. If one finds that the most common unit of fission, for instance, is the uterine sibling group, and then, in a given case history or social drama one discovers that the unit of fission is the minimal lineage or the elementary family, one is led to inquire into the reasons for this apparent anomaly. If the data relevant to the analysis are collected in terms of the social drama, the lines of alliance and cleavage in the specific village become visible ; and attention is focused on the particular norms which are observed and broken, on the actual motives which guide the behaviour of the participants, and on the detailed economic, political and other interests which unite and divide them. Apparent exceptions to structural regularities discerned in the numerical data are sometimes found to be the product of a combination of factors which taken alone, or in their unhampered expression in different situations, also possess regularity. Thus a series of marriages within permitted categories of kinship between two uterine sibling families or between two minimal lineages may decide whether these groups secede or remain together in a particular drama of fission. Indeed the dynamic interaction of specific persons and groups in the process which I have called the social drama falls within the province of the sociologist no less than the analysis of the statistical and ideal norms of social structure. In the social drama we see social structure in action. Our attention is drawn to the anomalous isolated instance, the apparent exception to statistical regularity, just as much as it is directed towards the manifestation of that regularity. In consequence, we are led to inaugurate a series of enquiries into the nature of the social mechanisms whereby regularities are maintained, and into what happens when regularities are broken. We are led to detect at just what points the fabric of the social structure is weakest, and what means are taken to solve problems of social integration posed by that weakness.

As an example of this social handling of structural vulnerability, let us take the recurrent situation of the exceptional persons or groups who transfer loyalty to the faction that opposes their own primary kinship allegiance in a conflict which terminates in fission. In Mukanza Village, Kayineha (I,G6), brother of Kafumbu's wife, was a case in point. We were led to inquire why he did not secede with his other siblings, and biographical data were presented which showed that he was a personal friend of Mukanza Kabinda, and that he had married Nyamwaha's daughter. We also found that in the fight between the Kafumbu and Mukanza factions, Kayineha acted as peacemaker. Later he assumed an intercalary role between the two settlements of Mukanza and Kafumbu. We found that Sondash's (III,F1) mother, who did not secede with her son, acted in a similar capacity as a link between Mwanawuta and Sondash villages. Matempa's (III,D3) sisters who remained behind at Nsang'anyi but whose children later went to their uncle, also occupied such an intercalary position, as did Mwanawuta's full brother who seceded to John's settlement.

In fact, persons who do not conform to the rule, may thereby acquire structural importance. Within the system of internal village relations these persons appear to be the exceptions to the rule that uterine siblings secede together. But a study of their behaviour at the point of fission leads to a retrospective inquiry into their motives for action, and an examination of their sub-role as intermediaries between groups to which they are connected by ties of close kinship, and groups where they actually reside. We learn that they perform an essential function in the wider system of inter-village relations, preventing the total estrangement of groups divided initially in anger. Thus apparent exceptions to statistical regularities obtained from genealogical data on village fission prove to be themselves regularities within a wider system of social relations.

Village fission which divides the basic unit of settlement, the village, tends on the whole to contribute to the integration of the wider system, the Ndembu socio-geographical region, by the provision of links of maternal kinship which join vicinage to vicinage, and senior headman's area to senior headman's area.

The wider system of social relations gains at the expense of the narrower.

Summary

Male kin form the residential core of villages : in a matrilineal society such male kin must import their spouses or separate from one another : virilocal marriage in a spatially mobile society prevents the formation of deep lineages and gives a high degree of cohesion and autonomy to the matricentric family which later becomes the principal unit of fission. The looseness of ties between matricentric families leads to a high frequency of fission, and their small size determines the small size and large number of settlements. *Within* the village other principles of social organization than the lineage become important, notably the oppositions and alliances of genealogical generations : *between* villages relations of spatial propinquity and affinity become more heavily weighted than relations of lineal kinship as factors making for cohesion in a vicinage. Ties of matrilineal kinship, on the other hand, are utilized to interlink separate vicinages. Ecological and structural factors, interlocking in a complex fashion, jointly determine the form of settlement, the mode of its fission, and the way in which settlements are interlinked within the wider social systems of vicinage and tribe.

CHAPTER VIII

THE STRUCTURAL IMPLICATIONS OF VIRILOCAL MARRIAGE WITHIN THE VILLAGE

THE first consequence of virilocal marriage in Ndembu residential structure is that the majority of village members tend to belong to a single bilateral extended family, consisting of the headman, his wives and children, and of his siblings, their spouses and children. There is no word in Lunda for ' elementary family ' but the term *ntang'a* connotes a group of bilateral kin and their in-laws who are dependent on some particular person.

Ntang'a, the singular, or *antang'a*, the commonly used plural form, is always used with a possessive pronoun, as in *ntang'ayami* or *antang'ajami*, ' my dependent kin group ' or ' my dependent kin (including in-laws) '. Its use can be extended to include all one's kin with whom one can trace genealogical connection, but in practice the term usually refers to one's local kin-group and is restricted to kin and in-laws with a junior status to oneself. Thus in Mukanza Village, all the villagers belong to Mukanza Kabinda's *ntang'a*. Kasonda's *ntang'a* includes his wife, his minimal lineage sisters, and his and their children and grand-children. It does not include his older sister's husband who is an older man than Kasonda and tends to move his residence between his own farm in Kanongesha Area and Mukanza Village. Sakazao's *ntang'a* comprises the whole of MALABU lineage, and the spouses and children of lineage members. Consequently his moral authority over junior kin overlaps with that of Mukanza Kabinda, since his sister Nyamukola is Mukanza Kabinda's wife, and Mukanza's children by her are his sister's children. The *ntang'a* is not therefore an independent, clearly demarcated corporate unit, but varies from senior member to senior member, as each is regarded as its point of reference.

Ntang'a or *antang'a* must be distinguished from *awusoku* (the plural form of *kawusoku*, ' a kinsman or in-law '), in that the latter term refers in practice to all one's kin and affines whereas *antang'a* is usually restricted to one's junior kin who reside with one. One's *awusoku* are, as it were, a pool from which *antang'a* may be drawn. But the term *awusoku* may be broken down into further subdivisions according to the context of situation. If one wishes to contrast one's kin from one's affines, one may refer to the former as *awusoku* or *wusoku wakuvwalika* (' kinship by birth '), and to the latter as *aku* or *mawuku,* and *mashaku* (singulars, *muku* and *ishaku*). *Aku* or *awuku* refer to in-laws of an adjacent genealogical generation ; *mashaku* describes in-laws of one's own genealogical generation. Both categories may be further subsumed as *wusoku wakusumbwang'ana* (kinship by marriage). But if one wishes to distinguish the category of one's kin who are respected (*ku-lemesha*) and feared (*ku-tiya woma*), or who respect or fear one, from other categories of kin, one also applies to them the terms *aku* and *awuku*. All one's relatives, including parents and children, may be so described who belong to an adjacent genealogical generation. Brother and sister may also sometimes refer to one another as *aku*.

To marry one's *muku* is incest (*chimalwamalwa, chipikapika* or *ku-shimuna*). But the concept *wuku* admits of a considerable range of behaviour patterns between complete avoidance, and respect tempered with affection and familiarity. In-laws of opposite sex in adjacent genealogical generations should avoid one another (*ku-dichina*) ; a member of the junior of two adjacent generations should ' feel fear for ' (*ku-tiya woma kudi*) his or her mother's brother or father's sister, his potential parents-in-law, who are often enough his or her actual disciplinarians ; and a person should ' respect ' (*ku-lemesha*) his or her parents and siblings of opposite sex. But one also ' loves ' (*ku-keng'a*) one's parents and siblings of opposite sex. In general the verb *ku-lemesha,* ' to respect ', is used to summarize the totality of respect-fear-avoidance attitudes regarded as appropriate between *aku*.

But the best way to learn the idiom of Ndembu kinship is to examine *local* systems of kinship, beginning with the *ntang'a* or bilateral extended family of the village headman.

I must repeat that, in its simplest and most fundamental form, the basic membership of an Ndembu village consists of a headman, his uterine siblings, and his and their children and grandchildren. In addition, it may contain spouses of some or all of these persons and perhaps some great-grandchildren of the headman. This group is the *ntang'a* of the headman. The spatial arrangement of the huts owned by its members gives the first clue to the character of their mutual interrelations. As I described in Chapter Three, members of the same genealogical generation tend to live in the same semicircle of huts while members of the adjacent generations live in the opposite semicircle. This means that members of alternate genealogical generations build together, and their huts are often interspersed. The arrangement of huts in fact suggests that the village is conceived not as a set of hierarchically organized lineages but as a single extended family ; for as a rule members of different lineages of variable span in well-established villages build adjacently, so that extended familial unity takes precedence over lineage differentiation in the spatial arrangement. In a small sibling village of the type we are considering, matrilineal kin, and the children and patrilineal kin of the headman, are interspersed. Within the *ntang'a*, EGO refers to his matrilineal kin either as *akwamama* or *mwivumu detu* (literally ' in our womb ' or ' in our lineage ', referring to matri-lineal co-descendants of a common ancestress), and to patrilineal kin as *akwatata*, which signifies persons descended through agnatic links from a common ancestor, almost invariably a common grandfather. These are not patrilineages ; but if men always bring their wives home, a man and his son and his son's children may all be living in one village.

The *ntang'a*, thus, has lineally two major components. Its vertebral members belong to the matrilineage of the headman. Female members of the matrilineage maintain its continuity through time, while its male members form the residential core of the village at any given moment. But through virilocal marriage, the headman, who is frequently polygamous, his brothers and his sons, have children who together constitute quite a high proportion of the population of a village (see Tables X and XI). In Chapter Two (p. 44) I suggested that there is a functional relationship of some importance between the size and structure of the local unit. Ndembu villages have a mean size of about ten huts, containing about twenty persons. In this small settlement, male village-kin outnumber female village-kin by more than two to one (see Tables X and XI). Since the children of brothers call one another siblings, the village membership has quite as much the appearance of an extended family as of a local matrilineage.

This virtual equality between family and lineage as principles of local organization is at least partially responsible for the merging of patrilineal and matrilineal kin as joint members of a single genealogical generation. Thus in many situations a man's father and his mother's brother have equivalent functions and are treated alike. Both should, according to custom, contribute the same sum or the same amount of goods to a man's bride-wealth. When a husband gives bride-wealth for a woman, he should give an equal portion to her father and mother's brother. A woman applies the same terms (*muku, mukwesanu* or *tatawenu*) to her husband's father and his mother's brother and must equally avoid (*ku-china*) both. Conversely, a man should avoid not only his wife's mother but also her father's sister, to both of whom he refers, and both of whom he addresses, as *muku* or *mawenu*. A man calls his own mother and also his mother's brother's wife *mama* (literally ' mother ') and greets them in the same way. He greets his father and his mother's brother in the same way also. The equivalence of father and mother's brother, and of mother and father's sister, is expressed in a number of other situations as well. This merging of lineally distinct members of the senior adjacent and authority-holding generations is a further index of the failure of the matrilineal principle to become indisputably dominant among Ndembu. It tends to strengthen the bonds between members of the same genealogical generation and at the same time, by the creation of a divided authority in the senior generation, to enable members of the junior generation to exploit the division between father and mother's brother to their own advantage. This division of authority and consequently limitation of unilateral control by either father or mother's brother undoubtedly contributes to the independent character orientation of Ndembu, which, in its turn, helps to account for the high frequency of fission.

The Ndembu village, then, in its social composition represents at once a veiled struggle between the two powerful principles of *familial* and *lineal* organization, and an attempt to reconcile these by a set of compromise formations between their modes of social control. In the course of the struggle these principles mutually inhibit one another, so that lineages remain shallow and extended families break up or lose their membership through the pull of matrilineal affiliation. This struggle is itself a manifestation of the deeper opposition between male and female in

Ndembu society. Each village represents an attempt to establish
a patriarchal settlement in the teeth of basic matrilineal descent.
But the male kin who reside together with their wives and families
are themselves interrelated by *matrilineal* ties which persist, while
ties with their children which interlink them in co-residence are
more tenuous and friable, snapping with the divorce of their
wives, with the marriage of their daughters, and with the frequent
defection of sons to their own matrilineal kin on attaining
maturity. On a village genealogy the line of descent, the spine
of village continuity, is through women whose brothers are
marginal to it. But in any given village at any specific point of
time the line is broken or in rare cases even invisible. For the
residential core of a village consists of men linked to one another
through women, most of whom may be absent at any one time,
or who are already dead. In the course of events, however,
nearly every village contains some female members of its nuclear
matrilineage, who have returned to it after divorce or widowhood, or reside there in cross-cousin or grandparent-grandchild
marriage, or whose husbands live uxorilocally. These women
betray by their presence the fundamentally matrilineal character
of the local unit.

Thus the kinship basis of a village is as much bilateral as unilateral and represents a compromise between familial and lineal
principles of organizations. In my opinion, the socio-spatial
grouping of village kin by genealogical generation, as noted
above, tends to neutralize some of the tensions arising from the
co-existence of disparate principles in a single local unit. Common membership of a genealogical generation aligns persons who
belong to potentially opposed descent categories, mother's
brother and father, wife and sister, husband and brother, son and
sister's son, daughter and sister's daughter, members of separate
groups of uterine siblings, or members of separate minimal or
minor lineages. In most Ndembu villages the headman is the
pivot of all three major modes of organizing kinship relations,
by lineage, by extended bilateral family, and by genealogical
generation. If he is an astute man he endeavours to reduce the
tendencies to disruption of the village, which originate in contradictions between these principles, by encouraging and taking part
in the growth of a network of affinal ties. These ties are formed
between persons belonging to opposed categories based on

different principles of social organization. Thus in Mukanza Village, the headman (I,F8) by his marriage with Nyamukola (I,H10) united the lineages of NYACHINTANG'A and MALABU. By the same marriage he strengthened the alliance between genealogical generations F and H (see Appendix I). By arranging cross-cousin marriages between his daughters by Nyamukola and his sisters' sons, Kasonda (I,G15) and Sandombu (I,G10), he simultaneously sought to increase the internal cohesion of NYACHINTANG'A lineage and of the village lineage of widest span, that of NYACHIPENDI, sister of the founder of the village. At the same time, both by means of his own marriage with Nyamukola and by means of the marriages of his daughters with his sisters' sons, he tried to overcome the dichotomy between his seminal children and his junior lineal kin. Since Nyamukola belonged to the village lineage his children by her were full village-members. Any children that Kasonda and Sandombu might have begotten on his daughters would also have been full village-members by matrilineal descent, and the rivalry between Kasonda and Sandombu might have been reduced by the fact that they had married sisters. Kasonda and Sandombu belonged to different minimal lineages, each of which represented a potential unit of fission. But their children by Nyamukola's daughters would have belonged to the same minimal lineage and would have been aligned with their grandfather Mukanza in the same linked-generation segment. Mukanza's other marriage, with Seliya, a remote matrilineal kinswoman, also ensured that his children by her would belong to the village matrilineage and at the same time strengthened his ties with Line (I,H17), a senior man of MALABU lineage who had married Seliya's sister. In this case too NYACHINTANG'A and MALABU lineages would have a joint interest in the children of these men. Kasonda's divorce of Mukanza's daughter and Sandombu's sterility thwarted some of these intentions. But Mukanza, like other headmen, clearly understood the necessity for forestalling by marital ties the potential disruption of his village. Sources of disruption were : divisions arising within matriliny, conflict between seminal children and sisters' children, and struggles between adjacent genealogical generations.

The contradictions between these three principles of village organization—lineage, family and generation—are implicit in the terminology of the Ndembu and influence the behavioural norms governing the interrelations of kin.   It is worth repeating that the simplest way to approach the analysis of Ndembu kinship is through the examination of the spatial structure of the typical village.   The village hut-circle consists of two semicircles, occupied respectively by members of adjacent genealogical generations, and composed respectively of members of alternate genealogical generations.   Each linked-generation segment calls all the members of the opposite segment collectively *aku*.   *Aku* of the senior generation levy respect from *aku* of the junior generation and exert authority over them.   Between *aku* who are in-laws, and, within this category, between *aku* of opposite sex, the relationship of respect is at its most formal and rigorous. *Aku* of opposite sex avoid one another, and *aku* of the same sex exhibit extreme constraint in one another's presence.   But affinal *aku* do not, in practice, enter into a relationship which confers a high degree of authority on the senior over the junior generation.   Hostility in the relationship predominates over the factor of social control, resulting in avoidance and constraint rather than in authority.   Not infrequently such *aku* physically attack one another.   For example, one of the prisoners at the Boma in 1950 was a man who had murdered his son-in-law after a fierce quarrel.   Benson of Ng'ombi Village (mentioned in connection with Social Drama II, p. 118) once beat his mother-in-law severely after she had upbraided him for taking a second wife and neglecting her daughter.

These examples indicate how near to the surface hostility may come in this relationship, and why the norms governing it stress the avoidance of mutual interaction as far as possible.   But a relationship of this kind can hardly be a suitable link in a chain of authority.   A relationship of superordination-subordination must also involve co-operation.   There is a chain of command. But there can be little co-operation between kin who *avoid* one another or experience extreme constraint in one another's presence.   Among Ndembu, authority relations are carried in the kinship structure.   Thus that category of *aku*, over whom one effectively exerts authority and whom one in practice obeys, is made up of consanguineal relatives of adjacent village genealogical generations.   Within this category, again, one finds a range of behaviour patterns. On the whole, matrilineal kin of the senior adjacent generation exert greater control over their junior relatives than do paternal kin.

But the sharp differentiation between the mother's brother as a severely authoritarian figure and the father as a benevolent protector found in many matrilineal societies, such as the Trobriand Islanders, is not made by Ndembu. Due to the partial assimilation of functions associated with the two positions, the mother's brother has much less control and the father rather more than among the Trobrianders. I have, for example, seen fathers administer beatings to their young children, and I have known sons who left the villages of harsh fathers to stay with their mothers' brothers. But the majority of fathers assist their own children financially ; help them to marry ; represent them in court ; teach them the skills of hunting, housebuilding, and the blacksmith's craft ; and instruct them in custom and law. The father is head of the domestic gardening team in bush-clearing operations, and may call on his children to assist him in hoeing his own garden. He takes his sons with him to carry his provisions and his kills when he goes on hunting trips.

There are a number of folk-tales which reveal the existence of tensions in the father-son relationship. One tale describes how a father killed his son in the bush when the pair failed to find game, and how the father was detected in trying to pass off his son's body as the dried carcase of an antelope. Another relates how a father cursed his son for walking beside him like an equal instead of behind him like an inferior when they went honey-collecting in the bush. As the result of that curse the son could not find a single hive. Eventually the lad's mother persuaded him to treat his father with respect and thus induce the father to revoke his curse. A son, other than an infant, may not sleep in his father's hut ; nor, by extension, may Chief Kanongesha spend the night in the village of any of his senior headmen to whom he stands in the perpetual relationship of ' father '. On the other hand, it is said that the father-son relationship is free from mutual sorcery accusations, although the case of Chibwakata and Kasamba (p. 160) where a classificatory son was alleged by his ' father ' to be trying to bewitch him, seems to be an exception to this rule. I have never heard that a father had been accused of bewitching his *own* son or vice versa, although in divination paternal kin of the victims are occasionally named as sorcerers or witches.

I have often witnessed acts of indulgence and kindness performed by men on behalf of their sister's sons. When, for instance, the uterine nephew of one man I knew carelessly wrecked his uncle's bicycle, the latter freely forgave him, telling me that if he were too severe on the lad, when the time came for him to make a village of his own his nephew would not come with him. ' People are more important than things,' he added. I have known men to pay their nephews' fines in adultery cases. But there is no doubt that uncles often punish nephews quite harshly. For example, Sakazao, usually the gentlest of men, grew exasperated one day in Mukanza Village by the persistent naughtiness of Chikimbu,[1] his sister's son, and twisted his arm out of joint. Sisters' children are usually at the beck and call of their uncles in the collection of firewood, the carrying of food from kitchen to *chota*, and so on. But the father is in the final issue his own child's protector. In Ikelenge Area I once saw a man angrily threaten his sister's son with a beating after the latter had knocked down the former's son. The case cited on page 189, in which a father refused to allow his wife's brother to sell his children into slavery, well expresses the difference between avuncular and paternal attitudes. The marked hostility between uncle and nephew emerges in many sorcery accusations I have recorded between these categories—most of them in connection with succession disputes.

The relationship of father (*tata*) to daughter (*mwana wamumbanda*) is often one of great affection ; indeed, I have only once seen a father beat his young daughter. In fact, such an action is roundly condemned by Ndembu who say that it is the task of the mother to punish the daughter and of the father or mother's brother to beat the son. Mothers' brothers may soundly rebuke nieces who have been involved in adultery cases, as may mothers, but fathers seldom do so.

Mothers frequently beat young children, but once a boy has been circumcised he comes under the general control of the men

[1] Chikimbu had transferred his allegiance from Sakazao's group to Sandombu's group. The relationship between uncle and nephew was strongly influenced by the political struggle between village factions. But the political factor did no more than exacerbate a relationship that was already tense.

of the senior adjacent generation and the mother loses her punitive role. But mothers exert quite a considerable authority over daughters, levying their help in gardening, the preparation of food and the carrying of water supplies. It is the mother who receives the greater share of gifts, as distinct from cash, bestowed for her daughter by a future son-in-law, and in the past it was for her that her son-in-law used to build a hut and make a gardens In the context of marital relations the mother is sometime. spoken of as the real ' owner of the child ' (*mwenimwana*). This close and authoritarian bond between mother and daughter is probably strengthened by the fact that lineal descent passes through women. This bond is not broken by death, since the ritual histories I have collected show that the mother's spirit is thought frequently to afflict her daughter with reproductive troubles or illness if the daughter neglects to mention her name when praying or to make her an offering of food or beer. Again a mother's spirit is thought to afflict her daughter if she quarrels with relatives. In fact, the mother-daughter tie is the second most frequent category of relationship between afflicting spirit and patient which I recorded.

The father's sister (*tata wamumbanda* or *tatankaji*) is in certain contexts equated with the mother, but she is treated with greater constraint, since, with preferred bilateral cross-cousin marriage, she is a potential mother-in-law. For that matter the mother's brother is a potential father-in-law, and this tends to diminish his authority over his sisters' children if they marry his children. After marriage of this kind, his nephews have little to do with him directly, and his nieces avoid him.

So far we have been considering relationships between *primary* kin who call one another *aku*. The *classificatory extension* of kinship terms tends to diffuse over the whole group of senior *aku*, the control exerted by primary kin over their juniors in the adjacent generation, thus mitigating its narrow severity in particular relationships. This control by a whole genealogical generation of village kin over another whole generation is especially marked in the case of men who form in some respect a separate moral community of males.[1] One of the most

---

[1] Women do not form a coherent moral community since with virilocal marriage many are unrelated to one another and do not belong to the matrilineal group of the village.

important functions of the boys' circumcision ritual of *Mukanda* is, in fact, to remove boys from the authority of their own individual mothers, in the sphere of the kitchen, and to bring them under the collective control of the men of their village, in the sphere of the *chota*, the men's court and forum. A girl remains largely under the authority of her own mother until her husband has made the *kazundu* payment, at a variable period after marriage, which enables him to remove his wife 'from her mother's knee'. This is because the basic format of a village consists essentially of a set of structured relationships between *male* kin who control and obey one another in economic and jural matters. Another aspect of this collective control is connected with the conception of a village as a unit which transcends its narrower components, the uterine sibling groups and elementary families discussed above.

Within each linked-generation segment in a village the most general behavioural characteristics may be said to be familiarity and equality. But the precise weighting of such characteristics varies in each segment. In the grandparent-grandchild segment,[1] the generation components are genealogically unequal and often differ considerably in the mean age of their respective memberships. This fact tempers the familiarity of their intercourse with respect, since it is a general principle of Ndembu social life that the eldest-born is entitled to the greatest respect. But these components have in common the fact that both are opposed to the intervening genealogical generation which endeavours to wrest control from the grandparent generation. With reference to the medial generation they stand allied. On the other hand, since the grandparent generation nearly always holds the headmanship in a village, and since ultimately all the authority relations are vested in this office, a certain tension exists in the relationship between alternate generations. Again, if we regard the village as a set of linked corporate groups, each a potential unit of fission, we find that members of alternate generations have different uterine sibling group affiliations and belong to different elementary families. This fact again, in view of the basic and

---

[1] By 'grandparent' is meant any member of the senior alternate generation with whom a person can trace genealogical relationship through any line.

PLATE V

THE ALLIANCE OF ALTERNATE GENERATIONS

All the children, with one exception, playing around Sakazao, the nominated
successor of Headman Mukanza, are daughters' children of his sisters Nyamukola
and Nyatioli. The exception is the little girl standing behind him and clutching a
maize-cob. She is Kasonda's daughter and is Sakazao's cross-cousin and joking
partner. All the children present in fact have a joking relationship (*wusensi*)
with Sakazao, their ' grandfather '.

ineradicable narrowness of Ndembu corporate group relations, is a latent source of tension between them.

That tension exists is again revealed by certain sorcery beliefs. I have been told that at night a sorcerer sends out his *ilomba* snake-familiar to listen invisibly to what his grandchildren (*ejikulu*) are saying about him in private and to report back to him any expressions of animosity. In ritual performed to placate female spirits who have returned to plague their living female relatives with infertility or illness, grandmothers form the largest category of punitive spirits.

On the other hand, in custom the grandparents are the genial advisers and instructors of the grandchildren in many matters. Especially is this the case where sex instruction is concerned. *Aku* and siblings of opposite sex may not speak openly to one another on sexual topics but must employ circumlocutory speech (*kudidyika*). But this prohibition does not extend to grandparents (*ankaka*). In fact many instructresses of girls undergoing the puberty ritual are 'grandmothers'. These women (*ankong'u*) instruct their novices *inter alia* in the techniques of sexual intercourse and in other matters connected with sex and reproduction. Grandparents and grandchildren may sleep in the same hut and witness each other's sexual activities. Young children who are considered too old to remain in their parents' huts at night for this reason are sent to sleep with their grandparents, sometimes in the same bed.

The relationship between grandparents and grandchildren, like that between cross-cousins, is summed up in the Ndembu term *wusensi*. *Wusensi* may be translated as 'joking relationship'. Joking partners may revile one another, exciting amusement but not anger. They may claim any articles of one another's property they may fancy or call on one another's assistance in work without payment or return. Joking partners of opposite sex may indulge in sexual play, even in public. But the joking relationship which exists between grandparent and grandchild is of a mild and restrained type, and tends to be asymmetrical. The grandparent tends to initiate joking activities such as reviling, or seizing food carried by the grandchild. Again, although a young child is often allowed to take considerable liberties with his or her grandparents, when the child reaches adolescence he or she must behave with greater respect towards them. The relationship

s

between grandfather and granddaughter tends to be more ribald and egalitarian than that between grandmother and grandson, approximating in fact to the behaviour between cross-cousins of opposite sex. By far the higher proportion of grandparent-grandchild marriages are between men of the senior and women of the junior genealogical generation.

In many of the simpler societies terminological equivalence is made between grandparents and grandchildren so that the two categories are regarded as siblings. But among Ndembu the two categories do not apply to one another a self-reciprocal term but each category is distinguished. A grandchild calls his or her grandparent *nkaka*, and a grandparent calls his or her grandchild *mwijikulu*. Furthermore, while grandparents and grandchildren of opposite sex may sleep in the same hut and indulge in sexual play together, such behaviour is rigorously forbidden between brothers and sisters (as in other societies where there is this terminological identification). Grandparents and grandchildren behave towards one another more as though they were cross-cousins than as though they were siblings. Yet in the case of grandfathers and grandsons kinship terminology and behaviour patterns determined by it do suggest that an approximation to the equivalence of brothers is involved in the relationship. For example, a man may call his mother's mother's brother's child and also his father's mother's brother's child, a person of parental generation, ' my child '; thus implying that the speaker is regarded as being in some sense the mother's brother of his own parent. The fact that a woman may also call her mother's or father's mother's brother's child ' my child ', suggests that she is regarded as the cross-cousin or potential wife of her classificatory grandfather. Thus, although all members male and female of the senior alternate genealogical generation are classified together as *ankaka* by all members of the junior alternate genealogical generation, who are collectively called *ejikulu* by them, cross-sexual relations between these categories tend to be modelled on cross-cousin relations, and relationships between members of the same sex on those obtaining between brothers or sisters. Between the categories as a whole, therefore, there is a range in the character of their interaction between equivalence and alliance, and equivalence and alliance are modified by the perceptible degree of authority exerted by the senior over the junior generation. Contradiction exists in the relationship in that a grandson who is regarded in one sense as a younger brother is at the same time a potential brother-in-law. Similarly a granddaughter who, as the sister of a kind of younger brother, must be regarded as a sister, is also a potential wife. Behaviour associated with these respective roles is contradictory. The consequent confusion is one of the elements in the joking relationship which is nearly always a *coincidentia oppositorum*.

This confusion and contradictoriness seems to me to bring out the essential nature of the principle of organization by genealogical generation as a compromise formation between the lineal and familial modes of organization. If paternal and maternal kin are partially merged as members of a single genealogical generation it is possible to preserve their distinctive kinship characteristics in that generation ; but in the following generation, given the continuing strength of the generation principle, such distinctions become blurred. In a society with strong lineage organization, one aspect of which is lineage exogamy, members of the generations junior to EGO are divided into two categories :

(1) Lineage fellows with whom copulation is incest.
(2) Others, certain of whom are potential spouses.

But among Ndembu, members of generations junior to EGO are divided into two other categories :

(1) Those in adjacent generations, with whom there is hostility, fear, formality, authority, etc.
(2) Those in alternate generations, with whom there is informality, trust, equality, and the like, and who are potential spouses except for own children's own children.

Marriage with one's own sister's daughter's daughter is frowned upon but sometimes occurs, as in the case of Nswanamatempa, who married his own sister's daughter's daughter Njonka (III,G1 ; see Appendix III).

But the generation principle triumphs over the lineage principle to the extent that a person may marry a quite close lineal kinsman or kinswoman belonging to an alternate generation. On the other hand, one may not marry a comparatively distant paternal or cognatic kinsman or kinswoman of an adjacent generation.

The joking relationship between alternate generation kin is made up of two major components. One such component is that in effect a person may marry someone regarded as his or her classificatory sibling ; for true siblings this is taboo, yet here it is perfectly legitimate to do so. Embarrassment is resolved by laughter. The neighbouring Lwena tribe regard this Ndembu custom with as much abhorrence as Ndembu display towards the reputed Lwena custom of wife-sharing. The other component consists in the fact that two categories of genealogically asymmetrical kin are regarded as equal and allied, in contradiction to the general principle that seniority by birth or genealogical order confers authority. Thus one's equal is at the same time one's inferior, a paradox again resolved by mutual joking.

In both linked-generation segments in a village one of the two component categories consists of primary and classificatory siblings. In many contexts siblings are equated, in others they play opposed roles. They are equated as members of a uterine sibling group, the basic unit of fission and nuclear unit of a new settlement. The term *mwivumu detu*, ' in our womb ', is most often applied to such a group, the children of a single mother, although it may be extended to all who claim descent through real or putative matrilineal links from a common ancestress or even to those who without remembering the name of that ancestress claim maternal relationship with one another. But basically *mwivumu detu* refers to one's own sibling group. There is no general term for ' brothers ', only terms for ' older brother ' (*yaya*) and ' younger brother ' (*mwanyika*). A man does not discriminate between an older or younger sister, but calls both by the term *muhela*. Older and younger sisters distinguish one another by the terms *yaya* and *mwanyika* respectively. A woman calls both older and younger brothers by the term *manakwetu*. *Kwetu* is the locative, not the possessive, form, and means ' at our place '. This is interesting, since it denotes that a woman regards her home as being where her brother is residing. The plural form ' *kwetu* ', ' at *our* place,' suggests that the sibling group is regarded as a spatial unit. Sometimes a woman will refer to her brother, whether older or younger, by the term *yaya* which is usually applied to an older sibling of the same sex as EGO. This implies that she recognizes his authority, since within the genealogical generation seniority goes with primacy by birth. In the past I am told that a woman used to call her brother *iyala*, literally ' man ', a term now sometimes used as a synonym for ' husband ' (*mfumu*).

Within a genealogical generation seniority in age and not in genealogical position determines whether parallel cousins call one another ' older ', or ' younger sibling '. On the other hand, sub-lineages of a village matrilineage are rated as senior (*ivumu damukulumpi*) or junior (*ivumu dakansi*) according to the sibling order of their apical ancestresses. Thus one might find a man in a senior lineage addressing his parallel cousin in a junior lineage as ' older brother ' since the latter was the earlier born of the two. Hence in each linked-generation segment there is a contradiction among lineal kin of the same sex between the principles of genealogical and chronological seniority. Both principles are invoked by candidates for village headmanship.

Nevertheless, despite the close and persistent ties that unite members of a single uterine sibling group, powerful tensions between its members exist. The closer the tie, the greater the ambivalence of feeling. Between older and younger uterine brothers mutual hostility is revealed by an analysis of sorcery accusations. By adelphic succession a younger brother may succeed to headmanship on the death of his older brother so that he is a natural target for suspicions which themselves may tend to influence the result of a divination. A further source of hostility resides in the fact that an older brother is regarded by Ndembu as his father's lieutenant within the sibling group. He may be delegated by his father with the task of punishing a younger brother or of admonishing him severely for bad be-haviour. In the boys' circumcision ritual, this role of the older brother is dramatized ; either a father or an older brother is considered to be the most suitable person to act as ' shepherd ' (*chilombola*) to a novice. Part of a shepherd's duties consist in administering punishment to his charge for breaches of lodge customs, on the instructions of the senior official of the seclusion lodge (*mfumu watubwiku*), who is himself usually the father of the greatest number of novices. An older brother can command the services of his younger brother in, for example, the carrying of loads, the collection of firewood, hut-building, and many other ways. But just as the shepherd at circumcision protects and attends to the wants of his charge, so also does the older brother give protection and assistance to his younger brother in the affairs of life. Once when Daudson Mwevulu's (I,H7) younger brother Sign [1] was insulted at an *Nkula* ritual as being too young to take part in the popular modern *chikinta* dance which today accompanies most rituals, and in which the younger element dominantly participate, Mwevulu immediately started a fight with Sign's detractor and then knocked down the latter's father who had intervened on his behalf.

In more formal matters older brothers will assist their younger brothers with bride-wealth, with court fines, and with death-payments, and will share their food and possessions with them without question. As brothers grow older their relationship becomes more egalitarian and reciprocal and often something like a division of skills emerges between them. Thus Mukanza Kabinda became a headman while his younger brother Kanyombu acquired a reputation as a ritual specialist and herbalist. In another village Mulila, the younger brother, acted as headman while Itota, the older brother, devoted most of his time to hunting. In Ikelenge Area Nswanandong'a was at once headman of a village and a hunter while his younger brother Makwayang'a participated fully in the cash economy at various times as a casual labourer, *kapasu* or Native Authority policeman, and cash-crop farmer.

Uterine brothers usually spend the whole of their lives together. Mothers and sons may be separated by the divorce and remarriage of the former. Sisters are divided from brothers by virilocal marriage. Children may be separated from fathers by divorce, sex, matrilineal pressures and virilocal marriage. Uterine brothers are united by descent and generation. Thus the link between brothers is deep and abiding, despite the possibilities of conflict inherent in it. When a man founds a new settlement his most faithful supporter is his brother, for their sisters have another loyalty—to their husbands.

In the relationship between parallel cousins the ties are less close and the cleavages more clearly evident. Parallel cousins belong to different matricentric families and may have been reared in different paternal villages. When different groups of uterine siblings build together and become co-members of a

---

[1] Manyosa's sons in Mukanza Village.

village genealogical generation, the divisions initially existing between them are not immediately or easily overcome. Even although it is customary when meat is divided to give an equal share to all kin who bear the same kinship term, in practice people tend to favour their closer at the expense of their more distant kin and this becomes a source of jealousy and back-biting, especially between sibling groups. Similarly, although it is expected that close kin should contribute and receive the bulk of marriage payments, fines, etc. and that distant kin should contribute and receive lesser amounts, much wrangling actually takes place between two or more uterine sibling groups within a minimal or minor matrilineage about the precise sums given and received. But it is when succession to office drops from the last living member of the senior village generation to the junior adjacent generation that relations between its component uterine sibling groups tend to become most strained. It will be remembered that in Mukanza Village the relationship most fraught with tension was that between Sandombu and Kasonda, parallel cousins belonging to different sibling groups. It was pointed out in the analysis of Social Drama I that according to Ndembu opinion succession to office in a chieftainship or in a well-established village should not be confined within a single narrow-span lineage, so that a man was succeeded by his uterine nephew. In point of fact, however, a headman's own sister's son often strongly urges his claim and this brings him into conflict with his male parallel cousins and also with their siblings who support them. This kind of conflict probably influenced the secession of Nswanakudya (II,D10) from Shika Village when his parallel cousin seemed likely to succeed, and that of Matempa (III,D3) from Nsang'anyi Village, when the present headman did in fact succeed to headmanship (see Appendices II and III; also p. 208 and p. 212).

The tie between brother and sister is also a very close one, and like the preceding tie, contains several possibilities of tension. Brothers and sisters are frequently reared together in their father's village, but the tie of spatial propinquity is usually broken by the virilocal marriage of sisters after puberty. Brother and sister are linked by descent and generation, but are divided by sex. In certain respects the relationship of brother and sister resembles that between *aku* (in-laws) belonging to adjacent generations.

Strong taboos against incest divide them and introduce constraint into their behaviour towards one another. Neither may speak overtly of sexual matters to the other. Only as very small children may they sleep in the same hut. A man was once strongly suspected of sorcery when on a visit to his married sister he sat on her bed and it broke beneath his weight. To obtain a peculiarly potent hunting medicine a man must commit incest with his sister, and the suspected possession of such medicine by a hunter causes him to be regarded with abhorrence. One Ndembu oath believed to be powerfully binding in a village court has the form, 'If what I say is untrue I have had sexual relations with my sister.' This is considered to be a statement of the impossible. Yet in spite of this incest barrier sisters are equated with wives in several contexts. At a chief's installation ritual, for example, the chief-to-be is secluded during the night before his accession either with his senior wife or, if she is in a state of pollution due to her pregnancy or menstruation, with his sister. Again, in the *Nkula* ritual, performed for women who are thought to be afflicted with menstrual disorders by the spirit of a deceased relative, the patient is escorted from the small spirit-hut built behind her dwelling-hut to the ritual fire by a male ' helper ' (*chaka chaNkula*), who may be either her husband, her brother or her son. At the boys' circumcision ritual either the mother or a father's sister of a novice may cook for him at the sacred fire (*ijiku daMukanda*).

In their own generation the principal conflicts of interest between brother and sister spring from marriage and the family. A brother desires his sister's children to swell his following, but, owing to the strong ties that interlink members of a matricentric family it is difficult to fulfil this wish unless his virilocally resident sister is divorced from her husband. I have recorded several cases in which a husband demanded compensation from his wife's brother in a Native Court for retaining her in his village when she had paid him a visit. On the other hand I have heard complaints from brothers that their sisters have remained with their children in their husbands' villages so that the brothers have been unable, though senior men, to found their own settlements.

When brothers and sisters inhabit the same village, disputes sometimes arise between them over their respective groups of children. Sisters accuse brothers of neglecting their nephews and nieces in favour of their own children. Quarrels arise between brothers and sisters over the distribution of bride-wealth received for daughters of the latter. I have often heard sisters bitterly scold their brothers for failing to assist them with money, and for giving cloth to their wives but not a rag to their sisters. The sister has considerable power in this relationship, and her threat to leave her brother's village often has the effect of bringing him to heel. For example, Chawutong'i of Mukanza Village, incensed that Kasonda, her first parallel cousin, had not bought clothing for her younger children, left the village for a while to stay at Mbimbi Village, a short distance away. She would not return until he had made up a dress for her daughter on his sewing-machine.

Despite the possibilities of discord inherent in the relationship between siblings, within each linked-generation segment primary and classificatory siblings, matrilineally related to the headman, confront the other members of their generation as a unitary group. Thus in the senior segment the headman and his matrilineal generation mates confront the adult members of the 'grandchild' category, who are usually numerically inferior and may be divided among themselves by varying maternal and paternal affiliations. Some may be matrilineal members of the village, others seminal children and children's children of male village members. In the junior segment primary and classificatory matrilineal siblings confront their cross-cousins, the seminal children of male village members of the senior segment. Since the matrilineage is to some extent a persisting corporate group while the tie to the father is personal and ephemeral, in this segment also the matrilineal sibling group tends to have greater internal cohesion. This group is linked to the co-members of its segment by cross-cousinship.

Cross-cousinship, like the grandparent-grandchild relationship, is a joking partnership. Perhaps on account of the egalitarian nature of the tie between cross-cousins in Ndembu society, the joking is of a more boisterous type than that between kin belonging to alternate generations. It is symmetrical, sexual in content, derogatory in manner, and often contains reference to the sorcery or witchcraft of the joking partner. Cross-cousins make free with one another's possessions, those of opposite sex indulge in sexual play, and cross-cousin marriage is the preferred form of marriage. Ndembu men appear to marry their patrilateral and matrilateral cross-cousins with equal frequency. But a distinction must be made between the kinds of behaviour that typically occur between close and distant cross-cousins. Cross-cousins who inhabit the same village behave to one another more as though they were brothers and sisters than joking partners. Their relationship exemplifies the statement previously made that in the village there is a convergence between lineal and familial principles of organization, and that the organization by genealogical generation represents a compromise between them. As members of a common generation cross-cousins are united in opposition to the adjacent generations. As children they are jointly under the authority of the senior adjacent generation, as adults they jointly exert authority over the junior adjacent generation. Together they co-operate in communal working-parties at the beginning of the gardening season. Male cross-cousins may hunt together, female cross-cousins may pound in the same mortar. Their familiarity in daily tasks and the similarity of their structural position in the organization by generation tend to reduce the element of unlikeness derived from their distinct lineal affiliations. If they lived in different villages the feeling of dissimilarity would be much stronger.

Unfamiliarity and hostility are components of the raillery between joking partners. Cross-cousins may be regarded as *unlike* and *equal*. Relations between siblings may be described as *parallel* relations. Siblings are regarded as *equivalent* to one another. They are *alike* and *equal*. Village cross-cousins also tend to interact in parallel rather than in complementary and opposed relations. They tend, in fact, to behave to one another like siblings. This may result in a reduction of joking and perhaps in a dampening down of the sexual attraction between opposites. Cross-cousin marriage between close kin is relatively infrequent. On the other hand marriage between persons who call one another cross-cousins (*asonyi*), but who cannot trace precise relationship between one another is quite common. This kind of marriage supports my previous statement that villages which claim common matrilineal descent soon forget their precise matrilineal link but can still class one another's members by genealogical generation. Thus the men of one village know

roughly which women in the other village fall into the marriage-
able category and which women fall into the forbidden categories.
Among the Lamba of the Ndola District of Northern Rhodesia
whom Mitchell and Barnes found to possess a high frequency
of virilocal marriage (38·1 per cent of extant marriages), and
among whom, therefore, cross-cousinship must constitute an
important ingredient of village kinship, primary and traceable
cross-cousin marriages formed an extremely low proportion of
the total marriages recorded (7 primary, 2 classificatory cross-
cousin marriages out of 360 extant and dissolved marriages,
or 2·5 per cent).[1] It may well be that among matrilineal peoples
with shallow local lineages and virilocal marriage an identification
tends to arise between the children of siblings of opposite sex
on the basis of co-membership of a genealogical generation which
inhibits frequent intra-village cross-cousin marriage. Among
Ndembu, at any rate, there is a markedly greater tendency to
marry distant than close cross-cousins. And it is a matter of
observation that joking behaviour reaches its fullest expression
between distant cross-cousins, and between cross-cousins,
whatever their genealogical distance, who normally reside in
widely separated villages. Each village contains a separate and
autonomous system of kinship relations construed on organizational principles which mutually modify one another. No one
principle then achieves its maximum expression. Concrete
behaviour is their mean working. In specific situations, however, one or other may become dominant. Marriages do in fact
take place between village cross-cousins. When children build
leaf-huts in the bush and 'play at husbands and wives', cross-
cousins but not brothers and sisters mime the marital roles. In
other kinship categories we have seen examples of the kinds of
situation in which, for instance, fathers stand opposed to mothers'
brothers, and children to nephews. But in order that the village
may be a going concern and a viable unit, it is necessary that
conflicting matrilineal and patrilateral loyalties should be reconciled. Organization by genealogical generation is the major
means by which this reconciliation is effected.

---

[1] Mitchell and Barnes, *The Lamba Village*, p. 41.

Summary

Virilocal marriage unites a number of narrow-span maternal descent groups within the bilateral extended family to form the local unit of residence.   Each such descent group is a matricentric family which in the course of the social process strives to disengage itself from all other ties of local affiliation and achieve residential autonomy.   It is possible to regard most other categories of local kinship ties as counterbalancing the centrifugal tendency of the matricentric family.   In its early stages the matricentric family is typically linked through its apical member, the mother, to a village lineage to which her husband belongs. Its members then have a personal tie of loyalty to their father, to the bilateral extended family (*ntang'a*) of which he is a member, and to his matrilineal village itself, regarded as something more than the sum of its parts, as a unit of social space which may bear an ancient and respected name.   If the father is a headman this tie to the village and to its dominant kin-group, his bilateral extended family, is exceptionally strong.   If he is not a headman, but the senior brother in a large uterine sibling group, his children's dominant attachment may well be through him to his own, narrow bilateral extended kin group which comprises his own siblings and their children.   If this group splits off from the village his wife and her children will go with them.   But even within this village to which they are linked primarily through their father, the children are divided from their parents by generation and united with their patrilateral cross-cousins, who, like their father, are members of the village lineage.   On the other hand, even while they live in their father's village, they pay regular visits to their mother's village, in which they have ties of corporate group membership.   It is in this village that some of them may one day succeed to office and inherit property.   On the divorce or widowing of their mother they may return to it. On their return, either in a compact group or severally in stages, they form within it a tight group which with the maturation of its membership becomes a potential unit of fission.   Their emancipation as a separate residential unit is prevented, or at least retarded, by the cross-cutting allegiances mentioned above, and by a division of their loyalties between the narrow group of uterine siblings and the wider groupings of minimal and minor matrilineages and of the village as a whole. Virilocal marriage which was at the root of their intense cohesion now operates to separate the siblings by sex. Nevertheless, as we have seen, the tendency to joint secession evinced by the group of mature uterine siblings frequently asserts itself to retard the growth of large villages.

CHAPTER IX

POLITICAL ASPECTS OF KINSHIP AND AFFINITY

WE have already discussed the way in which ties of maternal descent are utilized to establish links between villages in separate vicinages. Such ties have a political function. Because ties of kinship, which are often coterminous with ties of friendship, and of economic, ritual and jural co-operation, enjoin collaboration and are almost always means to establish residential affiliation, they have a high political value in a decentralized, mobile and unstable society. Even more important in this respect are affinal ties which interlink exogamous and potentially conflicting groups. In the preceding analysis of internal village relations, we have seen how intra-village marriage in a long-established village allies uterine sibling groups, belonging to the same generation, by means of cross-cousin marriage, and inter-links uterine sibling groups belonging to alternate generations by grandparent-grandchild marriage. In this case kinship ties, both lineal and cognatic, are supplemented by affinal ties within the settlement. In this chapter links of in-lawship between villages will be examined as a mechanism for establishing political relations between them.

Two major aspects will be considered : (1) the effects on inter-village linkages brought about by the particular form of marriage among Ndembu, and (2) the range of such ties, whether they interlink villages within a vicinage or whether they associate separate vicinages within a *connubium*.

Table XX, based on a sample of 165 extant marriages in my Village Census about which I was able to obtain information from both marital partners, shows to what extent virilocal marriage is the prevalent form. Nearly seven out of ten marriages were virilocal as compared with seven out of a hundred which were uxorilocal. Some uxorilocal marriages represented the first stage of a first marriage in which the husband was still conforming to the tradition of initial uxorilocality. Others, like the marriage of Ndeleki in Mukanza Village (see pp. 101-2), were special cases in which the husband had abandoned his matrilineal village on account of fears of witchcraft or because of serious disputes with his kin.

The structural effects of virilocal marriage within the village have already been discussed in Chapter Eight, where it was found that a relationship existed between this form of marriage, the close cohesion of the uterine sibling group, the shallowness of the matrilineage, the organization by genealogical generation within the village, the tendency towards the merging of familial

TABLE XX

RESIDENCE OF HUSBAND AND WIFE

Sample of 165 extant marriages :

Residence	No. in sample	Percentage
Virilocal	115	69·7
Intra-village . . .	27	16·4
Uxorilocal . . .	12	7·3
Other	11	6·6
Total	165	100·0

and lineal principles of intra-village organization, and the high rate of individual mobility. Between villages its principal consequence is to mesh together by ties of affinity, which ulti-mately give rise to links of consanguinity, a number of spatially distinct settlements, vicinages and even senior headmen's areas. Matriliny is the foundation of each village's continuity in time ; matrilineal descent is therefore the dominant mode of attachment by kinship. Virilocal marriage scatters the nuclear women of the matrilineal kin-group of each village through many other villages, so that the dominant bond of kinship is utilized not merely to consolidate the local unit, but to strengthen the ties between separate villages. Thus each village contains not only its own nuclear group of matrilineal kin but also a number of matricentric families belonging to the nuclear matrilineages of other villages. Conversely, through the virilocal marriage of its own women, the nuclear matrilineage of each village at any one time has a number of its cells, consisting of matricentric families lineally related to it, dispersed through other villages. It is as though each village entrusts other villages with the task of fostering its own future membership and simultaneously brings up the potential personnel of other villages. But there is no precise correspondence between the villages to which each village exports women and from whom it receives women. In other words, there is no marked tendency towards the formation of connubial clusters of villages which constitute closed inter-marrying groups. Interlocking ties of affinity connect separate chiefdoms. Kanongesha's Ndembu intermarry freely with Musokantanda's Kosa, and with Kazembe's Congo Lunda. And within Kanongesha's chiefdom, senior headman's area is inter-woven with senior headman's area by the busy shuttle of viri-local marriage. If we consider each remembered matrilineage separately we find that it has a local nucleus, consisting typically of a minor lineage in which male members outnumber females by about two to one, and a widely scattered peripheral member-ship in which the proportions tend to be reversed (if absentees, both male and female, at urban centres are excluded from the reckoning).

In certain matrilineal societies that practise virilocal marriage, such as that of the Trobriand Islanders described by Malinowski, it is customary for the sister's son to return to his mother's brother's village on attaining puberty or social maturity as defined by other criteria. No such custom exists among Ndembu. A son will remain with his father after attaining man-hood if he obtains any material advantage from so doing, or if he has a strong tie of affection with him. For example, Gideon of Mukanza Village, son of the headman, prefers to remain with his father, even although his mother, from Shika Village, has been dead for several years. Gideon is in his middle thirties and says that he will stay in Mukanza until his father dies. Daughters will often return to their fathers' villages after divorce, especially if their mothers also reside there, instead of taking up residence with their mothers' brothers. This duality of residential choice results in a state of endemic and barely concealed conflict between a man and his wife's village matrilineal group, who want his wife and children, and between him and his sister's husband's village lineage, who seek to retain his potential local following and heirs. This conflict only becomes acute as the children and sister's children grow up, but it exists at every stage of a marriage. There is really no way finally to resolve the situation except by divorce or death. In the final issue village continuity depends on marital discontinuity.

In practice, of course, since each village is in effect a set of variously linked uterine sibling groups with attached individuals, who may be kin or strangers, and since the units of affinal conflict are uterine sibling groups, losses in some groups are compensated by gains in others. For a time indeed marital continuity is an indispensable condition of village continuity, since children replace the lost sister's children, both in the uterine sibling group and in the village. But in the end, if the sisters' children do not return, the village will perish as a matrilineal descent group. The village of Mbimbi, for instance, close neighbour of Mukanza, was, in 1954, in a fair way towards becoming extinct, since Mbimbi's sisters' children were either living with their fathers or had gone to other villages, his only living daughter was living virilocally, and his son had left him to reside with his mother's brother for fear of the witchcraft of his father's senior wife, who was thought to have killed several children in the village.

Each village is linked to many other villages by single marital ties and in this way it extends the geographical range of its political interconnections. On the other hand, one finds the not infrequent establishment of a relationship of reciprocal marital exchanges between two villages. This arrangement aims at reducing conflict since each of the two intermarrying groupings rears the future membership of the other. It is in the interest of both villages to maintain in being the marriages that interlink them, since the breakdown of a marriage in one village may lead to the exertion of pressure by the matrilineage of the other on their virilocally resident kinswoman to leave her husband and bring her children to her own village.

Nevertheless, as we shall see, marital ties, far from establishing enduring friendship between villages, may give rise to frequent disputes between them.

In order to bring out the political function of inter-village marital linkages, the field of affinal relations of a single village with other villages will first be considered, followed by an analysis of the ties of affinity and of kinship affiliation, inaugurated

T

by inter-village marriage, existing between the headmen of component settlements in a single vicinage.

Since I have analysed the internal structure of Mukanza Village in some detail, I shall discuss the external relations of the same village constituted by affinity in similar detail. In most respects this village is typical of the consolidated and traditional Ndembu village. I regard all living members of NYACHINTANG'A and MALABU lineages, together with Nyawunyumbi and her children, of NYACHULA lineage, who have made their home at Mukanza, as 'village members'. Both extant and fruitful completed marriages, whether completed by death or divorce, between village members and members of other villages will be considered.[1] Persons who were absent in urban areas in November 1951 will be excluded from the investigation.

Reciprocal marital exchanges have taken place between Mukanza and Shika Villages for several generations. Shika Village matrilineage belongs to the wide matrilineal descent group from which the incumbent of the Kanongesha stool is elected. There is a distinct tendency for villages which participate in the Kanongesha chieftainship to intermarry with Kawiku villages. Thus Shika Village and its offshoot Nswana-kudya Village tend to intermarry with Nsang'anyi, with Kasai, and with Mukanza Villages, all Kawiku settlements. Similarly there is a tendency for Chibwakata and its offshoot Ng'ombi Village, both of Lunda origin, to intermarry with Kawiku villages. Both Shika and Chibwakata refer to themselves as 'the husband' (*mfumu*) of Nsang'anyi. Nsang'anyi, on the other hand, calls himself 'the husband' of Chibwakata. In actuality, although both parties, the one descended from the original invaders, the other from the autochthonous people, claim superiority over one another by the use of the term 'husband', both are able to make this claim by virtue of the fact that the chain of reciprocal intermarriage began with an exchange of sisters between the heads of the respective groups.

In one sense, therefore, the reciprocal intermarrying between Mukanza and Shika Villages is an aspect of the political relation-

---

[1] See Map 6, Mukanza Village Marriages, for spatial range of extant marriages and fruitful completed marriages of matrilineal membership.

ship between Lunda and Kawiku. But, more importantly it, is a relationship between two Ndembu villages. At one time Shika Village belonged to the same vicinage as Mukanza Village, and it was at this time that Mukanza Kabinda (I,F8), then a young man, married Nyatungeji (II,D3), sister's daughter of Headman Shika Ikubi (II,C2). In the same year Nyatungeji's brother Kahumpu (II,D1 ; see pp. 190–1) married Mukanza Kabinda's sister Nyamwaha (I,F7 ; see p. 118 et seq.), thus interlinking not only the two villages but also the uterine sibling groups of Mukanza Kabinda and Kahumpu by reciprocal intermarriage. Although I have not been able to trace the exact genealogical connection, Mukanza Kabinda called both Nyatungeji and Kahumpu his ' grandchildren ' (*ejikulu*), which suggests that previous intermarriages had taken place between the two villages.

Mukanza Kabinda's marriage was terminated by the death of Nyatungeji in 1943, and the circumstances associated with her death became a source of perennial discord in the relations between the two villages. When a death occurs among Ndembu the lineal kin of the surviving spouse have to pay the lineage of the deceased what is for them a substantial sum, called *mpepi*, or ' death-payment ', in compensation for the loss they incur of his or her labour potential, or in the case of a woman, of her fertility in addition. *Mpepi* also includes payment for various ritual services performed by the village lineage of the deceased for the surviving spouse, the most important of which is to rid the latter of the spirit of the dead spouse (*ku-fumisha mukishi windi*) which will otherwise cling to the survivor and afflict him or her with bad dreams and illness. Such a spirit may also jealously attack the survivor's next wife or husband with disease. Now in order to avoid paying *mpepi* [1] it frequently happens that a man or woman will divorce a spouse who is fatally ill. The lineage of the deceased cannot then claim that the death occurred while the marriage was extant, and that therefore according to Ndembu notions responsibility for the welfare of the deceased was vested in the surviving spouse and his or her village lineage. The practice of divorcing an ailing spouse has undoubtedly distorted

---

[1] It should be mentioned that Ndembu villagers believe that the payment of *mpepi* is forbidden under a Native Authority regulation, but they tacitly agree to maintain the custom clandestinely. But if a sick spouse is divorced there is no remedy at law.

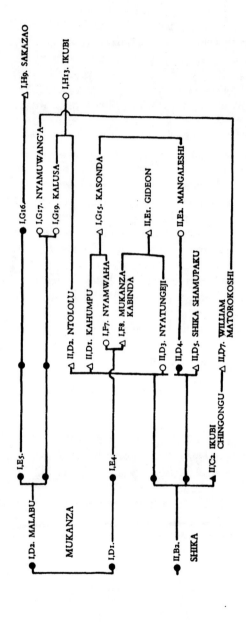

the divorce ratios in Table VII, since a significant proportion
of the divorces recorded must be in reality masked widow-
hoods.

When Nyatungeji seemed to be on the point of death, Mukanza
Kabinda divorced her, and carried her, with the aid of kinsmen,
back to Shika Village on a stretcher. He alleged that someone
among her matrilineal kin in Shika Village had bewitched her ' in
order to eat the *mpepi* ', hinting that Headman Shika himself was
to blame. He then affected to take umbrage because the
marriage-payment (*nsewu*) he had made for her in cloth was not
returned. In the long process through which an Ndembu
marriage becomes consolidated a number of payments in cash
and kind are made. They include the small *chijika muchisu*
' which closes the door ' (today about 2s. 6d.) which signifies
betrothal ; the *kazundu*, ' taking a wife from her mother '
(today about 5s.), which gives the husband his right to take his
wife to his own village ; and the most important, the *nsewu*,
' the arrow ', the marriage payment proper, formerly paid in
cloth, livestock or a gun, but now in cash. *Nsewu* is generally
regarded by Ndembu as a precaution against adultery ; informants have compared it with a fence round a cassava garden
to keep out wild pigs. If a man has paid *nsewu* for a woman he
is entitled to compensation from his wife's lover both in a Native
Authority Court and in a village court, if adultery is proven.
Moreover, a man is entitled to the return of his *nsewu* on divorce,
whichever party is adjudged culpable. If he wishes to retain
with him immediately one or more of his children he will not
seek the return of his *nsewu* from his wife's kin. Again, if he
wishes to maintain friendly relations with his wife's village
kin who will help to look after his children, he will ' leave the
nsewu with them '. In the case of Nyatungeji no death-payment
was made and no marriage payment was returned. Mukanza's
two surviving children, including Gideon (see Social Drama IV,
p. 148), by Nyatungeji, remained in their father's village.
Although no overt breach of social relations took place between
the two villages, an undercurrent of hostility remained which
manifested itself in subsequent situations.

Kasonda (I,G15), son of Kahumpu (II,D1) and Nyamwaha
(I,F7), married his father's classificatory sister's daughter
Mangaleshi (II,E2), of Shika Village lineage. She is known as

his cross-cousin on both father's and mother's sides,[1] has borne him five children, and their marriage is a stabilizing factor in the relations between the two villages. Kasonda's older daughters have both acted in the capacity of ritual handmaids (*tunsonselelu*) to girls undergoing the puberty ritual at Shika Village, and will themselves be secluded there. They pay frequent visits to Shika unaccompanied by either of their parents. Mangaleshi herself goes to Shika to take part in any major ritual that is performed there. Her classificatory brother Gideon and Kasonda have built adjacent huts in Mukanza Village, and Kasonda's connections with Shika have stood him in good stead both in his internal intrigues and in his intercalary role between the two villages. It is important for the Mukanza people to maintain friendly relations with Shika Village, for it is possible that a member of that village will some day succeed to the Kanongesha chieftainship.[2] The husband of Kasonda's classificatory sister Chawutong'i (I,G12), Ndeleki (II,D8), is also the son of a Shika man, and he and his wife have also built adjacently to Kasonda on the other side to Gideon. These persons, linked to one another through kinship ties of varying character with Shika Village, form a small pressure group under the leadership of Kasonda within Mukanza Village. Within Mukanza too they support the interests of NYACHINTANG'A lineage to which they are affinally or filially attached. At the same time they provide a number of linkages with Shika Village which by their multiplicity and strength prevented the conflict between Mukanza Kabinda and the elders of Shika Village from developing into a permanent breach of friendly relations between the two villages.

Two members of MALABU lineage were also affinally linked with Shika Village in 1951, and conflict arose from both relationships. Nyamuwang'a (I,G17 ; see Social Drama IV, p. 148) was married to William Matorokoshi, (II,D7), son of the late Shika Ikubi. In that year he divorced her on the grounds that she was a witch and wanted to kill him by her witchcraft. Since Nyamuwang'a was feared for the same reason in Mukanza

---

[1] Kasonda stresses this double tie to support a politically valuable marriage. But Mangaleshi is not his true matrilateral cross-cousin. She is classificatory sister to Gideon (II,E1), who is Kasonda's matrilateral cross-cousin.

[2] See pp. 207-8, 322.

Village itself, and since the pair had no children, little was said about the matter. But Sakazao (I,H9), senior elder of MALABU lineage, resented having to return William's *nsewu*, since he was a poor man. He was said to have upbraided Nyamuwang'a for her reputed occult activities and to have demanded that she contribute to the repayment of *nsewu*. I did not hear whether she did so, but it is probable that she did, since she was living in Sakazao's quarter of the village in the dry season of 1951 when Social Drama IV took place.

Nyamuwang'a's sister Kalusa (I,G19) was married to Kasonda's father's uterine brother Ntololu (I,D2), and this pair were the parents of Ikubi who, as described in the account of Social Drama IV, was supposed to have been killed by the witchcraft of Nyamuwang'a. Ntololu at that time was living uxorilocally in Mukanza Village, having quarrelled with his classificatory brother, the headman of Shika, Shamupaku (II,D5.) After Ikubi's death Ntololu returned to Shika Village with Kalusa, bitterly angry with Nyamuwang'a and in fact at odds with the people of Mukanza Village as a whole.

The death of Kalusa, sister of Nyamuwang'a, at Shika Village in 1953 touched off a social drama which made overt many of the hidden tensions both within Mukanza Village and between Mukanza and Shika Villages.

SOCIAL DRAMA VII

Two Headmen Dispute over a Death Payment
(my own observations)

On July 6th, 1953, a messenger arrived one somnolent afternoon at Mukanza Village with news from Shika that Kalusa (I,G19) was dead. Instantly wailing broke out from all the Mukanza women who rushed into the central clearing between the huts and sat or stood each separate from one another. In a short while the plaints became organized into songs of grief, led by Manyosa (I,G13), who sat with her hands crossed on her shoulders, shaking and nodding her head while tears ran down her face. Among her rhythmic cries could be heard brief phrases, ' She died all alone ', ' my father and mother and my uncle Kanyombu are dead', ' a death by *andumba* [a term for witchcraft familiars or *tuyebela*]'. At first all the women had been facing in the direction of Shika Village. When the last phrase was uttered all turned in the direction of Sandombu Farm with anger

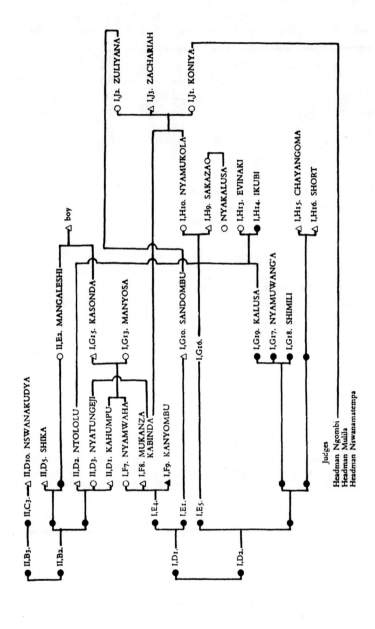

on their faces. Men had joined the bewailing group, although in keeping with custom they did not weep. Sandombu (I,G10) came slowly towards them from his own place. He came forward into the middle of the dispersed group and a harsh argument developed between him and Nyakalusa, the slave wife of Sakazao (I,H9), privileged as we have noted already by virtue of her role as an ' outsider ' to speak openly what was in the minds of all. Chayangoma (I,H15), classificatory sister's son of Kalusa and Nyamuwang'a (I,G17), and classificatory brother of Sakazao, all in MALABU lineage, also joined issue with Sandombu. Chayangoma since he was, as we have described, a blind man, as well as a close lineal kinsman of Kalusa, was also free to speak his views. They attacked Sandombu for harbouring a witch in his farm, meaning Nyamuwang'a. Nyamuwang'a had recently visited her sister at Shika Village and they recalled how Nyamuwang'a's sister Shimili (I,G18) had died at Chimbili Village after Nyamuwang'a had visited her, and how Ikubi (I,H14), Kalusa's daughter, whom in the words of Mangaleshi (II,E2), Kasonda's wife, ' Kalusa had followed ', had died after receiving a malediction from the old witch. Sandombu shouted back at them that there had been no proof that Nyamuwang'a was a witch. She had loved her sister, he said. He returned to his house in animated conversation with Chayangoma (I,H15) who was led along beside him by Kasonda's small son who was incidentally his father's confidant.

Later the men assembled in the *chota*. It was decided that they should send round to the other villages to buy beer for the funeral gathering (*Chipenji*) of Kalusa (I,G19) which would be held in Mukanza Village. It was also decided to send a small delegation to Shika to ascertain more fully the facts of the situation and to make arrangements about the funeral gathering. Feelings had calmed somewhat, following a rumour that Headman Shika (II,D5) was contemplating a witchcraft action in a chief's private court against unspecified ' Mukanza people '. It was suggested that in this way he wished to evade the payment of *mpepi* to Mukanza Village, since if he could get his charge upheld the latter would be culpable and his own group could not in any way be held responsible. *Mpepi* is paid by the kin of the relict, not in compensation for their witchcraft, but *inter alia* for failing to protect the deceased spouse from real or supernatural harm. But if her own kin had bewitched her, Kalusa's affines need not pay them *mpepi*. This rumour, which may have been inspired by someone in Mukanza, had the effect of uniting the village against Shika. They discussed the question of *mpepi*, which is divided into two consecutive payments, a small sum called *kutotafu* (' to take away the dead ') for ritual services rendered to the widow or widower, and the *mpepi* proper, and decided to ask only 2s. for the former since they could not obtain enough beer or provide enough food at that time for a long funeral gathering (in the past this sometimes lasted three or more months accompanied by elaborate ritual). The *mpepi* proper was to be left over for negotiation between the two villages after the all-night *Mudyileji* dance which concludes the funerary ritual. The emissaries to Shika were as follows : Mukanza's sons, Gideon (II,E1) whose mother came from Shika, and Zachariah (I,J3), uterine nephew of Sakazao (I,H9) ; Short (I,H16), younger uterine brother of Chayangoma (I,H15) ; Zuliyana (I,J2), Mukanza's daughter and Zachariah's sister ; and Nyakalusa. The women were included only because the deceased was a woman. Village unity had been restored to such an extent that Nyamuwang'a (I,G17) was nominated as executrix (*nyamufu*, ' mother of the dead '). She would receive and distribute Kalusa's property, sell her Shika gardens, and take charge of the *mpepi* paid by Headman Shika. This nomination was a demonstration of the solidarity of the Mukanza group in the face of the outside world. Normally this office would devolve upon the uterine brother or mother's brother of a dead woman but Kalusa had no brothers and Nyamuwang'a was her closest uterine relative. Sakazao, as head of MALABU lineage, might have been appointed but since he had recently been fined for not returning the marriage payment to the divorced husband of Kalusa's daughter Evinaki (I,H13) and was looking round desperately for cash from whatever source, it was thought inadvisable by the majority of village elders to entrust him with the office of executor.

By the mechanism, therefore, of the *chota* debate a crisis which threatened to activate the hostilities latent in the village was brought under control and the ranks closed against Shika Village.

The next stage of this social drama followed the month of the *Chipenji* gathering, during which Ntololu (II,D2) kept the customs of widowhood at Mukanza Village where a grass hut (*nkunka*) was built for him. On the night of *Mudyileji* (the final dance), Headman Shika and other elders of his village, together with many women, came to Mukanza. Nearly every village in the vicinage of Mukanza Village sent a contingent. The general atmosphere was euphoric and no hint was afforded of the acrimonious debate that was to take place on the following day. Both Mukanza and Shika danced, and much apparent good-humour characterized their relationship round the beer pots.

Next day the real business began, the controversy over *mpepi*. Three *mahaku* were called in to judge between the contending parties, Headman Ng'ombi (see p. 200), Headman Mulila who had come some years ago from Angola into the vicinage, and Headman Nswanamatempa. None of these men had close consanguineal ties with either Shika or Mukanza, although Ng'ombi had married Mukanza's daughter Koniya (I,J1). But Ng'ombi's reputation for scrupulous fairness made him immune from the charge of favouritism. Shika called in Headman Nswanakudya (II,D10), whom, it will be remembered, he called ' older brother ' (p. 208 et seq.), to assist him in putting forward his point of view. He was also supported by the widower Ntololu (II,D2) and by a classificatory sister's son from Shika Village. On the Mukanza side, Mukanza Kabinda himself spoke, assisted by Sandombu, Chayangoma, and Sakazao. Nyamuwang'a refused to discuss the question of *mpepi*, saying that she had been ' despised ' (*ku-sawula*) by the Shika people on many occasions and would not hear herself insulted again. Her place was taken, curiously enough, by Nyakalusa, who had originally accused her of witchcraft. Once more Mukanza people had closed their ranks.

The discussion took place outside the *chota* since it was not about internal village affairs. Sandombu opened the debate by demanding a sum of £5 as *mpepi*. Ntololu, he alleged, had made it clear during the *Chipenji* funeral gathering that he intended to retain with him in Shika Village his two daughters by Kalusa, so that their services would be lost to Mukanza. Furthermore, ' bad words ' had been spoken by Shika people about witchcraft in Mukanza and it was only just that they should make amends by paying a big *mpepi*. He went on to say that £5 was not such a large sum after all by modern standards and mentioned cases in which £7 and even £10 had been paid. Shika, a big, blustering man, who, it is said, had once tried to bribe Kanongesha to appoint him to the Chibwikaship (see Chapter Eleven), hotly disputed the sum named, pointing out that the two villages had for many years been in the habit of exchanging wives, and had come to be interrelated by many ties. It was an unfriendly act to make heavy demands on one's kin. Besides, he recalled that when Nyatungeji (II,D3) was on the point of death Mukanza had divorced her, paying only 2s. 6d. to Shika. Again, at the beginning of *Chipenji* he had sent 10s. to Mukanza by Ntololu to contribute to the cost of divination into the death. ' What did the chicken say ? ' he went on, referring to the poison test (*ng'ombu yamwaji*) administered to fowls in one mode of divination. It would appear that Mukanza Kabinda had not gone to a diviner but had ' eaten ' the money. Did Mukanza think that he was a *muloji* (sorcerer) to ask him for such a large *mpepi* ? Mukanza himself then spoke, saying that he had no quarrel with Shika but that the latter must know that it was the custom nowadays to pay a large *mpepi* since ' every kind of food and beer now cost money, and cloths, pots and pans were very dear '. He had not gone to a diviner, for, if such a matter came to the ear of the Boma, all of them might ' receive a very heavy case '. But he had taken the money already paid into account when he had decided in consultation with his fellow-villagers on the amount of *mpepi* he would ask for.

Other elders now spoke on both sides, presenting variants on the main arguments. After a time the judges were consulted and they suggested that Shika should pay £2 10s. Headman Ng'ombi said that bitter things had been said on both sides and it had to be taken into account that Mukanza had divorced Nyatungeji in order to avoid the payment of *mpepi*. But since many people in both villages were kin, it would be a bad thing if one group started to nurse a grievance against the other. He thought that Mukanza should be satisfied with half the amount demanded, in view of the Nyatungeji affair, of kinship relations between the villages, and of what Shika had already paid as a contribution towards a divination which had never taken place. Sandombu, speaking on behalf of Mukanza Village, refused to accept this, saying that while they would no longer press for £5 they would be content with nothing less than £3 10s. After more argument Shika agreed to pay this sum. But he told the Mukanza people that they were mean and selfish to drive such a hard bargain. He said that he could only pay £1 that day, as he was a poor man (*kazweng'i*) but that he would pay the rest later in instalments. He then left the village ' in a huff ' (*ku-fundamoka*) with his followers. Kalusa's children remained at Shika Village, and for more than six months there was a marked reduction in visiting between the villages, and much mutual backbiting. In the last chapter I shall describe how one of the functions of the *Chihamba* ritual I witnessed was to effect a reconciliation between the villages.

Analysis

Social Drama VII illustrates a number of points already made. Among these may be noted : (1) the way in which inter-village disputes help to promote intra-village unity—strikingly brought out by the change of front shown by Chayangoma and Nyakalusa, who began by accusing Sandombu and Nyamuwang'a of witchcraft and abetting witchcraft and ended by jointly arguing the case for Mukanza Village, and even, in Nyakalusa's case, by acting as representative for the one initially stigmatized ; (2) the interest shown by representatives of the wider social system of the vicinage in what was primarily a matter concerning two inter-marrying villages ; and (3) the role of matriliny in providing links between villages in different vicinages, exemplified by

Nswanakudya's advocacy of his classificatory brother's case. But its main interest for us in this chapter is the light it throws on the kinds of cleavages and ties between intermarrying villages. Every breach in a marriage, whether made by divorce or death, is accompanied by conflict between the villages, but the existence of other ties of affinity and kinship prevents the conflict from rupturing all ties between them. Cross-cutting affiliations ally those who are in conflict. Kasonda and Manyosa, for example, would not argue on behalf of Mukanza Village. They said that their father Kahumpu came from Shika Village and that he was the full-brother of Ntololu. Kasonda said that in addition his own children belonged to Shika Village through their mother. How then could he speak against men whom he called 'father', and who were grandfathers of his own children, i.e. members of the same linked-generation segment in Shika Village ? Again, Mukanza himself spoke with great moderation, for his three children by Nyatungeji belonged by matrilineal descent to Shika's following. By another reckoning, through Mukanza's marriage with Mangaleshi, he was a 'co-parent-in-law' *(nkulu nami)* with Headman Shika, since he was *muku* to Mangaleshi, and Shika was, in the context of affinity, *muku* to Kasonda. Persons who call one another *nkulu nami*, may sleep in one another's huts, receive hospitality from one another, and in general behave with considerable familiarity, although there is no joking between them. To my mind this is another expression of the solidarity of genealogical generations. Sandombu, on the other hand, had no close kinship or affinal tie with Shika Village to prevent his speaking the Mukanza case unreservedly. Shika recognized in him the authentic voice of Mukanza Village, when he asked for £3 10s., and agreed to pay up to preserve peace between the villages because he knew Sandombu's demand to be a final offer.

But although the villages did not break off relations it was felt by the Shika people that Mukanza Village had had the better of the bargain. Resentment lingered ; Shika people complained in many villages of the meanness of the Mukanza group, coupling their reprobation of the village with disparagement of the Kawiku as a whole. The latent conflict between Lunda and Kawiku, the invaders and the indigenous people, never entirely damped down, began to smoulder. Moreover, the people of

Mukanza felt rather uneasy about their own conduct in the affair. Members of other villages hinted that they had not behaved well in demanding such a large sum as *mpepi*. When it was decided to hold the *Chihamba* ritual for Nyamukola [1] a special invitation was sent to Shika Village to attend. Ntololu's children came and a number of children linked to both villages were chosen as candidates for initiation. At the ritual level both villages were temporarily reconciled.

But outside this relationship of marital exchange with Shika Village the people of Mukanza had a wide and extensive range of marital connections with other villages. Even divorce and death do not break such ties, if the union has been productive of children, for children act as a focus of common interest between the maternal and paternal groups. Children who live with their mother often exchange visits with their father. In custom, a man must show no animosity towards his ex-wife's present husband whom he calls *nkulu nami*, the same term as he applies to his child's spouse's parents or uncles and aunts. This rather tense relationship of outward friendliness prescribed by custom enables a man to visit his own children at his divorced wife's home, whether she be living in her own or in her new husband's village. The customs are directed against the outbreak of physical violence due to jealousy. But if a couple have had no children, the relations between their respective villages will nearly always cease on their divorce. Affinal ties are strengthened enormously with the advent of children, in whose welfare the groups to which each spouse belongs by various principles of attachment have an interest.

I examine the extant inter-village marriages of Mukanza people and the fruitful marriages of present members which ended in divorce and death. Starting with members of NYACHINTANG'A lineage, in order of seniority, Manyosa (I,G13) was married to Chikasa, of Mpawu Village in the deposed Government Sub-Chief Ntambu's area. She had previously been married to Chisempi, whom she divorced and by whom she had five children ; he was a member of a village in the vicinage in which Nyaluhana (see p. 48) is principal headman, in Chief Kanongesha's

[1] See p. 310.

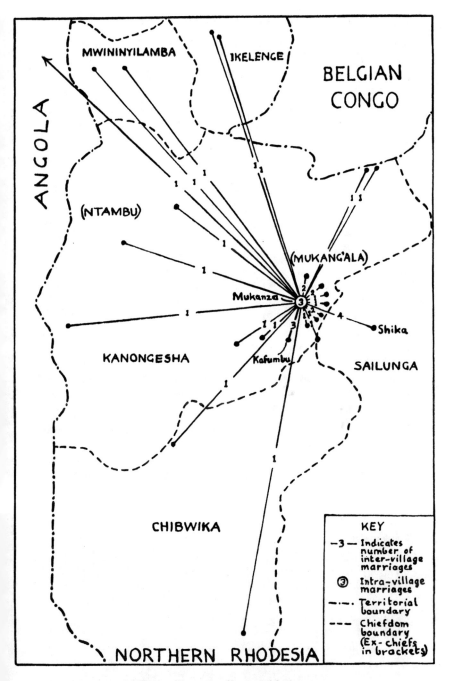

MAP 6. MUKANZA VILLAGE MARRIAGES

area.   Her oldest son lives with his father, although he sometimes
visits Kafumbu Village, and she goes to see him when she visits
Kafumbu Village which is near Sawiyembi Village, where her
former husband and her son reside.   All her other children,
except Rosina (I,H8) who lives with her husband in Kafumbu,
reside in Mukanza Village.   Chawutong'i (I,G12), whose
husband Ndeleki (II,D8) lives uxorilocally, provides a link with
Ng'ombi Village through Ndeleki's matrilineal connection there
and with Shika through Ndeleki's father.   Kasonda (I,G15),
by his divorced wife Mika, who had a baby by a lover, maintained connections with Ntambu's area.   These connections,
though snapped by divorce, between Kasonda and Mika, were
renewed by Kasonda's marriage with ex-Chief Ntambu's sister's
daughter's daughter Luciana.   NYACHINTANG'A lineage had
maintained relations by affinity with the NTAMBU chiefly lineage
for several generations.   The Ntambu chieftainship was reckoned
equivalent in status to that of Kanongesha in Lunda tradition :
Chief Ntambu sent tribute directly to Mwantiyanvwa as Kanongesha did in the past, and the two chiefly lineages interchanged
spouses just as Shika and Mukanza Village lineages did.   The
father of Mukanza Kabinda and Nyamwaha, Santapu, was the
younger uterine brother of an incumbent of the Ntambu chieftainship.   The marriages of Nyamwaha's son and daughter
maintained the connection.   Kasonda had in fact married quite
astutely.   His children by Mangaleshi might succeed or bear
successors to the chieftainship of Kanongesha.   His children by
Luciana might succeed to the stool of Ntambu.   Kasonda
cherished hopes that Government would eventually restore that
chieftainship to its former position in the Native Authority.
His son by Luciana might then perhaps become a Government
Chief in that case.   If Jerry, his son by Mangaleshi, became
Kanongesha, Kasonda might be the father of two chiefs.

   Sandombu kept up intermittent contact with the daughter of
his first wife Nyalundawu.   This daughter, regarded by Sandombu
alone as his, had married into a village in Ikelenge Area and had
a small daughter.   When Sandombu visited Ikelenge Area on
business he always stayed with his ' daughter '.   Sandombu's
sister Mangalita (I,G11) had formerly been married to a man from
nearby Nswanakudya Village, but in 1951 she was living at
Kafweku Village with her new husband.   Kafweku, formerly a

senior headman's village, had previously been linked with
Mukanza by the uxorilocal marriage of Kajata (I,F10), of MALABU
lineage. It is in Mwininyilamba Area, far from Mukanza, on
the border of Angola.

Bibiana (I,H4), mother's sister's daughter's daughter of
Sandombu, also lived with her husband, a crippled ex-askari, in
Chimbila Village near Ikelenge's capital village. She had three
sons and two daughters. The sons regularly visited Mukanza
in the school holidays, and when I left, Bibiana, divorced by her
husband in 1954, was talking of settling in Sandombu Farm.
Bibiana's first parallel cousin, Nyampesi, was married to a store
capitao working for a European trader, near the Boma. She
made frequent visits to Sandombu Farm. Her husband had a
useful role from the point of view of Mukanza Village in placing
the younger men in paid jobs.

Manyosa's oldest daughter Kandeleya was married to Makan-
jila, son of Headman Mbimbi, whose decrepit village immediately
adjoined Mukanza. Manyosa's son Daudson (I,H7) had two
wives. One was the daughter of an Ovimbundu immigrant
who had made a farm near Mukanza. The other was Sakutoha's
daughter (see p. 191 et seq.) from her father's adjacent settlement,
which paid tax through Mukanza. Her other daughter Rosina
(I,H8) was married to Kantamoya (I,H3), the younger brother
of the headman of Kafumbu Village.

In MALABU lineage Sakazao (I,H9) was connected to Kafumbu
by marriage through Nyaluwema (I,C4). His slave wife
Nyakalusa no longer seemed to maintain contact with her
Angolan home village. Nyatioli (I,H11), his sister, had lived
in Mwininyilamba area for many years with a husband from
Nyanseng'i Village. Her daughter Yana (I,J4) had married a
man from the neighbouring village to Nyanseng'i, Kambimbi
Village. In 1951, when Yana was still living virilocally, I
visited Kambimbi Village, far from the motor road along a path
winding over troublesome spurs of rock, with a number of
Mukanza people ; and we were all given hospitality by Yana
and her husband, in the form of food and beer. Yana's brother
Pearson (I,J5) was married to a girl from Ng'ombi Village in
the vicinage. Their younger sister Serita had previously been
married to a man from Ibulu Village in Chibwika Area, by whom
she had had a daughter who was living with her father. Recently

u

she married a man from Nswanakudya Village in the vicinage of Mukanza. Nyamuwang'a (I,G17) of Mukanza had formerly been married to a man from Kafumbu Village, by whom she had borne a daughter. This man subsequently died, and his death was popularly supposed to have been caused by Nyamuwang'a's witchcraft. But her daughter Ikayi (I,H12) still visited her father's village from time to time. Nyamuwang'a's subsequent marriage to a man from Shika Village has already been mentioned. Nyamalita (I,G20), the surviving uterine sister of Nyamuwang'a, lived virilocally for many years with her husband, a farm headman in Ikelenge Area, and later obtained work as a Ward Maid at the Kalene Mission Hospital. Her younger children, like those of Bibiana (see p. 164), frequently visited Mukanza Village in school holidays, and it was expected by Mukanza people that they would look on it as their home when they grew up.

Chinema (I,G21) and his uterine siblings remained in Ikelenge Area after Kahali Chandenda (I,F5 ; see p. 180 et seq.) had returned to Mukanza Village. Together with some disgruntled claimants for the Mukang'ala chieftainship he established a new composite village, called after him. He and his siblings married in Ikelenge Area and I shall not enumerate the marital and consanguineal ties that now interlink the matrilineage of Mukanza through Chinema and his siblings with villages in Ikelenge Area. Some of Chinema's uterine nephews have now returned to Mukanza, including Chayangoma (I,H15) and Short (I,H16 ; see Social Drama VII, p. 269 et seq.), neither of whom were married at the time of which I am writing. Line's senior wife came from Sawiyembi Village, near Kafumbu Village, and he frequently accompanied her on visits to her village. His junior wife, Maria, as noted on page 186, belonged to the lineage of NYACHULA, led off from Mukanza Village by Yimbwendi, as described in Social Drama VI (p. 181). Of the NYACHULA people who remained in Mukanza Village, Nyawunyumbi (I,G25) through previous marriages which were fertile provided links with villages in Chibwika and Kanongesha areas. Her son Kenson (I,H21), who resided at Mukanza Village, was married to a woman from nearby Chibwakata Village. She herself, as already mentioned, was married to Headman Mbimbi, and her youngest daughter (I,H20) was married to a man from Kasai

Village, a Kawiku village in another vicinage (see p. 191 et seq.).
Aram (I,J7), Line's sister's son, was married to a woman from
Chikang'a Village, in the same neighbourhood as Kasai Village.
Of Nyamukola's children, her daughter Koniya (I,J1) was
married to Headman Ng'ombi, while her son Zachariah (I,J3)
was married to the sister's daughter of Farm Headman Sakutoha
(see pp. 192–3), close to Mukanza Village.

Affinal ties, then, linked Mukanza Village to other villages in
the same vicinage, to villages in adjoining vicinages, and to
villages in distant vicinages and even in different Government
Chiefdoms. By marriage the village was interconnected with
villages in Chibwika Area forty or fifty miles to the south, and
with Mwininyilamba Area about the same distance to the north-
west. Genealogies suggest that similar wide ranges of marital
ties interlinked villages in pre-European times. Numerous close
ties of kinship and affinity with Shika Village can be placed at
one end of a scale, on the other end of which we find single
threads of connection radiating in all directions to settlements
near and far.

Table XXI, based on village census material, gives some idea
of the spatial range and dispersion of marital ties. I was unfortunately unable to work out in many cases what marriages
had taken place between members of villages belonging to the
same vicinage. Mukang'ala is classed as a 'chiefdom', although
the incumbent was deposed by the Government in 1947. The
high proportion of extra-chiefdom marriages in the Ikelenge
sample is probably due in large measure to the high immigration
into the area from Angola, the Belgian Congo and from other
parts of Mwinilunga District (see p. 9 and p. 59). The table,
despite its deficiencies, does show how widely the network of
affinity, which interlinks villages, vicinages and chiefdoms, is
spread.

Kinship and Affinal Connections between Headmen in a Vicinage

Before discussing the network of affinal and kinship ties
interlinking the headmen in the vicinage of which Mukanza
Village forms part, a few words should be said about polygyny
and about the polygynous marriages of headmen in particular.
Table XXII gives the age and conjugal status of all members of

TABLE XXI
SPATIAL RANGE OF MARRIAGE

Sample of 165 extant marriages :

Category of marriage	No. in sample					Percentage in each chiefdom				
	Chiefdom of residence					Chiefdom of residence				
	Muk	Nya	Mwi	Ike	Total	Muk	Nya	Mwi	Ike	Total
Intra-village	15	5	5	2	27	23·1	16·1	18·5	4·8	16·4
Intra-chiefdom	24	10	7	6	47	36·9	32·3	25·9	14·3	28·5
Sub-total	39	15	12	8	74	60·0	48·4	44·4	19·1	44·9
Other intra-Ndembu N.R. . .	15	5	9	18	47	23·1	16·1	33·3	42·8	28·5
Intra-Ndembu outside N.R. . .	4	7	3	13	27	6·1	22·6	11·1	3c·9	16·4
Other intra-Lunda	—	—	2	1	3	—	—	7·4	2·4	1·8
Extra-Lunda	—	—	1	2	3	—	—	3·7	4·8	1·8
Neither spouse a village member	7	4	—	—	11	10·8	12·9	—	—	6·6
Sub-total	26	16	15	34	91	40·0	51·6	55·5	80·9	55·1
Grand total	65	31	27	42	165	100·0	100·0	100·0	100·0	100·0

Legend

Muk Mukang'ala
Nya Nyakaseya
Mwi Mwininyilamba
Ike Ikelenge

24 villages and 6 farms, while Table XXIII compares the age and conjugal status of 28 headmen with those of 107 commoners of thirty years old and over.[1] More than half the headmen had two or more wives while only about a sixth of the commoners had two or more wives. Headmen have greater obligations than commoners to offer hospitality, and the more wives they have the better are they able to do this. But marital ties between headmen and members of other villages are politically stronger links than those between commoners, since the headman represents a group and sometimes inherits a time-honoured title. Men often, like Kasonda, anticipate headmanship by judicious polygynous marriage with important maternal descent groups ; others find that they must marry more than one wife to fulfil their duties after they have succeeded. Since also the children of headmen often remain with them, the polygynous headman with fertile wives is enabled to beget a following within the social system of the village of whose loyalty he can be almost sure.

Conflict and tension between co-wives is, however, a frequent cause or excuse for divorce so that polygyny, while it offers advantages to the ambitious, more than doubles the possibilities of conflict, never absent from the Ndembu marital relationship.

Before 1952 only five villages comprised the vicinage (*chitung'ili* or *itung'a*) to which Mukanza Village belonged. These were Nswanakudya, Chibwakata (in a different site, now in a Government Forest Reserve), Ng'ombi, Mukanza, and Mbimbi. Now Nswanakudya and Chibwakata were interlinked by a number of marital and consanguineal ties. The headman of Nswanakudya was the son of a Chibwakata man, Kaluwa, who was the mother's brother of the headman of Chibwakata. Thus the two headmen were cross-cousins. Headman Nswanakudya married Nyachipoya, classificatory sister of Headman Chibwakata. When Ng'ombi split off from Chibwakata, Nyachipoya's uterine siblings went with Ng'ombi. Headman Nswanakudya's oldest son by Nyachipoya later settled in Ng'ombi Village where he was *mulopu* or deputy of the headman. Headman Ng'ombi's mother was older uterine sister of Nyachipoya. Several other marriages interconnected the three villages but

---

[1] The lay-out of these tables is based on Table XIX in Mitchell and Barnes, *The Lamba Village*, p. 46.

TABLE XXII

AGE AND CONJUGAL STATUS

Sample of 24 villages and 6 farms:

Age	Number in sample									Percentage in each age group								
	Unw.	D	R	1	2	3	4	Married Total	Total	Unw.	D	R	1	2	3	4	Married Total	Total
Males:																		
0–Pu	95	—	—	—	—	—	—	—	95	100·0	—	—	—	—	—	—	—	100·0
Pu–19	18	—	—	—	—	—	—	—	18	100·0	—	—	—	—	—	—	—	100·0
20–29	15	—	—	31	5	—	—	36	51	29·4	—	—	60·8	9·8	—	—	70·6	100·0
30–39	3	2	—	29	5	—	—	34	39	7·7	5·1	—	74·4	12·8	—	—	87·2	100·0
40–49	—	3	—	21	6	1	—	28	31	—	9·7	—	67·7	19·4	3·2	—	90·3	100·0
50–59	—	—	—	14	14	2	—	30	30	—	—	—	46·7	46·7	6·6	—	100·0	100·0
60–	—	—	5	24	5	—	1	30	35	—	—	14·3	68·5	14·3	—	2·9	85·7	100·0
Total	131	5	5	119	35	3	1	158	299	43·8	1·7	1·7	39·8	11·7	1·0	0·3	52·8	100·0
Females:																		
0–Pu	99	—	—	2	—	—	—	2	101	98·0	—	—	2·0	—	—	—	2·0	100·0
Pu–19	20	—	—	31	—	—	—	31	51	39·2	—	—	60·8	—	—	—	60·8	100·0
20–29	—	8	—	49	—	—	—	49	57	—	14·0	—	86·0	—	—	—	86·0	100·0
30–39	—	3	—	52	—	—	—	52	55	—	5·5	—	94·5	—	—	—	94·5	100·0
40–49	—	4	1	27	—	—	—	27	32	—	12·5	3·1	84·4	—	—	—	84·4	100·0
50–59	—	5	3	19	—	—	—	19	27	—	18·5	11·1	70·4	—	—	—	70·4	100·0
60–	—	6	9	10	—	—	—	10	25	—	24·0	36·0	40·0	—	—	—	40·0	100·0
Total	119	26	13	190	—	—	—	190	348	34·2	7·5	3·7	54·6	—	—	—	54·6	100·0

TABLE XXIII

PART 1. AGE AND CONJUGAL STATUS OF HEADMEN

Sample of 28 headmen ·

Number in sample

Age	Unw.	D	R	Married 1	2	3	4	Total	Total
30–39	—	—	—	—	1	—	—	1	1
40–49	—	—	—	1	1	—	—	2	2
50–59	—	—	—	—	8	1	—	9	9
60–	—	—	—	11	4	—	1	16	16
Total ·	—	—	—	12	14	1	1	28	28

Percentage in each age group

Age	Unw.	D	R	Married 1	2	3	4	Total	Total
30–39	—	—	—	—	100·0	—	—	100·0	100·0
40–49	—	—	—	50·0	50·0	—	—	100·0	100·0
50–59	—	—	—	—	88·8	11·1	—	100·0	100·0
60–	—	—	—	68·8	25·0	—	6·2	100·0	100·0
Total ·	—	—	—	42·8	50·0	3·6	3·6	100·0	100·0

PART 2. AGE AND CONJUGAL STATUS OF COMMONERS (MALE)

Sample of 107 commoners :

Number in sample

Age	Unw.	D	R	Married 1	2	3	4	Total	Total
30–39	3	2	—	29	4	—	—	33	38
40–49	—	3	—	20	5	1	—	26	29
50–59	—	—	—	14	6	1	—	21	21
60–	—	—	5	13	1	—	—	14	19
Total ·	3	5	5	76	16	2	—	94	107

Percentage in each age group

Age	Unw.	D	R	Married 1	2	3	4	Total	Total
30–39	7·9	5·3	—	76·3	10·5	—	—	86·8	100·0
40–49	—	10·3	—	69·0	17·2	3·5	—	89·7	100·0
50–59	—	—	—	66·7	28·6	4·8	—	100·0	100·0
60–	—	—	26·3	68·4	5·3	—	—	73·7	100·0
Total ·	2·8	4·7	4·7	71·0	14·9	1·9	—	87·8	100·0

Legend

Unw.   Unwedded
D   Divorced, and not remarried
R   Relict ; widower or widow, not remarried
1, 2, 3, 4   1, 2, 3, 4 Spouses
Pu   Puberty

those mentioned were politically the most outstanding. Ng'ombi Village, it will be remembered, split off from Chibwakata Village in the 1920's.

Mukanza Village was linked with Mbimbi Village in a number of ways. The headman of Mbimbi was the son of a member of MALABU lineage in Mukanza Village, and his son was married to Kandeleya, daughter of Manyosa of NYACHINTANG'A lineage, the favourite ' granddaughter ' of Mukanza Kabinda. Mbimbi's second wife was Nyawunyumbi, mother of Mukanza Kabinda's second wife and Line's second wife. The primary relationship between Mukanza Kabinda and Mbimbi was that of classificatory ' father ' to ' son ', since Mbimbi's father Ibeleka was classificatory ' older brother ' to Mukanza. Through subsequent marital ties Mukanza could be considered the classificatory son-in-law of Mbimbi, since Mbimbi had married Mukanza's mother-in-law Nyawunyumbi. By matrilineal affiliation Mbimbi belonged to the descent group from which incumbents of the Mukang'ala senior headmanship were chosen.

Between these two groups of closely related and intermarried villages, Nswanakudya-Chibwakata-Ng'ombi on the one hand, and Mukanza-Mbimbi on the other, stretched threads of genealogical connection. Headman Ng'ombi was the husband of Mukanza's and Nyamukola's daughter Koniya, former wife of Kasonda, Mukanza's uterine nephew. Few marital ties directly interlinked Nswanakudya and Mukanza, but the close relationship of marital exchange which existed between Shika, from which Nswanakudya had seceded, and Mukanza, by classificatory extensions of kinship terms and behaviour, made it possible for Mukanza Kabinda and Headman Nswanakudya to call one another *ishaku*, ' brother-in-law '. Kasonda called Nswanakudya ' father ' since Nswanakudya was the classificatory ' older brother ' of his father Kahumpu. Through the marriage of his sister Nyamwaha to the previous headman of Chibwakata, Mulowa, Mukanza could also call the present headman of Chibwakata, Chonku, classificatory younger brother of the late headman Mulowa, his ' brother-in-law ' (*ishaku*). Kasonda's father's father came from Chibwakata. A few marriages between younger people interlinked the two villages. But on the whole few ties of kinship and affinity connected Mukanza Village with these three villages. Mbimbi once married a woman from

Shika Village who died many years ago, but on the strength of this former marital tie, he could call Headman Nswanakudya 'brother-in-law' (*ishaku*). I could not trace any genealogical connection between Mbimbi and Chibwakata.

In 1952 Government moved a number of villages out of the vicinage in which Nsang'anyi was the principal village when their former territory was declared a Forest Reserve. These villages were told to build in the vicinage of Mukanza Village. Map 3 (p. 21) shows the distribution of these villages and their gardens in 1953. It is instructive to note the way in which kinship, affinal and historical connections influenced the choice of their new sites. Nsang'anyi would not build near its offshoot Nswanamatempa, in view of the tension that still existed after the secession of the latter (see p. 212) as recently as 1940. Nor would Nsang'anyi build close to Mukanza, who claimed to be *mwenimbu*, principal headman, of that part of the vicinage adjoining the Government motor road. Nsang'anyi was the senior and most ancient Kawiku village and could not recognize the local pre-eminence of any of its offshoots. Nswanamatempa broke up as described on page 216 into three settlements, all of which built near Mukanza, a fellow-Kawiku but distantly-related village. Another group of villages and farms, settled on the very verge of the Forest Reserve, were interrelated with each other and with villages already in the vicinage. Itota, the headman of one, was married to the sister of the headman of another, named Lambakasa. Lambakasa and his sister were in their turn siblings of Headman Mbimbi. Their father came from Mukanza Village, from MALABU lineage. Lambakasa was a full brother of Mbimbi ; Itota's wife was their half-sister. Her full-brother Nsanji built a small farm opposite the road from Lambakasa, his half-brother by the same father, and on the same side of the road as Itota. In this group also was a farm founded by a woman headman Nyamumwema whose daughter was Lambakasa's junior wife.

Next to Nsang'anyi Village on the Itota side was Kanyabu Village. Headman Kanyabu had married Nsang'anyi's uterine niece. Kanyabu's own uterine niece had once been married to Sakazao of Mukanza Village, where; indeed, she had died. Her daughter by a previous husband was the wife of Gideon, the son of Mukanza Kabinda.

These villages then were intricately interlaced by affinal and kinship ties. No ties of either type existed between Mukanza and Itota. In this case, however, the headmen made the contract of blood-brotherhood (*wulunda*). Mukanza used this relationship to secure for nothing the services of Itota as senior ritual specialist in the *Chihamba* ritual, to be described in Chapter Ten.

After 1952 also, a few small farms grew up in the vicinage. Anderson Mulumbi (see Social Drama V, p. 160 et seq.), son of a former female slave of Chibwakata, made a farm between Mukanza and the Nswanamatempa group, and set up in business as a sewing-machine tailor. His wife was sister's daughter's daughter of Nsang'anyi, and many disputes arose between the Kawiku and Anderson over his cruel treatment of her. Anderson's sister, married to an Ovimbundu ritual specialist who had introduced the new ritual of *Tukuka* into the vicinage, occupied the next farm. Next to her again was another Ovimbundu, a petty trader whose daughter was married to Daudson, Manyosa's son, of Mukanza Village. Beside him was the small farm of Muchona whose wife belonged to the Nswanakudya village lineage. He was a close friend of the Ovimbundu witch-doctor and they jointly officiated at several kinds of ritual. Near Chibwakata, the younger uterine brother of the headman, Makayi, made a family farm with his two wives and children.

In the absence of strong overall political authority, such ties of kinship and affinity become of the utmost importance in giving some degree of cohesion to a fluid and volatile society. But since strong possibilities of conflict exist in these very relationships themselves, kinship and affinity, unsupported by other kinds of linkage, do not constitute reliable political bonds between villages. Even where, as in the case of Mukanza and Shika, conflicts which arose between two villages over a broken marriage could to some extent be contained by the countervailing influence of other ties of kinship and affinity which interconnected their members, tensions were set up which seriously reduced the frequency of interactions between them. Indeed, such tensions might, within each village, give rise to incessant bickering between its own nuclear lineage and affines and kin belonging to the lineage of the other. In other words, the instability in the marriage relationship, arising from the conflict between matrilineal descent and virilocal marriage, was at the same time a source of instability in the political relationships between groups allied by marriage. Kinship and affinity in such a society divide as often as they bind. They provide brittle foundations for a social polity. Time and again one notices the tenuity of the kinship and marital ties that hold together the component elements of local groupings of whatever kind. Villages constantly shed uterine sibling groups which become potential nuclei of new settlements. Sometimes they divide at a higher order of lineage segmentation. Individuals move from village to village in pursuit of their immediate interests. Most women marry out at least once. Between villages, strife is endemic at the level of consanguineal and affinal relations. The best neighbours are not one's closest kin. Since many kin participate in marriage and death payments, and since these are nearly always subjects of dispute in whatever context of social relations they may be considered, conflicts between villages over them are continually taking place. Such conflicts seldom reach a solution satisfactory to both parties. The contradiction between principles of social grouping *within villages* inhibits the growth of deep lineages, tends to rip the matricentric family prematurely from the matrilineage, sets adjacent generations at odds with one another, divides sisters from brothers, and enfeebles the bonds of marriage. Between villages, the same contradiction engenders disputes, makes of the vicinage an unstable grouping, and disperses kin throughout the whole Ndembu region. Unlike the societies described in *African Political Systems* as 'segmentary',[1] in which lineage organization forms the permanent framework of social relations, the cohesion of Ndembu society depends on the strength of its mechanisms for resolving conflict which arises from the weakness and instability of lineage organization and from the ambiguous character of kinship and affinal ties.

---

[1] Fortes, M. and Evans-Pritchard, E. E., ' Introduction ' to *African Political System* (1940), p. 10.

CHAPTER X

THE POLITICALLY INTEGRATIVE FUNCTION
OF RITUAL

IT has been suggested by Professor Gluckman [1] that in societies without governmental institutions, social cohesion ' appears to depend on [the] division of society into a series of opposed groups, with cross-cutting membership '. Again, he says, that ' social ties were . . . established to link together people who in other contexts were enemies '. We have seen how, in an Ndembu village, cohesion is to some extent maintained by the many-sided social affiliations of its component groups and persons. In the same way, villages are interlinked in vicinages, in senior headmen's areas, and in the Ndembu tribal region, by varying sets of ties : kinship, affinity, spatial propinquity, blood-brotherhood, and so on. Analysis of the social dramas has shown how persons and groups divided in one set of social relations are allied in other sets. But the analysis of social dramas has also shown that cohesion is by no means necessarily or invariably maintained in a group after an outbreak of conflict between persons or groups within it. For instance, we have seen that a village consists of a number of persons bound together by several principles of social affiliation, some of which become dominant in certain situations, *in spite of* the countervailing pressures exerted by the others, and which destroy the unity of the village.

Thus, in most cases of fission examined, the principle of the unity of the uterine sibling group prevailed against such principles as the unity of the minimal lineage, the unity of the genealogical generation, and the unity of the village. Again, the principle of the unity of the uterine sibling group came into continual conflict with the principle of the unity of the family : and the success of the former can be measured in terms of the high frequency of divorce. But we have also noticed how the unity of the widest political unit, the Ndembu people, gains at the

---

[1] ' Political Institutions ', in *The Institutions of Primitive Society*, p. 67. See also Fortes, *The Dynamics of Clanship Among the Tallensi*, pp. 241 et seq.

expense of its significant local unit, the village. Frequent fission, associated with wide-ranging spatial mobility of the seceding group, tends to create through time numerous sets of local kinship nuclei, each set consisting of villages which have arisen from a common source or from one another by fission. The villages in each set, though widely scattered in space, may be interlinked by belief in common matrilineal descent, or by knowledge of actual kinship connections. The separate sets are interlinked by affinal, vicinage and other ties. Thus fission and mobility, while they break up villages, interlock the nation, which has no effective overall political authority. But when we examined more closely the political role of ties of kinship and marriage enjoining co-operation we found that these ties too were of an unstable and friable nature.

It would seem then that links of kinship and of political and economic co-operation *per se* are insufficiently strong to hold together village and nation. And yet Ndembu are conscious and proud of their unity as a discrete group, and as a sub-group of the great Lunda nation, the unity of which is expressed in the king-ship of Mwantiyanvwa.

Such a consciousness of national unity obviously depends on the joint recognition by all Ndembu of a common system of values and a common set of norms regulating behaviour. Their unity is a moral, rather than a political, unity. By what social mechanisms are these common norms and values inculcated and periodically re-animated? In this book I shall say nothing about the educative process whereby young children are indoctrinated in the basic values of their group. Nor, except in passing, have I been able to deal with the juridical mechanisms. More im-portant perhaps than either as a means of keeping continually before the people their common norms and values, in terms of symbol, mime and precept, is the complex system of ritual.[1]

The profusion of types and frequency of performance of ritual in Ndembu society are, in a way, confessions of failure in the power of secular mechanisms to redress and absorb conflicts that arise in and between local and kinship groups. I have suggested

---

[1] I do not intend here to make a cultural analysis of Ndembu ritual but simply to isolate from the ritual complex those sociological features which are relevant in this book.

that the contradiction between virilocal marriage and matrilineal descent is a crucial determinant of structural instability at all levels of organization.   I would postulate that where the mode of post-marital residence is inconsistent with the mode of reckoning descent in unilineally organized societies, local groupings in such societies will be inherently unstable unless other factors intervene, such as limitations on access to resources.   I have tried to show how the tenacity and tendency to autonomy of the uterine sibling group are related to virilocal marriage, and how the tenacity of this group tends, in situations of conflict, to jeopardize the cohesion and continuity of villages.   I have also tried to trace a relationship between virilocal marriage and the high divorce rate, which, in its turn, impairs political relations between inter-married villages.   So radically disruptive of local cohesion is this contradiction that not infrequently the combined operation of all countervailing relations is powerless to prevent absolute schism in villages.

Most Ndembu rituals tacitly recognize the instability of villages and of the relations between villages, but posit the ultimate unity of all Ndembu in a single moral community.   The instability of kinship and political relations is recognized in the fact that the dominant social element in the composition of ritual assemblies is not a kinship group but an association of adepts who belong to many kinship groups.   Also, the dominant symbols in the cluster of symbolic objects and activities associated with each ritual do not reflect or express major aspects of the social structure, but rather the values which *all* Ndembu possess in common, such as, for example, the fertility of women, crops and animals, huntsmanship, health, and the power of the ancestors to bestow or withhold such benefits.   The ultimate unity of all Ndembu is expressed in the composition of ritual assemblies.   Thus, all Ndembu, all Lunda even, have the right to attend any perform-ance of ritual of whatsoever type.   Indeed, if they have been initiated into its special techniques and esoteric knowledge, its ' mysteries ' (*mpang'u*), they have the right to participate as officiants (*ayimbuki*),[1] whether they are related to the principal subjects of the ritual or not.   It is also expressed in the recurrence

---

[1] Singular *chimbuki*.   This term has the dual significance of ' doctor ' or ' leech ' in so far as the ritual is regarded as therapeutic, and ' adept ' (perhaps even ' priest ' for a senior adept) in so far as it is a national cult.

throughout the ritual system of symbols representing the historical origin of the Ndembu in Mwantiyanvwa's empire and of symbols representing gerontocratic authority *in general* and of matriliny *in general* rather than specific political positions of authority or specific matrilineages.

The unity of all Ndembu is not maintained by political control from a strong centre of authority. Nor is their polity one consisting of homologous unilineal descent groups formed by a process of fission into structurally equivalent and juxtaposed segments. Moreover, there is no considerable overlapping of territorial and kinship groupings such as one finds in segmentary societies. In such societies force tends to be distributed according to the like but competitive interests of homologous segments. In both the pyramidal and segmentary types of society, ritual relations tend both to express and to buttress the major political relations, and ritual symbolism tends to express particular political offices or to stand for the unity of specific corporate groups of kin. In both states and segmentary societies, political, kinship, territorial and ritual relations tend to some extent to be coterminous.[1] In these respects, both types differ markedly from the Ndembu. Among Ndembu, relations established by ritual cut sharply across kinship and territorial ties, and even across tribal affiliation, since members of other Lunda groups, such as the Kosa of Musokantanda and the Ndembu of Ishinde (and even Lwena who practise analogous rituals), can participate in any cult into which they have been initiated. By establishing ties of co-participation in cults which operate independently of kinship and local linkages, the ritual system compensates to some extent for the limited range of effective political control and for the instability of kinship and affinal ties to which political value is attached. It would seem almost to be the consistent idiom of Ndembu social structure that certain basic sets of ties which tend to be interwoven so as to reinforce one another in many small-scale societies, should here be separated from one another ; further, the cohesion of the total society in some measure depends, not on the juxtaposition and correlative operation of the ties, but on their disjunction, and even on their opposition. Thus maternal descent groups have

---

[1] Fortes and Evans-Pritchard, 'Introduction' to *African Political Systems*, pp. 16 et seq.

no local centres, and vicinages are made up of villages most of which are unrelated by lineal descent. Descent and post-marital residence are not congruent. Spatial and social mobility throw territorial, kinship and political affiliations out of alignment. A few fixed points exist in the social structure to provide a measure of stability within the general flux. In the next chapter I discuss the politico-ritual roles of the chief and of certain senior headmen in this connection. But, by and large, the function of maintaining the unity of the widest social unit, the Ndembu people, devolves mainly upon the ritual system, although the ritual system spreads even wider than this.

Ndembu have two major categories of public rituals. These are life-crisis rituals, and cults of affliction.

Life-crisis rituals are performed in the first place to signalize important points in the social or biological development of individuals (whether these coincide or not), as these developments are interpreted by Ndembu culture. In the second place, life crisis rituals handle disturbances in the social structure set up by the change in social status of the principal subject or subjects of the ritual. In the third place, they provide occasions for a demonstration of the unity of all Ndembu. In the fourth place, they frequently act to reaffirm ties of local propinquity between villages in a given vicinage or sometimes between adjacent vicinages. The three most important life-crisis rituals are the boys' circumcision ritual (*Mukanda*), the girls' puberty ritual (*Nkang'a*), and the funeral ritual.

A detailed analysis of Ndembu life-crisis rituals is in preparation, and in this book I shall consider only cults of affliction. What I have called cults of affliction are performed for individuals, who are said by Ndembu to have been ' caught ' (*ku-kwata*) by the spirits of deceased relatives whom they have forgotten to honour with small gifts of crops and beer, or whom they have offended by omitting to mention their names when prayers are made at the village *nyiyombu* (sing. *muyombu*) (see p. 173) tree-shrines. People may also be ' caught ' for quarrelling with close kin or as representatives of kin groups torn by conflicts. Being ' caught ' means to be afflicted with bad luck at hunting in the case of men, with reproductive disorders in the case of women, and with illness in both cases.

A distinction is made by Ndembu between the spirit (*mukishi*) which afflicts, and its mode of affliction. The spirit that afflicts is a known and named deceased relative of the afflicted person or patient (*muyeji*). The patient is at the same time a *candidate* for initiation into the curative cult ; the *doctor* is an *adept* in that cult. The *mode of affliction* refers to certain characteristics of this spirit which are correlated with outstanding features of the sufferer's misfortune or illness. Thus a spirit which afflicts a woman in the mode of *Nkula* (or as Ndembu put it, which 'comes out in Nkula', as in the phrase *mukishi wami wedikilili muNkula,* 'my spirit emerged in *Nkula*'), 'sits in her back' (a euphemism for her reproductive organs), and afflicts her with menstrual disorders. These disorders include menorrhagia, dysmenorrhoea, and amenorrhoea. The woman may dream that her dead relative has appeared to her equipped like a hunter, wearing the red wing-feather of a lourie in her hair, as only those who have shed blood, such as hunters, manslayers and circumcisers, are entitled to do. Similarly the main symbols of the ritual fall into the class of red objects : red clay, the bark scrapings of a tree that secretes red gum, the blood and entrails of a red cock, lourie feathers, and the like. The name of the mode of affliction in this ritual is called *Nkula*. The name of the ritual performed to treat the afflicted person is also called *Nkula*. Now the treatment is carried out by a number of ' doctors ' or ' adepts ' (*ayimbuki* or *ayimbanda*), both male and female, who have themselves been closely associated with previous performances of the *Nkula* ritual. The women doctors must at one time have been patients themselves and may not become practising doctors unless they are generally considered to have been cured by the treatment. The male doctors must have previously acted in the capacity of *chaka chaNkula,* that is to say, male ritual assistant of the *Nkula* patient, a role which may be performed by her husband, brother or son, and involves the performance of a few ritual tasks, such as guiding the patient out backwards from the spirit-hut to the ritual fire. The doctors or adepts are arranged in a loose hierarchy of ritual prestige and each performs a different ritual task. Between doctors and patients there may be no ties of kinship or affinity at all. If ties interlink them, which in secular situations would be associated with mutual avoidance, these ties are reckoned inoperative in the context of the ritual, so that a man,

x

in his role of doctor, may splash with medicine the almost naked body of a woman whom he calls 'mother-in-law' or 'daughter-in-law', and whom he normally avoids. If a patient has been treated successfully, she is entitled to take part in future performances of the *Nkula* ritual as a junior doctor (*chimbuki wanyanya*, 'little doctor'). Her ritual status becomes higher the more she participates in rituals of this type, and the more she learns about the medicines and techniques. To whatever part of the Ndembu region she may move afterwards she will still be entitled to participate as a *chimbuki* (adept) in *Nkula*. The spirit which had once afflicted her is now thought to give her healing power (*ng'ovu yakuuka*) as a doctor, as well as to make her fertile. It is 'her spirit' (*mukishi windi*). This spirit is thought to have been itself an *Nkula* patient and doctor during its lifetime.

The ritual itself has exoteric and esoteric phases. During the exoteric phases, which typically take place in the village clearing, a big secular dance often accompanies the curative process proper, and as many people as are able to leave their other tasks in the vicinage, and, indeed, in villages in other vicinages who have received tidings of the ritual, come to dance, sing, drink, gossip and look on. The headman of the village and the close kin of the patient buy and brew as many calabashes of beer as they can to satisfy the clamorous demands of the throng of dancers. If the secular dance is a success, the prestige of the headman will temporarily be high, but if there is insufficient or unfairly distributed beer and food for important attenders, it will sharply decline for a time, whether the patient recovers or not. The esoteric phases of the ritual are attended by doctors and adepts only. They take place either in the secrecy of the patient's hut, or in the bush, where medicines (*yitumbu*) are collected with song and symbolic action, and where towards the end of several phases of ritual, a chicken or goat is sacrificed. In the past doctors drove the uninitiated away, by threatening them with bows and arrows, from areas in the bush which they had sacralized for ritual purposes.

Each culturally-defined mode of affliction by a spirit is associated with a cult whose adepts collaborate to placate the offended spirit. Since the most common cause of affliction is the neglecting or 'forgetting' (*ku-vulamena*) of the spirit, the most important aspect of the process of placation is to bring it back to memory, ' to make it known before many people ' and ' to mention its name in their hearing '. In sociological terms, this means that in a mobile and fissile society there is a strong tendency towards structural amnesia, which is countered by rituals which continually revive the memory of dead persons through whom the living are significantly interconnected. When the senior doctor addresses the afflicting spirit at various points in a ritual he mentions a number of significant kinship connections of the deceased. Sometimes he gives a brief outline of the kind of behaviour which divination has suggested as the cause of the spirit's anger. (This outline, incidentally, gives the anthropologist valuable information about the kinds of conflict that often arise in the kinship system.) In the context of the ritual situation, this citing of genealogical ties and discussion of contemporary conflicts has the dual effect on Ndembu of reviving kinship and affinal linkages which are beginning to wear thin, and of invoking the participation of the wider society, represented by the adepts drawn from all over the Ndembu region, in the conflicts of the narrower unit of the village. By means of ritual, the immediate past and the politico-kinship relations originating in it are kept alive, in spite of the social forces working in the opposite direction.

The other cults have the same general structure and functions as *Nkula*.[1] In each, there is a band of doctors and adepts, who share out among themselves the various ritual tasks. In each, there is a patient or subject of ritual, who is at the same time a candidate for initiation into the cult. In each, a named, deceased relative of the patient is divined as the cause of the affliction. This spirit afflicts in a specific mode. The *mode* is common to all members of the society : the *spirit* belongs to particular persons and narrow kinship groups. The name of the mode is the name of the ritual. The same spirit may afflict the same living relative in several modes, or may attack several relatives in the same mode. For example, Nyaluwema of Mukanza Village was afflicted by her mother's mother's spirit with reproductive

---

[1] For a preliminary classification of Ndembu rituals see my ' Lunda Rites and Ceremonies ', *Occasional Papers of the Rhodes-Livingstone Museum*, New Series, No. 10 (1953). A detailed analysis of Ndembu ritual is in preparation.

troubles in the mode of *Wubwang'u*, and with illness in the mode of *Chihamba*. She is now an adept in both cults, and as we shall see an important doctor of *Chihamba*. On the other hand, Nyamukang'a of MALABU lineage in Mukanza afflicted her daughter's daughter Nyamasung'a, her daughter's daughter's daughter Nyamukola, and her daughter's daughter's daughter's daughters Zuliyana and Yana, with illness in the mode of *Chihamba*. The spirit is most frequently a mother or a mother's mother in women's cults. Thus the cults act as a mnemonic of direct matrilineal kinship links. Virilocal marriage, which may scatter women far from their matrilineal kin, is to some extent counteracted by cults that stress matrilineal ties between dead and living women. But sometimes a woman may be afflicted by a spirit from a different village sub-lineage from her own. Nyatioli, Nyamukola's sister, for example, of MALABU lineage, had twice been afflicted by Nyachintang'a, apical ancestress of the other village lineage, in the modes of *Isoma* and *Wubwang'u*.

Thus the cause of affliction is thought to be connected with a breach of kinship norms in some specific kinship group. But the treatment of the afflicted person is carried out by an association of ritual specialists who need not necessarily be related to him or her.

Since most adult members of any village are adepts in at least one cult, and since members of all cults may be found everywhere in the Ndembu and Kosa regions, it follows that the total ritual system provides a set of interconnections which in effect perform a political function. This will be clear if I present a highly schematized picture of the way ritual interlinks persons and groups in a vicinage, with reference to cults concerned with female reproduction only. There are four main cults which are today performed to placate spirits interfering with female reproduction : their names are *Nkula*, *Chihamba*, *Wubwang'u* and *Isoma*.[1] Let us for convenience call these cults A, B, C, and D. Let us suppose that there are four villages in the vicinage, each containing eight adult women belonging to the village descent group. Now let us suppose that in each village two women belong to each cult association. This means that the women

---

[1] There is another cult *Kalemba* which used to be frequently performed but is now extremely rare.

belonging to a single kinship group in each village are divided by membership in four cults, and that four cult associations interlink the four villages which, let us suppose, belong to four unrelated descent groups. Now let us suppose that in each village there are eight wives of male village members, each wife from a different village in a different vicinage. If two wives in each village belong to each cult association, each pair of wives is linked to two female village members by cult affiliation, and to female members and wives of male members in all the other villages in the vicinage. They themselves, since they originate in other villages and vicinages, act in effect as representatives of the Ndembu *as a whole* in the context of the ritual. Now let us suppose that in each village one man is a doctor or adept in each cult. In his own village he is linked through cult membership with two kinswomen and two female affines, none of whom, perhaps, is his own wife. He is cross-linked with one man and four women in each of the other villages in his vicinage, and divided from all the other men, and from three-quarters of the women, in his own village, by membership of a cult-association. Siblings and parents and children may be divided from one another by cult affiliation, while the status of members of adjacent genealogical generations may be reversed during the period of performance of a ritual. When ritual is being performed in connection with cult A, members of cults B, C, and D are *excluded* [1] from the esoteric phases of the ritual, although senior doctors of these cults may be given sacralized beer or food in token of their high ritual status in other situations. Similarly with the other cults. Thus in a society characterized by the poverty of its status system in secular social relations, the status differentiation within each cult and the exclusion of uninitiated persons, whatever their rank or standing in other contexts, from its central mysteries, provides some compensation for the frustrations of ambitious urges, or for the occupation of an inferior status in secular life.

I have only mentioned one section of the ritual system, in dealing with cults relating to female reproduction. In addition,

---

[1] Gluckman has shown in 'The Role of the Sexes in Wiko Circumcision Ceremonies', that exclusion from the *arcana* of a ritual is sociologically as significant as participation in them.

there are two distinct but interlocking categories of cults relating to huntsmanship (*Wubinda* and *Wuyang'a*), one of which (*Wubinda*) contains five separate cults. Social bonds of membership in the hunters' cult likewise interlink individuals in different localities, and even cross tribal boundaries. Then there are curative cults of various kinds, a cult which concerns itself with the initiation of diviners, and a number of anti-witchcraft cults. Today, new cults, often organized by Ovimbundu and Lwena immigrants, are directed against disease and misfortune caused by the malevolent influence of living and dead Europeans, and, in some areas, these are beginning to oust the traditional cults. To the manifold ties interconnecting people in these cults must be added the links created by the boys' circumcision ritual, which join men in opposition to women,[1] and by the girls' puberty ritual, which join women in opposition to men. Furthermore, there is the *Mung'ong'i* association which carries out important duties during the funeral rituals of its members and which carries out an elaborate initiation ritual of its own in connection with the funeral rituals.

These cult-linkages can be politically effective only if ritual is frequently performed. I do not know whether there has been any increase in the frequency of performance of rituals in recent years ; but I have personally witnessed thirty-one performances of no less than fifteen different categories of cults of affliction and anti-witchcraft cults, as well as many life-crisis rituals, and have been notified of the performance, in localities where I was staying at the time, of more than twice that number—mostly in my second period in the field. It is likely that rituals were performed at least as frequently in the past, for a number of rituals in the bow-hunters' cult (*Wubinda*) have become extinct, as well as ritual performed by the women's *Chiwila* funerary association, and a cult called *Musolu*, performed by a chief or senior headman, to bring rain if there had been a drought at the beginning of the rainy season. Many cults involve the performance of two successive rituals, separated by a period during which the patient undergoes partial seclusion from secular life. The first of these rituals is in the women's cults called *ku-lembeka*

---

[1] Cf. Gluckman, M., ' The Role of the Sexes in Wiko Circumcision Ceremonies '.

or *ilembi*, and the second, and more elaborate and important, *ku-tumbuka*. A candidate who has undergone *ku-lembeka* may play a minor role in the cult, but cannot become an officiant until she has passed *ku-tumbuka*. Often a person is considered cured, that is, freed from the ban of her fertility imposed by the spirit, after *ku-lembeka*, and may never undergo *ku-tumbuka*. The fact that most cults involve two separate performances of ritual multiplies the number of occasions on which each kind of ritual may be performed. Again, rituals are sometimes considered to have failed in their purpose for a number of reasons. The diviner who prescribed this or that ritual may have been deceived by a witch. Or he may have divined the right spirit but the wrong mode of affliction. Or several spirits may have been afflicting the patient simultaneously in different modes of affliction, so that rituals must be successively performed by several cult associations before a cure is effected. Thus, persons entitled to participate as adepts in cults are constantly being mobilized, and new candidates for initiation, as patients, or in the guise of patients, are constantly undergoing treatment.

Some women, such as Yana (I,J4), daughter of Nyatioli (I,H11) in Mukanza Village, have been initiated into all the women's cults. Yana, who was only thirty-four in 1954, was a patient in the *ku-lembeka* phase of *Nkula* when she was about seventeen years old. *Nkula* in this case had been performed after the miscarriage of her first child. Her husband had sought out a diviner who had named her mothers' mother Nyamasung'a as the afflicting spirit. Yana considered the treatment successful, for her next child was born successfully. After about ten years she had menstrual troubles and her husband went with Sakazao her uterine uncle to consult a diviner. He diagnosed the renewed anger of Nyamasung'a's spirit as the cause of her trouble and recommended that the *ku-tumbuka* phase of *Nkula* should be performed. After this, her mother Nyatioli, who had been the senior female doctor in the ritual, taught her the full ' mystery ' (*mpang'u*) of *Nkula*, and its full curative aspect (*wumbuki*). The following year she became ill during pregnancy, and divination indicated that her mother's mother's mother had afflicted her in the mode of *Isoma*. The *Isoma* manifestation of a spirit can cause abortions and miscarriage. To prevent these she underwent the full ritual, in this case called *ku-tumbuka*, of *Isoma*,

performed by Kanyombu, Mukanza Kabinda's brother, and at
that time her mother's husband. There is no *ku-lembeka* at *Isoma.*
But when she bore her child without mishap, the *kwidisha*, or
' causing to come out ' (i.e. from the grass seclusion hut), was
performed, to celebrate the success of the treatment.
    Yana also underwent as patient a performance of *Wubwang'u,*
ku-tumbuka only. *Wubwang'u* is most frequently performed for
a woman who has had twins, for her and their welfare, or for a
woman who is expected to bear twins because she herself or her
mother is a twin. Yana passed through *ku-tumbuka* only, because *ku-lembeka* is performed during pregnancy and not after
parturition. Once the twins have been born, *ku-tumbuka* is
enacted. Yana's twins both died and the treatment was reckoned
unsuccessful. Nevertheless, Yana claimed that she was entitled
to act as a junior adept (*chimbuki*) in *Wubwang'u* and had in fact
attended two performances since her own, in both of which the
patients were cured. She said that she had paid the senior woman
doctor, wife of the headman of her husband's village, where the
ritual took place, ten shillings for full instruction in the collection
and preparation of the herbal ' medicines ' (*yitumbu*) of *Wubwang'u.* Yana was also a candidate for initiation into the
Chihamba ritual at Mukanza which I am about to describe. In
a relatively short period then, between the ages of about seventeen
and thirty-four, Yana had undergone six performances of ritual
in four women's cults. She was entitled to participate as an
officiant, with varying status in each, in four cults. In *Nkula*
she was quite an important officiant ; in *Isoma* she played a
prominent role ; in *Wubwang'u* she was entitled to help in the
collection of medicine in the bush with other adepts but did not
prepare and apply them ; and in *Chihamba* she had acquired the
right to enter the sacred enclosure from which the uninitiated
are excluded. Her mother Nyatioli was an important officiant
in *Isoma* ; performed ritual tasks in *Nkula* ; was an adept, but
not an important one, in *Wubwang'u* ; and had never been
initiated into *Chihamba.* In *Chihamba*, then, Yana rated higher
than her mother, about equally in *Wubwang'u*, and lower in
Nkula and *Isoma.* Yana, however, had been initiated, but not
Nyatioli, into the new fashionable *Tukuka* and *Mwana Ipana*
rituals introduced from Angola and the Belgian Congo respectively. Yana displayed rather more than the usual interest in

ritual common in Ndembu women but it is no exaggeration to say that most Ndembu women are initiated into at least two cults concerned with female reproduction between puberty and the menopause.

Does the frequency with which such ritual is performed indicate a high rate of reproductive disorders ? I obtained the impression that it was indeed high, but not exceptionally high for Africa. I would like to postulate that the high frequency with which curative and 'gynaecological' ritual is performed by Ndembu is just as much socially as biologically determined. Misfortune, illness and reproductive troubles among Ndembu, if severe enough, are associated with the activities of spirits, witches and sorcerers. When these are regarded as the causes of affliction, one does not have to look very far before one finds conflict in social relations. Every one of the social dramas I have used to illustrate and carry forward the analysis contains at least one reference to a supernatural agency in connection with a social dispute. Ndembu society, as we have shown, is torn with perennial disputes, there is little harmony and much conflict between its dominant principles of social organization, and in secular life there is little to bind together more than a small number of people in habitual co-operation. Unity in such a society is maintained by making each outstanding case of personal misfortune the occasion on which the moral norms and values shared by all Ndembu are prominently displayed in a number of ways—in prayer, precept, symbol, mimetic action, and in the ritual association of those who have suffered regardless of their kinship or other interlinkages. The common misfortunes of mankind are made occasions for restating the common values of Ndembu.

Among the Ndembu, as we have seen, each little mobile local unit is torn with continuous dissension. Nevertheless out of conflict itself unity is engendered. Each severe case of illness brings into the open some rankling dispute within a particular group, between specific persons with opposed interests. Many such disputes are irresoluble since they spring from contradictions in the social structure itself. Since they are ultimately irresoluble the most that can be done is to bring about a temporary palliation, to produce, as it were, the illusion of harmony within the disturbed group. This is done by stressing in each little localized performance of ritual the common interests of the whole society, and what Fortes and Evans-Pritchard call ' the basic relations that make up the social order ',[1] such as matriliny, gerontocracy, the historical unity of the Ndembu, and so on.   Again, the ritual is carried out by an *ad hoc* association of cult initiates, who represent not this or that particular interest group but Ndembu society as a whole.   Such a group is too ephemeral to develop internal conflicts of a serious kind.

Thus, each individual's misfortune brings to light some specific and localized conflict in inter-personal or inter-group relations. Ritual is then invoked, under the pretext of curing the patient or removing his misfortune, to settle the conflict.   But the same ritual has far wider importance in that it affirms the common interests of all Ndembu, often expressing this community of interests in symbols representing pivotal aspects of a culture shared by all, however distant from one another they may be in space, however opposed to one another in political action.

I have suggested that there is a relationship between what was in the past a marked emphasis on hunting and the institution of virilocal marriage ;   and also that the contradiction between virilocal marriage and maternal descent in a context of semi-nomadic hunting and cassava-cultivation gives rise to many conflicts between sections and factions varyingly affiliated in the social system.   I have argued that therefore secular life is full of manifold and unceasing struggles, of schism and fission.   I believe further that the society exhibiting this turmoil and unrest could not maintain any sort of coherence for long were it not for its plastic and adaptable system of ritual.   This ritual, although it operates in a contingent and fitful manner in particular situations, and lacks great national, seasonal or regular performances, still contrives to stimulate in its members sentiments of tribal unity, of a general belonging together, which transcend the irreparable divisions and conflicts of interests in the secular social structure.

The affliction of each is the concern of all ; likeness of unhappy lot is the ultimate bond of ritual solidarity.   The adepts have themselves known the suffering the candidates are experiencing. The spirits who cause them to suffer themselves suffered in the

---

[1] *African Political Systems*, p. 18.

same way. But affliction is potentially a boon, not merely a present pain, for it is the royal road to ritual eminence in a cult. Affliction by a spirit follows a breach of regular customary relations between living and dead, i.e. relations of worship involving the mentioning of the names of the dead in prayer, or a breach between living and living, when kin quarrel, which is then punished by the dead. Thus the *unity of all* Ndembu is only perceived in situations arising out of the *breach* of *specific* relations, usually couched in terms of kinship. A society continually threatened with disintegration is continually performing reintegrative ritual. Ritual among Ndembu does not express the kinship and political structure as in a firmly organized society ; rather it compensates for their deficiencies in a labile society.

In order to bring out more fully the implications of this analysis I propose to examine in some detail the social background of an important ritual which took place near the end of my second tour of fieldwork at the village of Mukanza.

' Chihamba ' Ritual at Mukanza Village

In this analysis I try to isolate social relationships and processes from their cultural integument as far as possible. I hope to make a detailed examination of the cultural structure of Ndembu ritual in a separate study. But some account of the main cultural features of the *Chihamba* ritual is necessary, if we are to grasp clearly its sociological implications.

The *Chihamba* ritual is said by Ndembu to be a very important one (*chidyika chalema nankashi,* ' a very heavy ritual '). Some claim that it is more important than the boys' circumcision ritual, others deny this. But all agree that its *ku-tumbuka* phase is usually attended by many more people than come to any other ritual except boys' circumcision. Many calabashes of beer are brewed by the village sponsoring it, and a large amount in cash and kind is paid to the ritual officiants afterwards.

Chihamba is a specific manifestation of an ancestor spirit. It is an exceptionally dangerous one, for while most manifestations of spirits cause misfortune, infertility or disease only, a spirit that has ' come out in *Chihamba* ' can kill the person it afflicts.

The *Chihamba* manifestation of a spirit afflicts its victim in several ways. Most commonly it causes pains in the whole body, especially in the neck, and a feeling of extreme cold. Sometimes it is said to induce decay in crops planted by the object of its wrath. Again, a man who is 'caught' by *Chihamba* may experience bad luck in hunting. It may also afflict women with reproductive troubles. The *Chihamba* manifestation is, in fact, a sort of compendium of all the misfortunes that can happen to a person. But *Chihamba* is not simply the manifestation of an angry ancestor. Another category of supernatural being is also involved. At several points in the ritual a strange supernatural being is represented in various ways. It speaks indecencies in a throaty voice and brusquely questions the candidates. This being, called *Kavula* (a name known in theory only to initiates), is *not* the spirit of a dead person, but has 'his' own independent existence. *Kavula* is an archaic term for the lightning, and is perhaps etymologically connected with *nvula*, 'rain'. At one phase in the ritual he is said to enter the hut of the principal patient, as the lightning does, through the grass 'top-knot' (*ntung'u*).

On the evening of the first day of the *ku-tumbuka* phase, a doctor impersonating *Kavula*, screened from the view of adepts and candidates, addresses them in the principal patient's hut in a throaty voice. After enquiring of the candidates why they have come to visit him, and after reviling them, he confers on them ritual names which only *Chihamba* adepts are entitled to use. Next day a contraption is made symbolizing *Kavula* in a secret place called *isoli* within a sacred enclosure in the bush about a quarter-of-a-mile from the village. The contraption consists of an inverted meal-mortar containing symbolic objects and a framework of sticks to which rattles are attached. Over this is spread a blanket or skin whitened by cassava meal. A concealed string attached to the framework can be manipulated by a male adept to 'make *Kavula* dance'. Just before nightfall the candidates, each in order of ritual status, but women before men, are brought to 'greet *Kavula*', their 'grandfather', 'the one who knows everything and must be praised'. One by one they crawl on their stomachs to the leaf-hedge surrounding the white image of *Kavula*, banging their heads on the ground as they advance, first on one side and then on the other. Women squeeze their breasts 'to give milk to the chief' as they move forward. *Kavula* is compared with Mwantiyanvwa at this moment. When he reaches *Kavula*, each candidate is told 'to kill *Kavula*', by striking him on the 'head' (really the inverted meal mortar) with a *Chihamba* rattle—each candidate has such a rattle, of special form elaborately carved for him or her before the performance. The candidates are then led away by adepts and brought back to find the blanket gone and the mortar running with the blood of a sacrificed chicken. They are told by the adepts that they have killed 'the chief' (*mwanta*) and that they have seen *Kavula's* blood.

The whole of that day they have been driven, wearing only a waist-cloth, between the sacred enclosure and the principal candidate's hut by the adepts. They have been called 'the slaves' (*andung'u*) of *Kavula* and have been forced to wear symbolic slave-yokes (*mpanda*). *Nkaka* means 'owner' (of slaves and domestic animals) as well as 'grandfather'. It seems reasonable to infer that one of the many meanings of *Kavula* is gerontocratic authority in general. *Kavula* jokes (*ku-senseka*) with adepts and candidates, as a grandfather does with his grandchildren. He reviles them sexually in a thick, mirth-provoking, yet nevertheless, rather terrifying, voice. Some of his esoteric names, *Samaseng'a* for example, said by informants to be derived from *ku-seng'uka*, 'to multiply' (of fruit), suggest that he presides over fertility and that his authority has its benevolent side. His associations with the rains, with cassava, and with other cultivated crops, support this view. He can remove sickness and misfortune and bestow health and fertility after his mystical death. But it is clear that there is ambivalence in the relationship between *Kavula* and candidates. He it is who strikes like lightning with disease, who treats the candidates like slaves, who forces them to grovel before him, who taunts them with teasing questions and reviles them, and who finally is bloodily killed by them. This ambivalence is not surprising in view of the strains and conflicts in the kinship system, and between slaves and their masters.

Kavula is said to be a male. The spirit of the afflicting ancestor, on the other hand, is always female, and its name is found by divination. One informant told me that '*Kavula* is the husband and X (the afflicting spirit's name) is the wife. They join together to catch the patient.' In the *Chihamba* ritual there is normally a principal patient or candidate (the term *muyeji* has, of course, both meanings), always a woman, who has been ill or unlucky in the ways mentioned above. A divination has been made for her and the diviner has said that ' such-and-such a spirit has come out to her in *Chihamba* '. Other sick women in the village may then also be thought to have been afflicted by the same spirit and they are also nominated as candidates. On the most important day of the ritual, that on which the candidates are chased back and forth like slaves from the sacred enclosure to the hut of the principal candidate, the pursuing doctors may capture any persons of any age or sex who happen to cross their path and add them to the group of candidates. People often get caught deliberately in order to be initiated, in spite of the humiliations to which they are subjected. Parents urge their young children to get caught, for this renders them immune from capture at subsequent performances of *Chihamba* and gives them the right to enter the sacred enclosure, if not to approach closely to the central shrine. The chasing goes on all day until sunset. Each time the candidates are driven back into the sacred enclosure from the village, they are made to sit down with their backs to the central shrine in a long row, while adepts crouch beside them on either side asking each in turn a number of riddles all concerned with the identity of *Kavula*. Most candidates make ridiculous mistakes in their answers at which the adepts laugh derisively.

Each time they return they advance a little nearer to the central shrine where the symbolic representation of *Kavula* is being made. They are told that they will see ' something terrifying '. Until the final obsequious greeting of *Kavula* no candidate ever mentions his name. There is a fiction that only the initiated know it, although I have obtained evidence that uninitiated people have heard of it. Eventually they are told by adepts who are their friends to mention the name of *Kavula* when asked by the senior doctors, who are always male. The women claim that *Chihamba* was once their ritual but that the men ' stole it from them'. Male doctors and adepts concern themselves principally with the more esoteric aspect of the ritual such as the construction of *Kavula's* representation, while the women adepts act as a sort of police force guarding the sacred enclosure from desecration by the uninitiated, chasing the candidates and seizing those who cross the path between village and sacred enclosure. Thus men are the more important adepts, while women are the principal candidates.

PLATE VI

THE INTERROGATION OF *CHIHAMBA* CANDIDATES

The candidates sit modestly in a line with their backs to the small sacred
enclosure (*isoli*) where *Kavula* (see Chapter Ten) is represented. Nyamukola
is the candidate nearest to the camera. Manyosa stands on the right, arms
akimbo, holding her adept's rattle while other adepts ask the patients, riddles.
The child-candidates can be seen top-left, harangued by Headman Itota, who
enacted *Kavula* the previous night. Nyamuwang'a, the suspected witch of
Social Dramas IV and VII, is the bare-headed female adept near the centre of
the photograph.

Kavula is impersonated in the patient's hut behind by a screen by the most senior male adept or an experienced adept with a suitable voice for reviling in the style required. Another senior adept makes the blanket-covered framework that represents *Kavula* in the bush. Other male adepts take turns to manipulate the string that makes the structure shake and rattle. No woman may pass behind the screen of leaves where *Kavula* thus ' dances ', but the leading female adept may sit close to the front of it. Both men and women adepts may chase the candidates, although more women than men do this. Both men and women may question the candidates, although men ask the most esoteric questions.

After *Chihamba* is over, a special form of friendship similar to blood-brotherhood and blood-sisterhood (*wulunda*) is made between adepts and those who have been candidates in the ritual, called *wubwambu* or *wulunda waChihamba*. This *wubwambu* provides yet another means of interlinking members of different villages, for members of the same villages are seldom united in this way. The adept with whom a candidate is joined in ritual friendship is the one who has helped him or her to answer correctly the final riddles put by the senior male adepts, before the killing of *Kavula*.

This necessarily abbreviated account of the main features of the *ku-tumbuka* phase of *Chihamba* must suffice as an introduction to the sociological analysis of a specific performance of this ritual. It will be remembered (see Chapter Five, p. 164) that the village of Mukanza was rapidly approaching the crisis of fission in 1954, near the end of my second tour of fieldwork. It seemed likely that the village would undergo a three-way split, with Sandombu reviving the name of Kahali Village for his farm and obtaining his following from Bibiana and her children ; Kasonda dividing off with Manyosa and Chawutong'i and founding a farm ; while Sakazao, with or without Chinema, and supported by most of MALABU lineage, would succeed to the name and position of Mukanza. It will also be recalled that the relationship under most strain in this situation was the marriage between Mukanza Kabinda and Nyamukola which interlinked two village lineages and also two genealogical generations.

Mukanza and Nyamukola were a most devoted couple, were the parents of many children, and would never divorce one

another. Hostility between village lineages and generations did
not express itself in marital quarrels between them but in criticism
directed by other villagers against Nyamukola. Mukanza himself was rarely attacked ; in some ways he seemed to be above
the battle, as a personification of the values of village unity and
persistence. But Nyamukola became involved in several
quarrels, some of them quite sharp. Most of her disputes were
with members of the intervening genealogical generation. Social
Drama V (pp. 157-61) includes a quarrel between Sandombu
and Nyamukola. She also had a dispute with Chawutong'i which
led to the latter's temporary defection from Mukanza Village.
Nyamukola had complained publicly that when she had been
to Kalene Hospital for treatment of her leprosy, Chawutong'i's
sons, Kasenzi (I,H5), who worked for the European headmaster
of Sakeji School, with Kaseloki (I,H6), who was a schoolboy at
Kalene Middle School, had only given her a small piece of beef
between them. Chawutong'i, who had recently visited Kalene
Hospital, herself accused Nyamukola of lying, and claimed that
her sons had given Nyamukola a lot of meat. As the quarrel
progressed mutual recriminations became more and more savage.
Chawutong'i accused Nyamukola of witchcraft, claiming that
the latter had developed a grudge (*chitela*), the activating principle
in witchcraft, against Kasenzi, because he had once, on receiving
the present of a goat from his father- and mother-in-law after the
first pregnancy of his wife, charged Nyamukola and Mukanza
some money for a portion of its meat instead of giving it as an
obligation of kinship. After saying this she demanded compensation from Mukanza for the slander his wife had uttered
against her sons. Mukanza became angry himself at the accusation of witchcraft and refused to pay. Kasonda then came along
and said that it was true that Kasenzi and Kaseloki had given little
help to Nyamukola. Chawutong'i, by this time in a towering
rage, retorted that she could now see that she had no brothers
to help her in Mukanza Village, so why should she stay there ?
She promptly ordered her docile husband Ndeleki to carry the
family's scant possessions to Mbimbi Village where there was a
vacant hut. Later, Kasonda became alarmed that he would lose
Chawutong'i's support for his projected farm, and took her
part against Nyamukola who, he told me, was an inveterate
scandalmonger (*mukwakukapekelela*). It will be recalled that

Nyamukola had once accused Kasonda of bewitching Mukanza (p. 140) and that he had then been defended by Chawutong'i. Both quarrels bring out the strength of the combined lineal and generation attachments, and the opposition between adjacent generations. Nyamukola was at the centre of sundry other quarrels, and it is clear that she occupied a position in the social structure subjected to considerable strain.

In the latter part of 1953, Nyamukola's leprosy became worse and she began to suffer considerable pain from a large spreading sore on her left shoulder and upper arm. We sent her to Kalene Mission Hospital and when she returned she seemed to experience a slight improvement in health. But she was still unable to do a full day's work in her gardens and in the preparation of cassava meal. A private divination was made into the cause of her affliction, and the verdict was that her matrilineal great-grandmother Nyamukang'a (I,E5) had 'caught her in *Chihamba*'.

Nyamukang'a had been the daughter of Malabu and the apical ancestress of a minimal lineage which included Sakazao and his sisters and their children, and which was structurally opposed to another minimal lineage of MALABU lineage that included Nyamuwang'a and Line. But her role as afflicting spirit probably did not so much derive from the contemporary social situation as from the fact that when Nyamukola was a young girl she was initiated at the *ku-lembeka* phase of *Chihamba* performed for her mother Nyamasung'a. The spirit afflicting Nyamasung'a in *Chihamba* was then divined as Nyamukang'a. It was said in Mukanza Village that Nyamukang'a 'wished to make Nyamukola a full doctor' (*chimbuki wachikupu*) in *Chihamba*, and would make her ill (*mukishi wakamukatisha*) until the *ku-tumbuka* phase was performed for her.

But it is possible that Nyamukang'a was divined because her genealogical remoteness from the living enabled the inhabitants of Mukanza Village to assert their unity as a long-established village against the centrifugal forces of factional struggle that threatened to destroy it. The fact that Nyamukola, the person most involved in current disputes, was singled out as the senior candidate in an important ritual, as the focus of the unity of a big ritual assembly, also suggests that the people were intuitively aware of the threat to their cohesion and were dealing with it at its source.

Y

I suggest that the people of Mukanza Village had three main aims in sponsoring *Chihamba*. The first aim was deliberate : it was to cure Nyamukola and her fellow-patients and to initiate other members of the vicinage into the important cult mystery. The second aim, hardly conscious but proceeding from a collective sense of disturbance, was to reintegrate the village of Mukanza itself, torn, as we have seen, by many dissensions. The third, also hardly conscious, was to effect a reconciliation with villages with which Mukanza Village was at the time on poor terms, notably Shika and Kafumbu Villages. The first aim was directed towards the physical and moral welfare of individuals, the second towards the betterment of internal village relations, and the last towards the creation of a climate of friendliness and co-operation in the wider systems of inter-village dealings.

An analysis of the social composition of the ritual assembly on the day of chasing and questioning would clearly reveal, even if supporting evidence were lacking, that the last two aims were present. I list the candidates and adepts approximately in order of importance, and give the village affiliations of each, dividing them by sex.

CANDIDATES

Name	Village	Ritual Status
Women :		
Nyamukola	Mukanza	afflicted by spirit
Zuliyana	Mukanza (Sandombu Farm)	,, ,, ,,
Yana	Mukanza	captured by adepts
Masondi	Muchona Farm	,, ,, ,,
Kalusanzi	village in Ikelenge Area	,, ,, ,,
Girls :		
Seliya Sakwimba	Shika (mother from Mukanza)	,, ,, ,,
Sani	Mukanza (mother from Shika)	,, ,, ,,
Mwendiana	Mukanza (mother from Shika)	,, ,, ,,
Didiya	Kafumbu	,, ,, ,,
Delu	Shika	,, ,, ,,
Rene	Ntambu	,, ,, ,,
Rene's twin sister	Ntambu	,, ,, ,,
Monica	Mukanza (mother from Shika)	,, ,, ,,
?	Chibwakata	,, ,, ,,
Men :		
Makanjila	Mbimbi	,, ,, ,,
Chilayi	Nswanamatempa	,, ,, ,,
Mungongu	Nswanamatempa	,, ,, ,,
Wankie	Ng'ombi	,, ,, ,,

Name	Village	Ritual Status
Boys :		
Kafwila Munjila	Mukanza	captured by adepts
Chikimbu	Mukanza (Sandombu Farm)	,, ,, ,,
Samuwika	Mukanza	,, ,, ,,
Bisheki	Kafumbu	,, ,, ,,
Jerry	Mukanza (mother from Shika)	,, ,, ,,
?	Nswanakudya	,, ,, ,,
?	Kasai	,, ,, ,,
?	Chikang'a	,, ,, ,,
?	Chibwakata	,, ,, ,,

ADEPTS

Name	Village	Ritual Status
Men :		
H.M.[1] Itota	Itota	*Kavula*
F.H.[1] Sandombu	Mukanza (Sandombu Farm)	organizer of ritual arrangement
F.H. Sakutoha	Sakutoha	senior adept
F.H. Muchona	Muchona	,, ,,
Sachinjungu	Kasai	,, ,,
F.H. Lambakasa	Lambakasa	,, ,,
H.M. Kamawu	Kamawu	,, ,,
Biscuit	Kamawu	,, ,,
H.M. Kanyabu	Kanyabu	,, ,,
Kilisha	Kasai	,, ,,
F.H. Koshita	Chikang'a (Koshita Farm)	,, ,,
H.M. Nswanamatempa	Nswanamatempa	,, ,,
H.M. Ng'ombi	Ng'ombi	,, ,,
Chisanji	Nswanamatempa	junior adept
Mboyunga	Nswanamatempa	,, ,,
Ndeleki	Ng'ombi	,, ,,
Kapitula	Kamawu	,, ,,
Spider Chanza	Ng'ombi	,, ,,
Women :		
Katendi	Kafumbu	oldest adept (sat near *isoli*)
Nyaluwema	Mukanza (mother from Kafumbu)	principal female organizer
Nyakantemba	Itota (sister of Mbimbi and Lambakasa)	wife of Itota who impersonated *Kavula*
Nyamuleji	Shika	senior adept
Nyamuwang'a	Mukanza (Sandombu Farm)	,, ,,
Nyawunyumbi	Mbimbi	,, ,,
Nyamalichi	Chibwakata (mother from Kamawu)	,, ,,

[1] H.M. stands for Village Headman.
F.H. stands for Farm Head.

Name	Village	Ritual Status	
Nyamunyaka	Kamawu	senior adept	
Mandamu	Nswanamatempa	,,	,,
Mateng'ineng'i	Lambakasa	,,	,,
Makisa	Lambakasa (daughter of Nya-mumwema woman headman)	,,	,,
Nyakamboya	Nsanji	,,	,,
Nyawatwa	Nswanakudya	,,	,,
Nyaluwema	Chibwakata	,,	,,
Manyosa	Mukanza	,,	,,
Mangaleshi	Mukanza (mother from Shika)	,,	,,
Mika	Mbwambu (Ntambu Area)	,,	,,
Nyamuhemba	Ng'ombi	,,	,,
Kaluswika	Chibwakata	,,	,,
Nyakamawu	Chibwakata	,,	,,
Lumiya	Mpawu (Ntambu Area)	,,	,,
Mesala	Mukanza (mother from Kanyabu)	junior adept	
Disa	Ng'ombi (daughter of Lumiya)	,,	,,
Nyawatwa	Ng'ombi	,,	,,
Susanna	Nswanakudya	,,	,,
Nyamatong'a	Mbimbi	,,	,,

This list gives some idea of the scale of the ritual and of heterogeneity of composition of the ritual assembly. The 27 candidates of whom 13 were males and 14 females, and 9 were adults and 18 children, came from 13 different villages and farms (14 if Sandombu Farm is reckoned independent of Mukanza). Seven of these villages, including Mukanza, were in the same vicinage ; six belonged to other vicinages. Ten of the candidates were resident in Mukanza Village at the time of the ritual, but four of them belonged to the village lineage of Shika. On the other hand Kalusa's and Ntololu's daughter Seliya Sakwimba (see p. 272), resident at Shika but belonging to Mukanza Village lineage, was made captive by the adepts, and her younger sister came to the public dance.

There were 18 male and 26 female adepts present, from 19 different villages and farms, 6 (1 man and 5 women) being resident at Mukanza Village. 12 of these villages were in the same vicinage as Mukanza, but the remaining 7 came from 6 different vicinages.

Thus in all there were 71 adepts and candidates (to whom jointly we may apply the term *congregation*), drawn from 20 villages in seven different vicinages. In addition there was a large number of attenders at public phases of the ritual. At the night dance immediately preceding the chasing and interrogation of the candidates, I estimated that there were about four hundred people present. I noticed Ndembu from every part of the region, some married into the vicinage, some visiting kin and affines, others working at the Boma as labourers or clerks, and others in transit from one part of the region to another.

But *Chihamba* would not be such an important cult if there were not many uninitiated persons to be excluded from its *arcana*. In the vicinage of Mukanza Village alone the following headmen and farm heads had never been initiated : Nsang'anyi, senior headman of the Kawiku (see p. 210 et seq.), Chibwakata (see p. 45), Mukanza himself, Mbimbi (who was caught by the adepts and paid a sum of money to free himself, after having been chased once or twice, much to the amusement of everyone), Makumela, Mulongesha (mother's brother of Headman Ng'ombi), Makayi (younger brother of Chibwakata), Nsanji (younger brother of Mbimbi and Lambakasa), Nshimba (Ovimbundu efficient at *Tukuka* rituals), Nyamumwema (a woman headman whose daughter was an adept), and Anderson Mulumbi. The last, whose wife had entered the sacred enclosure as an adept, went to fetch her to cook for him. He was attacked by two adepts, Chisanji and Spider, and beaten up. But he managed to drag his wife away, shouting out that *Chihamba* was ' rubbish '. Everyone was scandalized and said that in the past he would have had to pay a heavy fine, perhaps a slave or a gun, and would have been compelled to become a candidate in which role he would have been beaten for his offence. But nowadays such punishments are forbidden by the Europeans. Anderson was an extreme example of the growing class of modern sceptics. But the old headmen excluded from the cult felt ashamed of their uninitiated state. Moreover, they knew very little of what actually took place in the sacred enclosure. All of them knew the name *Kavula*, but none knew who or what *Kavula* was or what were his attributes. The status of candidate can only be measured against the ritual exclusion and ignorance of highly respected and powerful members of the local community such as these.

This short analysis of the social composition of the ritual assembly at the *Chihamba* I attended at Mukanza Village brings out in detail some of the points made in the general account of

Ndembu ritual.   The allocation of ritual offices to members of
Mukanza Village reflects the contemporary balance of power
within the village.   Nyaluwema, representing Sakazao who was
ntondu (uninitiated), within the village stood for MALABU lineage,
as well as for Kafumbu, her matrilineal village.   The three most
important female candidates, Nyamukola, Zuliyana and Yana,
belonged to MALABU lineage.   Sandombu's increasing influence
was reflected by his office in the ritual, and by the fact that his
wife Zuliyana was one of the principal patients.   His wife was
thus put almost on a par with Mukanza's wife.   Kasonda was
not so happily placed in this ritual.   He was, in fact, nearly
turned back from the entrance (*mukoleku*) to the sacred enclosure
when he came with me on the day of chasing and was only
admitted on the payment of quite a considerable sum (*nyishing'u*,
' payment to attend an important phase of a ritual or to purchase
ritual privileges '), and then only on account of his position as
my henchman.   I was myself rated as a *muyeji*, ' candidate ',
although the only ordeal I had to undergo was to be chased
several times by the adepts.   Kasonda claimed that he had been
a child-candidate years ago in his stepfather's village in Sailunga
Area, and that therefore he might enter the sacred enclosure.
Wankie Soneka, likely successor of Headman Ng'ombi, was
nearly debarred from entering the enclosure by furious women
adepts, who resembled so many Bacchantes, but someone
remembered that his father Nswanakudya had carried him
beyond the *mukoleku* years ago, when he was a child in arms and
his father was still a pagan.   Wankie tried to participate with
the senior adepts in the construction of the *isoli* and of the representation of *Kavula*, but he was haled before an impromptu
court which met at the *isoli* or ' central shrine ', the site of *Kavula*.
It consisted of Lambakasa, Sandombu, Muchona and Sachinjungu,
who sentenced him to be chased with a symbolic yoke of *mudyi*
wood round his neck, and to make obeisance to *Kavula* towards
sunset.   The interesting point here is that Wankie, a recusant
Christian schoolmaster, was making a bid to be considered a
leading elder in the vicinage and went to considerable lengths
to be regarded as an adept in *Chihamba*.   The ritual had evidently
not yet declined into a mere formality but was still socially
significant.
Kasonda's wife Mangaleshi was an adept, and he saw to it that

PLATE VII

SANDOMBU MAKES A *CHIHAMBA* SHRINE FOR HIS WIFE ZULIYANA

In the early morning following the day of chasing, a personal shrine is made by senior adepts before the hut of each adult candidate. A chicken is sacrificed and its head and entrails are impaled on the shrine. The shrine is called *kantong'a* and consists of a cutting of cassava (a food plant elaborately ritualized in *Chihamba* tied to a bunch of twigs collected from various medicine trees, each of which has a symbolic meaning. Maize and beans are planted around its base and watered. In this photograph Sandombu has just finished praying to the spirit. He used a beer bottle I gave him to water the *kantong'a*, since I was his ritual brother. When the food plants sprout, food taboos will be lifted.

four of his children were captured by the adepts and initiated. His elementary family was well represented in the ritual. His sister Manyosa was an adept, though her husband Chikasa was not. It was rather pathetic to see Chikasa dress up in his hunter's gear, although he was not going anywhere, and walk along the path on which the candidates were being pursued, as though to dare the adepts to seize him. They did not lay hands on him in fact, although they had mocked old headman Mbimbi (see p. 313), perhaps because they sensed the brittleness of Chikasa's self-respect.

Nyaluwema also acted as a link with Kafumbu Village lineage, to which she belonged by descent. Her older sister Katendi was treated by other adepts, male and female, with the greatest respect. Katendi's eldest son, headman of Kafumbu Village, was a *Kavula* impersonator, but he was unable to attend the performance. Some Kafumbu children were initiated, and the ritual was generally reckoned by Mukanza people to have benefited the relations between the two villages, which had been a little strained for some time. I was given the *Chihamba* adept-name of Samlozang'a Ndumba, which made me a ritual namesake of Headman Kafumbu. We thus had the right and duty to exchange gifts with one another. In this way I became a social link between the two villages.

Several Shika people, too, formed part of the congregation, and many members of that village attended the public dances and beer drinks. The hostility that had sprung up over Kalusa's death-payment (see p. 269 et seq.) between the villages was to some extent reduced by common participation in the ritual.

The major social effects of the Chihamba ritual at Mukanza Village may be summarized as follows :

(1) It reduced the hostility felt by many village members, especially of NYACHINTANG'A lineage (including Sandombu, Kasonda, and Chawutong'i), against Nyamukola, the senior woman of the village, by making her an object of sympathy and the focal personality of a great public ritual.

(2) It was an attempt to close the breach opening between different factions within the village by establishing ties of ritual collaboration between leading members of each faction.

(3) It gave prestige to Mukanza Village in and outside the vicinage.

(4) It re-established friendly relations with villages traditionally linked by kinship and affinity with Mukanza, but which, for that very reason, were constantly quarrelling with Mukanza.

(5) It drew more closely together long and recently established villages and farms in the vicinage : it will be remembered (pp. 285-6) that in 1952 Government moved many of the villages mentioned in this account of *Chihamba* into the vicinage in order to make their former territory a Forest Reserve.

(6) It made a dramatic restatement of the values of an indigenous society which were beginning to fall into abeyance.

(7) It offered an alternative source of prestige to those with limited authority in secular life—daughters were in some cases candidates and adepts but not their mothers, wives but not their husbands, sons but not their fathers, nephews but not their mothers' brothers, commoners but not headmen, and so on.

(8) It afforded opportunities to ambitious persons such as Wankie and Sandombu to enhance their prestige.

Chihamba is only one, though a most important one, of a dozen or more cults which resemble it broadly in form and social function. Different aspects of human suffering and misfortune are ritualized, and the rituals have a politically integrative role. I hope to establish, in a subsequent book, how, in the course of a ritual, symbols and verbal behaviour are manipulated so as to discharge tensions in the social system and to reintegrate the members of the ritual assembly into the disturbed social groups to which they belong—at all events for a short time after the ritual is over. Here I can only state that the cultural structure of an Ndembu ritual is consistent with its social function. Ritual for Ndembu is closely associated with breaches in social regularities and their redress. It is not so much a buttress or auxiliary of secular social regularities as a means of restating, time and again, a group unity which transcends, but to some extent rests on and proceeds out of, the mobility and conflicts of its component elements.

In conclusion, it must be stated that the system of cults of affliction and of life-crisis rituals does not operate in complete isolation from the system of political ties between chief, senior headmen and village headmen.   Thus, if an important ritual, such as *Chihamba, Mukanda* or *Wuyang'a* is to be held, the headman of the sponsoring village sends a messenger (*ntemesha*) to the chief or senior headman of the area in which his village is situated with a calabash of beer, to ' obtain fire ' (*nakutambula kesi*)—in other words, to obtain permission from the senior to hold the ritual. This act is the point of intersection between two virtually autonomous systems, each of which has the function of maintaining the highest common values of the whole Ndembu people.   The chief and senior headmen, it will be shown in the next chapter, enshrine and embody in their titles and ritual functions Ndembu history and the link with Mwantiyanvwa—they represent the historical unity of the people.   The cult associations maintain common values and reaffirm norms in relation always to the contemporary situation, to local and transient breaches in social relations, to the here and now.

CHAPTER XI

THE CHIEFTAINSHIP

PROFESSOR EVANS-PRITCHARD, writing of the king-ship among the Shilluk,[1] summarizes the king's position as follows : ' The king symbolizes a whole society and must not be identified with any part of it. He must be in the society and yet stand outside it and this is only possible if his office is raised to a mystical plane.' In substance, this formulation also holds good for the traditional position of the Ndembu chief Kanongesha.

It is difficult to obtain a clear and coherent picture of the Ndembu chieftainship as it existed before the Europeans came. Ndembu territory has been divided between Britain and Portugal ; and rival Kanongeshas in Rhodesia and Angola have arisen, whose authority and functions have been considerably modified by the different theories of government espoused by the respective colonial powers. Nevertheless, it is certain that Kanongesha was in the past a ritual rather than a political head, and was never able to exert effective political control over his senior headmen. From accounts I have collected from both Kanongeshas and from all the Rhodesian Ndembu senior headmen it would seem that the first Ndembu did not all invade their present region in a compact body, but many came in separate groups led by senior headmen, and that, although they all recognized Kanongesha as their chief, each of these headmen continued to maintain a considerable degree of autonomy. Yet they collaborated in national ritual and each of them had a ritual function [2] to perform at the funerary and installation rites of a Kanongesha. If Kanongesha asked them to help him to send tribute to Mwantiyanvwa they would usually comply ' out of respect ', but were Kanongesha to try to exact it by force I have been told he would have been forcibly opposed.

---

[1] Evans-Pritchard, E. E., *The Divine Kingship of the Shilluk of the Nilotic Sudan* (1948), p. 36.

[2] For example, at the installation, *Kabung'u* placed the chiefly lion- and leopard-skins on Kanongesha's chair, while Ikelenge removed them afterwards, in virtue of his office as *Kalula*. Mwininyilamba, as *Ifwota*, ' the vanguard-leader ', chose the site of the new chief's capital village : and so on.

Already in the first half of the nineteenth century, before the period of slave-raiding and -trading on a large scale, the Ndembu must have presented the picture of a scattered, thinly-spread, highly mobile and locally autonomous people, similar to the Chokwe, Bangala and other Angolan groups described by Carvalho and Capello and Ivens. Yet they possessed great pride and fierce consciousness of their direct and exalted origin in the empire of Mwantiyanvwa. This consciousness of origin was epitomized in the office of Kanongesha chieftainship. But that office was much more than an index of tribal identity ; it represented tribal rights to the use of land. Although Kanongesha wielded hardly more political power, in terms of control over organized force, than any other important headman, the ritual component of his status was bound up with Ndembu rights in the occupation and exploitation of a large region over which Ndembu felt free to roam as they pleased. These rights had been reserved to them, according to tradition, by the mutual agreement of a number of free and equal Southern Lunda chiefs (who had conquered land both for themselves and also in order to extend the political influence, if not the direct rule, of their overlord Mwantiyanvwa), to define and henceforward mutually to respect the boundaries of one another's territories. Another party to the agreement, according to one tradition, was the Lwena chief Chinyama, who also traced his descent from the Mwantiyanvwa dynasty.

But Kanongesha reigned rather than ruled, and he reigned with many of the attributes of the Divine King as set forth by Evans-Pritchard and in classical ethnography. In this capacity his ritual powers were limited by and combined with those held by senior headmen of the autochthonous Mbwela people who made submission after long struggle to their Lunda conquerors. Power to confer and periodically to medicate the supreme symbol of chiefly status, the *lukanu* bracelet, made from human genitalia and soaked in sacrificial blood at each installation, was vested in the Humbu (a branch of Mbwela) headman Kafwana, called *Chivwikankanu*, ' the one who invests with *lukanu* '. He also had the title of *Mama ya Kanongesha*, ' Mother of Kanongesha ', because he gave symbolic birth to each new incumbent of that office ; Kafwana was also said to teach each new Kanongesha the medicines of sorcery which caused him to be feared by his rivals and subordinates—yet another index of deficient secular authority.

The first *lukanu* was said to have been given by Mwantiyanvwa to the first Kanongesha, Nkuba, and to have been a replica of his own. When Nkuba died, his younger brother Sakapenda and his son Kabanda reported his death to Mwantiyanvwa. Mwanti-yanvwa made a new *lukanu* and asked Sakapenda to advance between a gauntlet of warriors along a line of leopard skins to receive the *lukanu* from his own hand. But Sakapenda, afraid of treachery, would not move. Then Kabanda walked forward fearlessly to Mwantiyanvwa who gave him the *lukanu* and said that he should succeed his father, for he was a brave man, not a coward like Sakapenda. Later Sakapenda is said to have bewitched Kabanda out of jealousy, but then became reconciled, and Sakapenda and Kabanda jointly planted a *muyombu* tree to the spirit of Nkuba. Then Kabanda gave Sakapenda the office of *Ntete Mwenimajamu*, 'the one who looks after the nail-parings and the graves' of the Kanongeshas and allocated him some territory over which he might preside. But his descendants were excluded from the succession from that day. It was about this time, it is said, that Kafwana, who had fought against Kabanda, submitted to him and was given the office of *Chiv-wikankanu*, just as Nsang'anyi, the Kawiku headman, became *Chivwikankanu* to Kabanda's son, the first senior headman Mukang'ala (see p. 212). It would seem that in those early days Kanongesha's office conferred a higher degree of political power than it did at a later period, and that his political authority was set at the opposite pole to the ritual power possessed in different ways by Sakapenda, Mwenimajamu and Kafwana Chivwi-kankanu, in an opposed and complementary relationship.

The *lukanu* was ritually treated by Kafwana and hidden by him during interregna. The mystical power of the *lukanu*, and hence of the Kanongesha-ship, came jointly from Mwantiyanvwa and Kafwana : its employment for the benefit of the land and the people was in the hands of a succession of individual in-cumbents of the chieftainship. Its origin in Mwantiyanvwa symbolized the historical unity of the Ndembu *people* ; its medication by Kafwana symbolized the unity of the *land*—of which Kafwana was the original 'owner'. The daily prayers addressed to it by Kanongesha were for the fertility and continued health and strength of the land, of its animal and vegetable resources, and of the people. On the negative side, its use by Kanongesha in cursing—he touched the earth with it while uttering a formula—meant that the person or group cursed would become barren and their land infertile and devoid of game. In the *lukanu*, finally, Lunda and Mbwela were united in the joint concept of Ndembu land and folk.

In a political system as fluid and mobile as that of the Ndembu it would be a mistake to look for undue rigidity in structure. Ndembu say that the early Kanongeshas parcelled out specific tracts of territory among the leading Lunda who had accompanied them from Mwantiyanvwa. Later they gave further land to their sons. Thus Kabanda is said to have sent Mukang'ala to the Chitunta Plain area not far from the Kawiku Plain, to keep an eye on the Kawiku villages. Other chiefs' sons who were given territories were Kafweku (see p. 13) in Rhodesia, Mweni Ambeji (' owner of the Zambezi ') and Mulumbakanyi in Angola. A chief's son who was thus given a territory (*mpata*) of his own was called the chief's *Mwanawuta* and was debarred thereafter from consideration as a candidate for his father's chieftainship. Until the second half of the nineteenth century succession to the Kanongesha-ship had been modelled on succession to the Mwantiyanvwa stool. The first chief's sons by his two principal wives, supplied in the Ndembu system by the matrilineages descended from the original pair of wives Nyakaseya and Nyachilesya, succeeded him ; theoretically in order of birth, but actually according to the choice of a sort of ' electoral college ', consisting of senior headmen (excluding those called *Mwanawuta*), from all parts of the Ndembu region. Succession passed along a line of brothers, and then descended to the sons by the senior wives of the oldest brother. After this, theoretically, it should have passed to the sons of the oldest son by his senior wives, but in practice, the sons of former chiefs would assert their claim to succeed. Succession wars were said to have followed. In the reign of Kanongesha Ishima Watuta Menji (' well of cool water '), about 1890, the chief in council decided to change the mode of succession to matriliny, to bring it into line with the custom followed in the villages. Ishima also established the new position of Chibwika, the nominated successor of the incumbent, and appointed his sister's daughter's

son, Chababa, as the first Chibwika. By this means he apparently
hoped to divert against the Chibwika the current of intrigue
against the incumbent unceasingly maintained by hopeful successors. Ishima apparently had no sons himself, or own sisters'
sons. Much pressure had been put on him by his matrilineal
kin to change the mode of succession. Since his death matrilineal kin of former Kanongeshas have succeeded Ishima both
in Angola and Rhodesia.

Today, in Mwinilunga District, where there is also a Chibwika-
ship parallel to the one in Angola, the Chibwika is nominated
by the Kanongesha, but the nomination is made only after the
senior headmen have been consulted, and no Kanongesha would
dare to run counter to their wishes. There are a number of
villages belonging to the chiefly maternal descent-group in the
District, and there is a convention that the Chibwika-ship, and
hence the Kanongesha-ship, should circulate through them and
not be monopolized by a single village. Thus there should be
no close relationship between Kanongesha and Chibwika.
Kanongesha Mulumbi's successor in Rhodesia, Kafuleji, came
from Kalwiji Village in Chibwika Area ; the present Kanongesha came from Nyakanschila Village in Kanongesha Area
proper ; the present Chibwika from Wachikeka Village in
Chibwika Area ; and it is thought that the next Chibwika will
be chosen from Nswanakudya Village (see pp. 207-10). The
fact that chiefly villages are scattered through the Ndembu
region—there are some in Ikelenge and Mwininyilamba Areas—
and that each is situated in a different vicinage from the others,
gives the whole people an interest in the chieftainship. Thus, if
a member of Nswanakudya Village became Chibwika (and
thereafter Kanongesha), senior men in the vicinage, from such
villages as Chibwakata, Mukanza, Ng'ombi and Nswanamatempa
for example, would seek appointments at court as councillors,
assessors, kapasus, road capitaos, etc., or would build in the
vicinity of the new chief in order to obtain privileges as his kin
and affines, giving him in return their support and protection
against his rivals and enemies. Paternally-linked kin of a chief
are often singled out for special favour and provide him with his
most trustworthy support. In the capital villages of Lunda chiefs
where succession is matrilineal, one often finds a compact block
of paternal kinsmen of the chief near the chief's own enclosure.

Uterine kin of the chief are also trusted, but not matrilineal relatives from other chiefly lineages. When a chief dies the inhabitants of his capital village often break up into small groups, each usually a minimal matrilineage or a uterine sibling group, and found new villages some distance away from the capital of the new chief.

Beneath Kanongesha in the traditional political system were the senior headmen or *ayilolu*, who consisted of the matrilineal descendants of the first Ndembu leaders who entered the area and the sons of chiefs who had been given an area (*mpata*). *Chilolu* is a term indicating relative social position when one person refers to another.[1] In a village a *chilolu* is a person who does not belong to the village matrilineal descent group. Thus Ndeleki (see p. 101) in Mukanza Village may be described by Kasonda or Sandombu as our 'chilolu'. In the same way Kanongesha refers to headmen who do not belong to his maternal descent group or who are unrelated to him by paternal ties as his 'ayilolu'. By an extension of meaning *ayilolu*, when used by Kanongesha, came to mean important headmen within his territory who might not enter into the succession to his chieftainship. The term then came to be applied to senior headmen. Such headmen were not called 'Sub-Chiefs'[2] among Ndembu, although the occupants of similar positions in Ishinde's area in Balovale District were called *anyanta yamutayi* ('branch chiefs').[3] The term 'mwanta', 'chief', can be applied to the head of any local unit of whatever span, qualified by the nature of the unit of which he is head. Thus Kanongesha may be known as *mwanta wampata*, 'chief of the country'. Senior headmen such as

---

[1] C. M. N. White (personal communication) holds that the basic meaning of *chilolu* is 'a headman upon whom a chief relies for support, information, etc.' The village usage I cite he considers to be a slang one and not the primary sense. He writes that 'ayilolu are sometimes referred to as *mbwambu jamutung'a*, "the nails that keep the country together"'. But if the village usage is a slang one it is very widespread. When I collected census material about marriage, my informants, if they had not married kin (cross-cousins or 'grandchildren') would tell me they had married 'a *chilolu*', i.e. a person not of their descent group.

[2] See, however, page 11, footnote 1 for discussion of this point.

[3] Thomas Chinyama, *The Early History of the Balovale Lunda* (1945), p. 8. I expressly raised this point with Ndembu informants in discussing Chinyama's book.

Ikelenge, Mwininyilamba, Nyakaseya and Mukang'ala may also be so termed. Sometimes Kanongesha is distinguished from the others by the adjective 'great' (*weneni*) while the others are 'small' (*wanyanya*). The head of a village is usually called *mwanta wamukala* ('chief of the village', pl. *anyanta anyikala*) whether he is a *chilolu* or not. Other terms used for a village head are *mweni-* or *mwini-mukala* ('owner of the village'), and *ntung'i*.

But the political system of the Ndembu is no simple pyramid of authority, at the top of which is Kanongesha, beneath him the *ayilolu*, and beneath them again the *anyanta anyikala*. It is true that according to custom the *ayilolu* had the right to tribute from the headmen living in their areas and certain joints from game killed in their areas, half of which they were supposed to send to Kanongesha. It is also true that they were entitled to display certain insignia such as a short sword, a bead crown (*chibang'ulu*), a slit-gong (*chikuvu*), a xylophone (*mudyimba*), and a bangle. They also presided over courts to which were summoned the best *mahaku* of their areas and which served as appeal courts within the areas. They had more elaborate installation rituals than village headmen, and certain headmen gave them tributary wives. They possessed special medicine not known to ordinary village headmen, for protecting their capital villages from witchcraft; and they were held to know many sorcery techniques for punishing those who offended them. Nevertheless it was difficult for a *chilolu* to enforce his rights on proud and independent headmen who, like Mukanza Kandulu in Chief Ikelenge's area (see p. 105), would unhesitatingly quit his area if he tried to gain his ends by force or even by the threat of force.

The social composition of a *chilolu's* area was always changing. It might consist of two or more vicinages, each composed of villages belonging to various maternal descent groups. In each vicinage there might be one or more villages belonging to the *chilolu's* maternal descent group. In his own vicinage would be found his closest matrilineal kin, a group belonging to his father's maternal descent group, and a number of 'strangers' (*ang'eji, antu acheng'i*) whom he had given permission to settle in his vicinage. In other vicinages (*ayitung'ili*) within his area (*mpata*) might be found villages whose nuclei consisted of his more remote matrilineal kin, others founded by members of his predecessor's capital village, notably paternal relatives of his predecessor, and villages of 'strangers' (*ang'eji*). In vicinages other than his own within his area one headman was usually recognized as the moral leader, if not as the political head. This was usually the headman of the village which had been established longest in the locality, and which had most abandoned residential sites, gardens and graves in it. Its headman was called the *mwenimbu*,[1] and he usually, though not invariably, sponsored the boys' circumcision ritual when it was decided to hold it in his vicinage. He, rather than the *chilolu* of the area, conferred or withheld permission to an incoming group to build and garden in his vicinage. But he might not give such permission without first consulting the other headmen and *mahaku* of the vicinage. Each *mwanta wamukala* had direct access to the *chilolu* of the area, each paid him tribute (*mulambu*, or more commonly in the plural, *nyilambu*) directly ; the *mwenimbu* of a vicinage did not act as the *chilolu's* agent. When the people of a village elected a new headman the *chilolu* and not the *mwenimbu*, of the vicinage confirmed their choice,[2] although the *mwenimbu*, and indeed any elder of the vicinage, might speak on behalf of any candidate in the election.

The giving of tribute was regarded as a moral obligation rather than as a compulsory matter—ultimately as a recognition of the historical origin and unity of Ndembu in Mwantiyanvwa. It is said—probably as a pious statement of the norm—that whenever Kanongesha asked his *ayilolu* for tribute to send to Mwantiyanvwa, and the latter asked their village headmen, it was never refused. Their Ndembu-hood was an aspect of their Lunda-hood, and both were maintained by what amounted to a voluntary recognition of their traditional leaders.

I have spoken of the Ndembu as being extremely individualistic, even anarchistic in their tribal character. This tendency, fostered by the individualism of their economy, is strongly offset by elaborate conventions enjoining formal respect in the matter

---

[1] The primary sense of *mwenimbu* is a person who lives at a village and has his domicile there. Thus a child is a *mwenimbu* at his own village. The antonym of *mwenimbu* is *ng'eji*, 'a stranger'. *Ng'eji*, like the Latin *hospes*, means 'stranger' and 'guest'.

[2] In the past, I am told, a headman was given a piece of cloth by the *chilolu* as a token of recognition.

z

of greeting and in behaviour at a chief's court. Greetings between headmen express their relative status in terms of criteria based on traditional history, and do not reflect their present circumstances. The chieftainship is a ritual and moral structure which epitomizes the unity of Ndembu. It is a fixed emblem of a moral unity which is dynamically if indirectly maintained by the cult associations.

Although respect is shown to the chief and *ayilolu* in formal situations, Ndembu village headmen had no hesitation in fighting them in the past. It is said that the Angolan Ndembu headman Kapanga attacked Kanongesha Nkomesha in the nineteenth century to loot his capital village and take his people as slaves. Matembu Village attacked Ikelenge, one of Kanongesha's principal *ayilolu*, in alliance with several villages from the area of Mukang'ala, another *chilolu*, but without Mukang'ala's participation in the rebellion. When the Chokwe invaded Ndembu territory, resistance was organized not by Samuhang'a the Kanongesha, but by Chipeng'e, a village headman. Chipeng'e later married Kanongesha's sister and as chief's brother-in-law acquired the title of *Sambanza*. The chief was afraid of him and for a time Chipeng'e established something like a dictatorship over part of the Ndembu area. If two persons or groups were engaged in a dispute one party would attempt to invoke Chipeng'e's aid by means of gifts. If he was satisfied by the presents or if he thought the case of the donor was just, he would force the other party to give compensation to his 'client'. But Chipeng'e was said to have respected custom and loved justice. Once he became involved in a dispute which put him into opposition to the powerful *chilolu* Mwininyilamba, his own close matrilineal kinsman. 'Mwininyilamba' was a famous historical title and Chipeng'e refused to fight against its holder. In this he was bound by tradition when he might well have established a new dynasty of his own. He would not attack either Kanongesha or Mwininyilamba because they represented the unity of the people for whom he had fought so well against the slave-raiders.

Yet chieftainship and the possession of a senior headmanship did give their holders a greater degree of political control and economic advantage than an ordinary village headmanship. For this reason also such offices were struggled for and in the past tenure of them was typically short. Faction fights, poison, assassination, took their toll of incumbents. Chieftainship and senior headmanship seem to have become exceptionally coveted positions in the period when the Ovimbundu slave-traders made frequent visits to the Ndembu region. These traders set up posts near the chief's and senior headmen's capital villages, and made agreements with them to give them preference in the purchasing of guns, cloth and other goods. The traders even encouraged these powerful Ndembu to raid their own village headmen to obtain slaves for sale. Perhaps this is one reason why the chief and senior headmen could not rally their people later against the Chokwe raiders who did not discriminate between senior headmen and other Ndembu in their depredations.

Even in these circumstances, however, the *chilolu* seems to have been little more than a village headman writ large, unable to coerce the headman in his area to obey his will. Most cases at law were settled in the vicinages. Self-help was resorted to in the event of homicide. As far as I have been able to ascertain, the senior headman possessed only two functions in which he acted as acknowledged leader of his area. Recourse to his poison-oracle could be made by any person named as a sorcerer or witch by divination. If the senior headman's poison-oracle reversed the diviner's decision the accused—no longer stigmatized as a sorcerer—had to pay a slave or a gun to the senior headman. The senior headman's other function also was of a ritual nature and consisted in his officiating at the *Musolu* ritual, at which he was assisted by the important elders of his area, led by his 'emblem-purifier' (*Chivwikankanu*), to bring on belated rains and restore the fertility of crops and animals. Both these functions were ritual rather than political, although in consonance with the general orientation of Ndembu society, the ritual had political aspects.

In its general form, then, Ndembu society falls into that category of societies of which Professor Evans-Pritchard writes that [1] 'the political organization takes a ritual or symbolic form which in politics with a higher degree of organization gives way . . . to centralized administration'.

---

[1] Evans-Pritchard, op. cit., p. 37.

CHAPTER XII

POSTSCRIPT

THIS book represents an attempt to combine two kinds of anthropological examination. The first is a synchronic analysis of Ndembu village structure. The second is an experiment in diachronic micro-sociology. My spatial unit of study has been the village, my unit of time the social drama. I have tried to marry the general to the particular by analysing a series of social dramas in the history of a single village. That village's membership was organized by the structural principles isolated during the synchronic study of a number of villages. But these principles were there interrelated in a unique way. In the social dramas I have tried to show how in specific situations certain principles came into conflict, and how attempts were made to maintain the unity of the disturbed group despite such conflict. Three main types of conflict became visible in the course of the social dramas : (1) conflict between principles of organization, receiving behavioural expression as choice between conflicting loyalties ; (2) conflict between individuals or cliques for power, prestige or wealth ; and (3) conflict within individual psyches between selfish and social drives. I have tried to handle these different kinds of conflict within a unitary analytical framework not only by examining social relationships within a convenient local system, but by examining changes and breaches in those same relationships over a period of time. I have looked for systematic interconnections in successive interactional events within a single spatial system. I have attempted to show how the unique, the haphazard and the arbitrary are subordinated to the customary within a single, if changing, spatio-temporal system of social relations. I considered it necessary to take a single village as my universe. My main aim was to show how the general and the particular, the cyclical and the exceptional, the regular and the irregular, the normal and the deviant, are interrelated in a single social process. I could only do this by examining the vicissitudes in time of a social group that wás in some sense 'a going concern ', a social entity with a certain

measure of cohesion and continuity, towards which its members
felt strong sentiments of loyalty. When members of a social
group attach a high value to its persistence, one is likely to find
that redressive machinery is brought into action by its foremos.
members to resolve crises that threaten its crucial relationshipst
Crises are the overt expression of any of the kinds of conflict
just mentioned or of any combination of them. Each kind of
conflict represents a challenge to some norm governing the
behaviour expected between occupants of positions in the social
structure of the group. Redressive mechanisms re-establish
norms, and they do so by scrutinizing deviant behaviour of all
types. Deviant behaviour becomes structurally relevant behaviour during the redressive phase of the social drama. For it
is against the background of deviance that conformity is assessed.
The norm derives strength and definition from condemnation
of its breach in the public situations of ritual and law. The
deviant, the haphazard and the contingent can only be recognized
to be such where consensus as to what is typical, orthodox,
regular, exists. And vice versa. It is for this reason that I
decided to use a single village as my unit of diachronic study,
rather than to illustrate the synchronic analysis by examples
taken at random from a number of villages.

Mukanza Village, the spatial system of social relations chosen
for detailed study, seemed exceptionally suitable from this point
of view. I have shown from numerical data how fissile and
subject to fragmentation most Ndembu villages are. Ecological
conditions, modern political and economic changes, and conflicting principles of social organization, all militate against the
continuous growth of large cohesive social units. Those villages
which have managed to persist for several generations acquire
great prestige, and their members attach a high value to their
maintenance. Mukanza, as a long-established village, that had
weathered many crises threatening its unity, afforded an example
of a group capable of holding together in the teeth of fissile and
centrifugal tendencies of all kinds. Since the disruptive trends
here were confronted by powerful reintegrative mechanisms,
the social crises I observed and had described to me in the history
of this village had an intensity which threw into relief most of
the features of Ndembu village structure.

The motto of this book, 'General Forms have their vitality

in Particulars ', well summarizes the method I have employed. The social drama is a description of a series of unique events in which particular persons, impelled by all kinds of motives and private purposes, interact in many different ways. But the very uniqueness of these events illuminates the structural regularities that interpenetrate them. Redressive custom absorbs particularities of behaviour and re-establishes the primacy of regulative custom, if only for brief periods.

I have made frequent reference in this book to certain social aspects of ritual. But the dominant stress of the investigation has not been laid on ritual but on how people conduct their social life in villages. I have tended to regard ritual in this connection as a mechanism of redress. At least I have so regarded rituals of affliction and the village ritual of *ku-swanika ijina*. I have postulated that ritual mechanisms tend to come into play in situations of crisis where conflicts have arisen in and between villages as the result of structural contradictions, rather than of the law-breaking activities of malicious or ambitious individuals or cliques. In particular situations principles of organization come into conflict within single groups. There are conflicts of loyalties, and there is therefore anguished choice between opposed goods, not between good and bad. In ritual the ideal unity of the disturbed social unit in question is counterpoised against its real internal divisions, which arise from situationally incompatible rules of custom. Ritual sometimes restores the unity of a village torn by structural cleavages.

But the majority of local groups in Ndembu society are transient and unstable. Nevertheless the principles of grouping on which they are formed and re-formed are persistent and enduring. The wider Ndembu society, as we have seen, persists within the framework of the ritual cults. These stress likeness of interests and characteristics as the basis of association rather than commonness of descent or common occupation of particular localities. Ritual performed by these cults is conspicuous for its content of dominant symbols which represent principles of organization and not corporate groups. Life-crisis rituals similarly emphasize general principles rather than particular corporate units. Particular groups break up, and divide or disperse ; but the structural form of the Ndembu village persists. And the very dispersion of particular groups helps to maintain the structural form of the wider Ndembu society. Ritual attempts to redress crises in villages, but if schism is irremediable ritual restates in what are usually emotionally charged circumstances the highest common values of Ndembu society.

A sequel to this book is in preparation which will make Ndembu ritual its central topic. A series of rituals will be analysed within a single field of social relations. Greater weight will be given to the cultural aspects of Ndembu ritual than in the present volume, especially to the symbolism.

BIBLIOGRAPHY OF WORKS CITED AND CONSULTED

ALLAN, W., *Studies in African Land Usage in Northern Rhodesia*, Rhodes-Livingstone Paper No. 15, London : Oxford University Press (1949).

ALLAN, W., GLUCKMAN, M., PETERS, D. U., *and* TRAPNELL, C. G., *Land-Holding and Land-Usage among the Plateau Tonga of Mazabuka District: A Reconnaissance Survey*, Rhodes-Livingstone Paper No. 14, Cape Town : Oxford University Press (1948). (*Tonga Report.*)

ARNOT, F. S., *Garenganze, or Seven Years of Pioneer Mission Work in Central Africa*, London : Hawkins (1889).

—— *Bihé and Garenganze, or Four Years' Further Work and Travel in Central Africa*, London : Hawkins (1893).

BARNES, J. A., *Marriage in a Changing Society*, Rhodes-Livingstone Paper No. 20, London : Oxford University Press (1951).

—— 'The Fort Jameson Ngoni', *Seven Tribes of Central Africa* (ed. by Colson, E., and Gluckman, M.), London : Published on behalf of the Rhodes-Livingstone Institute by Oxford University Press (1951). Reprinted with amended title by Manchester University Press for the Institute for Social Research, University of Zambia (1968).

—— (*with* MITCHELL, J. C., *and* GLUCKMAN, M.), 'The Village Headman in British Central Africa', *Africa*, xix. 2 (April 1949).

BAUMANN, H. VON, *Lunda : bei Bauern und Jägern in Inner-Angola*, Ergebnisse der Angola-Expedition des Museums für Volkerkunde, Berlin : Würfel-Verlag (1935).

BRELSFORD, W. V., *Fishermen of the Bangweulu Swamps*, Rhodes-Livingstone Paper No. 12, Livingstone (1946). Reprinted by Manchester University Press for the Institute for African Studies, University of Zambia (1971).

BUCHNER, M., 'Das Reich des Mwata Yamvo und seine Nachbarländer', *Deutsche Geographische Blätter* (1883).

BURTON, R. F., *The Lands of Cazembe : Lacerda's Last Journey to Cazembe in 1798. Journey of the Pombeiros, P. J. Baptiste and Amaro José, across Africa from Angola to Tette on the Zambesi*, translated by B. A. Beadle, London : published together by John Murray (1873).

CAMERON, V. L., *Across Africa*, London : George Philip & Sons (1885).

CAMPBELL, D., *Wandering in Central Africa*, London : Seeley Service and Co. (1929).

—— *In the Heart of Bantuland*, Philadelphia : Lippincott (1922).

CAPELLO, H., *and* IVENS, R., *From Benguella to the Territory of Yacca*, translated by A. Elwes, London : Sampson Low (1832).

CHILDS, G. M., *Umbundu Kinship and Character*, London : Oxford University Press, for International African Institute (1949).

CHINYAMA, T., *The Early History of the Balovale Lunda*, African Literature Committee of Northern Rhodesia, Lovedale Press (1945).

COLSON, E., 'The Plateau Tonga of Northern Rhodesia', *Seven Tribes of Central Africa* (ed. by Colson, E., and Gluckman, M.), London : Published on behalf of the Rhodes-Livingstone Institute by Oxford

University Press (1951). Reprinted with amended title by Manchester University Press for the Institute for Social Research, University of Zambia (1968).

COLSON, E., 'Rain Shrines of the Plateau Tonga of Northern Rhodesia ', *Africa*, xviii. 3 (October 1948).

—— ' Residence and Village Stability among the Plateau Tonga ', *The Rhodes-Livingstone Journal*, xii, London : Oxford University Press (1951).

—— ' Social Control and Vengeance in Plateau Tonga Society ', *Africa*, xxiii. 3 (July 1953).

CRAWFORD, D., *Thinking Black*, London : Morgan and Scott (1912).

CUNNISON, I. G., *A Social Study of a Bantu People* (Unpublished Thesis for the degree of D.Phil. at Oxford University) (1952).

—— ' Perpetual Kinship : a political institution of the Luapula peoples ', *The Rhodes-Livingstone Journal*, xx (1956).

DIAS DE CARVALHO, H. A., *Ethnographia e Historia Tradicional dos Povos da Lunda : Expedição Portuguesa ao Muatianvua*, Lisbon : Imprensa Nacional (1890).

EVANS-PRITCHARD, E. E., *The Divine Kingship of the Shilluk of the Nilotic Sudan*, Cambridge : at the University Press (1948).

FORTES, M., *The Dynamics of Clanship among the Tallensi*, London : Oxford University Press (1945).

—— *The Web of Kinship among the Tallensi*, London : Oxford University Press (1949).

FORTES, M., and EVANS-PRITCHARD, E. E. (editors), *African Political Systems*, London : Oxford University Press (1940).

FRANKENBERG, R., *Kinship and Community in a Welsh Border Village* (Unpublished Thesis for the degree of Ph.D. at the University of Manchester) (1954).

GANN, L., ' The End of the Slave Trade in British Central Africa ', *The Rhodes-Livingstone Journal*, xvi (1954).

GLUCKMAN, M., *Rituals of Rebellion in South-East Africa*, Manchester : Manchester University Press (1954).

—— ' The Role of the Sexes in Wiko Circumcision Ceremonies', in *Social Structure : Essays Presented to A. R. Radcliffe-Brown* (ed. by M. Fortes), Oxford : The Clarendon Press (1940).

—— ' Political Institutions', in *The Institutions of Primitive Society*, Oxford : Blackwell (1954).

—— (*with* MITCHELL, J. C., *and* BARNES, J. A.), ' The Village Headman in British Central Africa ', *Africa*, xix. 2 (April 1949).

—— *The Judicial Process among the Barotse of Northern Rhodesia*, Manchester : Manchester University Press (1955).

—— *Custom and Conflict in Africa*, Oxford : Blackwell (1955).

—— ' Kinship and Marriage among the Lozi of Northern Rhodesia and the Zulu of Natal ' in *African Systems of Kinship and Marriage* (ed. by A. R. Radcliffe-Brown and C. D. Forde), London : Oxford University Press (1950).

HARDING, C., *In Remotest Barotseland*, London : Hurst and Blackett (1904).

HILTON-SIMPSON, M. N., *Land and Peoples of the Kasai*, London : Constable (1895).
JOHNSTON, SIR H. H., *George Grenfell and the Congo*, London : Hutchinson & Co. (1908).
LIVINGSTONE, D., *Missionary Travels and Researches in South Africa*, London : John Murray (1857).
—— *The Zambezi and its Tributaries*, London : John Murray (1865).
McCULLOCH, M., *The Southern Lunda and Related Peoples (Northern Rhodesia, Angola, Belgian Congo)* (Ethnographic Survey of Africa), London : Commercial Aid Printing Service Ltd., for the International African Institute (1951).
MAGYAR, LASZLO, *Reisen in Süd Afrika in den Jahren 1849–1857*, Pest and Leipzig (1859).
MARWICK, M. G., ' The Social Context of Cewa Witch Beliefs ', *Africa*, xxň. 2 and 3 (April and July 1952).
MELLAND, F. H., *In Witchbound Africa*, London : Seeley Service (1923).
MITCHELL, J. C., ' The Yao of Southern Nyasaland ', in *Seven Tribes of Central Africa* (ed. by Colson, E., and Gluckman, M.), London : Published on behalf of the Rhodes-Livingstone Institute by Oxford University Press (1951). Reprinted with amended title by Manchester University Press for the Institute for Social Research, University of Zambia (1968).
—— (*with* GLUCKMAN, M., *and* BARNES, J. A.), ' The Village Headman in British Central Africa ', *Africa*, xix. 2 (April 1949).
—— (*with* BARNES, J. A.), *The Lamba Village : Report of a Social Survey.* Communications from the School of African Studies, New Series No. 24, University of Cape Town (1950).
—— ' A Note on the African Conception of Causality ', *The Nyasaland Journal*, v. 2 (July 1952).
MONTEIRO, J. J., *Angola and the River Congo*, London : Macmillan (1875).
POGGE, P., *Im Reiche des Mwata Yamvo*, Berlin : Dietrich Reimer (1880).
PRÉVILLE, A. DE, *Les Sociétés africaines*, Paris : Firmin-Didot (1894).
RICHARDS, A. L., ' Mother-right among the Central Bantu ', *Essays Presented to C. G. Seligman*, ed. E. E. Evans-Pritchard, R. Firth, B. Malinowski, and I. Schapera, London : Kegal Paul (1933).
—— *Bemba Marriage and Modern Economic Conditions*, Rhodes-Livingstone Paper No. 4 (1940).
—— ' The Bemba of North-Eastern Rhodesia ', in *Seven Tribes of Central Africa* (ed. by Colson, E., and Gluckman, M.), London: Published on behalf of the Rhodes-Livingstone Institute by Oxford University Press (1951). Reprinted with amended title by Manchester University Press for the Institute for Social Research, University of Zambia (1968).
SERPA PINTO, A. A. DA ROCHA DE, *How I Crossed Africa*, London : Sampson Low (1881).
SINGLETON-FISHER, W., ' Burning the Bush for Game ', *African Studies*, vii. 1 (1948).
—— ' Black Magic Feuds ', *African Studies*, viii. 1 (1949).

St. Hill Gibbons, A., *Exploration and Hunting in Central Africa*, London : Methuen (1898).

—— *Africa from South to North through Marotseland*, London : John Lane (1904).

Tilsley, G. E. *Dan Crawford. Missionary and Pioneer in Central Africa*, London : Oliphants (1929).

Torday, E. (with Joyce, T. A.), 'On the Ethnology of the South-West Congo Free State', *Journal of the Royal Anthropological Institute* (1907).

—— *Les Pays et les Populations du Bassin du Kassai et du Kwango Orientale.* Annales du Musée du Congo Belge, ii. 2 (1922).

—— *Camp and Tramp in African Wilds*, London : Seeley Service and Co. (1913).

Trapnell, C. G., and Clothier, J., *Ecological Survey of North-West Rhodesia*, Lusaka : Government Printers (1937).

Turner, E. L. B. (with Turner, V. W.), 'Money Economy among the Mwinilunga Ndembu : a Study of Some Individual Cash Budgets', *The Rhodes-Livingstone Journal*, xviii (1955).

Turner, V. W., 'Lunda Rites and Ceremonies', *Occasional Papers of the Rhodes-Livingstone Museum*, New Series, No. 10 (1953).

—— 'The Spatial Separation of Adjacent Genealogical Generations in Ndembu Village Structure', *Africa*, xxv. 2 (April 1955).

Verhulpen, E., *Baluba et Balubaisés de Katanga*, Anvers : L'Avenir Belge (1936).

Watson, W., 'The Kaonde Village', *The Rhodes-Livingstone Journal*, xv (1954).

White, C. M. N., 'The Ornithology of the Kaonde-Lunda Province, Part I. Climate and Ecology', *Ibis* (January 1945).

—— 'Witchcraft, Divination and Magic among the Balovale Tribes', *Africa*, xviii. 2 (1948).

—— 'Material Culture of the Lunda-Luvale', *Occasional Papers of the Rhodes-Livingstone Museum*, New Series, No. 3 (1948).

—— 'Stratification and Modern Changes in an Ancestral Cult', *Africa*, xix. 4 (1949).

—— 'The Balovale Peoples and their Historical Background', *The Rhodes-Livingstone Journal*, viii (1949).

Wilson, G., 'The Nyakyusa of South-Western Tanganyika', in *Seven Tribes of Central Africa* (ed. by Colson, E., and Gluckman, M.), London : Published on behalf of the Rhodes-Livingstone Institute by Oxford University Press (1951). Reprinted with amended title by Manchester University Press for the Institute for Social Research, University of Zambia (1968).

Wilson, M. H., 'Witch Beliefs and Social Structure', *American Journal of Sociology*, lvi. 4 (1951).

INDEX

abolition of slavery, 64n., 180-1, 183, 192-4
accretion, 197
adelphic succession, 87-9, 199-200 ; in Mukanza, 99
— group of male uterine parallel cousins, 68-9, 73
adepts, 293 ; in *Chihamba*, 311-12
adjacent genealogical generations, 207, 235, 237, 240
adjacent siblings, 209
adult males, residence of, 66
affinal connections, 281-6
affines, 235, 237, 240
African Political Systems, 287, 291, 302
age-seniority, 89
agriculture, 20-1
Akosa, 1n., 13
Allan, W., on carrying capacity of land, 21 ; on Lamba village size, 39
alliance of alternate generations, 80-1, 106, 167, 199 ; in Mukanza, 106-7
— between lineage segments, 109
ambition for headmanship, 99, 218
ancestor cult, 173, 195-6 ; associated with the bush, 173
— shrines, 35, 173 ; Tale and Ndembu, 172-3 ; *see muyombu*
Anderson Mulumbi, 160, 164
avunculocal, definition of, xviiin.

Bangala, founded by a hunter, 26 ; village size, 42
Barnes, J. A., 128n. ; on Ngoni village size, 39
Bashi-lange *riamba* cult, 26
Baumann, H. von, on Mbala and Chokwe hunters, 25-6 ; on Chokwe villages, 42
beer as payment at work-parties, 22 ; for rituals, 116, 118, 294
Belgian Congo, 1 ; trade with, 9
beliefs regarding the dead, 173
Bemba village size, 39 ; clans, 86 ; uxorilocal marriage, 76-7
Bibiana, 107, 277
Biscuit, 89, 217, 230
' black liver ', 98

blindness, 159
blood-brotherhood, 214, 286 ; for *Chihamba*, 307
Boma, 8
boundary of Northern Rhodesia, 1-2 ; arbitration, 7
boys, residence of, 53-4, 64-7
breach, of norms, 113, 115, 120-1, 123-4 ; of social relations, 91, 187 ; caused by natural calamity, 138-40, 142
Brelsford, W. V., on Unga village size, 39
British Government, and position of chiefs, 11n., 15 ; and Nyakaseya chiefdom, 3 ; and social change, 211-13, 218-20 ; and suppression of slavery, 192-3 ; and witchcraft, 114 ; and changes in lineage depth, 229
British South Africa Company, administration of, 7 ; and abolition of slavery, 64n.
brother-in-law, conflict between husband and, 189, 198
brothers, 249-50 ; conflict among, 79 ; separating to found adjacent settlements, 206 ; division of skills between, 250 ; gardens of, 22
brother-sister tie, 78, 251-3 ; *aku*, 235, 251-2
budgets, 23

Campbell, D., on colonial expansion of Lunda, 5n.
candidates, 293 ; for Chihamba, 310-311
Capello, N., and Ivens, R., on Luunda capital, 4-5 ; on Jinga hunters, 25 ; on Chokwe and Bangala villages, 41-2
capitals, 322-3 ; *Musumba*, 4-5
carrying capacity of land, 21, 45-6
cash crops, 9, 23
cash economy, 9, 51, 135-6
cassava, varieties, 20 ; and hunting, 26-7 ; and descent and residence, xviii-xix
causes of misfortune, 142-3

50-1 ; considered a calamity, 177 ;
renewed relations after, 176-8,
184, 197
fission of Mukanza Village, 178-82 ; of
Kafumbu Village, 182 ; of Yimbwendi Village, 182 ; further
possibility of in Mukanza Village,
101, 164-7, 307; of Shika
Village, 207-10 ; of Nsang'anyi
Village and offshoots, 210-18 ;
of Chibwakata Village, 49 ; of
Kawiku villages, 49-50
following, 15, 134 ; an embarrassment
to cash earners, 135 ; Sandombu's,
99, 153-4, 164; Kasonda's, 164-5;
Yimbwendi's, 181, 188
food, 23-4, 31-2
Forest Reserve, 20, 216, 285
form and process, xviii
Fortes, M., on concept of social system,
xxii ; on Tallensi, 82, 84, 170-2
fragmentation of villages, 45, 169
Frankenberg, R., on role of the
stranger, 147
funeral rites, 119, 267-71 ; and village
movement, 46

game, 19, 29 ; control, 19-20 ; drives,
29-30 ; resources as factor in
village size, 43, and movement, 46
Gann, L., on Angolan slave trade, 7 ;
on introduction of guns, 28
gardens, 20-1 ; the social organization of gardening, 21-3
genealogical recall, 82-4
genealogies, 37, 69-70
generation separation, 73-4, 236-7,
245 ; principle of, 175-6 ; effect
within the village, 175-6, 199 ;
and the extended family, 236-7
geographical location of Ndembu, 1
ghosts, *nyisalu*, 141, 143, 145
Gideon, 148, 153, 165, 265
girls' initiation, *see* ritual, girls'
puberty
girls, residence of, 53-4, 64-5
Gluckman, M., on cross-cutting alliances, xxii–xxiii, 288 ; on role of
sexes, 298 ; on Lozi judges, 122 ; on
divorce in patrilineal societies, 223 ;
on exclusion from ritual, 297n.
goats, disputes over, 132, 163
Government Tax Register, 74

grandparent-grandchild relationship,
80, 244-6 ; marriage, intra-
village, 79-80, 167 ; marriage,
inter-village, 176
grass huts, hunters', 29 ; early dwel-
lings, 35, 41-2
graves, 173
graveyards, ownership of, 217
greetings, 326
growth of small villages, 42-3
grudges, factors in sorcery/witch-
craft, 127
guns, introduction of, 28n.

Harding, C., on Lunda ' fortress ', 41
headmen, and their kin, 70-6 ; personality of, 52, 84, 200-2, 217 ;
privileges of, 129n. ; longest
established headman, *mwenimbu*,
217, 285, 325 ; polygyny of,
279-83 ; as hunters, 32, 202-3 ;
situation after death of, 178
hereditary titles of villages, 104-5
Hillwood Farm, 8-9
historical development of Ndembu
villages, 43-4
history and traditions, 2-18, 212-13,
318-27
hoe agriculture, 20, 22
hospital, 8, 141-2
hospitality, of headman, 200-2, 281 ;
between members of hunters' cult,
29 ; between Lwena clans, 85-6 ;
Sandombu's, 99, 136
Humbu, 4
hunters, training of, 29 ; aristocratic
rank of, 25-6 ; and headmanship,
32, 202-3 ; ideal personality of,
202 ; regarded as sorcerers, 32
hunting, a masculine occupation, 25-8 ;
social organization of, 28-31 ;
and the conflict between the sexes,
27-8 ; and descent and residence,
xviii, 27-8 ; and span of matrilineages, 227 ; and village size, 42,
173
huntsmanship, cults of, *see* ritual
husband, and wife-beating, 118, 120 ;
as witchcraft familiar, 145 ; in
conflict with brother-in-law for
wife, 192, 198
husband and wife, co-operation in
work-parties, 22

342 *Index*

Kawiku, 11, 18, 218 ; the name, 3–4 ; origins in Nsang'anyi, 210 ; village mobility, 45 ; village fission, 49–50, 183 ; and Ndembu, 4, 160, 163, 273 ; intermarriage with Ndembu, 262
Kayineha, 181 ; his friendship with Mukanza, 184–6, 232
Kazembe Mutanda, Chief, 3n. ; departure from Luunda, 2 ; chiefdom of, 1n.
Kimberley-brick houses, 10, 35–6, 45, 133, 138
kin, categories of, 70–2 ; absence of, 108, 152, 199
kingship, Shilluk, 318
kinship and affinal connections between headmen in vicinage, 279–87
kinsman, *kawusoku*, 234–5
ku-swanika ijina, see ritual, succession to a name

labour migration, 17
Lamba village size, 39–40 ; village structure, 61 ; clans, 86 ; cross-cousin marriage, 255
land, utilization, 20–1, 46 ; allocation, 217
law-cases, village : Nyamukola *v.* Sandombu (slander), 157–61 ; Sandombu *v.* Chibwakata (slander), 160 ; Mukanza Kabinda *v.* Shika (death payment), 270–2
— chief's court : Anderson Mulumbi *v.* Mukanza Kabinda (loss of goat), 163
law-men, *mahaku*, 16, 159 ; Kasonda, 103 ; Kahali Chandenda, 111 ; Chayangoma, 159, 269 ; Ng'ombi, 201, 271 ; of vicinage, 159–60, 270–1 ; of senior headmen, 324
law, skill in, 103, 201
life crisis rituals, 292
Line, 136 ; makes a farm, 136–8 ; marital ties, 186, 278
lineages, xix, 82–6 ; unstable structure of, 79, 174–6, 198–200 ; and individual mobility, 176–7 ; compared with Tale lineages, 170–3, 222
— depth of, 82–3, 172 ; factors limiting depth, 227–30 ; and village size, 82–3

lineages, attached, 170, 210–11, 222
lineal and familial principles in conflict, 237, 247
literacy, 103
Livingstone, D., on limited power of Lunda chiefs, 5 ; on stockaded villages, 41
local autonomy of villages, 6
local matrilineage as an ideal goal, xx, 84, 199
long-established and recently established villages, 74–6 ; and lineage depth, 82–4
Luba hunters, 25
Luchazi village size, 39
lukanu bracelet of chieftainship, 319–321 ; theft of, 14
Lukolwe, 6
Lunda, see Southern Lunda
Lunda of Luapula, clans, 86
Luunda, the name, 2n. ; centralized political system, 4–5 ; Lunda origins in, 2–3 ; clans of Luunda peoples, 85
Lwena, chiefs, 5–6 ; village size, 39 ; clans, 84–5

McCulloch, M., 2n.
maize, 20, 35
Makumela, 216–18
Malinowski, B. M., on the 'mythological charter', 98–9
Manyosa, 101–2 ; succeeds to Nyamwaha's name, 119–20 ; accuses MALABU lineage, 141 ; mourns Kalusa, 267 ; marriage, 164n., 165 ; marital ties, 274–5, 277
marital status, see conjugal status
marriage, spatial range of, 275, 280 ; between chiefdoms, 260 ; brittleness of, 62, 78 ; payments, 265–7 ; service for in-laws, 23 ; tradition of marriage between villages, 261–3
masked dancer, *ikishi*, 157
Matempa secedes, 212–13 ; fission in Matempa village, 216–17
matricentric family, xix, 68, 75–6, 82, 84–5, 222–3 ; as unit of secession, 79
matrilineages, major, minor and minimal, definition of, 80n. ; as units of secession, 205–6

Printed in the United States
55976LVS00002B/271-282